PUBLIC ADMINISTRATION IN TRANSITION

PUBLIC ADMINISTRATION IN TRANSITION

A FIFTY-YEAR TRAJECTORY WORLDWIDE

Essays in Honor of
Gerald E. Caiden

Edited by
Demetrios Argyriades
O.P. Dwivedi
and Joseph G. Jabbra

VALLENTINE MITCHELL
LONDON • PORTLAND, OR

First published in 2007 in Great Britain by
VALLENTINE MITCHELL
Suite 314, Premier House,
112–114 Station Road,
Edgware, Middlesex HA8 7BJ

and in the United States of America by
VALLENTINE MITCHELL
c/o ISBS, 920 NE 58th Avenue, Suite 300
Portland, OR 97213-3786

www.vmbooks.com

British Library Cataloguing in Publication Data
A catalogue record has been applied for

ISBN 978-0-85303-754-5 (cloth)
ISBN 978-0-85303-755-2 (paper)

Library of Congress Cataloging-in-Publication Data
A catalog record has been applied for

Typeset in 11/12.5pt Times NR by FiSH Books, Enfield, Middx.
Printed in Great Britain by Biddles Ltd, King's Lynn, Norfolk

Contents

Acknowledgements

A Festschrift is, by its very nature, a labor of love. The people who have joined in this enterprise gave selflessly of their time and patiently cooperated in the long and arduous process of getting the book published. To all of Gerald's friends, who helped in this initiative, the editors would like to express their deepest gratitude. They wish to single out the several contributors, authors from many lands – many where Gerald worked – who have, between them, given this Festschrift a global perspective, as well as historical depth.

The Editors are also greatly appreciative of the steadfast support received from Frank Cass, Mark Anstee and Vallentine Mitchell Publishers. Completing all the stages of production in good time would never have been possible without their strong commitment to the goals of the enterprise. To Gerald, Naomi and family, our heartfelt thanks are due for making this endeavor both possible and worthwhile.

Last but not least, the Editors express sincere appreciation to Marietta B. Monzon who, for the past two years, has served as the essential hub of a complex team effort, and whose exceptional skills and matchless dedication have made possible the timely execution of this multi-faceted project.

Finally, to our readers, we express our thanks and hope that they will share our sense of the profound importance of Public Administration and of the Public Service – both strategic institutions that are truly in transition, worldwide.

D. Argyriades
O.P. Dwivedi
J. Jabbra
February 2007

Preface

When Gerald Caiden graduated from the LSE with a BSc degree in 1957, the universe of values appeared to his contemporaries as firmly set. Fascism had been defeated, democracy had triumphed, a new world organization, the United Nations, had seen the light of day. With the Beveridge plan the modern welfare state had earned a high degree of acceptance. Something such as the final stage of political development in British and western societies appeared to have been reached; at least this was the message that social science faculties often communicated in the early postwar years. For university graduates, careers in the public service became avenues of choice. Public administration thus came in its own, both as a major discipline and as a great profession. The annual civil service competitive examination presented itself as a challenge to the top of the graduates' list. Administrative reform was in the air and it acquired new salience with decolonization and the emergence of new states in the 1950s, 60s and 70s. There was something very definite about its goals, which clearly had to do with the objectives of development and modernization in light of the prevalent models of democratization and nation-building. When Gerald started teaching, administrative development and the administrative state were in the air. His first book on reform (1969) reflected the mood of the times.

THE EARLY POSTWAR DECADES

Few in 1957, or even twelve years later, could have anticipated the sea change that occurred during the 1980s and 90s: the onslaught on the state, the denigration of government, the decline of public trust, the rapid spread of corruption and the erosion of public service. As all this happened, however, administrative reform and public administration, both as an area of study and as a field of work, changed drastically in nature and direction. The models and the narratives underwent a transformation reflecting the ascendancy of new political goals and value systems different from those that had prevailed in the early postwar years. Although we are now experiencing a new swing of the pendulum, it is probably too soon to tell how far this switch in public mood as well as more informed scholarly opinion will take us. Both as a field of study and as an occupation, public administration is clearly in a state of transition.

Conceived as a celebration of Gerald's fifty years of service to this field, this volume will attempt to trace this evolution, now half a century old. It will highlight the trends which in this troubled period significantly enhanced the scope and diversity of public administration. At its inception, the field was at best Eurocentric or North-America-centric. Descriptive or prescriptive, it accounted for developments, traced the configuration and explicated the functions of a set of institutions established, in most cases, for constitutional government under the rule of law. Though democratic patterns and rule-of-law concerns largely predominate, diversity of perspectives and a broad geographical spectrum have replaced the uniformity and narrow range of views that prevailed in the past. This volume demonstrates, and the list of contributors clearly shows, the extent to which the subject-field of public administration has been diversified and become truly universal.

Comparative analyses and developmental perspectives were added to the study of public administration, as Gerald's generation plodded through textbooks on 'government' during their final undergraduate years. A galaxy of new authors significantly broadened the scope and applications of public administration, thematically and geographically. Many are still household names: Lynton Caldwell, Alfred Diamant, Ferrel Heady, Albert Lepawsky, James Mosel, Fred W. Riggs, Walter Sharp, William Siffin and Robert Dahl (Siffin 1959). Most of them had tried their hand at 'technical cooperation', an emerging field, which served to demonstrate the range of possibilities the discipline could offer and the many practical uses to which it could be put. Both as an area of study and as an occupation, public administration was changing and expanding in ways seldom foreseen and hardly anticipated before World War II. This rapid evolution was captured in the title of Gerald's early book *The Dynamics of Public Administration* (Caiden 1971), which came just on the heels of his first major opus, *Administrative Reform* (Caiden 1969). It may be safely assumed that first the welfare state and then decolonization and the development effort occasioned this expansion and diversification. The parallel growth of a web of international agencies in varying areas of work added to the complexity of this emerging field and greatly enhanced its dynamism, vitality and appeal.

To use a favored expression which gained a lot of currency during the early 1960s, public administration, when Gerald was completing his BSc (Econ) degree, was readying for the take-off stage. In 1950s England it was still taught as a subfield of government. Across the Channel, in France, it was considered part of administrative law. The normative approach which was preferred on the Continent contrasted with the mostly historical perspectives that students gained in Britain. Our learning process started with the Act of Settlement in 1701. We then proceeded to study the Northcote & Trevelyan Report as presage to the reforms which laid the foundations of the civil service profession in the UK. This offered opportunities to mention Woodrow Wilson and the Pendleton Act and to take a cursory look at developments in Europe. Administrative systems were viewed and analyzed within a very specific political context, which seemed to obviate or even to preclude a systematic comparison of administrative structures across the board.

This was about to change as the 1950s gave way to the 60s and as Gerald moved to Canada and, later, to Australasia. Comparative administration was a shot in the arm of public administration, it aided its emancipation. Public administration now came to be considered as a distinct phenomenon of universal dimensions. The focus on the subject revealed its inner diversity. Increasingly, attention was paid to its subfields of which local self-government probably topped the list. Significantly, however, the 1950s saw the emergence of town and county planning and, naturally in an era of nationalization, of public corporations. In Manchester, London and Leeds, a process of fissiparity was generating subfields in what had been a subfield only a few years before.

The administrative state had come into its own, and students would be taught public administration not merely as one course in a much broader curriculum but chiefly with the intention of making a career of it. Administration had grown into a promising field. It was viewed as the key to socioeconomic development but also as an expanding professional category. The central role of government in economic development played an important part in this remarkable shift. Technical cooperation became a budding discipline during the 1950s and 60s and, with bilateral aid programs and multilateral programs in active search of consultants and experts for the field, young men and some young women discerned career opportunities as specialists in management and public administration.

Though it now seems self-evident, the work and contribution of experts in the field of public administration must have been less than obvious to the community at large in the early postwar years. Decolonization and the development programs of the 1950s, 60s and early 70s changed all that. Quite rapidly, not only applications like Organization and Methods (O&M) became much in demand but issues of reform in comparative perspective took on major importance in international fora. What was the right agenda for administrative reform? What was a proper strategy to make reform effective? What was the role of skills in the development process?

Without a doubt, a feature of the intervening change was renewed concern for education and training in public administration. Schools and institutes mushroomed in all developing countries, as programs of pre-entry and in-service training took off and multiplied. They called for both practitioners and scholars, initially from countries of North America and Europe, later also of the subcontinent, East Asia and Latin America. Not surprisingly, those programs, of in-service training especially, generated a debate on the scope, content and methods of such training both at the junior level and the senior management level.

With bilateral and multilateral technical assistance on the upswing, public administration emerged as a growth area and object of attention of an expanding network of international agencies and universities across the world. A small operational unit that was part of the overall management of the UN Technical Assistance Program was upgraded in the 1960s to form the UN Public Administration Division, with sections for Local Government, Organization & Methods, Development Administration and Personnel and Training. The Division served as model for similar establishments in the regional UN commissions in Bangkok, Santiago and Addis Ababa and arguably for programs on training and development in public administration run by the ILO, UNITAR, the OECD and the World Bank.

Institution-building concerns held center stage. These included civil service laws and practices, training resources development, the administrative aspects of central planning and administrative reform.[1] A certain predilection for practical pursuits, which made good sense in light of the development programs' overall objectives, meant that the subject itself, public administration, was treated *in abstracto* as mostly a set of principles, techniques and tools. The growth of comparative models and studies notwithstanding, these principles, tools and techniques were viewed as universal, as applicable, in fact, with little adaptation and differentiation to Africa, Asia, Central and South America (Mailick 1974). Though the vehicular languages English, French and Spanish brought significant cultural differences in their trail, the prevalent approach remained a tacit assumption that there was 'one best way' to modernize the world of public administration.

There cannot be any doubt that practical considerations – both supply- and demand-driven – account for this propensity. With limited capacity to take informed decisions on institutional change, many recipient countries inclined in the direction of cutting-edge solutions reputed to be the best. This understandable tendency received a powerful boost from the related bent to view the development process mostly in the form of convergence – all countries moving forward towards contiguous goals, albeit at different speeds. This general idea or predilection persisted in the subsequent decades of the 1980s and 90s, but in a drastically changed international environment.

THE RISING COUNTERCULTURE

The New Public Management (NPM) was the outcome of this change of environment. It resulted from the effects of a prolonged recession produced by the energy crisis during the 1970s, the rise of the radical right in Britain and America in the persons of Margaret Thatcher and Ronald Reagan respectively, and, above all, the dismantlement of the USSR. The failure of one system was soon taken as sure proof of the ascendancy of the other. 'Big government', the welfare state and socialism suddenly stood in the dock and word spread that the world had now changed course decisively, that it was irreversibly committed to reform but in the direction of a 'hollowing out' of the state, converting public management to private sector ways and globalizing capitalism.

Central planning went by the board as decentralization, devolution and downsizing largely replaced the stress on central coordination, direction and control which had marked the postwar efforts at administrative reform, expansion and modernization. Entrepreneurial management, allied to an overarching emphasis on efficiency and effectiveness, necessarily brought in its wake new methods and approaches and drastically altered the ways in which careers in the public service had been structured. Indeed, the very identity of the public service profession was now called into question as people argued forcefully that, management being management, work in the government service was like any other job. 'Deprivileging' the service became the favored slogan of Thatcherite reformers. It came with insistent demands to 'let the managers manage', increase their discretionary powers and free them from the shackles of rules and regulations or safeguards for the staff. Developments in training reflected this concern. The focus on technologies, 'management tools' and methods obscured all other dimensions. Interpersonal effectiveness and process skills seemed to prime all other pursuits. The 'how' now topped the list. It was as if all questions of substance had been answered, all policy issues resolved. The NPM perspectives played down the many differences between the public sector and private enterprise but also resurrected the old Wilsonian dichotomy of politics/administration, arguably on the grounds that it was not for managers 'to reason why', but only 'to do or depart'.

Comparative perspectives and interdisciplinary studies not surprisingly went under. Gone were the days of Oakshott and W.A. Robson at the LSE when public administration was studied in the context of history, philosophy, political science and ethics. The new prevailing doctrine placed it squarely in the framework of finance and applied economics. The premise underpinning this new approach, which was still going strong when the century drew to its close, betrayed the firm belief that management is a technique, a branch of applied economics and usable, accordingly, in the same shape or form regardless of the context, culture or circumstance. The 'one best way' of Taylor and Fayol was replaced by the favored slogan 'one size fits all'. Pluralism and diversity, indeed questions of principle, were delegitimized.

We are currently reaping the whirlwind of this approach, mostly in the form of failures but also of inequity, abuse of power and corruption. Not surprisingly at this stage, the tendency remains to focus on the downsides in terms of costs and benefits, seeking to limit the former but not at the latter's expense. Public integrity and ethics have been broached in practical terms as 'law and order' issues, with punishment meted out, typically, to 'little guys' in an attempt to stop the spread of this pandemic. Much damage has been done around the world, as policies and measures purported successful in Europe and America found their way to developing countries, either imposed by donors in the form of 'conditionalities' or savvily packaged and sold by highly-priced consultants. The world may be gradually awakening to the dangers of outsourcing policy advice and hence to the need to develop and maintain homegrown capacity for crafting and implementing informed decisions on policy. As one might well expect, not only comparative studies but also administration in the broadest sense of the term may gain from this awakening. A new critical mass of seasoned educators and scholars has emerged in all parts of the world, reluctant to look for ready-made policy transfers from distant, alien places or uncritically adopt savvily marketed models and highly priced 'best practices' which soon prove out of place in the recipient country.

A twenty-year perspective on the New Public Management offers an opportunity to weigh the costs and benefits of its varied contribution to administrative reform. On the plus side, the main gain to the world has come from the introduction of quantitative measurements or, at the very least, from our awakening to the importance of such measures. Not content with preaching the need to secure 'value for money', a generation of managers trained in economics endeavored to introduce the tools which made that possible. In the words of Naomi Caiden:

> For over fifty years, efforts have been made to measure the results of government activities. During the 1980s and 90s, these efforts accelerated as a key component of more civil service reforms. There is increasingly urgent enquiry into the means by which government programs may be evaluated, their quality improved, and performance standards created or maintained. These efforts have met with varying degrees of success and have encountered many obstacles. However, they form an integral element in a movement to redirect government towards a result orientation. (Caiden 1999)[2]

Not exactly a new approach, in developed countries especially, this invited the public and governments to focus on results, on the tangible outcomes of policies, the effectiveness of programs and less on the modalities and legal instrumentalities which gave shape to these policies. Such concepts came to the fore as inputs, outcomes of products and services, workload activities levels, costs, productivity, outputs, service quality and timeliness, customer satisfaction and long-term impact measurement. These concepts had been sparsely used in the early postwar era. Their novel currency showed not merely a new impatience with 'bureaucratic waste', but equally with claims and statements of performance which did not prove susceptible to quantitative measurement.

Sometimes this useful tendency and the attitudes to which it gave rise were carried to extreme lengths in value-laden dogmas which under the guise of pragmatism preached disregard for principle, the primacy of results and ethical indifference to the modalities used in their pursuit. 'Results over process' suggested that, in the last analysis, any which way was good that gets you where you want to go; that 'ends', in other terms, do justify the means. Invented in the process of 'reinventing government' (Osborne and Gaebler 1992: esp. ch. 6), this pithy but misleading maxim summed up a frame of mind which soon proved very damaging not only to public integrity but also to professional ethics and even, one may argue, to the quality and consistency of democratic governance. The 'erosion of public service' and the decline of 'public trust' (Caiden and Caiden 2002) to which Naomi and Gerald Caiden have often drawn attention during the past half century may be a product of this mindset; the quest for easy victories (as in Florida 2000), the priming of style over substance and the occasional triumph of salesmanship and spin over scholarly concerns might also well be attributed to this underlying approach for which nothing really matters, provided we get what we want.

Replete with costly failures, the experience of the past (the recent past especially) may be pointing the way out of such erroneous thinking, gradually guiding our footsteps towards both more constructive and less radical approaches to administrative change. It may be safely asserted that such return to normalcy would also be consistent with Gerald and Naomi's abiding concerns and quests around their chosen field. This should be hardly surprising knowing Gerald's overall professional orientation as well as the ideology and ethical convictions in which his thinking is grounded. A professional trajectory which spans more than five decades has, as one might expect, taken him many places and, like Ulysses of old, through many management cultures. In the process, it has led him to explore many different facets of public administration through arguably varying perspectives. Remarkably, however, in all these fifty years, which have seen drastic changes in both the subject field and the public service profession, certain abiding values, guidelines and preoccupations have marked his chosen way.

It was said of President Clinton that, unlike Reagan, he criticized bureaucracy but not the public servants, all too often vilified as 'problem bureaucrats' (Light 2006). Like Clinton, Gerald Caiden has criticized bureaucracy, or rather certain tendencies in public administration which render it impervious to modernization, resistant to change and, more than anything else, irresponsible and irresponsive to the needs of the general public. His list of bureaupathologies, beginning with 'abuse' and ending with 'xenophobia', reads like a veritable 'alphabet of woes' prepared for recitation on all appropriate occasions (Caiden 1991: 127). But it should be emphasized that this critique of pathologies has never served as a prelude or excuse for an attack on government, the administrative state or organized society. 'Society does not exist' is an aside attributed to Margaret Thatcher. It does not represent Gerald Caiden's way of thinking. Indeed, it goes against his deeply held convictions. In Gerald Caiden's world-view, society, not nature, has been the point of reference and source of legitimation of the principles we observe, the values to which we adhere. What makes us civilized is membership of a community defined by structures and a culture predicated on shared laws and rules of accepted behavior.

GERALD CAIDEN'S ETHICAL COMPASS

Arguably, in this regard, the fundamental principles underpinning Gerald's thinking and running through his writings on public administration have been profoundly Jewish. Deeply internalized and pervasive through his writings are the Ethics of the Fathers: 'If I am not for myself who is for me? And if I am only for myself, what am I?' (Pirkei Avot 1:14). The values he projects are community-based values. The measures he proposes, the institutions he defends, the reforms which he seeks to promote, all ultimately rest on a concept of a common good and the related notion that the administrative state is needed, in part, to protect those no one else will champion, the vulnerable segments of the community.

Advocacy of the needs of the poor, the sick and the weak has been a central theme of his writings and concerns, which again is deeply embedded in Gerald's religious convictions. He has internalized the wisdom of the Prophets and teachings of the Pentateuch in this regard. He has learned from Isaiah to 'seek justice, relieve the oppressed, judge the fatherless, plead for the widow' (1:17), and from the Psalm of Asaph to 'deliver the poor and the needy, rid them out of the hand of the wicked'. And he constantly reminds us of the duty not to 'wrong a stranger or oppress him, for you were strangers in the land of Egypt' (Exodus 22: 21).

No one could fairly argue that such important maxims have ranked among the values of neo-liberal thinkers. But that is where the advocates of the New Public Management and Gerald Caiden part ways. Both may be largely driven to 'reinvent' the state for economic development and social progress. However, to this date, the twenty-year campaign of the New Public Management has done little to reduce the level of injustice or alleviate the plight of the dispossessed. Quite on the contrary, in fact, it may be rightly affirmed that an unbending pursuit of economic orthodoxy and the cult of the 3Es have principally advantaged the powerful and the rich, exacerbated the incidence of human insecurity, increased inequality gaps and multiplied such maladies as corruption, social exclusion, marginalization, arbitrariness and the abuse of power.

Gerald Caiden, his friends and disciples are certainly not hostile to efficiency and effectiveness. However, in contrast to the followers of the New Public Management they do not accept the 3Es as ends in themselves; they do not view downsizing, deregulation or even decentralization as absolute goods. The difference between them could be summed up, in fact, as the distance which separates Social Darwinism from social justice.

As opposed to New Public Management, the principles and teachings of social justice are mostly very old. Some draw their inspiration from biblical injunctions. Take the following, for instance:

> 19. When you reap your harvest in your field, and you forget a bundle in the field, you shall not turn back to take it: it shall be for the proselyte (foreigner), the orphan and the widow.
> 20. When you beat your olive tree, do not remove all the splendor behind you; it shall be for the proselyte, the orphan and the widow.
> 21. When you harvest your vineyard, you shall not glean behind you; it shall be for the proselyte, the orphan and the widow (Deuteronomy 24:19–21).

Or the following:

> 14. You shall not cheat a poor or destitute hired person among your brethren, or a proselyte who is in your land, or one who is in your cities.
> 15. On that day shall you pay his hire; the sun shall not set upon him (with his pay in your hands), for he is poor, and his life depends on it (Deuteronomy 24: 14–15).

Such are not among the values or concerns of the NPM, for which 'results over process' and 'let the managers manage' have entailed ethical indifference, a measure of opportunism and frequent abuse of power. For Gerald Caiden, by contrast, these hallowed ancient values express the very essence of what he likes to call the 'civilizing mission' of public administration. It helps us to remember that, as opposed to 'management', administration flows from the Latin *ministrare* which simply means 'to serve'. Service is of the essence but must be addressed primarily to those in need of help. In spite of much rhetoric and lots of good intentions, this has hardly been the experience of the USA and the world in the past twenty years.

If society did not exist, we might have to invent it. Without it, 'all is permitted' (*pace* Camus and Nietzsche). In fact, without society and the underpinning values of shared responsibility, community, compassion and solidarity, public administration the way we know it today has virtually no place, and management becomes a tool of naked power. Such in fact has been the criticism expressed by Gerald Caiden in the chapter which is published in this book, a volume dedicated to his scholarship and his career. In fifty years, his output has covered many topics, from comparative perspectives on discrete administrative systems through administrative development to the ombudsman institution and the fight against corruption. Running through these themes, however, as a constant leitmotiv, is what he likes to call 'the civilizing mission of public administration', the duty to save life, to enhance the quality of life, to add to social capital and to contribute to human development. This civilizing mission also encompasses the duty to defend the weak and the poor, to contain predatory behavior, to seek to 'right the wrongs' and to encourage public virtue.

Such values and concerns have underpinned his study and advocacy of reform and, more recently, his efforts on behalf of public integrity and the ombudsman institution. Though efficiency and effectiveness also form part of the equation, one may safely assume that Caiden accords them secondary importance to the overarching causes of promoting social justice and enhancing the quality of life. To advance these core objectives and effectively fulfil its civilizing mission, public administration must reinvent itself and rescue the public sector, but, more than anything else, it must restore to the institutions of government and governance the capacity to plan, to think, to 'weave the future' (to use a favored expression of Plato (*The Statesman*) and Yehezkel Dror (2001)) and, of course, to lead responsibly.

If accomplishing these functions takes on the measure of urgency and importance which he accords them, then we would surely agree with Caiden that one area of government that greatly needs strengthening globally is what he terms 'the thinking part'. And yet, according to Caiden, it is the very part which in the recent past has been entrusted mostly to 'inexperienced, unaccountable and untrustworthy nongovernmental entities depending on public subsidies and other favors'. This is a telling indictment as well as a sad commentary on two decades of changing and reinventing the public service profession. There can be little doubt that, lip-service notwithstanding, not much has been accomplished in the past two decades to enhance the capacity of government to 'attract, retain, develop and motivate the right people and to direct their energies towards the public good'.[3] It is no exaggeration that, to this 'capacity deficit', a very great contributor has been the sharp decline in public service professionalism with attendant repercussions on performance, prestige and integrity (Caiden, 1999: 121–132). Quite apart from fraud and venality, what one cannot but find extremely disconcerting (Gerald Caiden certainly does) is the lack of disposition to 'speak truth to power' and the corresponding prevalence of what he aptly calls 'research for hire'. Sadly, 'spin', soundbites and slogans have invaded the field of research insofar as the advancement of the frontiers of knowledge is all too often surrendered to highly priced consultants or 'scholars' who convert themselves into troubadours of power.

There can be little doubt that implicit in professionalism is integrity and authenticity. These, in turn, are predicated on the will to establish, preserve and defend a certain measure of distance from lucrative concerns and political activity. If fifty years of scholarship and professional development have produced with Gerald Caiden a significantly valuable yield, this may well be on account of the fact that he has maintained that distance. He has always kept his sights on key professional values; these have always conditioned the quality of his output.

REFERENCES

Caiden, G.E. (1969). *Administrative Reform*. Chicago, IL: Aldine Publishing Co.

Caiden, G.E. (1971). *The Dynamics of Public Administration*. New York: Holt, Rhinehart & Winston.

Caiden, G.E. (1991). *Administrative Reform Comes of Age*. New York: de Gruyter.

Caiden, G.E. (1999). 'The Essence of Public Service Professionalism'. UN Department of Economic and Social Affairs, *Public Service in Transition: Enhancing its Role, Professionalism, Ethical Values and Standards*. New York: UN.

Caiden, G.E., & Caiden, N. (2002). 'The Erosion of Public Service'. Paper presented at the Van Riper Panel at the National Conference of the American Society for Public Administration in Phoenix, Arizona.

Caiden, N. (1999). 'Public Service Professionalism in Performance Measurement and Evaluation'. UN Department of Economic and Social Affairs: *Public Service in Transition: Enhancing its Role, Professionalism, Ethical Values and Standards*. New York: UN.

Caiden, N. (2006). 'Perspectives on Improving Organizational Performance'. *Public Administration Review* 66.

Dror Y. (2001). *The Capacity to Govern*. London: Frank Cass.

Light, P.C. (2006). 'The Tides of Reform Revisited: Patterns in Making Government Work, 1945–2020'. *Public Administration Review* 66 (1).

Mailick, S. (Ed) (1974). *The Making of the Manager: A World View*. New York: Anchor Press & the UN Institute of Training and Research (UNITAR).

Osborne, D., & Gaebler, T. (1992). *Reinventing Government: How the Entrepreneurial Spirit is Transforming the Public Sector*. New York: Plume Books.

Siffin, W.J. (Ed) (1959). *Toward the Comparative Study of Public Administration.* Bloomington, Indiana: Indiana UP.

NOTES

1 See in the UN 'Handbook Series' notably the *Handbook of Civil Service Laws and Practices* (1966) and the *Handbook on Training in the Public Service* (1966).

2 See also Caiden, N. (2006). Especially noteworthy are the contributions by S. Nicholson-Crotty, N. Theobald & J. Nicholson-Crotty, K. Yang & M. Holzer, M. Barzelay & F. Thompson, and G.E. Caiden on some limitations and downsides that such measurements present.

3 See UN, *Work of the 15th Meeting of Experts on the UN Program in Public Administration and Finance* (Report E/2000/66), Recommendation 19.

Public Administration in Transition: An Introduction

> In an increasingly turbulent environment, public administration has been experiencing a very bumpy journey. From the prospect of globalization, international cooperation and the dire need for universal action to tackle many of the current challenges facing humanity, the future beckons and the means of transportation will need to be remodeled and adjusted accordingly... Unless current trends are quickly reversed, the world seems to be heading toward disasters that may well overshadow anything that has happened in the past. Unfortunately, nobody can forecast with any accuracy how the craft of public administration will fare in future storms.
>
> Gerald E. Caiden (1990)

I

Written eighteen years ago, these words, nevertheless, sound as contemporary as if they had been spoken only a few days ago. The world in which we live remains full of uncertainty; the road to the future is bumpy. In a turbulent environment, the need for innovation, initiative and leadership in public administration is greater than ever before. In sixty years of progress since the end of World War II, the field has known developments that, globally, have changed it out of all recognition. Remarkably, however, both nationally and internationally, its scope and role, its values – indeed its very identity – remain in doubt and as contested today as at any other time since it emerged, with Woodrow Wilson and Taylor, in the late nineteenth century or, arguably, earlier still.[1]

The paradox and challenges which such doubts represent cast this collection of essays in a particular light, but also add to the value of the task that we have undertaken. In this volume, we have assembled essays in Gerald Caiden's honor, that hopefully will serve to bring into relief his major contribution to public administration since 1957, which is when he obtained the BSc (Economics) at the LSE and started a career which, with remarkable constancy, he has pursued to date. The field and the profession he chose to join and serve have undergone transformations, thematically and otherwise.

In this volume we propose to identify some of these changes. To carry out this task, we have assembled a team of eminent practitioners and scholars in the field. They come from North America, Europe, South Asia, East Asia and Australia, all regions of the world where Gerald Caiden worked and where the field and profession of public administration have made significant strides in the past fifty years. Indeed, the wide diversity of inputs to this study highlights the main dimensions of the intervening change: a shift in the center of gravity away from North America and Western Europe, the creation of new areas of specialization requiring new technologies and methods of research, as well as new concerns.

THE BEGINNINGS: FROM WILSON TO FRED RIGGS

Two major epistemological developments gave shape to the new discipline of public administration at the dawn of the twentieth century. One was the stress that Woodrow Wilson and Frank W. Goodnow laid on the need for separation of administration from politics, as the single most essential reform with a view to achieving efficiency and abandoning the practices of patronage and spoils. Thus, public administration emerged as a self-contained world with its own separate values, rules, and methods, obeying principles which were seen as universal.

The second, related development was the quest for scientific approaches to the discipline. While the origins of scientific analysis in social science disciplines can be traced back to the Enlightenment, slowly the two core elements of scientific method started influencing philosophy and the human sciences. These core elements were rational objectivity and quantification. The main purpose of these elements was, and to this day remains, the removal of possible biases by searching for 'hard' data, which can be measured, and then presented in an objective and rational manner. In this context, academics and practitioners were considered to be scientists dispassionately indifferent to culture, values and ethics. For them, administration was a machine, and efficiency an end in itself. It was also thought that the scientific study of administration could lead to the discovery of universal principles of an analogous nature to the principles – or laws – of the physical sciences. And finally, it was assumed that the principles of administration determined the way in which specific administrative values could be realized. In such a task environment, the merit principle became the main ingredient sustaining the operation of government administration.

It was against the backdrop of these early beginnings that comparative and, later, development administration made their entry into the discipline in the 1950s and 1960s. World War II, the emergence of the UN, the Marshall Plan for Europe and later decolonization added strength to this momentum. In the US, such scholars as Dwight Waldo, Lynton K. Caldwell, Fred Riggs, Ferrel Heady, W.J. Siffin and Fritz Morstein Marx, to name but a few, started teaching and writing about comparative administration beyond what L.D.

White had initiated, back in the 1930s. But the main spurt of scholarly activity came when the Ford, Carnegie and Rockefeller foundations offered generous grants to American universities to support research on the problems of public administration – not only in the industrialized West, but also among the newly independent developing nations. Concurrently, the International Institute of Administrative Sciences in Brussels was taking the lead in Europe to encourage research and publications in the comparative field.

A quantum leap was taken, in 1962, when a Ford Foundation grant to the American Society for Public Administration enabled its Comparative Administration Group (CAG) to organize regular seminars and conferences, encouraging a spate of publications on this subject matter. A flood of scholarly activities engulfed the field (Caldwell, 1965; Heady, 1962; Henderson, 1971; Raphaeli, 1967; Riggs, 1961; Siffin, 1957; Waldo, 1964). This was further supplemented by many contributions made by scholars from across the Atlantic and also in interaction with the developing countries' researchers. Among scholars, it was the energy and innovative leadership provided by Fred Riggs that offered the required theoretical underpinnings to the discipline.

Riggs discerned three trends in comparative administration: (1) a movement from the normative to more empirical approaches, (2) a movement from idiographic to nomothetic approaches, and (3) a shift from a non-ecological to an ecological form of study (Heady 1962). These trends stressed the need for empirical description and explanation, a distinction between unique case studies, as opposed to those aimed at testing general propositions; and a shift from the isolated study of administrative institutions to study placing them in a larger institutional context or societal framework.

The 1950s and 60s were, actually, the days of great visions and the hope that the whole world might eventually speak the same administrative language. However, within a decade and certainly by the mid-1970s, a serious crisis emerged in the field partly due to a decline in funding by American foundations, which constrained research, and partly to the failure of the American dream materializing in the transfer of administrative technology to the developing countries. Not only did CAG go out of existence in 1973; even its flagship, the *Journal of Comparative Administration*, ceased publication in 1974, after only five years of existence (Heady 1979: 23). Remarkably, however, development administration had seen the light of day and made its mark already, principally with reference to countries of the Middle East, East and South Asia, Africa and Latin America emerging from the process of decolonization and seeking to secure the benefits of aid under either bilateral or multilateral programs of economic and social development.

A NEW CONCERN: DEVELOPMENT

Development became an intellectual concern in American social science during the 1950s. Following Walter Rostow's *The Stages of Economic Growth: A Non-Communist Manifesto* (Rostow 1960), political development literature tried hard to identify the non-economic conditions for an accelerated – and orderly – economic growth. As far as the role of public administration, in this process, was concerned, two interrelated visions prevailed. One originated within the Committee on Comparative Politics of the Social Science Research Council (SSRC), especially within its Political Development Group; the other principal vision of public administration in development came from the Comparative Administration Group (CAG) of the American Society for Public Administration. While both shared many assumptions, they differed in terms of their focus.

For those in political development, public administration was perceived as an institution contributing mainly to stability and *systems maintenance*. In their view, bureaucratization was a functional condition for stability and legitimacy in the political order (i.e., political development). For those in the comparative administration group, modern administration was essentially a mechanism for the attainment of developmental goals. This way, the key role of bureaucracy was that of processor in the institutional framework converting inputs of objectives, capital and know-how into developmental outputs.

Such characterization of development administration emphasized the formal and technical aspects of the government machinery. Developmental goals were assumed to be self-evident and, therefore, broadly agreed upon by the local, Westernized elites. Their names were: 'nation-building' and 'socio-economic development' (Esman 1966). Swerdlow identified two interrelated tasks in the development process: *institution building and planning* (Swerdlow 1975). Other authors outlined a number of other development-oriented activities, such as the management of change, establishing an interface between the 'inner' environment and the larger intra- and extra-societal context, and mobilization of human and physical capital for development objectives and related political action.

The 1950s and 60s were decades of hope and prosperity. It was confidently expected that, armed with modern technology, the administrative state would overcome the challenges of poverty and backwardness. The rapid reconstruction of Europe and Japan reinforced this conviction. Almost throughout the world, the approach was technocratic. The assumption was that problems, whatever their nature, lay *with* and *at* the periphery; by contrast, the solution was always locked in the center. In a way, the prevalent attitude was that developing countries not only *had* the problem, but really *were* the problem. Conversely, the West claimed both to *have* and to *be* the solution. It was tacitly taken for granted that traditional societies had to be saved, both from the appeal of communism and from themselves (Nef and Dwivedi 1981).

A developmental creed soon emerged which posited that, in order to attain development, a country's administrative structure ought to be overhauled in order to conform to the standards of the most advanced industrial societies. The issue, thus, consisted in the reorganization of the existing traditional machinery into a new entity. This needed to be accomplished through administrative development: the modernization of the public service machinery through exogeneous inducement, the transfer of technology and the training of local staff by foreign so-called experts. For this task, there was already a neat prescriptive model to be found in Western traditions. This was based on the dichotomy between politics and administration; a system which exemplified a pyramidal hierarchy, unity of command, political neutrality, recruitment and promotion based on the merit principle, public service accountability, objectivity and integrity. In reality, these principles co-existed in most places with local traditional methods. Thus, a parallel value system gained currency in those parts of the world where Western models were set up, but operated alongside traditional economies and black markets. Rarely were the principles of development administration, as recommended by 'experts', seriously questioned in theory; they were generally accepted at face value by the indigenous elites, especially in those countries where a relatively smooth transition to nationhood had taken place.

The post-independence political and bureaucratic elites rapidly moved to replace colonial administrators. A Western education was widely perceived to be the vehicle both for personal advancement and for acceptance into the global community of Western-trained professionals. Thus, it is not surprising to find that an administrative machinery progressively took shape which was incapable of implementing developmental goals, particularly in dealing with poverty and scarcity. In spite of their modern rhetoric, administrative systems continued to be imitative and ritualistic. Practices, styles and structures of administration generally unrelated to local traditions, needs and realities succeeded in reproducing the symbolism, but not the substance, of a British, French or American administrative system. Even where a relatively large contingent of trained functionaries existed, as in India, Pakistan, Sri Lanka, Kenya, Nigeria or Ghana, perpetuation of the colonial administrative culture prevailed. For most of the local elites, technical solutions appeared more palatable than the substantive political options needed to bring about real socio-economic change. Reorganization and rationalization soon became ends-in-themselves, far more than the means to development, or development administration.

FROM HOPE TO GROWING DOUBTS

Not surprisingly, euphoria in the 1950s and the 60s gave way to a rude awakening during the 1970s. With the energy and debt crises bringing two decades of prosperity to a rather abrupt close, the very foundations of development administration were badly shaken. Not only was its usefulness to the Third World suddenly called into question, but an intellectual crisis also spread among the students of development administration in Western countries. The gap between the center and the periphery was widening rather than narrowing, in both relative and absolute terms. Instead of development and nation building, turmoil and fragmentation proliferated throughout Africa, Asia, the Middle East and Latin America. Urban crises, drastic cessation of growth, resulting unemployment, breakdowns of public institutions and decline of civic morality dashed earlier hopes that First World administrative technology and science would solve all problems globally.

During the fourth development decade, the New International Economic Order (NIEO) became an important new symbol in the development arena. Its demand for a basic realignment of the world economy through changes in trade, aid and technological transfers was praised but generally ignored by the richer donor nations. In fact, there was no consensus concerning NIEO objectives and some commentators felt that it might even harm certain countries. While the World Bank and the International Labour Organization (ILO) symbolically endorsed this approach, the monumental change demanded by NIEO did not occur. In the absence of shared strategies, the NIEO soon went the way of earlier concepts. But by the end of the 1980s, another major event shook the existing order badly: the withering away of the USSR, and the related entry of former communist states into the ambit of the Third World. Soon, attention was diverted and a share of aid resources channelled towards these countries, now denoted as 'transitional'; for how long, no one ventured to say.

Cataclysmic events in the East coincided, in the West, with an impressive revival of ultra-conservative ideologies. First, the rise of Margaret Thatcher and later of Ronald Reagan added a powerful impetus to the New Public Management. NPM dominated the scene during the 1980s and into the 1990s. Its recipes emphasized drastic reforms predicated on a number of standard prescriptions: (1) accent on results, both in the planning and in the evaluation of programs and people; (2) treatment of the public and citizens as customers; (3) delegation of authority as close to the action level as possible; (4) empowerment of 'clients' (devolution); (5) greater attention to cost through comprehensive auditing, contracting out (outsourcing) and introduction of competitive practices into the public space; and (6) private-sector techniques calculated to motivate employees, such as merit/performance pay, mission statements and quality circles (Dwivedi and Gow 1999: 130). Other key operational 'principles' included budget restraint and 'downsizing' bureaucracy. NPM also introduced the notions of corporate management, corporate culture and market-driven rhetoric. This paradigm was based on the premise that by reducing 'bureaucracy' and 'monopolistic practices', corruption would decline; that by narrowing down the scope of government activities, an efficient, transparent and accountable system of governance would necessarily emerge. It was thought that with 'less government' there would be fewer bureaucratic problems.

In retrospect, we know that this did not happen. However, in the 1980s and well into the 1990s, NPM became a fixation in the Anglo-Saxon world, as well as in some important financial institutions. Its advocates did not realize that their precepts would soon prove to be a 'recipe for disaster by advocating measures that encourage information distortion and public risk-taking, stifling voices of caution, experience and independence' (Hood and Jackson 1991: 478). To many theoreticians and practitioners, the greatest charge against the type of managerialism promoted by NPM was its reductionism and lack of imagination. It tried to encapsulate a complex prismatic phenomenon into a single model drawn from an idealized version of the private sector which, in reality, existed in only a limited number of capitalist countries. It turned the public servant from being a steward of the state into an entrepreneur, for whom the moral constraints of public accountability were formalistic irritants. Carried to extremes, the NPM techniques created an *ethical vacuum* and an *amoral state*. It may not be inappropriate to say that the NPM produced a sort of 'MacDonaldization' of development, with multinational corporations joining forces with international agencies to demand similar laws, access to state apparatus, fewer rules and regulations, 'outsourcing' and privatization, all in the name of freedom and 'debureaucratization'.

As a prescriptive model to solve the problems of government and open the road to development, this left no scope for diversity. During the 1980s and well into the 1990s, it underpinned the programs of structural adjustment with which development agencies sought to address the needs of countries in the Third World. At present better known as '*one size fits all*' solutions, New Public Management recipes seldom benefited the countries for which they were intended. Rather, they contributed to a legacy which earned the 1980s the name of 'lost decade'.

The Golden Age of the 1960s turned into an Age of Pessimism during the 1980s and early 1990s. Developing nations were disillusioned when they found that, instead of being treated truly as recipient countries, they were compelled to make net transfers of their meager resources to the West. In order to service their debt, several countries came very close to bankruptcy. Restrictive trade practices prohibited poor nations from exporting their products. The problem was further compounded when commodity prices fell to their lowest level in fifty years, while the prices of manufactured goods from rich countries kept rising. It is no wonder that poverty, inequality, oppression and despair have continued to rise in the South. Nevertheless, there were new rays of hope from the worldwide awareness displayed at the Earth Summit in 1992 and the Millennium Summit at the United Nations, in New York, in September 2000. Both of these events affirmed the need for greater solidarity worldwide, and shared responsibility in addressing and meeting the challenges confronting all countries and all peoples in this twenty-first century.

II

An unintended consequence of the New Public Management and neo-liberal thinking was the abrupt decline of both comparative studies and development administration. The end of the Cold War, which followed on the heels of the unforeseen implosion of the USSR, was generally perceived and indeed sold to the world as truly '*the end of history*' (Fukuyama 1993). This lent credence to the view that the dawn of a new era for humanity had come. It presaged a new creed, one aptly articulated in the *Washington Consensus* (Stiglitz 1998), which dominated the scene during those critical years. The 'myth of global convergence', which accompanied this trend (Pollitt 2001), saw administrative development mostly in terms of approximation to the '*shrinking state*' ideal (World Bank 2002: xvi). The premise underpinning this model betrayed a belief that management is a technique and, therefore, applicable in the same shape or form, regardless of context or circumstance ('management is management'). It lent support to an attitude that favored one-size-fits-all solutions, ignored the task environment and completely disregarded the cultural dimension in public administration. Pluralism and diversity were delegitimized. Departures from the norm were critiqued as aberrations, as errors in the past, no doubt to be corrected with the progress of modernization and globalization. Such prospects of convergence and pressures for reform have tended to promote a veritable industry of 'best practices', cleverly packaged for export and, like the 'New Zealand model', aggressively marketed worldwide during the 1990s.

THE MYTH OF GLOBAL CONVERGENCE AND ITS AFTERMATH

The myth of global convergence had serious implications for public administration on both the theoretical and practical levels. It lent legitimation to forcible policy transfers, which as 'conditionalities' became a staple feature of structural adjustment programs in several parts of the world. The results of such policy transfers seldom proved salutary (Hesse 2000: 15; Mossberger and Wolman 2003: 429; Newland 1996: 382–389). On the theoretical level, the myth of global convergence and the New Public Management accounted, as we saw, for a signal loss of momentum in the comparative study of public administration during the last two decades of the twentieth century. Particularly in the United States, where keen interest in the thought and practice of other countries had been much in evidence since Woodrow Wilson or earlier, a powerful counterculture set in (Heady 2001: 392–93). Suddenly, context and culture, what Fred Riggs had aptly denoted as the 'ecology of public administration', appeared to lose all meaning. The focus on techniques, tools, and cost-effectiveness obscured all other dimensions. Even the term 'public administration' itself went out of style, yielding to the much trendier 'public management'.

With 'management' triumphant, the fortunes of development administration also began to sink. Its fate was sealed when Milton Friedman and Hayek replaced John Maynard Keynes in the economic pantheon. Likewise, one might well argue that gradual loss of interest in the comparative subfield coincided with 'donor fatigue' (a favorite catchphrase during the 1990s), and the erosion of public services in several Western countries at about the same time (see Caiden and Caiden 2002; Taylor 1994: 61). Strident attacks on government, faith in the private sector as model for the future, the myth of global convergence, and the idea that management is all one and the same appeared to obviate the need for comparative studies and development administration.

It is hoped that, at long last, we may have turned the corner; that lessons from the failures of 'lost decades' are slowly beginning to surface, pointing to rediscovery of the value of diversity, the dangers of conformity to 'one best way solutions', but also and most importantly, the need for fresh approaches showcasing new departures in different parts of the world. A number of new books, which have made their appearance during the past two years,[2] offer some ground for optimism. Quite apart from acceptance of differences and rejection of facile generalizations in the name of 'global norms' or 'universal principles', what recent publications may indicate is the re-legitimization of '*culture*', as well as some renewed concern for public service reform and the problems of development. Rediscovery of culture in public administration takes on singular importance (Hofstede 1997). It may well represent a wholesome new beginning that could revitalize the comparative study of public administration. The prospects are currently good. The questionable dependency on largely exogenous models, which was probably inescapable during the 1950s and 1960s, has now become unnecessary and seems to have subsided. In Africa as elsewhere in the so-called Third World, there is a critical mass of scholars and literature that can be put to this task, bringing interdisciplinary and cultural dimensions to the study of public administration. In this connection, it may be worth recalling what Robert Dahl observed nearly 60 years ago:

> It follows that the study of public administration inevitably must become a much more broadly based discipline, resting not on a narrowly defined knowledge of techniques and processes, but rather extending to the varying historical, sociological, economic and other conditioning factors that give public administration its peculiar stamp in each country. (1947: 11)

THE CONTINUED NEED FOR COMPARATIVE AND INTERDISCIPLINARY APPROACHES

The present book, consisting in a collection of essays authored by several scholars from different parts of the world, belongs to this tradition. As has already been stated, it attempts an overview of significant developments in the study, teaching and practice of administration during the past half-century, which also marks the presence and signal contribution of Gerald Elliot Caiden to the profession of government and public administration, his chosen field of research. The inputs to this volume are written by practitioners and scholars, who have known and worked with Gerald Caiden during these critical years. They fall into three categories. The first group represents the *historical perspective.* This includes three contributions by Argyriades, Newland and Burke, respectively. It is followed by *case studies* from India, Bangladesh, China, Korea, Japan, Australia and Singapore. These are the chapters contributed by Jain, Khan, Ma, Yong-Duck Jung, Denise Conroy and Quah. Then prominence is given to *new and emerging concerns*, viewed from comparative angles. Europe, the USA, Canada and East Asia become the points of reference in the exploration of issues which take on special relevance throughout the world today, and which Professor Caiden helped bring to public attention several years ago. Corruption and integrity hold center stage with essays by Aufrecht, Huberts, Chapman, et al. A critical review of the ombudsman institution, by Professor Donald Rowat, comes as a timely reminder that, old though it may be in Scandinavian countries, the ombudsman institution still needs to be refined and defended in other parts of the world and organizational contexts.

Last but not least, the volume concludes as it begins, with chapters encapsulating fifty years of insights on the subject of public administration, by two veterans of the field: the honored scholar of course, but also one of the editors. They offer complementary approaches and ideas, which sum up, in effect, this overview of developments over the past half-century. Characteristically, they share a central theme: *values for public service.*

THE CONTENTS, ANALYTICALLY

Analytically, on the contents the following introduction would be in order.

In the first group of essays, Demetrios Argyriades begins with the topic '"Resisting Change": Some Critical Remarks on Contemporary Narratives about Reform'. The essay demonstrates how reform initiatives have been an enduring feature of national public services, over the past two centuries. Argyriades aptly encapsulates public administration and public service reforms into four major stages, which coincide respectively with one principal dimension of the nature and role of the modern state. The essay critically assesses the momentous impact of the '*market model of government*' which came to dominate administrative reform in several Western states. New Public Management ostensibly undertook to eliminate budget deficits and to reduce inflation. However, in this process it engendered a number of negative externalities, which, unfortunately, many public administration scholars have chosen to ignore. The essay concludes by tackling some of the critical weaknesses associated with the New Public Management paradigm, such as problems of accountability, the erosion of public service, decline of professional ethics and crisis in the rule of law. The essay's central message is the crucial importance of narratives and the dialectic relationship between public service reform and political ideology.

Chester Newland's essay, which follows, is a veritable *tour de force*. In highly compact style, Professor Newland traces the singular development of public administration in the United States, highlighting its point of departure and the fundamental concepts which shaped the course of its evolution. Firstly, he identifies a conflicted but enduring *Self-Image* in American nation-state perspectives. Significantly, despite the absence of a concept of 'the State' among most Americans, identification as 'a Nation' with an accountability to Enlightenment ideals and an enduring *Mission* emerged quite early and continues to persist. Secondly, he opens perspectives on current Facilitative State concepts that are akin to those early governance ideals. They are related to political accountability ideas that started to become powerful in the last decades of the nineteenth century. The reform of politics, which stormed to center stage, followed years of *laissez-faire* economic rampage and transactional political corruption. Transformations then gave rise to the American Administrative State, which dominated the middle half of the twentieth century.

Self-governance ideals survived those momentous decades, but, ultimately, many Americans considered themselves overly dominated by Big Government. Facilitative governance ideals, reflected in global trends, again took prominence in the late 1970s and early 1980s, except in the areas of American security and international affairs. Thirdly, American accountability in twenty-first century foreign and defense affairs is touched upon. One focus is the powerful Garrison (Warfare) State practices that re-emerged as a sequel to the explosion of terrorism after September 11, 2001. Another is the paradoxical assertion of a *Mission* to remake the world in America's *Self-Image*. Important in these developments is a perception among domestic and foreign critics that American unilateralism and exceptionalism have now prevailed over internal and external accountability to the rule of law.

The third essay in this group is by Catherine G. Burke, on 'Administrative Theory and Practice'. It is a paper which begins with an analysis of contributions by Gerald Caiden to the study of public administration, but quickly passes on into a discussion of the relationship between theory and practice with a focus on the ability to create a 'science' of public administration. The author provides what, she thinks, represents a useful distinction between leadership in an association and an employment hierarchy. She argues that her distinction clarifies much of the literature which frequently muddles these two types of leadership and their associated behaviors. The author concludes with an assessment of Professor Caiden's output over the past half-century.

The second group of essays includes case studies of selected nation states which, in the majority of cases, gained independence in the wake of the Second World War, after decades or centuries of foreign domination. The first essay in this section is by R.B. Jain on 'The State of the Study of Comparative Public Administration in India'. The author touches on a number of issues relevant to the study of comparative public administration, including trends and models that have defined the discipline, the Indian contribution to comparative administration, and experiences with teaching comparative public administration in India. He suggests emerging frontiers for such research. The essay also provides a brief discussion of some of the new challenges for the study of comparative public administration, namely issues related to corruption and good governance.

The second essay in this section is by Mohammad Mohabbat Khan on the topic 'Public Administration Reform in Bangladesh: Incremental Changes, Reform Resistance and Lack of Political Will'. The author traces the evolution of the Indian Civil Service during the British Raj as the foundation of the administrative structure of Bangladesh. He then examines various efforts undertaken while Bangladesh was still a part of Pakistan and, even at a later date, when independence came in 1971. A major administrative reform was launched in January 1997, based on the principles of New Public Management. Towards the end, the essay discusses the devastating consequences of corruption in Bangladesh and of large-scale decline of public trust in government on the satisfaction of citizens' expectations.

The third essay is by Stephen K. Ma, who explores 'Public Ethics in China: Toward a More Transparent Government and More State Capacity to Confront Corruption'. He sets out three research questions worthy of detailed analysis with respect to the issue of administrative corruption in China: (a) emergence of transparency in the Chinese administrative system; (b) the extent of administrative capability to deal with corrupt activities; and (c) the degree to which Chinese experience can be used for the guidance of other countries. The author demonstrates that China, despite its centuries-old history of being a closed society, has made significant strides in terms of achieving more transparent government due to the emergence of a citizenship culture. Of course, the author acknowledges the numerous examples of high-ranking Chinese officials ostensibly responsible for anti-corruption initiatives, who were themselves involved in graft. He takes the view, however, that, as the public becomes better informed, there will be greater openness, transparency and accountability in government, so as to ensure that Chinese officials are promoting the public interest rather than their own narrow self-interest.

The fourth essay is by Yong-Duck Jung on 'The Challenges of Public Administration Reforms in Japan and South Korea'. In essence, the author compares the administrative reforms that Japan and South Korea have conducted since the late twentieth century. According to the author, these reforms have been linked not only to domestic factors (post-industrialization and post-democratic transition), but also key international developments, such as the end of the Cold War, globalization and increased economic competition. Overall, the essay offers a sound comparative study of administrative reforms in Japan and South Korea, in retrospect and prospect.

The fifth essay, by Denise K. Conroy, deals with 'The Australian Public Service in Transition, 1972–2004'. The author provides a thorough and detailed account of public administration reforms that have been introduced in Australia from the decade of the 1970s to the beginning of this century. The essay is so structured as to examine the reforms undertaken by successive prime ministers, beginning with Gough Whitlam (1972–1975). It underlines the fact that Australia and New Zealand were among the first industrialized countries which adopted administrative changes based on New Public Management. The essay analyzes its principal dimensions: marketization, regulation, political control, privatization, decentralization and corporate management.

The sixth essay is by Jon S.T. Quah on 'Administrative Reform in Singapore: An Evaluation of Public Service 21 (1995–2004)'. Jon Quah evaluates the success of the Public-Service-for-the-Twenty-First-Century reform initiative in Singapore against its own stipulated goals. These he identifies as the improvement of service delivery and of the attitudes of members of the civil service towards change. He describes what, in effect, is the most comprehensive civil service reform ever introduced in Singapore. While focusing on this specific reform, the author also traces the history of earlier reforms. He suggests that it may be too early to provide an objective assessment of the impact of PS21, although it has reinforced the commitment of the government to organizational change, excellence and quality service delivery.

The third group of reports delves into two current challenges facing public administration and the public service profession. It opens with Steven E. Aufrecht on the topic of 'Balancing Tensions Between Personal and Public Obligations: A Context for Public Ethics and Corruption'. This briefly outlines a model with reference to the tension between the public and private lives of all public servants worldwide. The author then identifies some strategies for preventing unethical behavior and defines 'conflict of interest' as a tension between the civil servant's personal and official obligations. Conditions are listed which may incite an official to pursue personal needs and interests over his/her public obligations: (1) when his/her personal needs cannot be met legitimately; (2) when these needs can be met improperly, with relative impunity; (3) when there are weak controls that make detection unlikely; and (4) when, if caught, likely sanctions do not outweigh the benefits. Finally, the author advances a number of strategies for minimizing corruption, including early detection and swift punishment of illegal activities.

The second essay is by L.W.J.C. Huberts. This noteworthy contribution discusses the 'Pathology of the State: Diagnosing in Terms of Corruption or Integrity'. The author argues: (1) that conceptual clarification is required before any meaningful theorizing can occur regarding the subject; and (2) that researchers need to move beyond the standard definitions of corruption in order to provide better-informed assessments of bureaucratic transgressions. One area recommended by the author for further research is *public service integrity*. For this, the author presents a typology of integrity violations, from examples of corruption in Western democratic countries. One such example is that of the Netherlands, a country which has often been assessed as relatively free of corruption and yet is still beleaguered with a number of concerns about integrity in government.

The third essay, by Jeffrey I. Chapman, Colleen Byron and Min Su Kim, bears the title 'Justified Corruption in State and Local Finance'. It deals with the issue of public administration at the local government level. Specifically, it argues that local authorities, because of intense financial pressures to provide programs and services with insufficient resources, have tended to resort to using a number of CFIs (Complex Financial Instruments) as a coping mechanism. One of the side-effects of the use of CFIs has been an emerging situation which may be called '*justified corruption*'; a term which means activities by government departments and agencies which, while ostensibly legal, in the long run promote corruption of the system.

Last but not least, is an essay by Donald C. Rowat on the subject of 'the Dilution and Distortion of the Ombudsman Concept'. In it the author advances a distinct and important argument about the concept of the legislative ombudsman, which has become diluted when applied by several nations to their respective systems. Accordingly, he argues that reform is urgently needed to restore clarity to this important institution, which was created in order to protect ordinary citizens from administrative excesses and the abuse of power. The author comments on the relative success in the worldwide transplantation of this institution but laments the conditions in many countries, where the concept has been distorted. He explores what needs to be done to bring back its basic mission and its intrinsic merits. Thus, the essay ends with a number of recommendations for reform.

The volume's closing section carries two complementary inputs, respectively by one of the three editors and by the honored scholar. Writing about 'Spirituality in Public Administration: A Challenge for the Well-Being of Nations', O.P. Dwivedi discusses how the separation of values and ethics from public administration has damaged the moral fiber of the profession and has fostered the rise of an 'amoral' public service system in many places. Against this backdrop, the author attempts a historical review of the separation between ethics and public administration and underlines the need to bring back moral and spiritual dimensions into the modern governing system. The essay also examines the concept of the '*well-being of all*' as a part of sustainable development for humanity, and as a challenge for public administrators to fulfill their role in sustaining well-being for all through the process of good governance.

Gerald Caiden, for his part, builds on a theme which runs through many of his writings: 'The Civilizing Mission of Public Administration'. He discusses the development of public administration as a profession and notes that it has suffered from lack of political will. Few public servants today show a willingness to stand up and be counted, let alone defend their craft; while political leaders selfishly shift the blame from their own shortcomings onto defenseless public servants. Even the alluring prescriptions of the New Public Management have, if anything, eroded the traditional professional core, as well as the identity of public administration. These, in Gerald Caiden's view, are none other than enhancing and spreading civilization through professional integrity, hard conscientious work and civilized behavior. The author concludes by asserting that unless the civilizing mission of public administration is reinforced, the public service profession will be unable to achieve its potential for the greater good, quality public services, humanitarian deeds, and individual blessings. Sadly, if this were to happen, the ship of state would sail towards some form of authoritarianism as in the past.

It is indeed fitting to conclude with this perceptive essay by a trail-blazing scholar. This volume represents a veritable example of close cooperation in scholarly pursuits as evidenced by editors and scholars emanating from several parts of the world. The essays in this volume testify to the wide-ranging, scholarly and practical inputs that Gerald Caiden has made to the theory and practice of government and administration. His own interests and the subjects of his research and writing cover several areas. Among them, we have highlighted administrative reform and contemporary challenges such as accountability, professionalism, integrity, corruption and the abuse of power. The variety of approaches and vantage points, as well as the range of contributors, is a tribute to Caiden's position in the community of scholars and practitioners worldwide.

REFERENCES

Argyriades, D. (2006). 'The Rise, Fall and Rebirth of Comparative Administration: The Rediscovery of Culture'. *Public Administration Review*, 66 (12), pp. 281–284.

Caiden, G.E. and Caiden, N. (2002). 'The Erosion of Public Service'. American Society of Public Administration, National Conference, Phoenix, AZ, Van Riper Panel.

Caiden, G.E. and Caiden, N. (1990). 'Towards the Future of Comparative Public Administration'. In *Public Administration in World Perspective*, edited by O.P. Dwivedi and Keith M. Henderson, Ames, Iowa, USA: Iowa State University Press, pp. 363–399.

Caldwell, L.K. (1965). 'Conjectures on Comparative Public Administration'. In *Public Administration and Democracy: Essays in Honor of Paul H. Appleby*, edited by Roscoe Martin. Syracuse, NY: Syracuse University Press.

Dahl, R. (1947). 'The Science of Public Administration: Three Problems'. *Public Administration Review*, 7 (1), pp. 1–11.

Dwivedi, O.P. (2002). 'Challenges in Public Administration in Developing Nations'. In *The Turning World: Globalization and Governance at the Start of the 21st Century*, edited by Guido Bertucci and Michael Duggett, Amsterdam, The Netherlands: IOS Press, pp. 47–54.

Dwivedi, O.P., and Gow, J. (1999). *From Bureaucracy to Public Management: The Administrative Culture of the Government of Canada.* Peterborough: Broadview, Hadleigh.

Dwivedi, O.P., and Nef, J. (1982). 'Crises and Continuities in Development Theory and Administration: First and Third World Perspectives'. *Public Administration and Development* (UK), 2, pp. 59–77.

Dwivedi, O.P. and Nef, J. (2004). 'From Development Administration to New Public Management: The Quest for Effectiveness, Democratic Governance, Governability, and Public Morality'. In *Democracy, Governance and Globalization*, edited by P.L. Sanjeev Reddy, Jaideep Singh and R.K. Tiwari, New Delhi, India: Indian Institute of Public Administration, pp. 71–91.

Esman, M.D. (1966). 'The Politics of Development Administration'. In *Approaches to Development: Politics, Administration and Change*, edited by John D. Montgomery and W. J. Siffin. New York: McGraw-Hill.

Fukuyama, F. (1993). *The End of History and the Last Man.* New York: Morrow, William and Co.

Heady, F. (2001). 'Principles for 2001 and Beyond'. *Public Administration Review*, 61(4), pp. 390–395.

Heady, F. (1979). *Public Administration: A Comparative Perspective.* Englewood Cliffs, NJ: Prentice Hall.

Heady, F. and Stokes, Sybil L. (1962). *Papers in Comparative Public Administration*. Ann Arbor, MI: Institute of Public Administration.

Henderson, K.M. (1971). 'A New Comparative Public Administration'. In *Towards a New Public Administration*, edited by Frank Marini. Scranton, NJ: Chandler Publishing, 1971.

Hesse, J. (2000). 'Public Sector Report 2000, Central and Eastern Europe'. Report to the XVth Meeting of Experts on the United Nations Programme in Public Administration and Finance.

Hofstede, G. (1997). *Culture and Organisation: Software of the Mind*. New York: McGraw Hill.

Hood, C. and Jackson, M. (1991). *Administrative Argument*. Aldershot: Dartmouth.

Jabbra, J.G. and Dwivedi, O.P. (2005). Eds. *Administrative Culture in a Global Context*. Whitby, Ontario: de Sitter Publications.

Mossberger, K. and Wolman, H. (2003). 'Policy Transfer as a Form of Perspective Policy Evaluation: Challenges and Recommendations'. *Public Administration Review*, 63 (4), pp. 428–440.

Nef, J. and Dwivedi, O.P. (1981). 'Development Theory and Administration: A Fence Around an Empty Lot?' *Indian Journal of Public Administration*, 27 (1), January–March, pp. 42–66.

Newland, C.A. (1996). 'Transformational Challenges in Central and Eastern Europe and Schools of Public Administration'. *Public Administration Review*, 56 (4), pp. 382–389.

Pollitt, C. (2001). 'Convergence: The Useful Myth?' *Public Administration* 79 (4), pp. 933–47.

Raadschelders, J.C.N. (1998). *Handbook of Administrative History*. Brunswick, NJ: Transaction Publishers.

Raphaeli, N. (1967). Ed. *Readings in Comparative Public Administration*. Boston: Allyn and Bacon.

Riggs, F.W. (1961). *The Ecology of Public Administration*. New Delhi: Asia Publishing House.

Rostow, W. (1960). *The Stages of Economic Growth: A Non-Communist Manifesto*. Cambridge, MA: Harvard University Press.

Schaffer, B. (1973). *The Administrative Factor*. London: Frank Cass.

Siffin, W.J. (1957). *Towards the Comparative Study of Public Administration*. Bloomington, IN: Indiana University Press.

Stiglitz, J. (1998). *More Instruments and Broader Goals: Moving toward the post-Washington Consensus*. Helsinki: UN.

Swerdlow, I. (1975). *The Public Administration of Economic Development*. New York: Praeger.

Taylor, L. (1994). 'Hirschman Strategy at Thirty-Five', in L. Rodwin and D.A. Schon (Eds), *Rethinking the Development Experience: Essays Provoked by the Work of Albert O. Hirschman*. Washington, DC: Brookings Institution, pp. 59–66.

Umeh, O.J. and Andranovich, G. (2005). *Culture, Development and Public Administration in Africa*. Bloomfield, C: Kumarian Press, 2005.

Waldo, D. (1964). *Comparative Public Administration: Prologue, Problems and Promise*. Chicago: American Society for Public Administration.

White, L.D. (1964). *Civil Service Abroad*. New York: McGraw-Hill.

World Bank (2002). *Civil Service Reform: Strengthening World Bank and IMF Collaboration*. Washington DC: The World Bank.

NOTES

1 The study of public administration is hardly new. One can trace its origins in the contributions of Kautilya in India, Herodotus, Xenophon and Aristotle in Greece, Machiavelli in Florence, and Ibn Khaldun in the Middle East. Furthermore, most of the world scriptures have also outlined the obligations of rulers and their officials/servants (Raadschelders 1998). By contrast, modern comparative administration traces its origins after World War II, when a new field came into being as a sub-discipline of public administration. This is also our point of departure.

2 See Argyriades (2006).

My Basic Philosophy of Teaching: A Fifty-Year Trajectory

GERALD E. CAIDEN

> The university is not a business or a charity; its major task is the advancement of knowledge through research and teaching by employing people who think to engage others to think.
>
> The aim of education is not the memorization of information. It is teaching people to teach themselves by knowing where to find the relevant information, organizing and thinking about it, and presenting it in an attractive manner.

My philosophy of teaching was largely formed by the time I graduated from college in 1959 and started teaching at university level thereafter. Although I have adjusted it according to specific circumstances (such as the country and culture in which I was teaching, the age level and experience of the audience, the size and composition of courses and classes, ease of access to source materials, and detailed organizational requirements), its philosophical basis has remained fairly steadfast. It has been shaped by my own youthful experience with the good and bad of the British education system at the time. That system has since gone through many changes during which my college, the London School of Economics and Political Science (LSE), has progressed to be currently rated number two in the United Kingdom, overtaking one of the two universities (Oxford and Cambridge or Oxbridge) once thought invincible – while my boys' grammar school was turned into a mixed comprehensive school and eventually closed down altogether because of its poor teaching. Meantime, I had left the United Kingdom to teach at universities in Canada, Australia, Israel, and the United States, first in the San Francisco Bay area and later at the University of Southern California in Los Angeles where over half my teaching career has been spent.

I admit that most of my teaching philosophy was formed in reaction to my education and miseducation in fifteen years of British schooling and another five years at LSE, all of which I spent at home living with my parents in Clapton, part of the Hackney borough in northeast London, except for brief wartime evacuations in Huntingdonshire and Bedfordshire. That wartime period was disturbed and things did not quite settle down again until I joined LSE in 1954. Before then, and particularly before I joined Hackney Downs School in 1947, I consider much of my education to have been largely a waste of time, though not totally as obviously I learned my three R's in classes of over 50 pupils in lean times. Even so, arithmetic consisted of repeating out aloud in unison the times tables and doing 50 sums at a time. One mistake would entail another 50 sums. History was just memorizing lists of dates without explanation. Geography was tracing (when tracing paper was available) maps from an atlas without explanation. In English reading and writing, we learned poems by heart, again without explanation. For music, we danced around a maypole or sang folk songs. This kept us busy, things stuck, but we were passive learners, obediently doing what we were told to do and allowed almost no self-expression.

From very early on, we were streamed, that is, we were tested for ability and placed according to performance. The above average performers were presumably favored and allowed greater latitude, as no one could possibly keep track of all the comings and goings among students and staff. The big divide came at the age of ten or so when national examinations would determine which grade of secondary school to aim for. I was fortunate in being able to stay with the above average performers and scoring high enough in the 10+ examination to have a choice of grammar schools. The reality for most of us would be the nearest local grammar school. But there again after the first year, the pupils were graded and again in the early years the teaching was much the same as it had been in primary school. I suspect that the high flyers were once again favored and the rest were pretty much written off. I also suspect that at this stage, we learned more despite the system rather than because of it, simply because we (the above average performers) were able, had encouraging backgrounds with families keen on education for its own sake, and competed among ourselves to show how much we had learned from all sources. But I get ahead of myself.

EARLY CHILDHOOD

My pregnant mother was a sick lady. I was born sickly, certainly suffering from rickets that prevented my walking for several years. I lacked typical motor skills and for the first few years acted or reacted more like a vegetable. Except that there were signs of greater intelligence when my first spoken words took the form of a perfectly grammatical sentence. Later I had an instinctive flair for arithmetic, answering without showing any working out for which I was punished by the teachers, who thought I had cheated, although I had finished first. My family protected me and had faith that I would eventually catch up. Defying the doctors, my mother made me walk without supports. An older cousin with whom we were first evacuated insisted that I learn exactly what she was being taught and she was a hard taskmaster.

As an evacuee, I was bullied and resented for being teacher's pet. This country village school teacher had appointed me chalk monitor and inkwell monitor and gave me other chores that prevented my going out at play breaks and saved me from being teased and hit. The other children made up for this after school when my elder sister and I went back to the kind people with whom we lodged. The master of the house was also the Anglican churchwarden and he knew of our progress at Sunday school where we studied the Bible and where my schoolteacher also taught. One day, he saw us being chased from school by a crowd of children. Soon after, the ragging stopped and we were left alone.

These early childhood experiences never leave one. First, I discovered that nothing came or comes easy. One has to work hard, make sacrifices, suffer pain, and persist. I have watched so many others with superior natural gifts waste their time and fail to develop their talent. They gave up too quickly. They never really knew hard work because things came too easily to them. They did not seem to care until it was too late. To this day, whenever I see clever people fail to develop their superior talents, I feel great disappointment and find myself scornful because all of us lose when this happens.

Second, my heart always goes out to the disadvantaged, the handicapped, the backward, because I know what it was like being written off, disregarded, overlooked, and ignored. Everyone has something to contribute, some talent of some kind. It is just a matter of finding it, encouraging it, fostering it, and giving a person a fair chance. This does involve disappointment and frustration. One gets deceived, taken advantage of, one makes mistakes. But the reward of seeing someone do something for the first time, of achieving something that they once thought was beyond them, of realizing that if they only tried and made the effort, they could go on to the next step, is reward enough as every parent knows. The instructor should not expect to be rewarded. Better if people gain in self-confidence believing they did something by themselves unaided, even if this was not the case.

Third, I see little point in rote learning. I was always a poor rote learner. Why learn facts for their own sake? One can always find the facts when one needs them if one knows where to look. Why fill one's head with them? Better if one thinks about them, what they mean, what is the principle behind them, what is their context. Ramming facts down people's throats without explanation turns them off possibly for life. They become good at copying and repeating but they never truly understand; they have difficulty thinking things through, and their imagination and creativity can be driven out of them altogether. Imagination and creativity are precious. Of all the millions who play an instrument or read music, very few of them compose and even fewer have their compositions played after their deaths. So too of the millions who read and write, few are original enough to be recorded or published and their thoughts bequeathed to another generation. Too much imposed formal education suffocates real learning.

LATER CHILDHOOD

I was fortunate in being placed with the above average performers. I had the one prize teacher (Ms Smith) when evacuated to the village school, and she really stimulated me with her stories, mostly about British heroes and adventurers, and her encouragement. At the local Clapton primary school, Northwold Road, I had another (Ms Jones) who put up with my questions and with my sometimes peculiar stand. When once I was punished for not singing at the morning assembly as required, she actually asked me why I did not sing along. I replied that we had to sing this hymn 'All Things Bright and Beautiful' in which there was a verse saying that God makes the high and the lowly. I did not believe this to be true. Man makes the high and lowly. She told me that I did not have to sing and I would not be reprimanded again. This did not prevent me another time from being unfairly cornered by a playground monitor for supposedly teasing girls just as I emerged from where we drank our morning milk. I was marched up to the headmaster with several others and caned on the spot, despite my protestations, but nobody listened or cared. I never have gotten over the shame and the injustice to this day. I am told I was lucky that this happened only once, because for others this was a daily event – to be physically harmed by uncaring, insensitive teachers. Everyone should be given a hearing. Everyone should be protected from victimization and unwarranted punishment.

Hackney Downs School, formerly the Grocers' Company School, was a highly regarded secondary boys-only grammar school with a tradition of learning and a reputation for producing men of merit. Once a privileged school, it had been thrown open to all boys who had done well at the 10+ examination and who had been chosen after interview by its sterling headmaster (Mr T.O. Balk). It had superior facilities and the reputation of attracting good teachers. Actually more important at the time, many of its pupils drawn from the surrounding area were exceptionally talented and demanding. This was not so for the less talented; they were left behind and given a second-rate education. After the first year, each year was streamed into A, B and C with the last branded as inferior and made to feel so. They in turn took out their resentment in acting up, thereby justifying (?) the harsh treatment they received back. I suspect that they were not so stupid, as witnessed by their adult successes, just as conversely many in the A stream did not live up to their potential afterwards. Branding and stereotyping are wrong.

The A stream did have its share of real talent that egged on the others, not just in competition but also in genuine friendship. Some teachers delighted in having them around and encouraged them. Other teachers resented their gifts and tried sadistically to put the talented in their place. One pupil when bored composed poems. When caught, his poems were confiscated and destroyed without being read. The teacher did not stop to read them to see what they might show. That pupil later became one of Britain's foremost playwrights. That marked too much of the teaching system. One had to follow the rules regardless, copy, learn by heart, regurgitate without much opportunity to reveal one's talent. In the earlier years, one had to go by the book and stick to the straight and narrow. Anyone who deviated was reprimanded, demeaned and called some bad names, 'guttersnipe' being fairly common.

The later senior years were better. Already by this stage, some self-selection had taken place with parents withdrawing their sons from school, to go out into the real world and start earning a living. Those remaining knew what sacrifices were being made by their parents, who believed in education for its own sake. They also had their eye on higher education and the professions that were now, in Britain's new welfare state, more open to all the talents. The state and local authorities would pay university fees and subsistence allowances while the universities were prepared more than in the past to offer scholarships and places. By now many of the schoolteachers (particularly the newly college graduated) recognized that some of their pupils were cleverer than themselves and that they did not have much more to teach them. So they allowed the talented much more scope to study on their own and prepare themselves for higher education. Several tried their best to keep up, if not move ahead, and worked hard themselves so that they would not be outclassed or outdated.

I was one of those whose term work was always much better than my examination results, but it was the latter that counted most. How come the work that I was capable of doing was not reflected in the final examinations? Nobody knew how much work I had had to put into the school year, how many hours of homework I spent, how many libraries I visited to find sources, how many drafts I had discarded before I was satisfied.

Examinations were one-day affairs, mostly requiring rote learning (at which I was poor) or standard answers to standard questions. I did badly at the first set of statewide examinations, too badly to justify continuing on at school. But my parents had confidence in me that I would eventually make good. In response, I recognized that examinations had to be passed, like it or not. So, every weekend thereafter I practiced on past examinations, under examination conditions, in those subjects that most interested me and in which I had demonstrated I had some talent. Eventually, I grasped what areas were likely to come up, how answers had to be timed, and what might interest the examiners and the hard work paid off in the end.

What had I learned? First, that teachers can and do make a difference. They can kill interest or they can stimulate. The dull can ruin any topic. The creative can make anything interesting. One had to find some angle that would grip the audience and get people to change their minds. Second, teachers must respect all their pupils. Nobody should be written off. All should be encouraged to do their best and if that was not good enough, they should be instructed how to improve their performance. Do not condemn or insult. Be positive. Third, try to keep up with the brightest pupils. Go over their work carefully. Read every word. Point out errors but praise the effort and indicate willingness to see more. Fourth, remain human without becoming familiar. Do not be too stiff or too formal. Be relaxed. Apologize when wrong. Show trust but avoid showing disappointment when the trust is abused, as every so often it will be.

THE LSE UNDERGRADUATE YEARS

Higher education is indeed something different than high school. In my case, it was the exalted LSE, the queen of the social sciences. I had heard great things of it from relatives and friends and past and current students. One had to put aside Oxbridge images of rural landscapes, small neighborly towns, ancient colleges, intellects conversing with intellects at the frontiers of knowledge, High Table and all that tradition. LSE was in Aldwych, near the Law Courts, across from Bush House, but in the heart of downtown office-land and heavy London traffic. It was almost indistinguishable from the surrounding high-rise office buildings and if it were not pointed out, one could easily walk past it without knowing. It did not look like a university college at all. Its buildings had been altered and re-altered and at first it resembled a rabbits' warren. It was all utilitarian, nothing fancy, over-crowded, noisy, a busy hive of activity.

For first-year newcomers, LSE began on the first Wednesday of October at 10 am with an opening lecture in economic history. They all rushed in to get a good place in the Old Theatre to listen to the great professor who lectured from a podium on the stage, hard to hear from the back (and anywhere else when it was fully occupied). The lecturer read her notes for almost an hour without pause and without even looking up, and out she walked. There was no chance to question or interact in any way. Then off to the next lecture in another place, and so it went on. Having prepared myself beforehand, I had read the published work of the announced lecturers. What I heard was little different; they were regurgitating what they had already published and maybe added a few things here and there. The good were entertaining. The poor were just a bore, nowhere close to the quality of available texts. LSE, or rather its mass lecture system, was a let-down.

So after a few weeks, I rarely went to lectures again, excepting those of the celebrated and famous faculty and frequent visitors to LSE. Instead, I had discovered LSE's real treasure, its wonderful library of international renown, a storehouse for the social sciences. It was wonderful in its holdings, both open shelf and reserve stacks, but poor in accommodation. There were far too few places and to be sure of securing a seat, one had to be waiting outside when its doors opened promptly at 10 am. To keep one's seat, one had to resort to all kinds of tactics lest on taking a break, the seat were occupied by someone else with one's books and papers shoved aside. (As to finding books that could not be borrowed, that required a different set of tactics altogether.) There was never enough space in term time until late in the evening and before closing time at 10 pm. But weekends and vacations allowed Londoners like myself ample opportunity to browse.

Besides weekly lectures, LSE offered tutorials and seminars. One was allocated a tutor, usually a junior faculty member or a graduate assistant, who was free to direct his or her charges as he or she saw fit. They set exercises and research projects in their specializations and sometimes on anything they fancied. Some were excellent, everything one wished for in intellectual development, and deserved the highest praise. Others barely disguised their impatience with the slow learning and their contempt for the ignorant and lazy. But, on the whole, most had been carefully selected so they were challenging, stimulating, insightful and demanding. They kept one on one's toes and they could always find a topic that taxed one's abilities. The seminars and small classes varied in quality. The same groups of students would meet weekly under guidance to listen to presentations which were only as good as the presenters, some good, some not so good, and some a complete waste of everybody's time. Overall, the standard was not as high as expected. With most attendees unwilling to criticize the presenter (lest they be criticized in their turn), little interaction actually occurred. In the final year when one specialized, the seminars did not drag so much as there was more willingness to participate and students had something worthwhile to contribute. Again, it was luck of the draw. Some unlucky students found they learned absolutely nothing, while others could not wait for the next session to test their knowledge and wits.

But the year's work at LSE counted for very little. Examinations again dominated progress and degree grading. Part One of the BSc (Economics) degree required examinations in eight subjects after two years and Part Two required five examinations in one's specialization at the end of the third and final year. One could repeat Part One examinations, but only once. The sociologists suffered worse because all their examinations came only after three years. All the examinations were held day after day within the same fortnight in June, and the results would not be known until August. Nobody could tell what questions would be asked. Nobody knew who would mark the papers, or how. Nobody knew how the final grading would be determined. Theoretically, anything could be asked, whether or not a course had actually been completed as advertized. Political philosopher Michael Oakeshott, a star performer, never reached beyond the eighteenth century although his course of lectures was supposed to reach into the twentieth century, much to the disappointment of the student leftwingers. So one either crammed for the whole course or took a gamble on only selected parts in hopes that the choice would prove correct. In any event, one had to show in a handful of questions that one had mastered the field. It was do or die. Lapses of concentration and silly mistakes in the trauma of examination weeks could be fatal. Only one's answers on that day counted. Nothing else did.

My undergraduate years taught me different lessons from high school. The fundamental difference was to question the need for instruction. University students should be able to do without instruction, and prove capable of learning by themselves without guidance if necessary. That is what should distinguish them. If they could not go it alone, then they should be given remedial instruction until they could. Maybe this was wishful thinking. But other lessons were not. First, there is no substitute for reading, not just any old reading but the classics, the recognized authorities in the discipline whom everyone else copies with or without acknowledgment. Genius is rare but precious. Just reading the greats is not enough. One has to study them and think about what they have contributed that is unique. One has to master them, and go beyond them if possible. They may be already behind the times but they leave thoughts of lasting value. And they are so accessible, just a library or bookshop away (and these days just a computer program away), even if one has to wait a while when they are not immediately available. There is no substitute for the real thing. As I could not afford to start a library of my own or buy copies for myself, I made friends and relatives join public libraries and used their tickets, or I headed straight for the reference section and read sources on the spot.

Second, one-on-one teaching is superior to any other method. Lectures are too impersonal. They are good for just passing on information or introducing the audience to an exceptional performer. Otherwise, they are of limited value. When later I lectured to large audiences, I did not know how many could follow me, how many had switched off and were in their own dream world, how many had misunderstood what I had been saying, how many could not interpret their hasty notes afterwards. When as an experiment I did interrupt my narrative and pose questions to individuals, most minds were sure enough elsewhere. Seminars are too chancy. They have their place. With the right set of people prepared to do their homework, they can sparkle and incite top performances with intellectual rigor, something to look forward to and remember afterward. Too often, just a handful of participants can spoil it for everybody by showboating, interrupting, heckling and disrupting. Close intellectual intimacy is superior when minds interact and the line between instructor and instructed is blurred. To break down the barrier is difficult at first, and mistakes are likely until both become better acquainted and used to one another's style.

Third, examinations are rarely impersonal. The questions are set by somebody or some team with fixed agendas, usually without consultation with the examined so as to keep the examination secret. At LSE, as probably elsewhere, some of the best lecturers never completed their courses; but the examination had to cover the whole, and it was anyone's guess what might come up. This contrasted with other faculty who clearly set what personally interested them, sometimes quite selectively and narrowly, to the neglect perhaps of more important and significant areas central to the subject. Who marked and graded the examinations was a mystery. In those days at LSE, the answers were handwritten, poorly written too, some barely legible. Presumably, they would be marked in haste just as they were written in haste, and the great majority of answers, based on the same reading and lectures, would read much the same and send some examiners to sleep. It paid to write clearly, set out the plan of one's answer in case time ran out, and find some kind of different opening angle that would attract the examiner. After practising past examinations, I opted for a reinterpretation of the questions in order to write about what I wanted to write about, which I already had firmly in my mind before even seeing the examination paper. So much for impersonality and objectivity! None of this gamesmanship was a better indication of a person's worth than frequent exercises over a long period.

THE LSE POSTGRADUATE YEARS

I stayed on at LSE with a postgraduate bursary and jumped to the other side, becoming one of the instructors, although my main task was research for a higher degree under the supervision of a chosen faculty member, in my case a very eminent expert in my field who was austere, busy and distant. I actually only saw him maybe three or four times formally as a postgraduate student, once when we agreed on a research topic, another time after he had demanded to see my first chapter, a third to show me how he filed his research materials, and maybe once more when I submitted my final draft. Otherwise, he left me alone to go about my business, although he required me to attend his postgraduate seminars where we did discourse on key topics of the day. Once a year, he invited me to his home together with his other graduate charges.

The department to which we both belonged used me as a tutor for a handful of undergraduates every quarter. In addition, in order to keep body and soul together, I taught outside LSE. Graduates were allowed to teach in the school system under probation until inspected, when they would be fully certified. As my local area of London was always short of staff and needed substitutes whenever the permanent staff were absent, there were frequent vacancies, some one-day affairs, others could be for a term or more. One never knew where one would be sent or what age-level of pupil. One always hoped for one of the better schools and a subject one could teach at the drop of a hat. Usually, it was one of the poorer ('Blackboard Jungle') schools, and a subject that revealed one's ignorance or unpreparedness. One had to be ready to walk into any classroom and face a hostile audience. One had to learn quickly how to survive.

I consulted the experienced hands and asked how to handle difficult classes. I learned the tricks of the trade. After a series of one-day stands, I had regular assignments at the same schools until I eventually found a school, admittedly a tough one, on my route from home to LSE, so that I could teach during the day, take time off for crucial meetings at LSE, and do my research at LSE and elsewhere after school hours. My supervisor also recommended me to teach at colleges catering for foreign students, so I had a different audience from which I could learn about other countries. I was on a tough schedule trying to fit everything in and do well on my research at the same time.

What I learned about teaching was that I had to do my homework, prepare classes, and return written work as soon as possible and fairly graded. I had to keep the audiences interested and find ways to make them enthusiastic for more. I tried to appear as though I took a personal interest in everyone and that the individual's progress was my daily concern. The classes were not just anonymous groups but composed of individuals with different needs, interests, personalities, and ambitions. One could not fake interest; one had to show it by word and deed, in and out of the classroom, and take the initiative to organize class visits to places of interest, an easy thing to do in London with its multiple sites and its then first-class public transportation system. The foreign students saw a different London than the tourist. The schoolchildren had rarely been beyond walking distance from their homes, so the trips were a real adventure and enjoyable too. They showed their appreciation because, despite the fears and worries of other staff, they showed their best behavior and were no trouble at all.

ACADEMIC LIFE AFTER LSE

Thus, by the time I had graduated from LSE, my basic philosophy of teaching had been formed and tested under fire. It has never been set in concrete. At each subsequent university position, it was modified and reshaped. As Canada Council Fellow in Ottawa, I was allowed to teach part-time for the newly formed Carleton University where most of the students were much older than their instructor; but as many of them were career public servants and my research was on the federal civil service, we made a good fit. They learned academically from me while I learned a great deal from them about what it was like to work within the federal system. I brought the British Whitehall/Westminster culture and they presented Canada's reformulation of it.

Next, was my research in Canberra at the Australian National University which brought me even closer to the inside of how Australia was governed, while I brought a comparative perspective, much of my teaching again being with experienced career insiders rather than young political science undergraduates. Still, we spoke the same language and shared common values. The great contrast came at the Hebrew University in Jerusalem, where I was very much the outsider and had to learn the mysteries of the Israeli version of Middle East government and public administration. Here I taught mostly career public servants, and for the first time had large classes of undergraduates who harbored little intention of working in government. My whole approach to the subject was questioned by audiences who were not partial to the Anglo-Saxon view of governance.

I had to adjust once again when I taught in the United States, first in the San Francisco Bay area where and when the University of California at Berkeley and other local campuses were in uproar, and later in Los Angeles at the University of Southern California where, by that time, the campus itself was quieter than its School of Public Administration. In the 1960s, the counterculture of radicalized students and off-campus hippies made a target of the staid public bureaucrats of the establishment whom they saw as the lackeys of imperial capitalism. The audience for public administration was largely composed of students of varying ages who sought to rise in the public bureaucracy or were seeking to join its ranks as reformers. Getting to common ground was a trial. By the 1970s, things had quietened down but by this time it was the faculty who were split over what should be taught and how it should be taught, part of the intellectual crisis of that time. USC had the reputation of venturing into new areas, experimenting with new teaching formats such as the intensive course, and opening itself to large numbers of international students who brought quite different experiences and were not as enamored of American public management as their American counterparts. One had to learn new tricks.

1. Design an appropriate syllabus that covers the whole advertized subject, not just selected parts, not just the most interesting parts, while allowing for student choice of what they feel most important to them.
2. Choose the best available reading that is within the affordability of the average student, but ensure that multiple copies are available in the university library to be borrowed or held on reserve, and always keep a copy available for individuals to borrow even if they forget to return it. Do not set too much reading that overwhelms. Add up-to-date reading as it becomes available, so as to keep absolutely current.
3. Set a series of regular exercises and assignments to maintain a steady record on each student. Make each challenging, and expect higher and higher standards. Go over each exercise in detail to explain what was done collectively by quoting anonymously from the answers and explaining what was wrong.
4. Encourage participants to perform on their own, to show initiative, to be innovative in presentations. Explain how presentations could be improved in general and instruct the under-performers about what they personally need to work on.

5. Be generous in consultation and personal instruction where warranted. Be accessible by mail, phone, fax and email besides regular office hours.
6. Allow for personal contingencies, remembering that the students have other lives as well with their own problems and tribulations. They may need help to get through a bad patch.
7. Student grades should indicate fairly where they stand at any time. If they want to improve, allow them to do extra assignments and take home examinations which they cannot answer by copying, but must be their own unaided work.
8. Suggest that the participants get together in cooperative ventures to share the workload and help one another, also illustrating how it is more difficult to work with others than they imagine.
9. Get them to think outside the box, to look ahead into the future, and to anticipate what might be coming up.
10. Provoke participants with questions that require more sophisticated answers than usually given so that they can become highly qualified public service professionals, sensible, knowledgeable, enterprising, responsive and ethical.

But different levels of student require different consideration.

Doctoral candidates

Doctoral candidates have to be treated with special care from the very beginning. They are making real sacrifices that they probably cannot afford, financially, emotionally, socially and culturally (and that may never be compensated). Nothing really prepares them for the hard grind of the dissertation even if advances in technology have greatly reduced the clerical and physical burdens. It used to be that there was so much routine work involved that candidates were distracted from the intellectual side, which was demanding enough. On the other hand, candidates are rarely full-time. They have demanding jobs, families, communal commitments; they are very busy folk, spread wide, and impatient to finish. They do not comprehend the emotional rollercoaster that comes with original research, the highs when something new is discovered, the lows when things don't go as planned, designs fall apart, chaos reigns, results don't materialize and everything seems lost.

The doctoral supervisor has several roles. First, there is the obligation to the academic enterprise that candidates do complete their degree in good time. This means setting feasible and realistic timetables and schedules at every stage, and trying to make candidates stick to them by insisting on regular meetings to discuss progress and issues. Candidates underestimate just how much time is needed merely to write up what they have found, to revise drafts, and to assemble everything into the final dissertation. From the beginning, the supervisor must impress on candidates that they should be familiar with all the university rules and regulations on doctoral and dissertation requirements. They should familiarize themselves with what is expected by reading a sample of dissertations in the field. Some nagging will be involved.

Second, the supervisor has to keep things in proper perspective. Research carries candidates away into their own world. Things tend to be distorted and candidates too self-absorbed. When they drive themselves too hard or hit a wall, they have to be told to take a break and return refreshed. When they take out their frustrations on others, they must be told to ease up and devote time to restoring relations. There are things more important than finishing a dissertation, marital or parental obligations and duties being some of them. The supervisor has to be a wise counselor, trying to intervene without resentment yet offering helpful advice and, when unqualified, suggesting professional consultation.

Third, if there were difficulties before candidates began their doctoral studies, the stresses and strains are likely to make them worse. Mental illness is often not apparent although some symptoms may be clear to others. This is not something for amateur psychologists. It requires professional treatment. One of the hardest tasks of a supervisor is to detect mental illness and guide suspected sufferers toward obtaining proper help. Depression and loss of self-confidence are likewise difficult to handle. Sometimes, the candidate's imagination runs riot and difficulties are perceived where none exist or can be resolved by simple action. The supervisor has to be a good friend and trusted companion. If that relationship breaks down, the supervisor should suggest that someone else take over and confine his own role to purely academic advice.

Fourth, research has its surprises. Expected results do not materialize and sometimes nothing emerges despite much hard work and every attempt to prevent this occurring. The supervisor has to console the disappointed and the dejected, find a way of twisting things around and still produce a worthwhile dissertation, even if negative. The candidates did their best, demonstrated capacity for research and scholarship, and probably would have done better on another project. To some extent, the supervisor is responsible for not spotting an unfortunate outcome well beforehand and changing projects in time to avoid disaster. Where candidates have been warned and advised to change, but they persist because they are convinced they are right, there is not much one can do about such stubbornness except to avoid rubbing the fact in and to try to make lemonade out of lemons.

Fifth, sometimes, despite the misgivings of the supervisor, some candidates are bold and enterprising and embark on very ambitious research. They should not be discouraged. Because of the risks and expenses involved, too many dissertations are timid, sticking to the safe and narrow. As a result, they are probably only read by the candidate and the examiners, and no publication can be abstracted from them despite years of toil. The aim should be to turn the dissertation into a book or at least a couple of penetrating articles, and the candidates should often be reminded of this aim. The temptation is to leave the dissertation as it is and not bother with it again, simply because the effort of just getting there was exhausting enough. The supervisor should encourage the needed extra steps to be taken to justify the project to the world.

Master's level students

Doctoral candidates are the pick of the master's level graduates, most of whom do not intend to undertake further academic studies. In the case of public administration, they are more likely to be committed to a professional career in the public service. As pick of the undergraduates, they require little academic coaching except in research methods and presentation, and are probably more interested in career advancement than intellectual advancement. They want to know more about professional practice. They bring more experience, maturity and yen for career development than undergraduates, but like doctoral candidates they are likely to be busy people with many other interests and commitments. The subject matter for them has to be real, practical, hands-on, applicable and current. In response, I try to accommodate these busy people by teaching evenings, weekends, vacations, and compressed courses (intensives). However inconvenient to me, it is more convenient to them – although they may well come tired, hungry, out of sorts, and alas unprepared. I see this as a trade-off, for otherwise they might well drop out or not even register in the first place. Public administration needs every one it attracts, whether or not the students intend to become public officials (just as law schools benefit their students even though they may not want to practice law).

The instructor must be pragmatic. These students want to graduate and graduate fast. They are not going to be as knowledgeable as doctoral candidates, or willing to explore the subject as thoroughly. Unless the reading really grabs them, they are likely to skip; only the intellectually inclined will appreciate heaping the reading on them. They do not have time to keep current. It is the role of the instructor to see that they know about the burning issues of the day, what novelty is being employed or adopted, what works and what does not, and where the field appears to be heading. The exercises should be designed almost to force them to think about current events and developments and come to their own conclusions. They bring their own views, experience and ideals which they should be encouraged to share. This entails group participation and discussions which they can be relied on to organize for themselves. Indeed, they like to do so. They also have sufficient contacts to be able to obtain knowledgeable guest speakers who are valuable sources. Altogether, the learning experience should be enjoyable, mixing a variety of techniques and allowing the participants to have a say in what they want to study and how to organize themselves, including a course ombudsman to act as intermediary between instructor and instructed.

This all sounds good in theory, but circumstances are so varied that there is little telling beforehand what is likely to transpire. The instructor has to be flexible and understanding. Not every participant will fit in whatever is done. Not everyone will cooperate as expected. Not everyone will enjoy group work. Not everyone will see the purpose behind challenging exercises, even after repeated explanation; some want the answers beforehand so that they can regurgitate rather than think for themselves. Given the diversity of each group of participants and the uncertainties of postgraduate study, rarely will things go like clockwork; the instructor should expect the unexpected and be ready to adjust at a moment's notice. Few disciplinary problems should arise but those that do are likely to be messy, taxing and emotional, less academic (other than fear of failing) and more related to outside events and personal pressures, such as employer demands and family intrusions. Latitude is required but not to the extent of compromising academic requirements. The instructor has to keep a distance, much more than with doctoral candidates but less so than with undergraduates as the master's level students on the whole are more sophisticated, focused, self-directed, demanding and critical than the undergraduates.

The master's level students may not feel that they need individual attention, because they are expected to study alone, and they may believe that it is not right to draw attention to themselves. They do need academic assistance for a start and their career prospects may well be connected with their academic progress. While a distance should be maintained, it should not be so distant that they feel discouraged from consultations. The door must be kept open. Likewise, research does not come easy to those who have never done research before or whose work situation frowns on research. Master's level students should be required to demonstrate their research capability, which is what really distinguishes the postgraduate from the undergraduate. No doubt many working within the public bureaucracy (or any organization) are scared that they might reveal too much that is not supposed to be revealed to any outsider, and that might compromise their employer or themselves. Nonetheless, despite protestations, they should know that research is a requirement of postgraduate studies and that an essential part of being a master of any subject is to demonstrate proficiency in research.

Joint research may overcome individual qualms and help share the workload, but it introduces other problems of who really did what, who contributed and who coasted, who labored and who just put their name to the final product. Actually, these are minor problems as in practice, the dishonest who claim more than their fair share are easily detected by asking to see the documentation, reviewing the writing style, and listening to the complaints of the truthful with their backing evidence. Providing the participants know what is involved, there should be little objection to master's level students working their way together through the degree by taking the same courses together, forming their own study groups, and helping one another as they go along.

Undergraduates

Teaching undergraduates is the most trying of all. One wonders why they choose the courses they do. Some have no option; everyone is required to take certain selected/compulsory courses. For others, it is the only course that fits into their schedule; the time is convenient. The larger the class size, the more work is entailed in written assignments and the less chance of getting to know the students as much as one would like. One of the reasons I chose to teach at USC was that it limited the size of classes and although that cap has since been raised, I have not had to lecture to large anonymous audiences, relying on graduate assistants to act as intermediaries. Unfortunately, undergraduates expect to be lectured at and to take notes. It is difficult to persuade them that little real learning takes place that way. They are so busy taking notes that they do not listen; they hear and expect afterwards that their notes will convey the message. Without notes, they rarely remember anything after just a few days.

Because one assumes no knowledge at all or only scattered memories of related topics studied in the past, one has to lecture at first until sufficient time has passed to assume some reading has been done. The first exercises can determine which students should be there at all, that is, which students lack fundamental skills to do the required work. These should be counseled into remedial studies and warned that they will be expected to perform as well as anybody else. This preliminary sort-out also indicates roughly where everybody stands, from the high flyers who stand above the average down to the problem cases who lack skills or interest or concern. Early on, too, the students can tell who is who when they see who takes the initiative in discussion groups and who is nominated by their peers to report back to the class, as contrasted with those who remain silent and shy away from making presentations. This is not infallible, as some who push themselves forward are showboats without much substance behind them, and the quiet folk may be merely shy or feeling their way in what is for them a new subject.

The high flyers rarely give any cause for concern. They always seem to know what to do; they perform well at whatever they attempt; they can be trusted to do what is right. They are a joy to teach. What they need is to be encouraged to take full advantage of what the university offers outside the classroom, especially in student union leadership, student association activities, campus visitors, vacation employment and university connections that present uncommon opportunities to meet people and make contacts. Some of these activities are likely to be more important after graduation than their studies or degree.

In contrast, the problem cases slow the class down, somehow do not seem to know what is required and are content to drift along. Early on, they should be taken aside and told what to do to improve their performance. Some respond well, take heed of the advice and make good progress thereafter. Others shrug off any criticism, become very defensive, and blame others, not themselves. A poor grade at mid-term examinations does persuade some to drop out or to sit up. The rest are content with the lowest possible passing grade, doing only what is minimally required, but no more.

The number of those between varies considerably. They prefer a quiet life, not exactly over-exerting themselves but not slacking off either. Their major problem is that they have difficulty learning for themselves, and need to be guided. To help them, one tries to match them up with a high flyer but as this cannot be done obviously without branding, it does not happen that often. When it does, the impatient high flyer tends to take over and shield the partner, thus defeating the whole purpose of trying to get the average student to emulate the high flyer who usually does not tolerate being dragged down.

All undergraduates like to do something different, and welcome the opportunity to show what they can do. Their first presentations and exercises may be faulty, but once it is explained how their performance can be improved they do much better. Getting them to find things out for themselves is challenging and builds self-confidence. The assignments are designed to get them to do research on their own, assemble their findings for a presentation that keeps their peers interested, engaged and receptive, and write up their results after presentation for possible publication. Not everyone likes this approach, finding it too challenging, too self-directed, too ambivalent when used to being told exactly what to do. Learning should be fun, and it becomes so when the students believe they have done it all by themselves. The test is when they return five years later and say that they still have not forgotten what they were taught, even though at the time they felt they were doing all the work and not receiving sufficient direction.

The best reward of all is to see and follow the professional successes of one's former students. It must always be remembered that several will eventually outshine their instructors and were probably already ahead of them, though they tried not to make that fact too obvious. Others, never too happy in an academic environment, cannot wait to prove themselves in a different environment. And the late developers come eventually into their own and surprise everyone who never suspected their hidden talents. In any event, there is great joy in seeing all of them do well and even greater joy when they keep in touch, keep one informed of their achievements, and share their domestic as well as professional lives.

1

'Resisting Change': Some Critical Remarks on Contemporary Narratives about Reform

DEMETRIOS ARGYRIADES

> Public Service Reform (PSR) is a planned, deliberate program of intervention to achieve specific objectives, in spite of resistance. (Caiden 1969: 8)

INTRODUCTION

'Public Service reform', as a long-time observer and student of the field recently pointed out, 'never goes out of style' (Caiden & Sundaram 2004). In almost every country, it has been featured prominently on government agendas and the political platforms of the opposition parties competing for attention. Considering the risks, complexities and costs of most reform agendas, their slow implementation and very mixed results, we may be justified in pondering the frequency, ubiquity and undiminished appeal of public service reform.

We will leave aside for now the attacks against 'bureaucracy', invariably portrayed as 'bloated', 'unresponsive', 'rigid', and 'ineffectual'. It is symptomatic that such recurrent themes have been a *leitmotif* of populist rhetoric over the past two centuries, and that the stereotype of pompous, rules-addicted and paper-pushing bureaucrats remains a favored scapegoat of journalists and politicians and a caricature consistently popular among novelists and pamphleteers.

The currency of such metaphors can hardly be accidental. It invites us to reflect on the role that government plays in the daily lives of all of us, on the relevance of needs which public administration addresses or satisfies and our resulting dependence on 'officialdom'. Curiously, this dependency has not decreased substantially nor have the 'mounting costs' of government diminished as a result of reforms which in the past two decades have featured such prescriptions as downsizing, deregulation, 'outsourcing' and 'privatization'.

By contrast, the styles and narratives of public service reform have changed considerably over the years. Remarkably, these narratives have had much less to do with the avowed objective of bringing more efficiency, economy and effectiveness into the public service. Far more, both styles and narratives have been shaped and reshaped by shifting paradigms of state and public service, the scope and role of government and, in the last analysis, changing visions of society, redefinitions of citizenship and distinct conceptions of Man. Indeed, it would be plausible to argue, paraphrasing Paul Valéry, that all great new departures in government and public administration necessarily imply a different model of Man.[1]

SHIFTING MODELS OF REFORM

Contrary to the assertion that 'management is management', so often bandied about by NPM enthusiasts, the history of reform over the past two centuries suggests a different story. It shows that what has driven the agendas on reform have been ideas drawn from the realms of politics, philosophy, the law and, in the twentieth century, industrial engineering, psychology, sociology and economics. To illustrate this point, it may be worth our while to offer a cursory survey of dominant ideologies which furnished the underpinnings for successive waves of reform. The purpose of this exercise is not to argue their merits or to critique their flaws, but rather to place reform in an historical context and to emphasize the role of the sociopolitical and economic environment within which it unfolds. This approach will cast some doubt on the prescriptive value of models as guidelines for state action.[2] It will bring into focus the uses and abuses of cross-border international public policy transfers.

At the risk of some degree of generalization, it is possible to argue that public administration and public service reform have known four major stages during the past two centuries. Remarkably, every stage has been designed to address one main dimension of the nature and role of the modern state. The intellectual dominance and hegemony of European Powers (later of North America) during this period of time explains to a large extent the ubiquity of this pattern in some important aspects. Significantly also, all these stages left an imprint on public service systems, though their respective legacies do not coexist harmoniously in all cases. Indeed, the resulting friction and contradictions may be viewed as causal factors of subsequent reforms.

The Bureaucratic State

The bureaucratic state represents the signal legacy of enlightened despotism and of the Age of Reason. Peter the Great in Russia, Frederick II in Prussia, Richelieu and Napoleon in France associated their names with institution-building, which laid the foundations of public service systems in their respective countries (Argyriades 2001).[3] A very similar course took the United Kingdom, Japan under the Meiji and the Kingdom of Thailand down the path of reform during the nineteenth century (Sakamoto 2001).[4]

What all these reforms had in common was a vision of the state as the principal agent of progress and modernization. It was this powerful vision which acted as a catalyst of public service reform. It helped transform a band of courtiers and retainers into a great profession. Napoleon expressed this thought in the following eloquent terms:

> I want to constitute in France a civil order. To this day, there are in the world but two powers: the military and the ecclesiastic. More than anything else, I want a corporate body, because a corporation will not die [... a corporation] has no other ambition than to be of service and no other interest but the public interest [...] I want a corps whose management and statutes become so national in character that no one will ever lightly tamper with them. (Argyriades 1996: 49)

In his theory of the state, the German philosopher Hegel echoed Napoleon's sentiments:

> What the service of the state really requires is than men shall forgo the selfish and capricious satisfaction of their subjective ends. By this very sacrifice, they acquire the right to find their satisfaction in, but only in, the dutiful discharge of their public functions. (Argyriades 1996)

Implicit in these statements is the belief that a public service should be truly a public domain and that the state – because it is the state – should be a model employer. Open competitive examinations, close links between recruitment and public education and a career which offered rewards for industry and merit (*carrière ouverte aux talents*) were designed to give effect to these objectives.

The Democratic State

Related to this goal was an assault on jobbery and clientelism which became major concerns with the advent of democracy, as political parties competed for electoral support. Curbing executive patronage helped introduce a measure of probity and transparency into the conduct of government business. It also added momentum to the reexamination of policies and practices on the recruitment and staffing of civil service establishments. Such piecemeal steps, however, did not invariably strike at the root of the problem. This was succinctly expressed by the Northcote & Trevelyan Report in the following challenging terms:

> It may safely be asserted that, as matters now stand, the Government of the Country could not be carried on without the aid of an efficient body of permanent officers, occupying a position duly subordinate to that of the Ministers, who are directly responsible to the Crown and to Parliament, yet possessing sufficient independence, character, ability and experience to be able to advise and, to some extent, influence those who are from time to time set over them.[5]

One hundred and fifty years have elapsed since the issuance of this Report, yet its findings and conclusions have lost none of their relevance. The quest for men and women of talent and integrity remains an abiding concern of public service reform in most parts of the world. Now as in earlier days, governments must compete in the market for high-level skills fully conscious of the fact that, as in the nineteenth century, promising men and women will go 'where the prizes are to be found'.[6] What has drastically changed in the intervening period is the scope and scale of government and the degree of complexity which marks its operations. What has most certainly grown is the pressing need for people of 'independence, character, ability and experience to be able to advise and, to some extent, influence those who are from time to time set over them.' All are ultimately traceable to new definitions of citizenship and concepts of the state, which democracy brought in its wake.

Democracy and elections turned 'subjects' into citizens and the 'night-watchman state' into a welfare state which cares about its citizens and broad domestic issues, not merely about law and order, defense and foreign affairs. Democracy, however, also transformed the patterns, modalities and processes of governance on almost every level. With the progress of democracy, norms like accountability, responsiveness, transparency, due process, respect for human rights and for the rule of law gradually acquired new salience because they were now in demand and could also be enforced. These added to the qualities and competencies required of public servants. Though, like their predecessors in the days of absolute monarchy, they serve the executive power, they must now be aware not merely of the limits of the authority which may be vested in them but also of the propriety of the methods which they apply. Not only what they do, but also how they do it takes on major importance as the core of sound democratic governance. This salient trait of governance – the 'how', not only the 'what' – is sometimes overlooked.

Democracy, the Welfare State…

In most parts of the world, shifting political platforms are widely and rightly considered necessary features of democratic politics. The frequent change of governments and the rapid succession of ministers may well be facts of life in many countries. But they create conditions which might become intolerable without institutional frameworks and personnel ensuring the degree of consistency, coherence, continuity and credibility which the rule of law and survival impose as pivotal needs. Of course, it is no accident that securing these 4Cs under the rule of law became a major plank of public service reform, especially with the advent of democratic pluralism. The dangers notwithstanding of fostering 'careerism' and overly protecting the bureaucratic elites from 'the winds of change', the public service statutes which since the nineteenth century served as pivotal instruments of public service reform, accorded pride of place to the objective of safeguarding neutrality, professionalism and a certain degree of autonomy for public servants. This goal was closely related to institution-building concerns but also to the need to enhance the level of integrity in the political sphere and public life in general.

From the famous Pendleton Act (1883) in the USA to our own days, legislation has endeavored to protect public service employees against arbitrary power but also to design needed career structures which can attract, retain, develop and motivate talented men and women who direct all their energies to the single-minded pursuit of the long-term public interest and the good of the citizenry at large. In many parts of the world, the emergence of trade unions within the public sector has reinforced this trend. From the early twentieth century on, professional associations and unions of public servants became important partners and often vocal players in the process of reform.

Almost throughout the world, it was the period following World War II which saw the most decisive expansion and reform of state and public service. During the thirty years after 1945, the range of government functions was stretched to include provision of all the basic services, notably health, education, housing and social welfare. It should not be overlooked that these were also the years of decolonization, which began in South Asia and rapidly spread to Africa and other parts of the world.

On a global scale, the change was qualitative as well as quantitative. Nationally and internationally, the promise of reform, together with the challenges that come with independence, demanded vast new programs and institution-building on a scale almost without precedent. These significant departures in turn required professional cadres able both to design and to manage the policies and programs which marked the new profile of state and public servant. The postwar state emerged as primarily responsible not only for good governance and stewardship of the country's resources, but also for the welfare of each and every citizen 'from cradle to grave', as the popular expression of the 1950s and 60s suggested. True, this change was in the making for some time before the war, but triumph over fascism accelerated the process. Throughout the world, victory was perceived as a triumph over the forces of militarism, intolerance, repression and injustice. The establishment of the United Nations in June 1945, and the contents of its Charter and of the Universal Declaration of Human Rights three years later, strongly reinforced this view and added momentum to pressures for decolonization, national liberation and socioeconomic reforms.

Unlike its short-lived precursor the Covenant of the League of Nations, the Charter of the United Nations gave prominence to international economic and social cooperation (Articles 55–60). This meant that peace and development required collective action and consultation among the member states. The Marshall Plan for Europe was arguably the earliest and most ambitious experiment with this new approach in mind. At a cost which in 2003 (taking account of inflation) would amount to US$ 100 billion, the Marshall Plan exemplified the view that tackling the complexities of rehabilitation and reconstruction in war-torn Europe was a task of enormous proportions that could simply not be left to *laissez-faire* initiatives. The machinery of the state and the techniques of planning which had served to win the war against the Axis Powers were redirected toward this purpose. The success of this experiment soon turned it into a beacon and a model for the tasks of construction and development in the new states emerging from the process of decolonization.

. . . and Development Agendas

In 1994, looking back at postwar development, a group of MIT scholars revisited this model in an attempt to explain its nature and rationale:

> Post-World War Two development economists were neither naively pro-state nor diabolically anti-market; they just saw room for public intervention. How could they think otherwise, after experiencing the Depression and the war, and after being under the intellectual spell of John Maynard Keynes? (Taylor, in Rodwin & Schon 1994: 61)

Whether the model did exude an overweening confidence (as has been suggested by Rothschild, in Rodwin & Schon 1994: 113) or not, it caused a UN Group of Experts in 1951 to set eight preconditions of economic development. The group included both W. Arthur Lewis and Theodore W. Schultz. Its policy prescriptions were peremptory: the government should, for example, 'establish a central economic unit' and 'announce its programs for expanding employment'. Its historical theories were similarly grand: 'progress occurs only where people believe that man can, by conscious effort, master nature'. It incorporated the political conditions for growth: 'there cannot be rapid economic progress [. . . without] the creation of a society from which economic, political, and social privileges have been eliminated'. The group in effect demanded a revolution in moral and social life: 'ancient philosophies have to be scrapped; old social institutions have to disintegrate; the bonds of caste and creed have to be done away with; and large numbers of people who cannot keep up with progress have to have their expectations of a comfortable life frustrated' (Rothschild, in Rodwin & Schon 1994: 114).

Central planning became *de rigueur* (Galbraith 1964: 62) and with it a centralized administrative system. The concept of reform as a planned, induced, deliberate and orchestrated change, often against resistance (Caiden 1991: 67 and *passim*), encouraged the belief that progress with reform and therefore with development and modernization depended on the effectiveness of a central agency charged with the task of improving the administrative system. In an attempt to bolster its status, power and outreach, the apex and the center of the machinery of government became the choice location for its activities and the hub for units responsible for public service reform as well as development planning. In several countries, for instance, the president's establishment or the prime minister's office was greatly reinforced precisely on this account. Their role in the design, control and coordination of overall government policy received attention and prominence.[7]

These centralizing tendencies were as pronounced as they were ubiquitous. In retrospect, however, outcomes and expectations did not invariably match and in a number of cases the pursuit of central control produced many unintended consequences. According to a review of administrative reform in the Arab world,

> The problems of performance and deviations of practices are always dealt with by upgrading them to higher administrative levels, claiming to achieve more control in order to prevent problems from reoccurring, instead of getting the participation of all involved executive parties to study the specific reasons of these problems and hence take the proper procedures to eradicate them. (Al-Saigh 1986: 49)

Still, there is little doubt that for the best part of the 1960s and well into the 70s the central planning mechanisms, together with the functions of outreach, coordination and control, continued to attract the attention of reformers. They remained a principal focus of the UN Technical Cooperation Program in Public Administration and Finance (Argyriades 1995). Thus, a UN report on the *Administrative Aspects of Plan Implementation* observed:

> Studies reveal that the administrative machinery responsible for plan implementation is one of the most frequent obstacles to planning. The feasibility of plans depends not only on proper coordination of their objectives and instruments and on technical, economic and financial factors, but also on the administrative possibilities of implementing them. Hence the need to specify clearly the institutions, procedures and executive capacity which are to be used.[8]

According to the report, the human resources were often found wanting. Therefore, personnel development became a central pillar of the development effort as well as a major focus of the UN in public service reform. Pre- and in-service training emerged in the 1950s and 60s as pivotal concerns. In a manner which broadly reflected the spirit of the times, an institution-building approach was distinctly preferred. The 1950s, 60s and 70s saw the creation of centers, national schools and institutes of public administration for training and research in many parts of the world. Often they encountered opposition from university faculties of law and political science which cast doubt on the legitimacy of these professional schools and centers of research. Examples abound on both the national and regional levels. In the developing countries, many of these schools or institutes were sponsored by multilateral and bilateral technical cooperation programs.[9]

It needs to be emphasized that assiduous training during this period promoted a new profile of the public servant as both an accomplished adviser and able program manager. It exemplified the influence of prevailing development theories, especially in the way that they reshaped the contents and direction of the field for practitioners and scholars. The period in question – the 1960s in particular – is the high watermark of comparative and development administration, two areas whose emergence owe much to discontent with previous dogmatic approaches but also to decolonization and several bilateral and multilateral aid programs (Farazmand 2001; Siffin 1959; Frederickson 2004).

It may be safely affirmed that in this phase development concerns took center stage in the study and practice of public administration (Subramaniam 2003). Socioeconomic growth in quantifiable terms became the prime objective, requiring state initiative particularly in areas where private enterprise and civil society at large would not suffice or could not meet the challenge. The implications were far-reaching. For citizens at large, socioeconomic progress (later to be defined in terms of human development) (ul Haq 1995) carried the latent promise of growing opportunities for men and women alike, a rising standard of living and access to the benefits that civilization had hitherto vouchsafed only to very few.

RISE OF A COUNTER-CULTURE: THE MARKET MODEL OF GOVERNMENT

Already in the late 1970s and more emphatically during the 1980s, a powerful counter-culture asserted itself. It started in New Zealand but soon moved to Australia, the UK and the USA. The lingering global recession added to its credibility, and after the sudden collapse of the USSR (which was widely perceived as the demise of socialism) it came to be portrayed as *the* key to the future and as the official doctrine of the post-welfare state, post-Cold War ‘new world order’.

What started as a strategy to tackle budget deficits and reduce inflation developed into a full-scale offensive against ‘big government’, bureaucracy and the welfare state. The thrust of this attack, which has only very recently started to lose momentum, was to reverse a process which many people argued was leading to government failure. The tenets of this doctrine represented, in effect, a veritable antithesis to the trends which for more than a century had pushed in the direction of public sector growth. These tenets of the doctrine known as New Public Management (NPM) can be summarized in the following terms: decentralization, devolution and deconcentration, debureaucratization, deregulation, downsizing, outsourcing and privatization of public sector activities. Privatization and marketization took on a variety of forms which shared the common purpose of 'shrinking the state' and converting government, as far as that was possible, to private sector ways.

Both in theory and in practice, the implications of this posture were drastic and far-reaching. Central planning was quietly dropped as were the centralized approaches to personnel management that had previously been favored. Devolving responsibility meant surrendering control over decisions and inputs to the program action officer. It meant 'letting the manager manage'. To encourage a 'business mindset', competitive arrangements such as 'performance contracts', deceptively flattened hierarchies and such organizations as 'executive agencies' were preferred over more traditional patterns. The 'entrepreneurial manager' was lionized. Responsiveness to citizens was also highly prized on the principle that citizens, in fact, were the government's clients and should be treated as such. Efficiency and effectiveness ranked high in the hierarchy of values. By contrast, other principles received short shrift. In spite of much lip service to the contrary, professionalism, ethics, respect for the rule of law and due process lost ground. They were viewed by supporters of NPM as elements in 'the traditional structures of governance that needed to be minimized as [...] they might interfere with the effectiveness and efficiency of the performance of public administration in economic terms' (Sommermann 2001: 2). Legality and professionalism received belated attention and only as a reaction to the spreading pandemic of bribery, and mostly from the vantage point of safeguarding economy and efficiency in business and government.[10]

Models as maps ... or metaphors

In his critique of models, the famous US economist Paul Krugman has shown their strengths and weaknesses in shaping and promoting development agendas during the postwar decades:

> There is no alternative to models. We all think in simplified models, all the time. The sophisticated thing to do is not to pretend to stop, but to be self-conscious – to be aware that your models are maps rather than reality [...]
>
> In fact, we are all builders and purveyors of unrealistic simplifications. Some of us are self-aware; we use our models as metaphors. Others, including people who are indisputably brilliant and seemingly sophisticated, are sleep-walkers; they viciously use metaphors as models. (Krugman 1994: 51–52)

For more than twenty years, the market 'model' of government has guided the discourse of public administration and public service reform. The perils of its legacy did not take long to surface. 'One size does not fit all', yet uniform perspectives and one-dimensional thinking encouraged an approach to public service reform to which all factors other than management and economics appeared as largely irrelevant. It has been pointed out that the best guides for action are prevalent traditions and practices in governance (Bevir, Rhodes & Weller 2003). Only on the rare occasions of total system breakdown, when readiness to accept any way out comes with complete rejection of the old status quo, can 'made abroad, ready to wear' approaches and related radical strategies be preferred. Otherwise, homegrown solutions and feasible gradual reforms should be the order of the day. Other than in reforms which target the introduction of standard new technologies or the adoption of new tools, administrative mimetism seldom brings forth results.

The Importance of Context and Culture

Failure to grasp the meaning of the rule of law has been one major fallacy of this approach.[11] Lack of appreciation of the historical background, the social context and culture has been another. Often reforms proceeded as if the human factor and sociopolitical context could be overlooked, as if re-engineering was really all that mattered. In reality, however,

> Interventions operate in complex social systems, with their attendant conflicts, disparate interests, loose connections, and long and multifaceted causal chains... [reducing] our capacity to predict and control behavior. This is bad news for managers who are looking for interventions that will produce specific, intended effects. It is also bad news for social scientists who believe they can develop such interventions and for those who are laboring under the delusion that the interventions they already developed work like that. And it is bad news for consultants who want to sell neat solutions and quick fixes [...] An evolutionary perspective does not provide human resources practitioners with the comfort of a best way or with the illusion of certainty [...It] settles, instead, for improving adaptive processes, maintenance, and limited improvement, ever mindful of context and conflict. (Colareli 2003: 318, 321)

Lack of historical depth and radical proclivities are particularly in evidence when the adoption of new practices comes along with strings attached and the effects of mimetism are forced upon recalcitrant but also resourceless 'customers'. Often such impositions came from major donor agencies in the name of science and technological progress or globalization.

It may be pointed out that, as experience shows, public administration and public service reform are very seldom limited to simple exercises in technological innovation. Because of their distinct ideological bent, in the 1980s and 90s especially, the entire public sector and government system were targeted. The term 'public service reform' was intentionally used to cover a broad spectrum of employees paid out of public funds. Like 'civil service reform' (the term preferred in the past), it was meant to convey the impression of systemic efforts to modify and improve the institutional framework, terms and conditions of service, as well as, in some cases, the vision, mission and functions of public employees.

Rhetoric and Reality

Like so frequently in the past, such administrative reforms have been externally driven. Arguably, on that account they may have been envisioned as deliberate 'forced entry' and consequently planned with the certain expectation of encountering resistance. Indeed, how far 'resistance' is an essential feature of administrative reform – whether, in other words, the long-professed belief in the necessity of conflict is a *sine qua non* of the process of reform – remains an open question. There is reason to believe that practitioners and scholars have been prisoners of narratives which, over the past one century, dominated the discourse on administrative reform. In the words of an eminent scholar on the other side of the Atlantic:

> La réflexion sur l'administration se coule dans le moule des modèles d'administration. Ces modèles alimentent, par leur vision de la situation et du futur de l'administration, les analyses théoriques qui sont faites et les scénarios imaginés sur ses évolutions et ses transformations (Gérard Timsit, 1986).[12]

THE FORCE OF IDEOLOGY

There can be no denying the force of ideology in giving those narratives shape. Nor is there reason to doubt the significant impact of models in determining the course and contents of the discourse on public service reform and human resources management in general. We need to be reminded, however, of who the 'movers and shakers' of these models have been, where the discourse took place and which parts of the world served as a point of reference or source of inspiration in this regard.

I have already pointed out that the main early contributors to the discourse, on both sides of the Atlantic, were lawyers and philosophers, industrial engineers like Taylor and Fayol, and later, social scientists. Psychologists, sociologists and social anthropologists dominated the scene from the 1930s through the 60s, which also marked the heyday of the Human Relations Movement. As we have seen, this movement was later superseded by the New Public Management which to all intents and purposes represented the triumph of neo-liberal thought. The noted American scholar Ferrel Heady described it as 'representing the most recent urge to develop a science of administration, with principles of universal validity' (Heady 2001: 391).

Contrary to such pretensions, New Public Management theory remains an emanation of economic thought, a common law tradition and a management culture specific to an important, certainly, but still small group of countries. Whatever one may think of its prescriptive doctrines, their relevance to the problems and needs of developing countries has been increasingly questioned. Its early successes and outreach can largely be attributed to the degree of support which it received from certain Western governments and major international financial institutions.

It was against the effects of hasty and uncritical international policy transfers and the negative results of administrative mimetism that comparative and developmental administration emerged as a new field during the 1950s and 60s (Siffin 1959; Farazmand 2001). During those two decades, the focus of attention shifted towards the context or what was termed the 'ecology' of public administration (Riggs 1961). Acceptance of diversity brought in its trail a stress on the indigenization of administrative practices. It lasted twenty years and gave the UN development programs the distinctive approach which marked an era of decolonization and institution-building.

Coming into its own during the 1980s, the New Public Management represented, in effect, a drastic reversal of course. It presaged a departure from well-established legacies, rejection of the assumptions on which they had been founded and a return to principles which typified approaches to management theory and practice of the early 1900s. A focus on technique, the quest for standard tools and stress on cost-effectiveness went in tandem with 'reinvention' of scientific management married this time, however, to neo-liberal economics. Intolerance of pluralism provided the underpinnings for belief in 'one best way'. It led to propagation of the so-called 'best practices' – 'one size fits all' – solutions deemed to provide the answer to problem situations in a wide range of contexts.

The Strangely Resilient Myths of 'Irreversible Progress' and 'Global Convergence'

'Convergence' was the myth which lent support to such practices and belief systems (Pollitt 2001). Reinforced by the conviction that the end of the Cold War had also spelled the end of ideological pluralism, NPM offered its model – the market model of government – as *the* key to the future. The market model of government, it was assumed, pointed the way to reform. The pioneers of change, that is to say New Zealand, Australia, the UK and the USA, provided an example for all other countries to follow. A universe of cultures largely defined by history, geography, tradition, religion, custom and law (Hofstede 1997) was neatly subdivided into a descending order of quality and efficiency. It featured 'heroes and villains, or leaders and laggards (all) in the march to the land of plenty' (Premfors 1998: 143).

According to this line of thought, administrative reform was viewed in terms of convergence. Divergence from the 'norm' was correspondingly ignored, discounted or critiqued as an aberration, as errors of the past no doubt to be corrected with the advance of globalization (Premfors 1998). Implicit in this doctrine is an idea, of progress, Progress with a capital P. Hardly a new idea, it represents a feature of Western European political thought since the early nineteenth century, or arguably much earlier. This idea of Progress, propelled by historical forces in one direction only and quasi-irreversible, has been largely criticized as resting on false premises (Popper 1960; Nisbet 1993). Remarkably, however, it continues to exert a formidable influence across the political spectrum. Worse still, it has been exploited as a powerful marketing tool. Undoubtedly, it responds to fear of ambiguity as it appeals to people's strong desire for certainty and predictability.[13]

Over time, as we have seen, such ideas of progress and irreversibility have divided the bulk of humanity into 'heroes' and 'villains'. They have pitted the forces of 'progress' against those of 'backwardness', proponents of reform against 'old-guard reactionaries', 'revolutionaries' against 'counterrevolutionaries'. In this light, 'resisting change' has been portrayed invariably as worse than ill-advised, as mostly futile and pernicious. All militant ideologies have shared in the proclivity to bifurcate humanity in this simplistic manner. Differences notwithstanding, they have shared a common language indicative of both rejection of the past and the identification of 'new' with 'virtuous' or 'progress' with 'reform'. Disdain for 'old' and 'past' has always gone in tandem with a claim to supersession amounting to a monopoly over the future. 'Unser die Zukunft' was the motto of radical rightwing ideologies during the 1930s. Was it perhaps the implosion of the USSR that inspired *The End of History and the Last Man*? (Fukuyama 1993). Its author Francis Fukuyama was a cosignatory of the 'neo-con' manifesto significantly entitled 'Project for the American Century'. Wholesale rejection of models that hail back to the past resonates in the following passage of an Australian advocate of the New Public Management:

> The traditional model of administration is obsolete and has been effectively replaced by a new model of public management. This change represents a paradigm shift from a bureaucratic model of administration to a market model of management closely related to that of the private sector. Managerial reforms mean a transformation, not only of public management, but of the relationships between market and government, government and the bureaucracy, and bureaucracy and the citizenry. (Hughes 1998: 242)

From Welfare to Warfare

What is novel in New Public Management is neither its embrace of reform nor its claims to innovation, neither hopes of global outreach despite its ethnocentricism nor its scientific pretensions. Rather, in spite of *non sequiturs*, inconsistencies and contradictions,[14] its originality lies in its lack of historical depth (history is simply ignored or discarded as obsolete) and the sweeping radicalism of its political message.[15]

Over time this political message has shifted. Its thrust and contents have changed in line with the goals served and sources of support or inspiration. Viewed as an emanation of the economic doctrines of the Chicago School, it was identified with policies pursued by Margaret Thatcher in the UK and Ronald Reagan in the USA. Especially in the latter, it has been closely tied to the political fortunes and militant ideology of the Republican right. During the past five years, or roughly since the election of George W. Bush, a surge of fundamentalism – religious and political – has given a twist to the 'reinvention movement', which is New Public Management in an American context.[16]

Spilling over into management, the force of fundamentalism has been felt on several levels. In very basic ways, it has altered many assumptions which underpin the policies and practices of management. Perhaps more than anything else, it undermined the positive, Promethean and progressive view of Man which represents the legacy of the Human Relations Movement but harks back to the Enlightenment and arguably beyond. The tendency thereafter has been to revert to approaches which lay stress upon discipline, dependency, hierarchy and control. A sharp swing of the pendulum appeared to reinstate ideas on human nature which, in the early 1960s, a classic management textbook had summed up characteristically as 'Theory X' (McGregor 1960: ch. 3).

Thus, as the century drew to its close, the prevalent approaches veered back to fundamentally negative authoritarian and pessimistic perceptions of the human personality. In this light, the human factor was now considered mostly as a 'tool' and a cost of production. This view brought in its trail 'downsizing' as the core of public service reform. It also drastically altered the whole configuration of public personnel policies away from the benign, development-oriented approaches of the past toward more disciplinarian, 'lean and mean', 'take it or leave it' stances. The tendency to envision the workforce as a 'cost' which ought to be contained gradually prevailed over the one which looked upon it more as an 'asset', indeed, as the resource on which 'all else depends' (Likert: 1).

This change, however, came with an important difference. The latest conservative tide reinstated with full force the 'leaders/laggards cleavage' (Premfors 1998: 143), which, as we have just seen, represents a standard accoutrement of Theory X-approaches. Predicated on the assumption that 'most people must be coerced, controlled, directed (and) threatened with punishment to get them to put forth adequate effort toward the achievement of organizational objectives', the 'mediocrity of the masses' (McGregor 1960: 34) is viewed as going hand in hand with the ascendancy of the few to whom, in the light of this doctrine, all virtues and all competences are vouchsafed.

Though seldom stated so bluntly, such elitist doctrines were now allowed free rein. They have been especially effective in two major areas of policy: 'comparative rewards' and 'management prerogatives'. Discussing the erosion of public service in their keynote address to the ASPA National Conference in Phoenix, Arizona, in March 2002, Gerald and Naomi Caiden had this to say on this matter:

> Despite the measures taken in the 1990s to revamp public service career systems, many of them long overdue, they came too late to prevent the situation described by the Volcker and Winter commissions from getting worse and worse, year by year, as they had predicted. This was not just in the civil service, but in the armed forces, the police and intelligence services, not only for public sector agencies, but also for non-profit organizations, and not just in the United States, but in Canada, Western Europe and elsewhere. Meanwhile, the business sector has gone from strength to strength, especially for top executives of multinational corporations whose compensation packages, always superior to anything in the government sector in their home countries, have taken off beyond anything foreseen a decade earlier.

The spread of this phenomenon, the level of disparities and their tendency to grow at an accelerating pace have recently been the cause of some concern even in business circles and among supporters of free enterprise. In the words of one such advocate,

> The highest profile cases of excessive pay, unfortunately, are not isolated exceptions. Bosses' pay has moved inexorably upwards, especially in America. In 1980, the average pay for CEOs of America's biggest companies was about 40 times that of the average production worker. In 1990, it was about 85 times. Now this ratio is thought to be 400. Profits of big firms fell last year and shares are still well down on their record high, but the average remuneration of the heads of American companies rose by over 6%.[17]

The amount of income growth devoured by corporate profits contrasts with 'the low share [...] accruing to the nation's workers in the form of labor compensation'.[18] Visibly, such disparities are self-perpetuating. They migrate into other areas of public life and arguably open the way for oligarchic influences on policy formation and the life of society as a whole. It can be seen accordingly that, far from promoting good governance,[19] the market model of government advanced by NPM has legitimized policies and practices which have not only furthered the erosion of public service and public trust but undermined many of the critical values of democracy itself. The capture of the state by private interest groups operating as powerful lobbies represents an ominous trend especially pronounced in very recent years.

It may not be accidental that this reformist effort, in the name of NPM and the reinvention movement was 'driven primarily by practitioners and private sector consultants rather than academics or theoreticians'. Long lists of 'do's and don'ts' for 'creative public managers' have been marketed, accordingly, on the assumption that such principles can equally be applied to public sector agencies and private enterprises (Thomas 2000: 146–156; Kamensky 1996). The principles in question were taken to be universal and axiomatic.

'Let the managers manage' has been the movement's battle cry. Simple, direct and catchy, this motto exerts a strong appeal. The need for flexibility and freedom of maneuver which it conveys make some sense in a world where change and discontinuity have become facts of life; where rigid structures are rightly seen as things of the past and where adaptability and rapid response to contingencies are *sine qua non* conditions of survival and success. It must be pointed out, on the other hand, that criticism of rules has often served as a subterfuge to brush aside or weaken important institutional and legal safeguards in areas of vital concern to vulnerable segments of the population (Terry 1998: 194; Light 1997). It has opened the floodgates creating the conditions where the abuse of power, corruption and arbitrariness can flourish. Recent events in Iraq, the conduct of the war and the 'privatization of warfare' to which Professor Newland refers in the following chapter all point to such great perils.

Of strategies and measures ostensibly designed to foster flexibility, cost-containment and rapid response, none have been so controversial as outsourcing, offloading and marketization. The actual savings accruing from such debatable practices have often been doubted (Caiden and Caiden 2002). What those measures have induced is a certain attenuation of government controls and dilution of accountability, as well as further erosion of the idea that the state, because it is the state, should be an exemplar of virtue as well as a model employer. On the pretext of non-interference, governments have allowed their private subcontractors to get away with practices which would have been considered as downright reprehensible in a public sector context. Studies have shown that unchecked deregulation, downsizing and outsourcing have serious repercussions on labor, economic, fiscal and monetary policies which adversely affect society, though they may yield some benefits to private interest groups in the short run (Oman, Gabriel, Garrett and Malmberg 2002).

The unprecedented surge of massive graft and corruption which has visited the world in recent years bears witness to the dangers of governments neglecting, abdicating or outsourcing their overarching role in setting proper standards and enforcing those same standards in a consistent manner. Discounting or downplaying the normative functions of government went in tandem with attacks on 'rules-bound administration' which the New Public Management contrasted with the merits of 'entrepreneurial government' (Osborne and Gaebler 1992: esp. chs. 7 and 10; Argyriades 2003). Over a period of years, such narratives have helped promote a type of mindset for which anything goes. 'The end justifies the means' (Sommermann 2001).

From Enron, Arthur Andersen, World Com, Xerox and Cisco through Halliburton to Parmalat and Hollinger, massive corruption scandals have shaken public trust and positive perceptions of private sector practices. The magnitude moreover and the frequency of these crises strongly suggest that the problem is systemic: one that cannot be addressed through spot checks or punitive measures alone. Increasingly, the view has been gaining ground which discerns a strong connection between, on the one hand, the market model of government and, on the other, the rise and prevalence of what has been described as a 'cheating culture' (Callahan 2004). A lesson which emerges from the last two decades worldwide calls into question the wisdom of privatization of the public domain and what a noted scholar has called the 'seamlessness of politics, business and administration' (Newland 2002).[20] Clearly at fault are a confusion of values and a disregard of boundaries best rendered by the aphorism that 'management is management' (Argyriades 2003; Argyriades 2006).

CONCLUDING REMARKS

The concept that 'anything goes', that results should be prized over process, represents a signal derivative of the market model of government. In twenty years or so, the concept has migrated from business and economics to politics and governance, sweeping away the vestiges of contrary ideas encountered in its path. Its impact has been visible on the national, sub-national and international planes. Not only has it served to undermine respect for the rule of law and due process but, as already suggested, it has assiduously contributed to a bottom-line mentality which lies at the antipodes of ethics and professionalism in the public service (Kakabadse, Kakabadse and Kouzmin 2003; Argyriades 2003; Makrydemetres 2002) as well as of integrity in public life (Cox 2004). A reductionist perspective which rejects all values other than the self-centered pursuit of short-term financial gain and personal success, this bottom-line mentality feeds into a kindred doctrine which in the name of patriotism rejects all higher virtue, all 'raison d'humanité'[21] and all international order (Cox 2004: 321).

Currently in the ascendant, this militant approach to domestic and global affairs endeavors to arrest and reverse a process which, gradually and painstakingly over the past two centuries, has moved us somewhat closer to an open society founded on freedom, equality, tolerance, compassion, solidarity and shared responsibility.[22] With single-minded tenacity, it has pursued reforms to 'hollow out' the state of social welfare functions only to reinforce its military capacity. 'The fundamental ingredients remain the same: the emphasis on simplistic and self-interested moralizing [...] jingoism and brinkmanship, and placing national security above legal and human rights concerns – the hallmarks of neo-realism' (Cox 2004). Sadly, as the poet reminds us, empires and wars need enemies... imagined or real (Cavafy 1974).

In this and other regards, this rising counter-culture has staked, as we have seen, its claims to originality (Hughes 1998). Such claims are open to question. In one respect, however, the market model of government and the New Public Management may well be said to adhere to the reform tradition which prevailed in the 1950s and 60s:[23] a tradition which depicts administrative reform as a Herculean labor pitting a small elite of driven *cognoscenti* against the unenlightened but long-established masses and interest groups. It is a reform tradition which has been known to spawn 'one size fits all' solutions, visions of 'brave new worlds' and promises of more. 'One size fits all' solutions may be a good selling pitch. In retrospect, however, it did a lot of damage to strategic institutions in developing countries, especially those countries whose core structures of the state were mostly still in the making.[24] Worse still, 'one size fits all' and 'one best way' pretensions may have perversely encouraged administrative mimetism in the mistaken belief that the so-called 'best practices', which had been tried successfully in one part of the world, could be replicated in others.

The lesson we may draw from this unending saga of administrative reform is that there is no alternative to 'do-it-yourself' reform. This means creating indigenous capacity precisely for this task. Building homegrown capacity to plan, design and program and to direct and implement administrative reforms, as well as the capacity to monitor their progress and evaluate results, must be considered not only central to the establishment and maintenance of a modern public service but really also critical to a country's dignity and independence. Of course, this should not mean administrative chauvinism. In the global village where we live, the study of foreign practices and the constant exchange of experience among organizations within and across borders serve both a critical need and a good purpose. It means also that national organizations must be the final arbiters of their future; that weaving the future and shaping a country's destiny and fashioning its institutions form a core function of governance.

Lastly, in light of all the above, we need to reconsider our image of reform. The language we have used has quite perversely induced a vision of reform in confrontational terms as an ongoing battle or a crusade. A more appropriate narrative would represent reforms as cooperative efforts and incremental processes, often spanning several years. It would highlight the need for input from diverse sources, support from many disciplines and diverse stakeholders. Reform is not a task best left to experts and specialists, though, to be sure, many experts coming from several disciplines will be required to help. It is a task requiring sound analytical skills; deep knowledge of a country, its history, culture and institutions; good planning and sound strategies. More than anything else, it calls for a clear sense of purpose and direction, but also for a disposition to listen, to debate, to question and to compromise.

REFERENCES

Al-Saigh, N.M. (1986) (Ed). *Administrative Reform in the Arab World: Readings*. Amman: Arab Organization of Administrative Sciences.

Argyriades, D. (1995). 'Technical Cooperation in Public Administration and Finance'. *International Journal of Technical Cooperation* 1 (2). pp. 223–262.

Argyriades, D. (1996). 'Neutrality and Professionalism in the Public Service'. In H. Asmeron, & E. Reis (Eds), *Democratization and Bureaucratic Neutrality* (pp. 45–73). London: Macmillan.

Argyriades, D. (2001). 'Bureaucracy and Debureaucratization'. In A. Farazmand (Ed), *Handbook of Comparative and Development Public Administration* (2nd ed) (pp. 901–917). New York: Marcel Dekker.

Argyriades, D. (2003). 'Values for Public Service: Lessons Learned from Recent Trends and the Millennium Summit'. *International Review of Administrative Sciences* 69 (4), pp. 521–533.

Argyriades, D. (2006). 'Good Governance, Professionalism, Ethics and Responsibility'. *International Review of Administrative Sciences* 72 (2), pp. 155–170.

Bevir, M., Rhodes, R.A.W. & Weller, P. (2003). 'Traditions of Governance: Interpreting the Changing Role of the Public Sector'. *Public Administration* 81 (1), pp. 1–17.

Caiden, G.E. (1969). *Administrative Reform*. Chicago: Aldine.

Caiden, G.E. (1991). *Administrative Reform Comes of Age*. New York: de Gruyter.

Caiden, G.E., & Caiden, N. (2002). Keynote Address to the 63rd National Conference of the American Society of Public Administration, Phoenix, AZ, March 2002.

Caiden, G.E., & Sundaram, P. (2004). 'The Specificity of Public Service Reform'. *Public Administration and Development* 24 (1).

Callahan, D. (2004). *Cheating Culture: Why More Americans Are Doing Wrong to Get Ahead*. New York: Harcourt Brace & Co.

Cavafy, C. (1974). R. Dalven (trans). *Expecting the Barbarians*. Orlando: HBJ.

Colareli, S.M. (2003). *No Best Way*. Westport, CT: Praeger.

Cox, R. III (2004). 'Going to War: A Commentary on Ethical Leadership and Politics'. *Public Integrity* 6 (4), pp. 319–331.

Drew, E. (2003). 'The Neocons in Power'. *New York Review of Books* 50 (10), pp. 1–9.

Dror, Y. (2001). *The Capacity to Govern*. London: Frank Cass.

Farazmand, A. (2001). *Handbook of Comparative and Development Public Administration* (2nd ed). New York: Marcel Dekker.

Frederickson, H.G. (2004). 'A Weber for our Time: The Life and Work of F.W. Riggs'. *PA Times* (August).

Fukuyama, F. (1993). *The End of History and the Last Man*. New York: Morrow, Williams & Co.

Galbraith, J.K. (1964). *Economic Development*. Boston, MA: Houghton Mill.

Heady, F. (2001). 'Principles for 2001 and Beyond'. *Public Administration Review* 61 (4).

Herbert, B. (2004). 'We're More Productive: Who Gets the Money?' *New York Times*, 5 April, op-ed page.

Hofstede, G.H. (1997). *Cultures and Organizations: Software of the Mind*. New York: McGraw Hill.

Hughes, O.E. (1998). *Public Management and Administration: An Introduction* (2nd ed). New York: St Martin's Press.

Institute of Public Administration for Turkey and the Middle East (1965). *Organization and Functions of the Central Government of Turkey, Report of the Managing Board of the Central Government Organization Research Project*. Ankara: Is Matbaalick ve Ticaret.

Kakabadse, A., Kakabadse, N., & Kouzmin, A. (2003). 'Ethics, Values and Behaviors: Comparison of Three Case Studies Examining the Paucity of Leadership in Government'. *Public Administration* 81 (3).

Kamensky, J.M. (1996). 'Role of the Reinventing Government Movement in Federal Government Reform'. *Public Administration Review* 56 (3), pp. 251–252.

Kristoff, N.D. (2004). 'Militant Christianity versus Militant Islam'. *International Herald Tribune* (19 July).

Krugman, P. (1994). 'Conceptualizing Development'. In L. Rodwin & D.A. Schon (1994) (Eds). *Rethinking the Development Experience*. Cambridge, MA: Brookings Institution & Lincoln Institute of Land Policy.

Leach, E. (1974). 'Models of Man'. In W.A. Robson (Ed) *Man and the Social Sciences*. Beverly Hills, CA: Sage.

Light, P. (1997). *The Tides of Reform: Making Government Work, 1945–1995*. New Haven, CT: Yale University Press.

Likert, L. *The Human Organization*. New York: McGraw-Hill.

Lynn, L. Jr. (2001). 'The Myth of Bureaucratic Paradigm: What Traditional Public Administration Really Stood For'. *Public Administration Review* 61 (2), pp. 144–157.

Makrydemetres, A. (2002). 'Ethical Dilemmas in Public Administration'. *International Review of Administrative Sciences* 68 (2), pp. 251–266.

McGregor, D. (1960). *The Human Side of Enterprise*. New York: McGraw-Hill (Ch. 3, 'Theory X: The Traditional View of Direction and Control').

Newland, C.A. (2002). 'The Facilitative State, Political Executive Aggrandizement and Public Service Challenges'. Keynote Address to the 63rd National Conference of the American Society of Public Administration (ASPA), Phoenix, Arizona.

Nisbet, R. (1993). *History of the Idea of Progress* (new ed). Brunswick, NJ: Transaction Books.

Oman, R., Gabriel, R., Garrett, J., & Malmberg, K. (2002). Paper for the ASPA National Conference, Phoenix, Arizona.

Osborne, D., & Gaebler, T. (1992). *Reinventing Government: How the Entrepreneurial Spirit is Transforming the Public Sector*. New York: Plume Books.

Pagaza, I.P. (2004). *Modernización administrativa: Propuesta para una reforma inaplazable*. Mexico City: Universidad Nacional Autónoma de México.

Pollitt, C. (2001). 'Convergence: The Useful Myth?' *Public Administration* 79 (4), pp. 933–947.

Popper, K. (1960). *The Poverty of Historicism*. London: Routledge & Kegan Paul.

Premfors, R. (1998). 'Reshaping the Democratic State: Swedish Experience in a Comparative Perspective'. *Public Administration* 76 (4).

Riggs, F.W. (1961). *The Ecology of Public Administration*. London: Asia Publishing House.

Riggs, F.W. (1966). *Thailand: The Modernization of a Bureaucratic Polity*. Honolulu: East-West Center Press.

Rodwin, L., & Schon, D.A. (1994) (Eds). *Rethinking the Development Experience*. Cambridge, MA: Brookings Institution & Lincoln Institute of Land Policy.

Rosenbloom, D.H. (2001). 'History Lesson for Reinventors'. *Public Administrative Review* 61 (2), pp. 161–165.

Sakamoto, M. (2001). 'Public Administration in Japan: Past and Present in the Higher Civil Service'. In A. Farazmand (Ed), *Handbook of Comparative and Development Public Administration* (2nd ed) (pp. 349–301).

Siffin, W.J. (1959) (Ed). *Towards the Comparative Study of Public Administration*. Bloomington, IN: Indiana University Press.

Sommermann, K.P. (2001). *The Rule of Law and Public Administration in a Global Setting*. Report to the 25th International Congress of Administrative Sciences.

Subramaniam, V. (2003). 'Quality Governance for Sustainable Development: India's Obligations to Set a Model'. *International Review of Administrative Sciences* 69 (4), pp. 471–481.

Terry, L.D. (1998). 'Administrative Leadership, Neo-Managerialism and the Public Management Movement'. *Public Administration Review* 58 (3).

Thomas, P.G. (2000). 'Mintzberg on Public Management'. In H. Mintzberg & J. Bourgault (Eds), *Managing Publicly*. Toronto: IPAC.

ul Haq, M. (1995). *Reflections on Human Development*. New York: Oxford UP.

Valéry, P. (1962). *History & Politics*. New York: Pantheon.

World Bank (1994). *Governance: The World Bank's Experience*. Washington, DC: World Bank Publications.

NOTES

1 'All politics', wrote Paul Valéry (1962) 'implies a certain idea of Man'. On this subject, see also Leach (1974).

2 'Managerialism has had a significant impact on public administration. The essence of managerialism lies in the assumption that there is something called "management" [...] embodying a set of principles that can be applied (universally)'. Boston, quoted by Kamensky (1996).

3 See also Argyriades (1996).

4 See also Riggs (1966).

5 Report of the Northcote & Trevelyan Committee on the Organization of the Permanent Civil Service (January 1854) Paper 1713, B.P.P. 1854.

6 Ibid.

7 See, for example, the Institute of Public Administration for Turkey and the Middle East (1965).

8 *E/CN/.12/807* December 1968, 5.

9 UN (1966). *Handbook of Training in the Public Service*. Document ST/ITAO/M/28.

10 For a thorough overview of the salient characteristic features, tendencies and contribution of the New Public Management, see Pagaza (2004), esp. ch. 6, 'La Nueva Gestión Pública (NPM)', pp. 165–199.

11 'To a certain extent, this can be explained by the erroneous understanding of the rule of law as legalism and not as a dynamic concept of institutional and procedural principles which [...] protect human dignity and [...] foster development of the personality of each citizen' (Sommermann 2001: 77).

12 *Théorie de l'Administration* (p. 125). Paris: Economica.

13 Remarkably, Karl Popper's above-mentioned book has been dedicated to the 'countless men and women of all creeds or nations or races who fell victim to the fascist and communist belief in Inexorable Laws of Historical Destiny'.

14 This point was also made by Lynn (2001), and by Rosenbloom (2001). Characteristically, Rosenbloom concludes: 'The reinvention movement's key literature *is* deeply flawed. It *is* wholly unclear whether the reinventors know what they are reinventing [...] their concepts of democracy and its relationship to administration are muddled. They claim to favor democratic values. But they also disparage elections, representative institutions, and legal requirements for representation, participation, transparency and fairness in administrative decision-making'.

15 Ibid.

16 On religious fundamentalism, see Kristoff (2004). Here, reference is made to the latest in a series of evangelical fiction depicting 'The End of Days', with 'Jesus returning to the Earth to wipe out all non-Christians from the planet'. With more than 60 million copies sold worldwide, the 12 books in this series represent the fastest-selling adult fiction ever. On the political front, militantism has been the mark of the 'neo-conservatives', the American Enterprise Institute (AEI), etc. On this subject, see Drew (2003).

17 'Where is the Stick?' *The Economist*, 11–17 October , p. 13. See also: 'Fat cats feeding', in the same issue, pp. 73–76.

18 'The Unprecedented Rising Tide of Corporate Profits and the Simultaneous Ebbing of

Labor Compensation – Gainers and Losers from the National Recovery in 2002–2003'. Quoted in Herbert (2004).

19 For definitions of 'good governance', see World Bank (1994).

20 See also Chapter II in this volume.

21 Expression borrowed from Yehezkel Dror (2001), ch. 9.

22 Values recently highlighted in the United Nations Millennium Declaration (A/RES/55/2 dated 18 September 2000).

23 Vid. supra p. 8.

24 On this point, see United Nations: Report of the Meeting of Experts (1997), E/1997/86 para 60 et seq.

2

Accountability for Responsible American Governance in Today's Facilitative State/Garrison State Era

CHESTER A. NEWLAND

INTRODUCTION

Domestic and international accountability for US governance – social, economic, and political – is the subject of this three-part analysis honoring Professor Gerald Caiden's life-long devotion to 'The Civilizing Mission of Public Administration' (Caiden 2005).[1] Firstly, and at greatest length, an often-conflicted but enduring 'self-image' and transitions in US nation-state perspectives are discussed. Despite the absence of a concept of 'the state' among most Americans, identification as 'a nation' with accountability to Enlightenment era ideals as a 'mission' emerged early and it generally persists. Secondly are perspectives on current 'facilitative state' concepts that are akin to those early governance ideals. These are also related to political accountability ideas that started to become powerful in the last decades of the nineteenth century. Reform politics then stormed to center-stage following years of *laissez-faire* economic rampage and transactional political corruption. Transformations then gave rise to the US 'administrative state' which dominated the middle decades of the twentieth century. Self-governance ideals survived those decades but ultimately many Americans felt dominated by 'big government'. Facilitative governance ideals reflected in global trends and then again took prominence in the late 1970s and early 80s, except in US security and international matters. Thirdly, US accountability in twenty-first-century foreign and defense affairs is touched upon. One focus is powerful 'garrison (warfare) state' practices that reemerged following the explosion of Terrorist War in 2001. Another is a paradoxical assertion of 'mission' to remake the world in the USA self-image. Important in these developments is a perception among domestic and foreign critics that US unilateralism and exceptionalism now prevail over internal and external accountability to a broadly shared rule of law.

US SELF-IMAGE AND TRANSITIONS AS A NATION STATE

Searches for responsible social, economic and political governance held accountable under the constitutional principle of conjoined popular sovereignty and limited government have characterized the USA since the Enlightenment era out of which the country emerged. Paradoxes – sometimes rising to levels of boldface contradictions – have filled Americans' history as they searched among ideals and realities for workable frameworks of accountable governance in their ever-changing country. Nation-state concepts have now forced their way into the consciousness of some attentive Americans, and the nation's place on the planet has become the subject of an increasingly intense, ongoing search for accountability and responsible international as well as domestic governance.

Consider recent examples: (1) America's actions in warfare in Afghanistan and Iraq, during the Balkan war and in peacekeeping, and on the Korean peninsula more than half a century after rugged defense of the South against the North; (2) accountability for corruption among US-based global enterprises such as Enron, Arthur Andersen and WorldCom, and for facilitation of responsible and open global commerce; (3) the American Patriot Act's expansion of national government-powers and massively expensive efforts to cope with a regime of fear triggered by terrorists (Barber 2003; Kettl 2004); and (4) facilitation of constructively creative developments in sciences, technologies, arts and humanities, and balancing of related changes with stability of varied indigenous cultures and broadly shared global culture.

To facilitate an understanding of the USA and its complicatedly varied accountability provisions to sustain responsible governance (private and governmental) in the twenty-first century, historical transitions in Americans' perspectives of their country are briefly summarized here. Three sets of developments that overlap historical periods are noted: (1) early constitutional struggles for nationhood, the embrace of Manifest Destiny as a nation-expanding theme and the off-and-on pursuit of a 'national mission' to extend its self-image abroad; (2) domestic reform ideals in creation of the US administrative state that emerged in the centennial era and that came to characterize the mid-twentieth-century's idealization of rationality – and both coincidental and connected conflicts between international ideals and frequent US isolationism; and (3) transitions of the US welfare state and garrison state (key features of the administrative state) into a nation that now almost comfortably takes pride in its status as the momentarily lone global superpower, with what many Americans accept as accountability to an enduring mission and what many other people view as a sometimes recklessly self-indulgent machismo.

Constitutional Creation, Manifest Destiny and Mission

In the twenty-first century, many political leaders talk broadly of the US mission to spread popular democracy, and particularly freedoms, in the world (Bacevich 2002; Daalder and Lindsay 2003). Less is said of constitutional and other restraints of international and domestic law on US and other governments, economic enterprise and social conditions. By contrast, while America's founders stressed freedoms, after disappointing years of failure of the articles of confederation following the independence of the original 13 states, they struggled to create a constitutional framework of conjoined popular sovereignty and limited government that was not initially broadly democratic and in which government continued to be of little concern to most people. The founders sought a more perfect union through an empowered but limited federal government to create viable national conditions for security, economic commerce and some shared freedoms in social affairs within then-prevailing conditions. Although those included female-gender limitations and bond slavery in that period, some seventy years before the Civil War that would free slaves, the Constitution that took effect in 1789 reflected an ambitiously evolving culture of 'The People, Yes', celebrated 146 years later in Carl Sandburg's epic poem of that title (Sandburg 1936), sustaining a popular vision of expansion of liberties through yet more decades.

In short, to understand the US and its perceptions of accountability for responsible governance (including public policies and administration) in the twenty-first century, one must know that a widely accepted American ideal (a powerfully sustaining but paradoxical myth) is that, although 'the Nation' was founded in Enlightenment era aspirations (later idolized as perfection), 'the People' must continuously search to perfect themselves further and thereby elevate their country and the world. Many *feel* accountable for 'progress' in spreading their basic values and their means to achieve them. Considered deeply, these basics are human dignity, sensitivity to varied and multicultural contexts in the twenty-first century and a rule of law through constitutional democracy's search for reasonableness and responsible self-governance. Treated lightly, those basics often appear to boil down to force-fed freedoms of *laissez-faire* economics, unrestrained global social values (McWorld) and political/governmental institutions structured like those in the USA.

Although the geographically large nation founded in the eighteenth century with few people would in the future be populated by ever more varied nationalities and many people without such identities, the popular culture has continued to be one of 'The People, Yes', fundamentally conjoined in a general spirit of 'The State, No'. As late as the end of the twentieth century, Walter Kickert and Richard Stillman's well-documented conclusion was that this culture still persisted:

> The United States differs from Europe in most administratively relevant measures. In America, the concept of 'State' does not exist, at least in the minds of most of its citizens. The democratic system is typically viewed as 'pluralistic', with many competing interests and pressure groups. (Kickert and Stillman 1994: 4)

While the USA clearly became a nation in 1789 – if they had not earlier made that transition during the Revolutionary War – it was not until after the Civil War that questions such as whether states had sovereign authority to withdraw from the nation were settled. Thereafter, the Fourteenth Amendment to the Constitution through decades of legislative, executive and judicial interpretation vastly empowered the national government. Nonetheless, American references to 'the state' continued to refer not to the nation-state but to a particular state within the Union, i.e., the State of New York, Kansas, California, etc. A typical example is a scholarly analysis published in November 2003 in the highly respected *American Political Science Review*: 'The Difference States Make: Democracy, Identity, and the American City' (Hayward 2003). The article examines the role of sub-national American states in definitions of 'difference' among people.

From their constitutional era onward, Americans have commonly embraced identity as a nation, even though most have never or rarely considered applying the term 'state' to their Union. A sense of mission – later termed Manifest Destiny – became a justification for expansionism as early as the Louisiana Purchase in 1803 by the Jefferson Administration, which catapulted the American nation from the Atlantic Ocean to the Pacific. This powerful doctrine soon carried the nation through Texas and into California at the expense of Mexico. In 1867, it supported purchase from Russia of Alaska. In 1898, Hawaii was annexed by the USA following 50 years of economic domination. In the Spanish–American War of 1898, expansionism forced Spain to grant Cuba independence and to cede Puerto Rico and a Landrone island (later designated as Guam) to the USA. In the reach across the Pacific, Spain ceded the Philippines to the USA in 1899. Manifest Destiny (and accountability to a 'mission' to promote commerce) supported construction of the Panama Canal starting in 1903. US control continued until 31 December 1999 when it was terminated by a treaty of 1978.

Manifest Destiny reached a wavering end with regards to the imperial accession of territories but never with respect to a sense of 'mission'. During and after World War I, the USA disavowed territorial expansionism, demonstrating hesitancy to get involved in European affairs except to join a 'War to End All Wars'. President Wilson forcefully advocated national self-determination to redraw the map of Europe against European alternatives of 'conquer and then divide' (that ultimately won out in the 1920 Treaty of Trianon) and a League of Nations to advance accountability of nations to international law (rejected by the US Senate as subordination of the USA). Much earlier, political support of Philippine independence had been vigorous (starting in the presidential campaign of 1900), and in 1935, when the Philippines adopted a national constitution modeled after the US example, President Roosevelt immediately accepted it with a ten-year commonwealth period for nation-state transition. Japanese invasion and World War II subsequently forced postponement of independence until 4 July 1946. Clearly by then, US territorial expansionism had ended but an imperial 'mission' to spread its self-image of ideals had not. Economic, social and political expansionism assumed other forms. Most idealistically, following World War II the USA dutifully embraced responsibilities to help Europe rebuild itself through the Marshall Plan. It also sought to facilitate development by Japan of a constitutional democracy and economic and social reconstruction. The myth/ideal of accountability to universalize political democracy, generally linked with relatively *laissez-faire* economics and congenial social practices, came increasingly to define the USA on its way to becoming a global superpower.

The American Administrative State (the Regulatory, Welfare and Warfare State)

The rise of the American administrative state started as a fragmented design in the late nineteenth century. Dramatic changes took shape in the 1880s, with domestic political reforms designed to regulate rampant economic plunder and corruption in *laissez-faire* enterprise and later also to clean up similar, often-related political corruption in local, state and national governments. During and after World War I and, off and on, through and after World War II, closely connected idealism also resulted in widespread US aspirations for a responsible world order through broadly embraced human benevolence (as in actions in Europe and Japan, as noted above) under shared responsibility and accountability to international law (as in the Nuremberg Trials for war crimes after World War II). Domestic developments of the American administrative state are noted in this subsection. Related intervals of international idealism are briefly touched upon thereafter.

To understand current facilitative state and garrison state practices, it is useful to reflect upon the two phases of the US administrative state: the 'fragmented regulatory state' of the 1880s into the 1920s, and the 'bureaucratic administrative state' that started emerging nationally from the 'Budget and Accounting Act' of 1921 and which became dominant in the welfare state from the 1930s through the 1970s, and the garrison state of World War II and more than four decades of Cold War.

Accountability of private entrepreneurs and their business organizations for irresponsible economic self-governance and related human indignities and social degradation became a wildfire issue in the 1876–1889 Centennial era of the American Revolution. The constitution state governments first attempted to regulate actions of so-called Robber Barons, but the US Supreme Court (influenced by Darwinian/Spencerian theories of social and economic accountability – survival of the fittest in 'free enterprise') considered their efforts unconstitutional burdens on interstate commerce which only the federal (national) government could regulate. An agrarian political revolt followed, electing to Congress members who adopted legislation to create an Interstate Commerce Commission in 1887, the year of Woodrow Wilson's pioneering article 'The Study of Public Administration' (Wilson 1887). That was followed in 1890 by the 'Sherman Antitrust Act', which was designed as a robust effort to deal with private monopolies. Numerous other governmental regulations followed in efforts to hold economic enterprise accountable to law, thus ending unrestrained freedom. In short, *laissez-faire* self-governance of capitalism failed; Americans chose to modify market capitalism and to retain it as their economic system, limiting free enterprise by laws to encourage accountability for responsible market governance.

Nonetheless, market failure became massive in the Great Depression that began in 1929 and stretched to World War II. Starting with Franklin Roosevelt's New Deal, the US national government embraced the welfare state as a supplement to a greatly expanded regulatory state to try to achieve a workable market economy and a society consistent with human dignity. Together, these two strategies were adequate to preclude the rise in the USA of the state socialism that came to dominate much of the world in the middle of the twentieth century.

The bureaucratic state design of the US administrative state, highlighted in the Brownlow Committee formulations of the Roosevelt years and subsequently extended by the Hoover Commissions of the late 1940s and early 50s, was based on 'enhanced Executive Branch performance' through a balance of transparently responsible politics and professional expertise. This resulted in the great accountability paradox of the USA in the twentieth century: 'Democracy and Bureaucracy' (Mosher 1968). Economy, efficiency and effectiveness were standard under legislative authorizations and oversight, including direct reporting to Congress by the US General Accounting Office (now the Government Accountability Office), with requirements of neutral professional expertise and disciplined professionalism in public administration under the bipartisan independent Civil Service Commission. Those concepts had been pioneered earlier in progressive-era reforms of local governments. Focused legislative authority commensurate with responsibility became a mantra of civic affairs and the emerging field of public administration. Council-manager government became one favored means to bring professionally responsible expertise to public service. These frameworks were well known by Louis Brownlow and his associates Luther Gulick and Charles Merriam, who worked to extend them into the federal level before World War II.

Upon America's entry into preparations for war at the end of the 1930s and her subsequent defense engagements through five decades of 'Hot' and 'Cold' War, the strong executive model of the US administrative state took on a character of extensive aggrandizement of presidential power, with some similar trends at state and local levels. Accompanying political changes in the late 1960s and 70s under Presidents Nixon and Carter, executive-dominated spoils and corruption became concerns at national, state and local levels. In the following facilitative state years (to be discussed later) those accountability challenges multiplied.

Examples from Intervals of Ideals of International Community and Accountability to Law

Accountability for responsible social, economic and political self-governance under shared values of human dignity and reasonable law became something of an international ideal that was closely connected to American public administration. Woodrow Wilson's ideas, noted earlier, and some failed struggles by other Americans in support of the League of Nations and an international rule of law, are the best-known evidence of linkages. Space here allows for only two other classic examples with special relevance to twenty-first-century concerns about US accountability, to be followed by a note of contemporary reliance on international nongovernmental organizations (INGOs).

A leading classic example is that of Mary Parker Follett, who set forth her ideals in her 1918 book *The New State*. She elaborated upon human community in social, economic and political endeavors, advancing concepts that became cutting-edge several decades later in business management and in public administration. Follett applied ideas of group psychology and neighborhood/community democracy to what she called 'The World State', arguing that 'the aim of internationalism is a rich content of widely varying characteristics and experience'. She continued:

> There is not room on this planet for a lot of similar nations, but only for a lot of different nations. A group of nations must create a group culture, which shall be broader than the culture of one nation alone. There must be a world-ideal, a whole-civilization, in which the ideals and the civilization of every nation can find a place. (Follett 1918: 345)

Fundamentally, Follett advanced faith in self-governance as a foundation for a world community of shared multiculturalism, similar to formulations in parts of the USA in the twenty-first century but in contrast with America's current international image of forcing its conceptions of governance on others as a universal standard. Follett argued that

> We need a new faith in humanity, not a sentimental faith or a theological tenet or a philosophical conception, but an active faith in that creative power of men which shall shape government and industry, which shall give form equally to our daily life with our neighbor and to a world league. (Follett 1918: 360)

Such international idealism peaked after World War I but quickly faded. Calvin Coolidge ascended to the presidency upon the death of President Harding and was elected by a landslide in 1924 on a platform of isolationism. Nazism and fascism only slowly moved America to mobilize to help Britain in the late 1930s; the attack on Pearl Harbor seemed required to stir American action, based less on accountability to ideals than on defense necessity. The war that followed nourished renewed idealism that supported the creation of the United Nations as an international nongovernmental organization (INGO), with hopes among many that it would become facilitative of a shared embrace of international law, peacekeeping and human betterment.

Professor Arthur Holcombe of Harvard University has provided a classic example of the idealism of that time, expressing perspectives that are of interest now. In his 1950 book *Our More Perfect Union*, Holcombe advanced detailed prescriptions for enhanced US constitutional government. In particular, he argued that

> To bring the authority of the American presidency under an effective reign of law in the field of foreign affairs, it is necessary to delegate, to a world federation, the powers which are appropriate for the protection of the rights of men regarded as citizens of the world. (Holcombe 1950: 427)

Holcombe's concerns were about President Roosevelt's exercises of powers, similar to some critics' worries about President Bush II and his doctrine of preemption. Holcombe praised the UN Participation Act of 1945 as a useful step. His advocacy of world federation won few adherents, however. His international idealism, like Follett's, missed the mark for most Americans, who commonly hold their nation primarily accountable to ideals of its self-image as its 'mission'. In 1918, in 1950 and again today, a widespread US perception is not that it acts outside of authoritative international law (such as when it declines the authority of the International Court at the Hague), but rather that it is accountable, if necessary, to act preemptively to advance a higher law of its understandings of freedom and (constitutional?) democracy.

Complexities of US global involvements and accountability for them are broader and deeper, and narrower and shallower, than visions of international law among nations following World Wars I and II. Today, at least 238 international organizations (IOs) have responsibilities for varied issues, and many include extensive US involvements. These range from the United

Nations and its instrumentalities to old IOs such as the International Postal Union and more recently created ones such as the Organization of Supreme Courts in the Americas which was formed by charter in October 1995. US interests are visibly highly represented in such key IOs as the World Bank, the IMF, the World Trade Organization (WTO) and UN organizations, but engagements are large in others also, supporting some contemporary vision of 'a New World Order' (Slaughter 2004), reminiscent of but stretching far beyond Follett's enduring images.

Authority frameworks of IOs include rational-legal, delegated, expert and moral concepts and structures. They exercise their authority to regulate/facilitate international activities as instruments of their members. They also constitute reality, developing constitutional foundations for subsequent regulation, often with limited transparency. Michael Barnette and Martha Finnemore document findings of 'undemocratic liberalism' and worrisome contrary accountability challenges among IOs (Barnette and Finnemore 2004).

In the twenty-first century, war to produce a regime change in Iraq has brought such standards into focus through concerns about massive aggrandizement of presidential power, stretching well beyond Holcombe's worries of six decades earlier. An explosively crucial example for the 2006 congressional inquiry grew out of President Bush's assertion in December 2005 that as president he is not bound by the legal provisions of the 'Foreign Intelligence Surveillance Act' which requires judicial oversight by the Surveillance Court of government wire/wireless tapping of private communications. Such assertions of legally unrestrained executive power have stirred conflicts between US ideas of the nation's responsibility (destiny?) to extend its ideas of governance abroad, and opposing concepts and practices of international law and multilateral community of varied nations. This accountability problem and related counterterrorism efforts are touched upon again in the final part of this analysis. Before that, however, I will now summarize facilitative state developments of the final decades of the twentieth century and today.

ACCOUNTABILITY FOR RESPONSIBLE FACILITATIVE-STATE GOVERNANCE

Two dimensions of facilitative state developments are noted here: (1) US embrace and/or support of global transitions away from what many people perceived as domination of nations by 'big' and 'do-it-all' governments of the socialist/communist/welfare state era; and (2) facilitative state changes in US public administration, including practices associated with New Public Management (NPM) and complaints against them.

Transitioning from Dominant Governments to Facilitative Governance

Transitions of many nation-states from democratic socialism and more revolutionary changes among republics of the former USSR have resulted in widespread efforts to facilitate responsible social, economic and political governance. Regime theories advocated by the USA have stressed relatively limited and decentralized nation-state governments as well as devolution of key responsibilities and commensurate authority to regional and local levels. Domination of market economics, supported by such INGOs as the International Monetary Fund (IMF) and the World Bank under forceful US leadership, often characterized these transitions in the early 1990s, with a deficient attention to the creation of workable legal frameworks for accountable and successful economic and social changes.

Although the USA never embraced socialism, 'big national government' and large state and local governments were developed to implement extensive welfare and warfare responsibilities. The bureaucratic administrative state and its intergovernmental management apparatus fell increasingly into disfavor in part because of its complexities, because of some failures of policies and programs, and especially because of a powerful political shift in favor of market economics for provision and/or performance of many activities formerly dominated by governments. This political shift toward extensive reliance on market mechanisms was associated with the globalization of economics, communications and related social mobility. Thatcherism, which dismantled much of British socialism, and like-minded changes in Australia and New Zealand were embraced by the Reagan Administration as applicable to the USA. Before Reagan, President Carter had already won election on an anti-Washington platform. He had established a framework that would facilitate extensive dismantling of the professionally expert federal civil service of the administrative state. It also increased partisan politicization through presidentially dominated spoils and outcontracting of government activities. That paved the way for ever-growing reliance on political appointees in government and on private enterprise and other NGOs throughout the Reagan, Bush I, Clinton and Bush II Administrations. How can these private organizations and governments that finance them be held accountable for responsible performance?

Ideally, the optimistic answer to that is found in US traditions of social, economic and political self-governance: old facilitative state ideals that reach back through history to US origins, the optimistic political faith of constitutional democracy that people are capable of self-discipline in social interactions. This faith is joined with a similar optimism that market economics functions in the broader public interest with minimal governmental facilitation. This optimism has been elevated to a US doctrine as the hallmark ideal of today's facilitative state notions not only domestically but, in particular, abroad. For example, implementation of America's mission in

Iraq relies extensively on private, for-profit contractors such as Bechtel and Halliburton.

To recall an example quoted earlier: following Soviet collapse, rapid privatization of economies in the absence of an established rule of law became a disastrous prescription to restructure the former republics of the USSR, leading to widespread despoiling of economic and social institutions. In short, the facilitative state doctrine that has largely dominated the USA, and that has also been popular in many nation-state transitions elsewhere since the 1980s, mostly contemplates 'do-the-minimum' but not 'do-it-all' public bureaucracy to encourage and help sustain dispersed responsibility and authority consistent with optimistically idealized market economics (if not outright *laissez-faire* capitalism) and democratic freedoms. In the absence of a culture of constitutional law, this ideal rapidly dissolves into a Hobbesian 'state of nature'.

In the USA, a key facilitative-state example is an extensive welfare reform pushed into law by the Clinton/Gore administration, 'The Personal Responsibility and Work Opportunity Reconciliation Act' of 1996. That Act's title accurately reflects its purpose and provisions – to facilitate reduced welfare dependency by supporting employment and personal self-governance (Mead 2004). Medicare for the elderly provides another example, both old and new. From its outset in 1965, Medicare was designed to be insurance-funded with an ear-marked employment tax plus a beneficiary fee to pay to private providers of health care. In amendments pushed through by the Bush II Administration in November 2003, an exceedingly complicated Medicare prescription-drug 'benefit' to commence in 2006 was added, but again with fees to be paid by most beneficiaries and with opaque choices to be made among numerous private entities. Geraldine Dallek, a health policy analyst who consults with George Washington University on Medicare issues, described the situation as follows: 'Many in Congress fervently believe that the best way to provide health care for the seniors and disabled on Medicare, while holding down Medicare costs, is through private competition. This is faith-based health policy' (Dallek 2003: 8). It represents a traditional US doctrine of dispersed responsibility and accountability through market forces, even when such reliance results in private-enterprise processes undermining public purposes.

On the flip side of this rosy ideal are US political realities that have created powerful incentives for political parties, factions and leaders within them, as well as numerous special interests, to promote self-serving changes under the guise of facilitation of democratic freedom, self-governance and responsive customer services. Thus, the facilitative state resurrects ancient and enduring governance questions: facilitation of what, for whom, and how?

Among the major political forces behind US departure from the rational bureaucratic model of the administrative state in the mid-twentieth century are changes in partisan politics and elections – the USA's ultimate accountability mechanisms. Private contributions are used to pay the high costs of such campaign practices as polling, crafting policy positions and candidate images, producing and broadcasting commercials and staging events and manipulating public perceptions of benefits. Besides contributions from committed partisans, much money comes from interests seeking favorable regulatory and other policies, from organizations and people who profit from government contracts, and from beneficiaries of grants, tax exemptions and political appointments.

The Democratic Party's Bill Clinton and the Republican Party's Reagan, Bush I and Bush II, along with US Senators and Congress members (as well as many state and local politicians) appeared for years to inspire financial support by putting government out for bid. Public outrage over political buying and selling forced the adoption in 2002 of national campaign finance reforms (termed 'McCain–Feingold' after key sponsors), which were immediately challenged as unconstitutional. By December 2003, when the US Supreme Court upheld this law in a 5/4 ruling, money that could no longer go directly to parties and candidates was pouring into new clusters of old and new partisan interest groups. The Court majority acknowledged this and noted that problems of new outlets for political money are for Congress to solve.[2] Major problems remained during the 2004 elections and beyond, into the 2006 political campaigns.

A second major political reason for shifts away from the administrative state as an ideal is that, from the 1960s onward, and with sustained criticism by opponents, public employee unionization had increasingly displaced the rational, neutral public-service image with perceptions of self-serving, partisanly aligned and unresponsive bureaucracies. Following President Carter's opening doors to increased politicization of public service in 1978, political appointees at the top agency levels increasingly criticized labor-management rule systems as limiting 'customer responsiveness' and productivity while driving up costs. Despite the Clinton/Gore dependence on labor support, their administration engaged in unparalleled reductions in the civil service, cutting career ranks to early 1960s levels. Bush II has attempted to go even further.

In 2001, the Bush II White House directed each agency to open another 15% of its commercial-type jobs to contractor bidding (actually similar to a long-standing policy from the Lyndon Johnson years, known as A-76, but which usually has no across-the-board quotas); on 24 July 2003, the Office of Management and Budget (OMB) backed off of quotas, allowing flexibility for agency differences but still calling for opening 416,000 additional jobs to commercial competition. On 10 April 2003, Department of Defense (DOD) Secretary Rumsfeld proposed legislation titled 'The Defense Transformation for the Twenty-first Century Act' to allow DOD to hire civilians from outside the civil service system with incentives as high as $50,000 in annual bonuses and to transfer hundreds of thousands of uniformed-military jobs to such civilians or contractors. Subsequently, DOD was authorized to establish a new National Security Personnel System (NSPS) for implementation in 2006 with four career groups, all with pay bands structured to markets (Kauffman 2005: 1, 6). On 8 January 2006, the Government Accountability Office (GAO) also implemented a new personnel system of wide pay bands with pay based on 'competitive labor-market rates' (Ziegler 2005: 1, 4).

This marked the strong trend toward increasing fragmentation (flexibilitization) of the national government's public service. Similar trends characterize most state governments and many local ones, in which partisan mayors and councils have increasingly displaced the non-partisans of the administrative state years. The USA's 'progressive era' reforms had sought to make local elected offices few in number, highly visible for accountability and neutral with respect to parties. In recent decades, the vertical integration of political factions from national levels through state and local offices has become a dominant pattern, even in many council-manager local governments. In short, the accountability of American governments and the activities they finance is increasingly to partisan politicians, particularly the president and other executives, to facilitate parties' and officials' interests and advancement of their supporters.

Public Administration as an Accountable Field in the American Facilitative State

Along with this tendency to executive aggrandizement and related spoils, the constructive quality that distinguishes the facilitative state from the administrative state era is mostly an orientation to flexible responsiveness and varied choices to reduce bureaucratic rigidities. These changes, however, have facilitated glaring departures from the rule of law. Following the $450 billion in banking scandals subsequent to deregulation by the Reagan Administration, widespread corporate corruption during the Clinton Administration and damaging stock-market scandals during the Bush II years, the need for robust government (even though limited and flexible) to hold private interests accountable for responsible self-governance is again somewhat acknowledged. Since early US history, the means to such ends have been legal-accountability institutions that mostly exhibit integrity: information-reporting requirements; administrative-law venues; grand juries; prosecutors at national, state, and local levels; and empowered courts.

Within new facilitative and enduring legal contexts, US public administration has been significantly transformed. It has been both lowered and elevated in status in governments, in varied private organizations and in leading universities. The globally used name of the field – public administration – no longer appears in some catalogs of academic schools and departments, even when degree programs survive. Related changes started in the 1960s as policy analysis became fashionable first in DOD during the Kennedy Administration (as PPBS – Planning, Programming and Budgeting Systems) and then elsewhere as President Johnson's Great Society expanded social programs.

Policy studies were promoted as a 'discipline' said to be distinct from the 'field' of public administration by economists and others who emigrated into public affairs with limited knowledge of past developments, but with interests and useful expertise to apply to intricate programs and their fast-growing budgets. Within two decades, as New Public Management (NPM) developed among nations that were transitioning from socialism and other large-scale state structures, that development attracted many analysts and fast-multiplying partisan appointees in US governments (a few of whom had much economics expertise but many of whom lacked knowledge of law and public management) (Newland 1994). In these waves of change, many top universities – including the University of California System which had been involved in Kennedy-era DOD systems – dropped public administration altogether while continuing policy studies. Many other universities followed this trend.

While subject to escalated partisan politics and entrepreneurial enterprise in balancing competing interests in carrying out rule-making and other mandates (West 2004), much professionally expert practice of public administration continues among US governments. Increasingly, it also extends into for-profit and non-profit organizations that contract or that secure grants to perform functions financed by public funds and others that secure franchises/licenses to perform utility and other functions with direct charges to customers who may have no alternative but to use required services. Franchised public utilities, health-service organizations, religious institutions, charitable organizations, government-regulated organizations and businesses engaged in public contracts have employed public administration professionals for many decades. Lobbying organizations have done so also. But the scope of such activities and their public finances has expanded enormously under Clinton and Bush II. New forms of domestic NGOs have proliferated (Goldsmith and Eggers 2004; Mead 2004), and so have INGOs, as noted earlier. Domestically, faith-based dependency on public funds has grown; private contractors in homeland-security and defense technologies have mushroomed. As the privatization of provision and/or performance of functions has transferred increasing responsibilities and extensive public financing to these varied organizations, more public administration experts have joined them rather than entering the government.

Which accountability changes have accompanied these developments? In addition to partisanly political bottom lines (as noted above), leading managerial standards are increased reliance on market mechanisms of competition, performance-based contracting and compensation, and people's confidence (responsiveness to customers in NPM terms).

Fundamentally, as ideals, these are aspects of the facilitative institutional/organizational culture that do not define accountability in traditional *gotcha* terms of constraints but rather in terms of performance – the bottom line for facilitative state governments, involving both policy/program design and implementation/accomplishment. Participative management is an ideal. Donna Shalala, Clinton's Secretary of Health and Human Services, was nicknamed 'the accountable juggler' by Beryl Radin and has been broadly acclaimed as a masterful leader in these respects (Radin 2002).

Accountability through market competition between federal government agencies and private businesses preceded issuance in the Johnson Administration of the Bureau of the Budget (BOB, later OMB) A-76 rule, noted earlier. Performance management was stressed in the Eisenhower Administration, for example, and the Kennedy Administration initiated a project which culminated in the classic 1964 report 'Measuring Productivity of Federal Government Agencies' (US Bureau of the Budget 1964). Forced competition between agencies and external providers then compelled use of measures of in-house governmental performance, including 'whole overhead costs' (space, utilities, personnel retirement benefits, etc.).

In short, performance measures have been the central elements of accountability in American government for over half a century. In their early development, detailed costing prescriptions were formulated, along with rules on employees' qualifications and status (veterans, minorities, etc.), environmental factors, etc. Public employees and external interests competed for more and more rules favorable to their conflicting interests, and often performance outcomes were neglected. In short, Clinton's and Bush II's outcontracting for performance of government functions was old (although much more limited), long before the emergence of facilitative state notions and NPM. However, procedural accountability changed to provide for flexibility in rules to facilitate substantive performance accountability.

Performance-based contracting and internal performance-based management are means widely preferred today to escape detailed micromanaging, while ideally (but too often not) upholding accountability. Both take the form of specifying a satisfactory range of products/services (outputs, outcomes), commonly with bonus and penalty provisions for contractors for surpassing or failing to meet those specs but performing within range, while leaving many details up to the contractor or agency. In 2002, the Bush II Administration set a government-wide goal of spending 20% of services-contract dollars on performance-based contracts. A year later, eight agencies reported surpassing that goal: Energy 75%, Education 63%, Agriculture 34%, Transportation 33%, Interior 27%, Defense 25%, Treasury 24% and HHS 23% (Federal Procurement Data Center 2003: 1). Less visible trends have been to resort to restricted-source negotiated contracting (as with Halliburton for services in Iraq) and other non-arms-length relationships, particularly for exotic technologies and services. GAO and agencies' audit oversight seek to achieve accountability of such practices, but corruption is widely reported, both nationally[3] and internationally (Argyriades 2005).

With respect to internal governmental management, President Carter's 'Civil Service Reform Act' of 1978 required performance-based appraisals and merit pay as its centerpiece, and accountability for performance continues. The Clinton Administration established the National Performance Review (NPR) as its sustained theme under the vigorous leadership of Vice-President Gore. In 1993, the Government Performance and Results Act (GPRA; Public Law 103-62) became the ongoing framework for congressional oversight and executive-branch accountability. The GPRA was intended to enhance continuity of managerial systems and timely congressional involvement to limit wild changes and aggrandizement of executive powers that have accompanied presidential transitions. Continuity of performance management, with variations, has characterized Bush I (pre-GPRA), Clinton and Bush II accountability frameworks.

Bush I stressed Total Quality Management with a strong customer orientation and a relatively strong emphasis on the quality of work life. The Clinton/Gore National Performance Review (NPR) continued the customer orientation while drawing mostly on the Osborne and Gaebler book *Reinventing Government* (Osborne and Gaebler 1992) with touches of NPM. The NPR and NPM were (and still are) strongly criticized on two grounds. The first, as articulated most forcefully by Ronald Moe and Richard Gilmour, is failed accountability to lawful processes expected in performance of functions, especially those associated with sovereign authority (Moe and Gilmour 1995). The second criticism, penetratingly advanced by Denhardt & Denhardt, pertains to the twin themes of

> Dignity and worth of public service [. . .] and values of democracy, citizenship and public interest as the preeminent values of public administration. [. . .] Public servants do not deliver customer service; they deliver democracy. (Denhardt and Denhardt 2003)

This sort of criticism by US professionals of NPM's customer-focus as demeaning of citizens and their governance responsibilities is deep and wide. The most perceptive international critiques of NPM and the most penetrating analyses of the broader global thinking and practices are by Demetrios Argyriades (Argyriades 2002).

ACCOUNTABILITY FOR US INTERNATIONAL ACTIVITIES

Two sets of developments in international affairs and US culture require consideration in order to understand twenty-first-century accountability for

US international governance. Firstly, there are the internationally powerful conceptual frameworks of globalization and localization, and of governance (not simply government) (Klingner 2004) that had spread already for a decade before the collapse of the Soviet system. In the same set with these international concepts, from historic and current experience, is the US self-image discussed in the first section of this analysis. Secondly, there are the conflicting developments since the terrorist attacks of 11 September 2001 (National Commission on Terrorist Attacks upon the United States 2004) and the war on terrorism (including connections to the USA's sense of 'national mission').

International Conceptual Frameworks and America's Self-Image

Globalization has been vastly transformed by advances in electronic communications, knowledge/information systems and varied technologies. The World-Wide Web and the Internet have made nation-state boundaries seem irrelevant to many people. They have revolutionized domestic and international affairs – including accountability frameworks – of the nations whose borders they commonly ignore. Old distinctions between some tangible and intangible goods of economics and societies have been greatly ruptured if not excised along with international borders. Internal combustion engines and the airplanes they fuel advanced globalization tremendously in the twentieth century but they have been vastly augmented by digital-era advances. In these contexts, as noted in the first part of this analysis, the responsibilities and accountability of the USA and other nation-states have changed dramatically across a broad spectrum of sciences, technologies, arts and the humanities.

The digital globalization revolution has been accompanied by a vast restructuring of economics with the coincident rise to dominance of supranational entrepreneurial organizations. Herbert Simon said that these now define economics more than markets (Simon 1995). Consider Microsoft as an example. Thinking such as Simon's and realities created by Bill Gates and others have resulted in dramatically changed global dynamics. Most notably, the World Bank's policies on development have shifted from the generally *laissez-faire* posture of the 1980s and early 90s to vigorous support for *Building Institutions for Markets* (the title of the World Bank's *World Development Report 2002)* and social concerns, as in *Equity and Development* (the title of its *World Development Report 2006*) (World Bank 2002; World Bank 2005). Today's development experts stress interdependence of social, economic and political/governmental institutions to facilitate accountable markets of responsible enterprise for human, physical and macroeconomic advancement. Following the damage to the US and world economies from domestic and international corruption among leading US banks, corporations and stock-market institutions that contributed to the sustained global economic downturn at the outset of the twenty-first century, the crucial importance of accountability for the integrity of governance institutions (both private and governmental) appears to have caught the attention of many leaders in the USA besides those at the World Bank.

During the same period of the global electronic revolution and the rise to dominance of supranational business organizations, localization and upholding of values of place(s) and of varied indigenous cultures have expanded as standards of accountability. Deep currents of place values broke into global attention as an aspect of the Soviet Bloc collapse. Historic ethnic, religious, and national (in the Latin sense of *birth*) groupings more or less successfully sought self-determination and social, economic and political self-governance.

Soon, long-suppressed Balkanization emerged into open Balkan warfare and fragmentation and, after years of bloodshed with minimal European intervention, the USA pushed for Serbian accountability for atrocities, especially in Kosovo (Schnabel and Thakur 2001). A combination of place and planet values was involved, in part from the Global Civil Society and human-rights notions that had expanded somewhat globally since the 1980s alongside growth of NGOs and INGOs (Glasius, Kalder and Anheier 2002), in part from alarms about heavy damage to international social and economic commerce even in an idyllic Winter Olympics site, and most importantly among Americans, a sense of accountability to responsibilities to uphold their image of freedoms and human dignity which television continuously showed were being trampled by varied partisans, not Serbians alone. Among many Americans, what appeared to be ineffective European conceptions of international law (respecting Yugoslav national sovereignty), along with limitations on UN peacekeeping, cried out for accountability to a 'higher law' of human dignity and reasonableness in the US 'self-image', through coalition forces of NATO.

Terrorist War, American Sense of Mission and Accountability

International terrorism currently undermines the world order of nation-states and of constitutional democracy within those that are most threatened (Barber 1995). It has created far greater forces of change for the USA than those behind transitions of the state from the late 1970s through the 1990s from dominant-government models to dispersed facilitative-state governance. Consider the new reality. Conventional conflicts among blocs of nations preceded both World Wars and the Cold War. By contrast, before it exploded into inescapable consciousness on 11 September 2001 (9/11), today's Terrorist War was preceded by years of increasingly bold asymmetrical skirmishes. It is waged by non-nation-state forces, largely religious and tribal fundamentalists and criminal mercenaries who mostly oppose global social and capitalist consumerism and other Western and global intrusions into traditional cultures and revered places, such as Palestine and Saudi Arabia.

The USA and other nation-states attacked by terrorists lack sufficient agreement to sustain unity among them although changing coalitions take form. Conflicts include wars in Afghanistan and Iraq that have vestiges of conflicts over state regimes. But asymmetrical threats by non-state terrorist forces and countermeasures range from Western Europe, Russia, Turkey and Saudi Arabia to Pakistan, Indonesia, the Philippines and the USA. Homeland Security measures in America have greatly limited personal and organizational liberties and routines formerly associated with constitutional democracy, while awesomely elevating the garrison-state powers and actions, not in the ideological sense analyzed between 1937 and 1962 by Harold Lasswell (Lasswell 1997) but vastly exceeding what most Americans experienced in previous wars. Military and civilian specialists and industries devoted to advanced technologies and cultures of violence and countermeasures to them now consume hundreds of billions of US dollars, contributing to a national 'on-budget' deficit in 2004 of $568 billion (4.9% of Gross Domestic Product – GDP). This is an American political culture of growing fiscal irresponsibility, according to Comptroller General David Walker of the US Government Accountability Office (Walker 2005).

Accountability of terrorists and of nation states opposing their threats following 9/11 was initially considered optimistically possible through international law. Envisioned was an ongoing coalition of interdependent facilitative states and UN peacekeeping and nation-building, with extensive reliance on the USA as superpower (Newland 2001). Actions against the Taliban in Afghanistan more or less took on that form. In Iraq, however, it took the shape of a preemptive war against a nation-state by America and Britain along with a limitedly weak coalition of other nations. This was considered extensively long before the 9/11 attacks (Suskind 2004). France, Germany, Russia and other critics strongly held that America and the 'coalition of the willing' acted contrary to international law and without convincing intelligence and informed strategies to transform Iraq (Fallows 2004). As a typical scholarly criticism, Benjamin Barber in 2003 faulted Bush II's actions as making rogue states (the Axis of Evil, proclaimed on 29 January 2002) stand-ins for uncaught terrorists (Barber 2003). Barber concluded that America has become a costly 'realm of fear'. Furthermore, critics observe that instead of dealing with the roots of terrorism, the USA conveys a negatively self-righteous image and is seen to be seeking to impose by force on others her political institutions and her social and economic materialism.

By contrast, others discern constructive continuities in the foreign policies of Bush I, Clinton and Bush II. Continuities are found in a US doctrine of openness, as through NAFTA (North American Free Trade Agreement) and support of the European Union in order to facilitate economic expansion and an integrated global order (Bacevich 2002). In 2003, two Clinton

Administration National Security Council directors of key staffs, Ivo Daalder and James Lindsay, reviewed Bush II foreign policy in highly positive terms (Daalder and Lindsay 2003). Such analysts find support for the deliberate departure from previous policies of deterrence and containment and the embrace of preemption because asymmetrical terrorism compels offensive actions. Daalder and Lindsay stress precedents since the Wilson Administration in support of Bush II's policies of accountability to spread US-style freedoms and institutions globally. They caution, however, that resentments abroad entail high risks and that, even as a superpower, the USA needs a broader concurrence in order to achieve her goals.

CONCLUSIONS

Accountability for responsible American governance, both domestic and international, most fundamentally involves the substantive and procedural values and disciplines of constitutional democracy, sustained searches for human dignity in an increasingly multicultural society, and reasonableness (most particularly government under the rule of constitutional law). Such accountability is especially facilitated by the freedoms of speech and the press, along with robust academic inquiry. Domestically, US constitutional democracy requires leaders to be 'accountable jugglers' (as noted earlier in reference to former HHS Secretary Donna Shalala, whose standards went far beyond formal and legalistic provisions to sustain high values and self-governance disciplines among HHS people and those served by them). Responsible social, economic and political self-governance in international affairs requires similar juggling (searching with confidence balanced by humility) among people and their institutions generally. This represents a sustained current in the USA's usually pragmatic culture where 'the greatest realism is in the practice of ideals' (Newland 1984).

One basic rule of US constitutional democracy has always been that individuals, groups, organizations and other entities cannot be the final judges of their own actions. As observed in the 1776 Declaration of Independence, 'a decent respect for the opinions of mankind' is expected; accountability must ultimately be, in a significant measure, through the judgment of others. Their consent is sufficient. Enthusiastic support is infrequently expected, even for the continued authority of a juggler who is generally perceived to be searching to be responsible. In the War on Terrorism, the USA are a juggling lone superpower against asymmetric threats, and Bush II policies have sought extensive freedom from the constraints of some traditionally allied nation-states and international institutions as well as from domestic US law. These policies assert that, against terrorism, realism exists in a 'mission' to defend values defined in terms of the president's perceptions of the US 'self-image', even when actions are contrary to constitutional standards and when widespread international consent is lacking. Supporters define these policies in terms of national duty – even accountability to 'Destiny'. Critics shudder that this is a dangerously exceptionalist, unicentric and unevenly applied standard of accountability that contradicts both US and broad international ideals. In these conflicted contexts, the search for reason and human dignity in constitutional democracy persists.

REFERENCES

Argyriades, D. (2002). 'Governance and Public Administration in the 21st Century: New Trends and New Techniques'. *Governance and Public Administration in the 21st Century: Proceedings of the 25th International Congress of Administrative Sciences, Athens, 2001* (pp. 31–64). Brussels: International Institute of Administrative Sciences.

Argyriades, D. (2005). 'Rebuilding Public Service – Restoring Public Trust: Combating Corruption and Fraud'. Paper read in Yerevan, Armenia, 29–30 November 2005.

Bacevich, A.J. (2002). *American Empire: The Realities and Consequences of US Diplomacy*. Cambridge, MA: Harvard University Press.

Barber, B.R. (1995). *Jihad vs. McWorld: Terrorism Challenge to Democracy*. New York: Ballantine Books.

Barber, B.R. (2003). *Fear's Empire: War, Terrorism and Democracy*. New York: Norton.

Barnette, M., & Finnemore, M. (2004). *Rules for the World*. Ithaca, NY: Cornell University Press.

Caiden, G.E. (2004). 'A Cautionary Tale: Ten Major Flaws in Combating Corruption'. *Southwestern Journal of Law and Trade in the Americas* 10 (2), pp. 269–293.

Caiden, G.E. (2005). 'The Civilizing Mission of Public Administration'. Manuscript presented at the National Conference of the American Society for Public Administration in Milwaukee, Wisconsin (5 April).

Caiden, G.E., & Caiden, N. (1977). 'Administrative Corruption'. *Public Administration Review* 37 (3), pp. 301–309.

Daalder, I.H., & Lindsay, J.M. (2003). *America Unbound: The Bush Revolution in Foreign Policy*. Washington: Brookings Institution Press.

Dallek, G.A. (2003). 'Prescription for Confusion'. *Washington Post National Weekly* (5–21 December).

Denhardt, J.V., & Denhardt, R.B. (2003). *The New Public Service: Serving, not Steering*. Armonk, NY: M.E. Sharpe.

Fallows, J. (2004). 'Blind into Baghdad'. *Atlantic Monthly* 293 (1), pp. 52–71.

Federal Procurement Data Center (2003). 'Still Managing'. *Federal Times* 39 (27 October).

Follett, M.P. (1918). *The New State: Group Organization the Solution of Popular Government* (1965 reprint). Gloucester, MA: Peter Smith.

Glasius, M., Kalder, M., & Anheier, H. (Eds) (2002). *Global Civil Society*. Oxford: Oxford University Press.

Goldsmith, S., & Eggers, W.D. (2004). *Governing by Network: The New Shape of the Public Sector*. Washington: Brookings Institution Press.

Gorman, S.P. (2005). *Networks, Security and Complexity*. Cheltenham, UK: Edward Elgar Publishing.

Hayward, C.R. (2003). 'The Difference States Make: Democracy, Identity, and the American City'. *American Political Science Review* 97 (4), pp. 501–514.

Holcombe, A.N. (1950). *Our More Perfect Union: From Eighteenth-Century Principles to Twentieth-Century Practice*. Cambridge, MA: Harvard University Press.

Kauffman, T. (2005). 'DOD's New Pay Scales'. *Federal Times* 41 (42) (5 December).

Kettl, D.F. (2004). *System under Stress: Homeland Security and American Politics*. Washington: CQ Press.

Kickert, W.J.M., & Stillman, R.J. II (1994). *The Modern State and Its Study*. Cheltenham, UK: Edward Elgar.

Klingner, D.E. (2004). 'Globalization, Governance and the Future of Public Administration: Can We Make Sense of the Fog or Rhetoric Surrounding the Terminology?' *Public Administration Review* 64 (6), pp. 737–743.

Lasswell, H. (1997). *Essays on the Garrison State*. New Brunswick, NJ: Transaction Publishers.

Mead, L.M. (2004). *Government Matters: Welfare Reform in Wisconsin*. Princeton, NJ: Princeton University Press.

Moe, R.C., & Gilmour, R.S. (1995). 'Rediscovering Principles of Public Administration: The Neglected Foundation of Public Law'. *Public Administration Review* 55 (2), pp. 135–146.

Mosher, F.C. (1968). *Democracy and the Public Service*. New York: Oxford University Press.

National Commission on Terrorist Attacks upon the United States (2004). *The 9/11 Commission Report*. New York: Norton.

Newland, C.A. (1984). *Public Administration and Community: Realism in the Practice of Ideals*. McLean, VA: Public Administration Service.

Newland, C.A. (1994). 'A Field of Strangers in Search of a Discipline: Separation of Public Management Research from Public Administration'. *Public Administration Review* 54 (5), pp. 486–488.

Newland, C.A. (2001). 'Fanatical Terrorism versus Disciplines of Constitutional Democracy'. *Public Administration Review* 61 (6), pp. 643–650.

Osborne, D., & Gaebler, T. (1992). *Reinventing Government: How the Entrepreneurial Spirit is Transforming the Public Sector*. Reading, MA: Addison-Wesley.

Radin, B.A. (2002). *The Accountable Juggler: The Art of Leadership in a Federal Agency*. Washington: CQ Press.

Sandburg, C. (1936). *The People, Yes*. New York: Harcourt & Brace.

Schnabel, A., & Thakur, R. (2001). *Kosovo and the Challenge of Humanitarian Intervention*. New York: UN University Press.

Simon, H.A. (1995). 'Organizations and Markets'. *Journal of Public Administration Research & Theory* 5 (3), pp. 273–294.

Slaughter, A-M. (2004). *A New World Order*. Princeton: Princeton University Press.

Suskind, R. (2004). *The Price of Loyalty: George W. Bush, the White House and the Education of Paul O'Neill*. New York: Simon & Schuster.

US Bureau of the Budget (1964). *Measuring Productivity of Federal Government Organizations*. Washington: US Government Printing Office.

Vest, J., & Rozen (2005). 'Cunningham Inquiries Not Finished'. *National Journal* 37 (50), pp. 3818–3819.

Walker, D.M. (2005). 'Ethics and Integrity in Government: Putting Needs of Our Nation First'. The Elliot Richardson Lecture presented at the National Conference of the American Society for Public Administration, Milwaukee, Wisconsin.

West, W.F. (2004). 'Formal Procedures, Informal Processes, Accountability, and Responsiveness in Bureaucratic Policy Making: An Institutional Policy Analysis'. *Public Administration Review* 64 (1), pp. 66–80.

Wilson, W. (1887). 'The Study of Public Administration'. *Political Science Quarterly* 2, pp. 197–222.

World Bank (2002). *World Development Report 2002: Building Institutions for Markets*. New York: Oxford University Press.

World Bank (2005). *World Development Report 2006: Equity and Development*. New York: Oxford University Press.

Ziegler, M. (2005). 'GAO shifts to market wages'. *Federal Times* 41 (41) (28 November).

NOTES

1 From among Professor's Caiden's 30 books and monographs and over 260 articles, examples on accountability to combat corruption include Caiden and Caiden (1977); and Caiden (2004).

2 *McConnell v. Federal Election Commission*, 124 S. Ct. 619 (10 December 2003).

3 With respect to critical infrastructure protection and market strategies that undermine both efficiency and security, see Gorman (2005). On more widely understood corruption, an example is reported by Vest, Jason, and Rozen (2005).

3

Administrative Theory and Practice

CATHERINE G. BURKE

INTRODUCTION

The signature characteristic of Gerald Caiden is his effort to make the transition linking theory to practice. Academics who did not understand the gritty basics of administrative practice could contribute little to a useable administrative theory. Practitioners who argued that all theory was worthless would find it difficult to change and reform their practices.

Gerald works on both sides of the divide and thus has made significant contributions to both theory and practice. Too often in public administration, we hear public administrators argue that the theories they read do not relate to their work and experience. Some administrators seem to pride themselves on their disdain for theory. These same administrators then go on to quote their own views of organizations and management, e.g., 'it is just common sense', or 'it's understanding the politics', or 'it's gut feeling'. Nonetheless, these people have basic and usually accurate ideas about cause and effect without which they could not turn intention into action and actually achieve the intended results. Thus they demonstrate Caiden's point that everyone has theories. Such theories are often tacit, neither articulated nor capable of articulation. When this is done exceptionally well, we may refer to the person as a 'charismatic leader' – a concept that always carries a hint of mystery and magic.

On the other hand, some academics articulate theories but never put them to the test of practice. These are the 'academic' theories, rightly scorned by many managers. Even where such articulated theories are put to the test, the methods too often reflect a distorted view of science that eliminates human intentions and values. Thus the disdain heard so frequently in discussions of administrative theory: 'that doesn't make any sense', 'it may sound good in theory, but it won't work here'; 'we tried [name your least favorite theory], and it created such a mess, we're still digging out from under'.

Few would argue that this is the problem with Caiden's work. He has continuously stressed the practical. He has developed theories on corruption and the need for reform. He has studied the ombudsman institution as a way of improving governmental practices (Caiden 1975, 1982a, 1982b). He has worked extensively on issues of police reform and revitalization (Caiden 1972, 1973, 1976a, 1976b, 1977). His work has had impact around the world, as he worked in Canada, England, Israel, Australia, the United States and many developing countries. He has made significant contributions to international bodies including the United Nations and the World Bank.

He has attacked mismanagement, waste, fraud and power abuse. He sees governments as necessary instruments of social policy with great potential for service to humankind. At the same time, Caiden recognizes the difficulties of people battling the forces of greed, corruption and maladministration. He has written over and over about the need for reform and the methods of reform, providing practical ideas on how to improve our public administrative practices (Caiden 1969, 1971, 2003, 2004; Caiden & Caiden 1982; Caiden & Siedentopf 1982; Caiden et al. 2001).

In relating theory to practice he displays clear understanding of the elements and relationships, as illustrated in Figure 1. This model was developed by Ian Macdonald (personal communication, 2001) and it is an evolving model of the way theory and practice need to be linked (Burke et al. 2006). Although he has not used the specific model, Gerald is very clear on the need to unite all these three elements in order to make progress in public administration.

The model is based on the recognition that all human beings have beliefs, values, dreams and aspirations. Any valid theory of human behavior must take these into account. Caiden makes his values clear in all his works. He

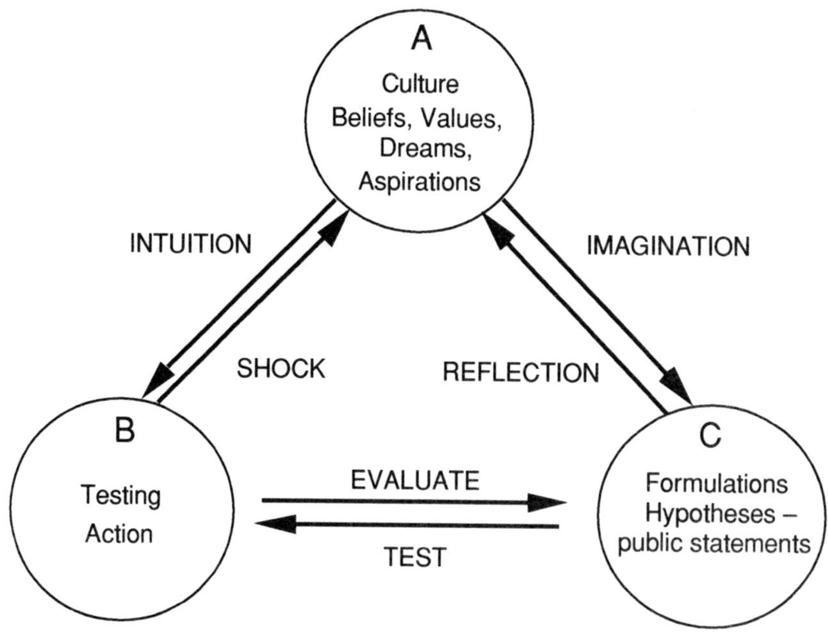

Figure 1

has attacked bureaupathologies wherever they are found. He fights for the universal human values of honesty, equity, fairness, respect for human dignity, courage and love (Burke et al. 2006). Caiden repeatedly emphasizes the importance of 'constitutionalism, rule of law, equal consideration, due process, equity, protection, access, competence, regularity, quality, fairness, responsibility, accountability, openness' (Caiden 1991a: 489).

In addition, in his philosophy of 'teaching public administration' (1991c) he writes that

> My heart always goes out to the disadvantaged, the handicapped, the backward, because I know what it was like being written off, disregarded, overlooked and ignored. Everyone has something to contribute, some talent of some kind. It is just a matter of finding it, encouraging it, fostering it, and giving a person a fair chance.

This humanity and concern for those less fortunate permeate much of Caiden's work, though not all may be aware of his deep feelings for others.

These are the values we hope would be shared by all public administrators, and experience suggests that a significant number do hold these values dear. Clearly this is not the case for all administrators, however, as we find abuse of authority, power and position, bribery and corruption, bias and arrogance, and lack of fairness and favoritism in many public organizations. Thus, the need for reform is the ongoing theme of Caiden's work. Nonetheless, in the Western societies of North America and Europe, public administrators do appear to share Caiden's values though they may work within governmental systems that are dysfunctional and with leaders who are incompetent, which makes attainment of those values difficult.

We need to remember that theories of public administration are not always helpful to practitioners. As a result, public administrators operate on the left side of the diagram, using cells A and B some of the time. Their actions are guided by intuition. When the intended result does not occur, they are forced to consider what happened and how they might change course to reach the intended goal. Unfortunately, if their theories are tacit and unformulated, they are largely untestable. Therefore, it is more difficult to replicate success than to avoid subsequent failures.

Even more important, it is impossible to articulate to others what the individual has learned and the theories now in use. This can become quite serious, as was observed by the author in a meeting with executives from a highly successful business.[1] The founders have long since retired, but in dealing with difficult issues the question came up more than once: 'What would Alan and Bill have done?' Executives recognized that these two founders had insights which others were struggling to grasp as they had not been able (or perhaps had not even been aware of the need) to pass on their insights to their successors.

In the public sector, rapid turnover of politically appointed executives makes the problem even more difficult. Often these newcomers want to make their own mark and are uninterested in what has been successful in the past. Long-term public administrators may endeavor to educate their new 'managers', but without a clear articulation of what worked and why, it is difficult or impossible to effectively suggest how new problems might be approached. Knowledge of cause and effect may be correct, but explanations as to why and under what conditions will be missing.

Academics, on the other hand, often get locked into A and C where the formulations are testable but left untested in a confrontation with action and reality – the worst of 'academic' theory. Where science is misunderstood as being value-free, as in the relationship between B and C, formulations and tests are devoid of human intention. Some of this research may be useful, but it is difficult to apply when the human dimension is omitted. It may also lead to tragedy, as when scientists become so disconnected from human ethical values that they are capable of the Tuskegee medical experiments or those conducted at Auschwitz.

What is required, of course, is that all three elements be inseparably linked. Sometimes this is accomplished within a single individual. More often, public administrators find consultants and academics to be valuable assistants in the formulation of testable theories and hypotheses. Caiden has played this role and it is reflected in much of his work. It is not so that managers cannot articulate their hypotheses, but the fact remains that they do not articulate them. They are usually too busy and time-pressured to clearly define terms and formulate clear hypotheses. Such formulations do not come easily or quickly. They require much hard work, and once articulated they often have to be modified as they are tested in practice.

That is why the work of Caiden has been so productive. He is continuously in touch with all three elements of the model. His efforts to improve public administration are never simply 'academic'. They have resonance for practitioners in rapidly changing environments. This dynamism means that there is a continuing need for revitalization and reform (Caiden 1982c, 1982d). As North American and Western European ideas of good administration have spread around the world, there is also a need to develop a common language to communicate our ideas more effectively.

LANGUAGE: SOCIAL AND SCIENTIFIC

One difficulty that all writers and practitioners involved in public administration theory and behavior often confront is that unlike in physics, chemistry, biology or engineering, there are few terms or concepts with generally accepted definitions. In the sciences, key concepts such as mass, volume, acceleration, DNA, cell, tensile strength or stress are agreed upon even where there are competing theories. Thus it is possible to share meaning quite precisely.

To study human processes such as public administration or management, two types of meaning need to be introduced. The first is 'scientific' meaning, where an entity or term has an agreed meaning by which we can determine whether an entity is 'one of those' or not. The second type can be termed 'social' meaning. In our everyday lives we approximate and assume an overlap in understanding without worrying too much if we mean precisely the same thing. Such terms as happy, leader, culture or friend are examples.

A problem in public administration theory is that concepts lie in the domain of social meaning. That is, we have a general understanding of terms such as manager, leader, authority, power, team, organization, abuse, injustice and reform, but there may be significant differences in the area of non-overlap. Is a manager also a leader? Is a leader a manager? Can one be a manager if one has no subordinates? Do you have a team if a manager appoints the leader or must a team select its own leader? Is 'severe interrogation' abuse or torture? Is helping a major campaign contributor corruption, or an abuse of authority?

In everyday conversations such details usually do not matter. To emphasize such details would appear at best pedantic, at worst bizarre. For example, if one person asks another 'what do you do', a typical reply might be 'I am a supervisor at the local plant'. It would be odd, indeed, if the first person then asked, 'So what exactly is the extent of your authority; how does it differ from that of a manager?'

In the workplace, however, such issues of authority are of utmost importance, especially to the worker who may be asked to carry out a task. He or she needs to know if this person has the authority to tell him, or her, what to do and within which limits. These are significant issues for both the worker and the supervisor, issues that may modify the response of the worker to the supervisor's direction. When trying to implement a new way of working, general social definitions can cause considerable confusion and difficulty.

The scientist Lavoisier developed the language of chemistry in the early eighteenth century, and it was only after his publication of a standard vocabulary that the science of chemistry began its rapid development. He wrote:

> We cannot improve the language of any science without at the same time improving the science itself; conversely, neither can we improve a science without improving the language or nomenclature which belongs to it. However certain the facts of any science may be, and however just the ideas we may have formed of these facts, we can only communicate false impressions to others, while we want words by which these may be properly expressed (Lavoisier 1789 in Bolles 1997: 380).

As public administrators struggle with the issues of our time, the absence of clear and agreed concepts is evident. Often there is lack of agreement on what constitutes reform, waste, fraud and abuse. Caiden (1979) notes that 'new public laws, new social controls, new rights, new functions, new roles, new organizations, new taxes, new paperwork, new public service occupations' do not necessarily make things better. Those who challenged the approaches of the 'progressive' reformers were not always wrong. Well-intentioned effort is no substitute for clear thinking and sound understanding.

THE PRACTICAL VALUE OF GOOD THEORY

A good theory uses defined terms and specifies the relationships between and among them. Without such theory we create mess and muddles from which we learn little or nothing. We see the result in the field of public administration where ideas are not specified clearly but left to general social understanding. Woodrow Wilson (1887) argued that there could be and should be a science of administration. Such a science would have to have general application and be based on clear concepts.

To illustrate the value of clear concepts, I provide an example that I believe can apply across societies using the concepts of 'association and employment hierarchy'. This example also suggests how the theories and methods of public administration that developed in the US, the UK or Europe might make the transition to other countries with different cultures and histories. I begin with the work of Max Weber (1946/1922) and Hernando de Soto (2000) to provide some insight into why generalizations from Western approaches may become universally applicable. In his study of types of authority, Weber wrote that as societies become more modern and democratic the dominant type of authority would be legal-rational. De Soto argues that the difference between developed and less developed societies is the influence of law. Without clear law regarding property rights, contracts, redress for damages and many other laws we take for granted in modern societies, development will be impeded and the poor will be unable to escape their poverty. While the character of the law will differ in different societies, de Soto (2000) believes the rule of law is essential for social and economic development.

According to Weber, the distinctive organizational form in systems of legal-rational authority is bureaucracy. Bringing his ideas together with those of de Soto, one can hypothesize that as societies develop and take on the characteristics of modernity – including law – bureaucracies will become the means whereby they organize to accomplish their goals. Therefore we may see the development of more universal theories of organization and public administration. The present author (Burke et al. 2006) has built on the work of Wilfred Brown (1971) and Elliott Jaques (1976) in order to clarify two concepts relevant to public administration: associations and employment hierarchies (bureaucracies). 'Associations are people coming together for a purpose. The purpose is either agreed to tacitly or expressed in a written document' (Brown 1971: 48). The written document may be a constitution, a charter, and articles of incorporation or authorizing legislation. Some associations such as neighborhood groups may not have a written document or formal rules, but they will have at least verbal agreements about who they are and what their purpose is for forming an association.

In developed societies almost all of us are members of associations. If you are a shareholder, you are a member of a business corporation. If you are a worker, you may be a member of a union. You may serve as a volunteer, a member of the Red Cross, which is a voluntary association. As a US citizen, you are a member of several governments: a city, a county, a state and a federal government. A partnership is a form of association, as is a university. Associations may be religious, athletic, medical or legal, or they may unite scientific endeavors.

Associations operate through consensus, voting, debate and persuasion. Except in the case of very small associations, members usually elect a few of their number to be their representatives in a governing body that is authorized to act on behalf of the members. These representatives set overall association policy within the limits allowed by their charters, and when necessary ask the membership to vote on changes which go beyond the charter or seek to amend the charter. When the workload of the association becomes too large to be handled by the Board and its members, the Board may be authorized to employ staff (employees) to carry out the association's purposes. Thus they create an employment hierarchy: 'that network of employment roles set up by an association of people to carry out work required to achieve the objectives of the association' (Brown 1971: 49).

Figures 2 and 3 illustrate generic patterns of member, representative, 'governing board' and employee relationships as found in business corporations and municipalities with the city-manager form of government.

In the US, city governments are termed incorporated municipalities and, therefore, often have a structure similar to that of a business. They are organized under the laws of their respective states which may have slightly different methods of incorporation and differing authorities granted to municipalities. The council hires a city manager who serves at the pleasure of the council. He or she may hire subordinate staff to run various city departments under rules set by the council or state law.

This simple corporate structure does not work well in large cities where political relationships usually include an elected mayor who, to a greater or lesser degree, is authorized to be the chief executive of the city, while a city

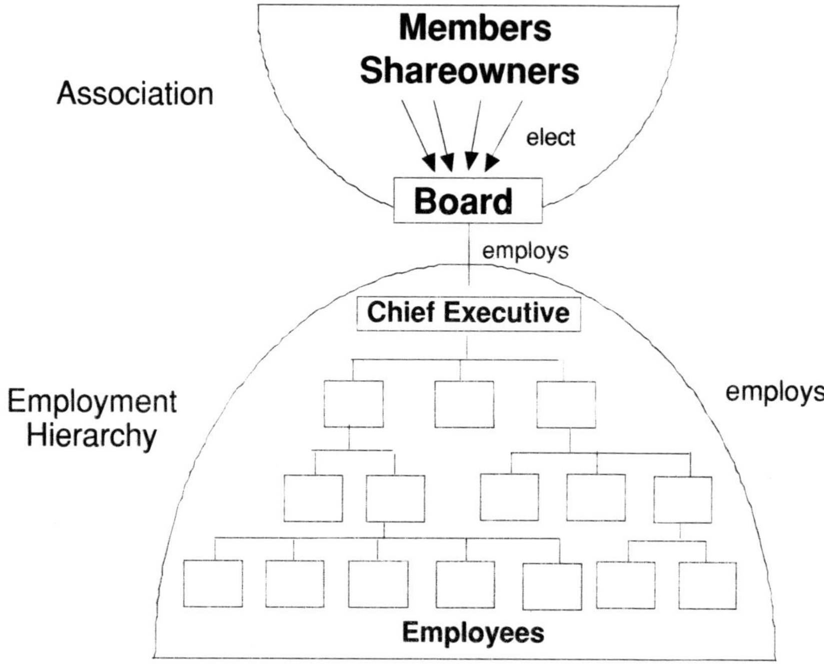

Figure 2 Corporate business structure

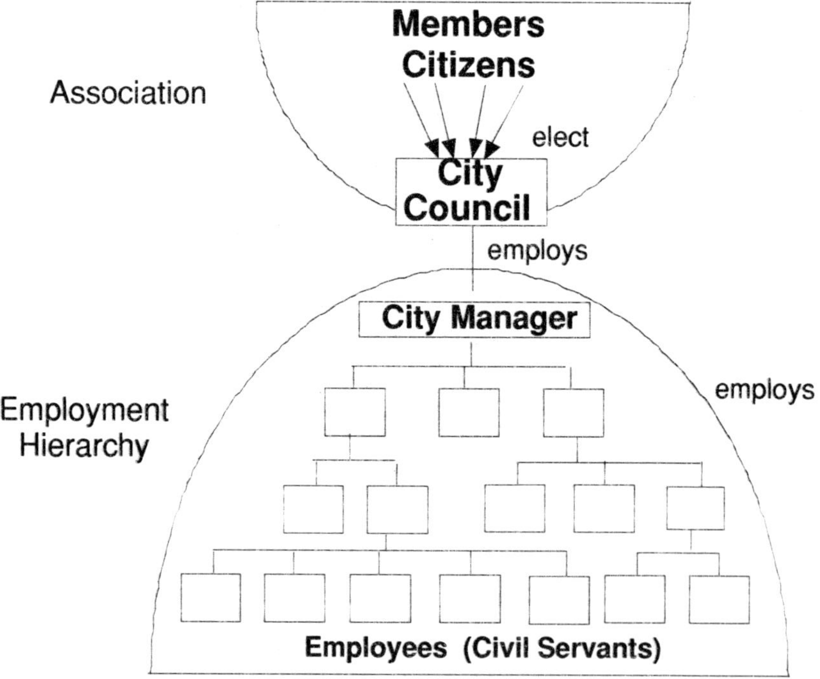

Figure 3 City-manager form of government

council acts as the legislative body. Figure 4 shows the structure of the city of Los Angeles, which has a mayor with relatively weak authority and a council with broad authorities. The gray areas show the political appointees, the white area shows the employees.

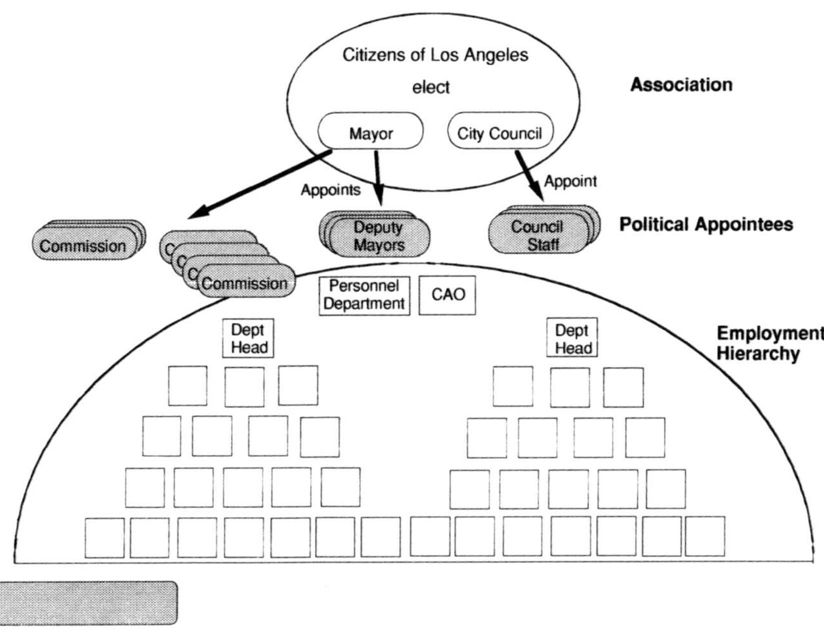

Figure 4 Generic structure city of Los Angeles

Political Appointees

In Los Angeles, Commissions head some departments while other departments have an executive department head. Other Commissions operate independently without departments. The Personnel Department and the CAO answer to the mayor, the city council and their staffs. It is a system that is vulnerable to power plays and favoritism.

Figure 5 is a simplified schematic of the types of divided governments found in the US. Drawn to indicate the basic structure of the federal government in the USA, it is a simplification but it does indicate the relationships among elected officials, political appointees and civil servants. The president appoints and the senate must approve the higher-level positions such as cabinet secretaries and their deputies.

In addition, there is a special group of civil servants called the Senior Executive Service. Political executives can move these high-level civil servants from position to position, but they retain their civil service status and cannot be removed from the service without cause. The SES carries out much of the management of federal agencies, and some members contribute policy recommendations. The jagged line between the political appointees and the SES demonstrates considerable interpenetration between these two groups.

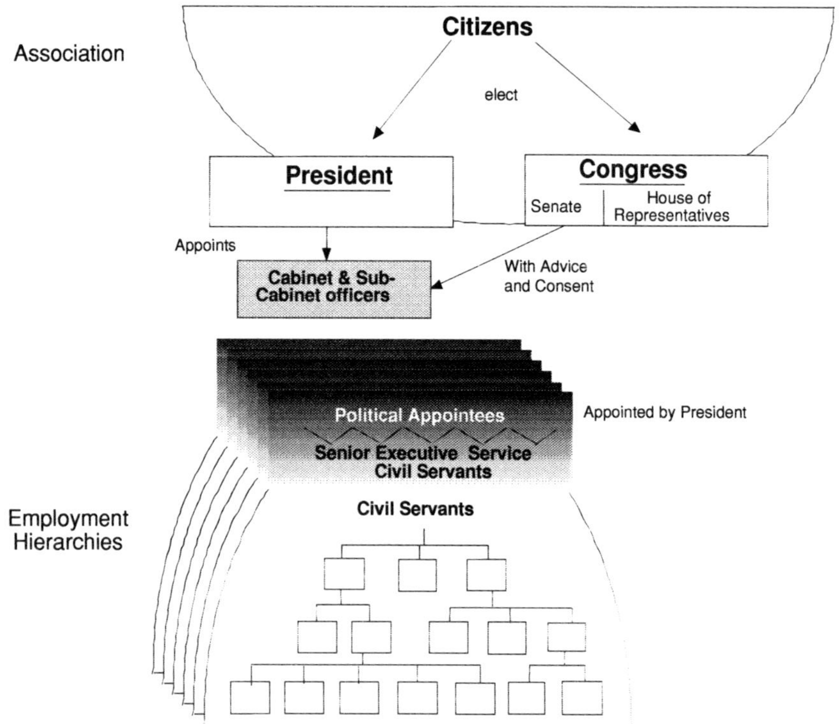

Figure 5 US federal government

A parliamentary system as shown in Figure 6 is less politically complex because 'the government' is made up of the leading officials of the party that controls the parliament. Government ministers head the departments and, in the case of the British system, the Permanent Secretary is subordinate to the minister and is the effective manager of the department. The Permanent Secretary, who needs considerable political skill, is still a civil servant with executive authority over other employees of the department, though he/she is constrained by civil service rules regarding the selection, promotion and dismissal of these employees.

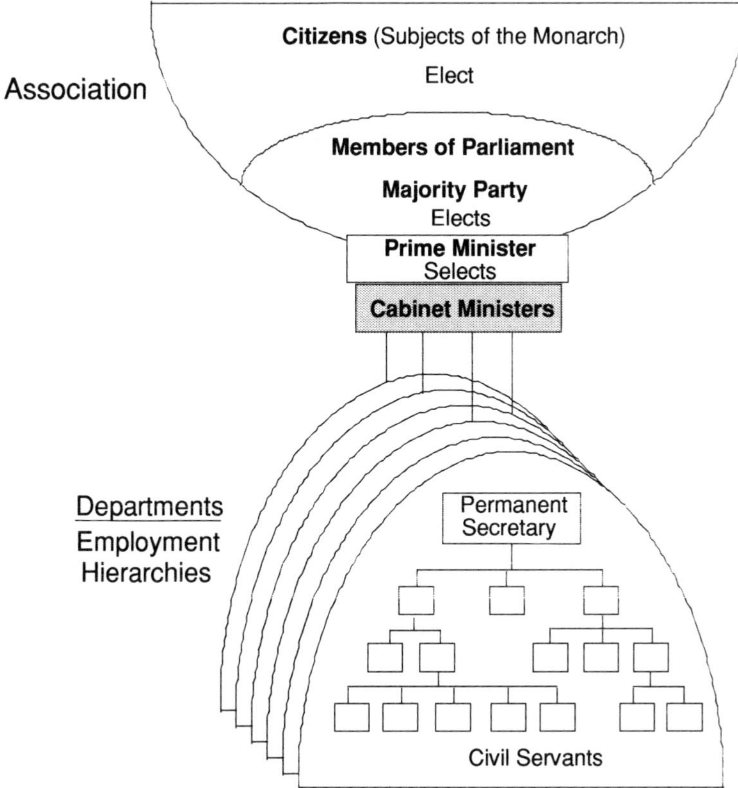

Figure 6 Westminster parliament form of government

Thus, all these associations may employ people to carry out the purposes of the association. These employment hierarchies have much in common with each other and are most effectively structured in a similar pattern (Jaques 1976; Burke et al. 2006).

If de Soto and Weber are correct in their respective analyses, the dominant form of organization will be the employment hierarchy or bureaucracy as societies become modern and democratic, i.e., based on legal-rational principles. These employment hierarchies are both secondary and dependent institutions (see Table 1). They are secondary in that they cannot be formed in their own right: there must first be an employing body that decides to establish an organization and provide the authorities within which employees carry out their work. They are dependent in that their continuity depends upon the continued existence of the employing body.

This example suggests that public administration deals with both associations and employment hierarchies, and that clarifying these concepts should improve our ability to develop a more general theory of public administration as it relates to different societies. Our associations may differ and a study of these differences should be fruitful for both scholars and practitioners. Employment hierarchies will display enough similarities that again we should be able to develop general principles of organization to guide administrative practice. No theory can substitute for good administrative judgment, but good theories inform and guide that judgment properly.

Table 1 indicates some of the practical implications for theory where associations and employment hierarchies are concerned. For example, the leader of an association is elected by his or her followers and held accountable by them. The leader of an employment hierarchy holds followers accountable and can select and dismiss them within the rules of the association. Keeping this simple distinction in mind helps clarify much of the literature on leadership that frequently muddles these two types of leadership and their associated behaviors.

Other issues are clarified by using these two concepts. Almost all employees of governments are citizens of that government, which creates serious dilemmas for civil servants when they are asked to act in ways that offend their concerns as citizens. Business employees can also have dual roles as shareholders and as appointment holders. There are other distinctions as well. In the US government, Congress is not a Board of Directors nor is the president a CEO. With the Supreme Court, Congress and the president form the core of US government with powers that are both separate and shared. This association makes governing the administrative departments (employment hierarchies) more complex and contentious. To what extent are departments controlled by the president and his appointees and to what extent by the Congress through its committees? Often their objectives are subject to dispute, and directions are unclear. Yet despite these significant differences between governments and other types of association, in democratic societies governments can be usefully depicted as associations (Jaques 1976; Tussman 1960; MacIver & Page 1960; Dewey 1927).

Caiden has also shown that associations and employment hierarchies – or, in Weber's terms, bureaucracies – are significant institutions worthy of careful study. If this illustration proves useful, perhaps we can start to develop a science of public administration with clear concepts and clear cause-and-effect relationships.

HUMAN BEINGS AND SCIENCE

If we are to develop such a science, it must be based in part on the nature of human beings. It has been argued, however, that where human beings are concerned there can be no exact science. Science deals with things we can observe, either directly or with the aid of various instruments. Human beings, on the other hand, have intentions: purposes that cannot be observed

Table 1 Characteristics of associations and employment hierarchies

Associations	**Employment Hierarchies (Bureaucracies)**
Primary	Secondary
Independent	Dependent
Authority relationships based on the Charter	Authority relationships based on the Charter
and social customs and practice	and the policies of the Board of Governors. Social customs and practice set limits on authority
Members	Employees
Members are equals	Employees are in superior/subordinate relationships
Act through representatives, who are held accountable by members	Act through employees, who are held accountable by higher level managers. Top manager held accountable by elected Board of the Association
Leaders held accountable by followers	Leaders hold followers accountable
Operate through consensus, debate, persuasion, voting	Operate through executive decision processes
Set objectives and policies of the association within the scope and authority of the Charter	Receive initial objectives and policies from the association. Formulate policies for Board
Where necessary seek vote of members	Decision/vote
Take instructions from members and advise	Listen to suggestions from subordinates, decide, give instructions
Representatives' relationships collegial	Manager/subordinate relationships hierarchical
Representatives have term of office	Employees have open-ended employment contract
Members need not perform in order to remain a member; only obey rules of the association	Employees must perform or lose job

but can only be revealed in the course of dialogue with others. Humans may or may not choose to reveal their actual intentions to an outside observer. Further, human beings have an opinion about being observed and this may influence their behavior.

When we observe human behavior we interpret what we see to provide meaning for ourselves. This may or may not reflect the meaning or intent of the person being observed. Nonetheless, we make such interpretations all the time. Those who become good at observing social processes often make what appear to be quite accurate interpretations. This appears to strengthen the argument that there cannot be a science of public administration; there can only be an art or a craft. We can agree that developing a scientific base for interpreting social phenomena remains difficult. Two possible reasons explain this.

The first has to do with our experience of life. We grow up learning how to predict the impact of our environment on ourselves. We learn to read our mother's behavior first, and over time we develop internal 'theories', that we term rules of thumb, hypotheses or prejudices concerning the way people behave as they do. We use these theories to order our own behavior so that it may produce the outcome we desire. Sometimes we are right, thus confirming our hypotheses; however, sometimes we are wrong. When we are wrong, we must decide whether our failure to predict was based on a wrong 'theory' or, if the theory was sound, because the event was really a 'special case'.

Thus, we develop our own ideas about human behavior. Consequently, such propositions as are made about organizations – which are essentially about human behavior – compete with our own – usually implicit – theories. This is very different from theoretical propositions in the natural sciences. We do not grow up with theories about aeronautical engineering, physics or chemistry. As they concern inanimate matter, it is easy to learn and to be objective about such matters. Of course, when scientific theories challenge ideas that are central to a given society, the propagators of such theories, such as Galileo, may find themselves in trouble. In our own time, biologists and teachers who use Darwinian evolutionary theory may find themselves in difficulty though they are not in danger of being burned at the stake for heresy.

However, when it comes to explicit and predictive theories of human behavior, we are likely to judge them true or false based on our own experience. This response is often quite emotional, because these are theories about us. New propositions may contradict existing and dearly held theories about our organizations and ourselves.

A second reason why scientific meaning remains difficult is that predictive theoretical propositions are necessarily based on statistical data. Scientific theories accurately predict what will happen to a particular entity always allowing for statistical variation. Predictions are based on general patterns of outcomes, not individual events. It is at this point that the natural and the social sciences converge. Like a subatomic particle, as individuals we are not entirely predictable. We know this and we resist predictions, especially if we see them as attempts at manipulation.

However unpredictable we may be as individuals, it does not follow that people or populations are totally unpredictable. We can make statements about how people, in general, react in given situations. Numerous experiments have shown that most people tend to agree with the majority view when it is made public, even if they disagree in private. We know people respond more positively and productively when given realistic feedback, be it positive or negative, than when they are given no feedback or only noticed when things go wrong. Although a few individuals do not react this way, this does not falsify the underlying proposition, though we may be interested to know why they are different from the norm.

We also have to recognize that individuals have the ability and, in democratic societies, the liberty to exercise their free will. Because a manager or leader can never know all of the inputs that influence the decision that his/her team members will make, there are times when a prediction made about an individual's behavior will be wrong. This is not necessarily a failure of the theory behind the prediction, provided always that the theory used as an analysis tool can be applied to explain the cause of the unpredicted outcome.

In the field of public administration, it is as important to observe and understand the social processes in human interaction as it is to observe and understand the technical and financial processes. Deming's work on quality in technical processes (1982) provides a useful insight. He pointed out the need to understand the process and to distinguish between common causes and special causes (exceptions). The same is true of social processes. To understand these processes, we must have shared definitions so that we may develop a clear and detailed understanding of the process. That should enable us to distinguish between common and special causes.

In making interpretations regarding social processes, we must also be careful not to assume that we know what another human being is thinking. We cannot know this. We can only make inferences or develop hypotheses based on what we observe, but we can never know what is going on in another person's head. The common use of such phrases as 'he has a bad attitude' or 'she thinks she's so smart' are at best careless; at worst they are insulting and demeaning, demonstrating lack of respect for another human's dignity.

Gerald Caiden has recognized the importance of these key human characteristics while developing a whole body of literature for discussing, thinking and working with propositions about public administration, administrative reform and how to implement a better society. Of necessity he uses words that have a common social meaning, but he has used them carefully, so that those who learn from them can have a semblance of shared definitions. This does not signify that other definitions are wrong. They are simply less useful for his purpose, which has been to advance our knowledge in the fields of public administration and administrative reform.

Most importantly, Caiden never lost sight of the core human values with which we must inform both our theory and our practice if we are to avoid the horrors produced by public maladministration and bureaupathologies. His integrity and persistence in the pursuit of sound theory and useful public practice is a model for all students in the field.

REFERENCES

Bolles, E.B. (1997) (Ed). *Galileo's Commandment: An Anthology of Great Science Writing*. New York: W.H. Freeman.

Brown, W. (1971). *Organization*. London: Heinemann Educational Books.

Burke, C., Macdonald, I., & Stewart, K. (2006). *The Work of Management*. London: Gower Press.

Caiden, G.E. (1969). *Administrative Reform*. Chicago: Aldine Publishing Co.

Caiden, G.E. (1971). *Impact and Implications of Administrative Reform for Administrative Behavior and Performance*. UN: Public Administration Division: ESA/PA/1/3.

Caiden, G.E. (1972). *Police Administration Today*. Netanya: Police Academy.

Caiden, G.E. (1973). *Police Administration Tomorrow*. Netanya: Police Academy.

Caiden, G.E. (1975). *To Right Wrong: The Ombudsman Experience in Israel*. Berkeley, CA: Institute of Governmental Studies. Revised (1980): *To Right Wrong: The Initial Ombudsman Experience in Israel*. Tel Aviv: Ashdown Press.

Caiden, G.E. (1976a). 'Systemic Corruption in Police Organizations'. Boston: Seminar on Police Corruption.

Caiden, G.E. (1976b). 'Reorganizing the Patrol: An Overview of the State of the Art'. Police Foundation.

Caiden, G.E. (1977). *Police Revitalization*. Lexington, MA: Lexington Books & D.C. Heath.

Caiden, G.E. (1979). 'A Letter from a Self-Styled Iconoclast to his Fellow Public Administration Theorists'. *Dialogue: The Public Administration Theory Network* 2 (2), pp. 4–6.

Caiden, G.E. (Ed) (1982a) *An International Handbook of Ombudsman*. Westport, CT: Greenwood Press.

Caiden, G.E. (1982b). 'The Ombudsman Institution in Israel'. In G.E. Caiden (Ed), *An International Handbook of Ombudsman* (pp. 123–130). Westport, CT: Greenwood Press.

Caiden, G.E. (1982c). 'Administrative Reform and Public Administration'. In G.E. Caiden & H. Siedentopf (Eds). *Strategies for Administrative Reform*. Lexington, MA: Lexington Books.

Caiden, G.E. (1982d). *Public Administration*. (Revision of *The Dynamics of Public Administration*). Los Angeles, CA: Palisades Publishers.

Caiden, G.E. (1983). 'In Search of an Apolitical Science of American Public Administration'. In J. Bowman & J. Rabin (Eds). *Politics and Administration*. New York: Marcel Dekker.

Caiden, G.E. (1991a). 'What Really is Public Maladministration?' *Public Administration Review* 51 (6), pp. 486–493.

Caiden, G.E. (1991b). *Administrative Reform Comes of Age*. Berlin/New York: de Gruyter.

Caiden, G.E. (1991c). 'My Basic Philosophy of Teaching Public Administration'. University of Southern California, Los Angeles, CA.

Caiden, G.E. (1994). 'Globalizing the Theory and Practice of Public Administration'. In J.-C. Garcia-Zamor & R. Khator (Eds), *Public Administration in the Global Village*. Westport, CT: Praeger.

Caiden, G.E. (2002). 'The Erosion of Public Service: A Warning'.Working Paper. University of Southern California.

Caiden, G.E. (2003). 'Reinvigorating Public Service'. Paper given at the ASPA Conference in Washington, DC.

Caiden, G.E. (2004). 'A Cautionary Tale: Ten Major Flaws in Combating Corruption'. *Southwestern Journal of Law and Trade in the Americas* 10 (2), pp. 269–293.

Caiden, G.E., & Caiden, N. (1982). *Administrative Corruption*. Tel Aviv: Ashdown Press.

Caiden, G.E., Dwivedi, O.P. & Jabbra, J. (2001). *Where Corruption Lives*. Bloomfield, CT: ILAS/Kumerian Press.

Caiden, G.E., & Siedentopf, H. (1982) (Eds). *Strategies for Administrative Reform*. Lexington, MA: Lexington Books.

Deming, W.E. (1982). *Out of the Crisis*. Cambridge, MA: MIT Center for Advanced Engineering Study.

Dewey, J. (1927). *The Public and its Problems*. New York: Holt & Co.

de Soto, H. (2000). *The Mystery of Capital: Why Capitalism Triumphs in the West and Fails Everywhere Else*. New York: Basic Books.

Gerth, H.H., & Mills, C.W. (1946) (Eds). *From Max Weber: Essays in Sociology*. New York: Oxford University Press.

Jaques, E. (1976). *A General Theory of Bureaucracy*. London: Heinemann Educational Books.

MacIver, R.M., & Page, C.H. (1960). *Society: An Introductory Analysis*. London: Macmillan.

Tussman, J. (1960). *Obligation and the Body Politic*. New York: Oxford University Press.

Wilson, W. (1887). 'The Study of Administration'. *Political Science Quarterly* 2.

NOTE

1 Names have been changed to disguise the organization.

4

The State of the Study of Comparative Public Administration in India

R.B. JAIN

INTRODUCTION

Perhaps no other discipline in social sciences has attracted such controversy over its nature as has public administration. Due to its growing significance and role in the system and processes of the organization of power, it has frequently been a subject of theoretical and practical deliberations from various disciplinary angles. A number of new paradigms, theories and models have now been added to the formerly accepted boundaries of public administration, invading related social science disciplines as well as the 'philosophy of science, epistemology and ethics'. The issues with which an educator, researcher and practitioner in public administration must now be concerned go far beyond the field's traditional compass. Some scholars have observed that the various problems before them now include:

> A phenomenological versus a positivistic administrative theory, incremental versus revolutionary patterns of scientific growth, normative versus empirical approaches to administrative research, structurally-based versus process-oriented concepts of administrative behavior and repressive versus liberating strategies of public policy formation and planning. (Dunn and Fozouni 1976: 5–6)

Administrative reality is, thus, conveyed today as a diffuse collection of multiple realities held by diverse individuals, groups and subcultures within the field. And yet, despite this tremendous growth in the contents and approaches to the discipline, a concerted theoretical foundation so far continues to elude the practitioners and theoreticians of public administration. The reason is that the task of interpreting public administration is, indeed, formidable. There are a number of ways and methods used by researchers to study public administration, each of them capable of revealing different facets of administrative reality in the context of differing environments, but no attempt has been made to consolidate these findings into coherent theoretical formulations.

EMERGENCE OF 'COMPARATIVE PUBLIC ADMINISTRATION' (CPA)

The search for the construction of a science of public administration brought home the fact that this depended, among other things, on success in establishing propositions about administrative behavior transcending national boundaries. In his 1947 essay 'The Science of Public Administration', Robert Dahl argued that 'the attempt to create a science of public administration with universal or even generally applicable principles was handicapped by the three basic problems of values, individual personality and the social framework' (Dahl 1947: 1–11). He pointed out that 'the comparative aspects of public administration have largely been ignored, and as long as the study of public administration is not comparative, claims for "a science of public administration" sound rather hollow' (ibid.).

The need for comparison presented many problems. To begin with, any attempt to compare national administrative systems must acknowledge the fact that administration is only one aspect of the operation of the political system. This inevitably means that comparative public administration is linked with the study of comparative politics. Work in comparative public administration has, thus, closely followed comparative political analysis. In the USA, both movements (comparative politics and comparative public administration) have been characterized 'by the comparative youth of their participants, by a general commitment to the outlook identified with behavioralism, by an effort to be interdisciplinary in interests and techniques and by an effort to arrive at concepts, formulas and theories that are truly universal, bridging and embracing all cultures' (Waldo 1963: 11–12).

Interest in comparative public administration also grew out of the fact that – beginning with World War II, continuing into postwar military occupations and accelerating with the many technical assistance programs of the USA, the UN and private foundations – US students and teachers of public administration found themselves engaged by the hundreds in professional work in foreign lands. This exposure to foreign (often non-Western) governmental systems and cultures stimulated a general sense of 'comparativeness' and raised questions about the appropriateness, or even the sheer possibility, of transferring familiar administrative devices or applications of what had been presumed to be good or scientific principles of administration to foreign settings (ibid.).

In order to meet the needs of new policy areas of technical assistance administration, important strides have been made in the evolution of the study of comparative public administration. Consequently, the students of comparative public administration, aware of the intellectual developments in comparative sociology, anthropology and other areas, became interested in developing theoretical constructs with a cross-cultural, cross-national and cross-temporal relevance in their field: 'They recognized that hypotheses developed in the American cultural context, in order to be valid [...] should be tested in cross-cultural settings' (Waldo 1968: 151).

The ultimate objective of the comparative public administration movement, as Caldwell observed, has been 'to hasten the emergence of a universally valid body of knowledge concerning administrative behavior – in brief to contribute to a genuine and generic discipline of public administration' (Caldwell 1968: 230). Comparative public administration thus delineates an area of concern and a methodological orientation that differs from the traditional approach of merely juxtaposing the description of a number of similar administrative institutions in different countries at one place. It offers to study the administrative processes and organizations for the purpose of answering common problems and questions. It attempts to identify the characteristics of various administrations in terms of certain established analytical categories, in the light of which identification of administrative phenomena becomes possible for as many administrative systems as possible. It further purports to not only examine similarities and differences in the norms, institutions and behavior of administrations, but also to account for them and aim toward the development of a body of knowledge so that policy recommendations can be made and trends predicted. It is in this sense that it becomes a matrix from which theories emerge. At the same time, it serves as a laboratory for their testing. As Dwight Waldo put it:

> To compare is to examine similarities and differences simultaneously; the effort is bent forward to two main ends: (i) to discover, define and differentiate the stuff (politics or administration) to be compared, wherever in the world it may be; and (ii) to develop criteria of differentiation that are useful in ordering and analyzing the 'stuff' once it has been identified. In this task, the contemporary stock of provoked or fashionable concepts in the social sciences, as well as those 'indigenous' to political science has been drawn upon extensively. The works of Max Weber and Talcott Parsons, structural-functionalism as conceived in various sources, the concept of culture, the decision-making scheme, communications theory and cybernetics, systems theory – all these and several more sources have been drawn upon by both movements. (Waldo 1963: 11–12)

TRENDS AND MODELS IN CPA

The Comparative Administration Group of the American Society for Public Administration (ASPA) did some pioneering work in strengthening the comparative public administration movement. A 1961 draft statement described comparative public administration as 'the theory of public administration applied to diverse cultures and national settings – and the body of factual data by which it can be examined and tested' (Heady and Stokes 1962: 4).

The study of comparative public administration gave rise to problems of methodological concern and conceptual focus. Scholars were greatly preoccupied with the construction of models and typologies of political regimes and institutions and the delineation of geographic-cultural areas – an activity prominent also in (and shared with) comparative politics. The range of concepts associated with the term 'bureaucracy' and its ideal type was extensively used. So-called 'action theory' and the concepts and language of structural functionalism were often involved, and the related and overlapping (but different and broader) concept of 'ecology' is also frequently set forth as important. Equilibrium theory, particularly the idea of a 'system' with 'inputs' and 'outputs', is prominent. Most of the popular concepts and phrases of contemporary behavioral science are being used, and reference is made to such matters as communications theory and multivariate analysis.

THE BUREAUCRATIC MODEL

The bureaucratic model has been enthusiastically adopted by students of comparative public administration in developed countries as a means of measuring the actual administrative institutions observed against an 'idea-type' model of rational administrative organization, that is, an organization perfectly developed to fulfill some set program objective. The model was first developed by Max Weber and has since been further developed, applied, criticized and altered. The model is so well known that it need not be elaborated here. Following Max Weber, political scientists have generally assumed that only an advanced society with a culture featuring legal-rational concepts of authority would be capable of sustaining administrative structures approximating the bureaucratic model.

Dwight Waldo found the bureaucratic model useful, stimulating and provocative, its advantage and appeal being that it 'is set in a large framework that spans history and cultures and relates bureaucracy to important societal variables, yet it focuses attention upon the chief structural and functional characteristics of bureaucracy' (Waldo 1963: 28–29). He rightly points out that not much empirical research has actually been done on the basis of the bureaucratic model.

However, US students of public administration – who had a tendency to resist the abandonment or serious modification of the bureaucratic model as they moved from the realm of advanced complex nations to that of the nations still undergoing modernization – have been beset with the malady afflicting comparative study in general: the tendency to put the structure first and to assume that the function performed by a given structure in one cultural-political context will carry over to a similar structure in another context. This accounts for the frustration of US specialists in public administration when they attempted to apply their expertise as technical advisors to the governments of Asian and African countries. Invariably, they found that the structure set up along the lines of classical principles failed to behave as expected, or even to display standard aberrations familiar in Western settings. Most perplexing was the difficulty of maintaining stable boundaries between administrative organizations and the political environment. On the one hand, achievement criteria were violated, often wholesale, as political considerations of personal loyalty, ideological parity or both became predominant as personnel policy. On the other hand, administrative agencies showed a tendency to step beyond the brands of their assigned functions and seek a role (sometimes in the absence of clear political initiative) in charting the direction and pace of modernization of their respective countries (Wood 1970: 616–17).

Among the scholars who contributed to the study of comparative bureaucratic systems are Monroe Berger, Alfred Diamant, Ferrel Heady, Robert Presthus and Michel Crozier. The emphasis in most writing on comparative bureaucracy appears to be on the interaction between the administrative subsystem and the political system in which it (the administrative subsystem) exists, although some attention has been paid to other dimensions of administrative ecology.

RIGGS' PRISMATIC *SALA* MODEL

The most prominent contemporary model-builder in the comparative administrative movement is Fred W. Riggs. As his thinking evolved, he developed not only a model but a series of overlapping and interrelated models. Riggs is well-known for his model of the 'prismatic society' (for an introduction to the prismatic *sala* model, see Riggs 1962 and 1964). In this model, Riggs changed the key terms from '*agraria-transitia-industria*' to 'fused society', 'prismatic society' and 'refracted society' (later redesignated as 'diffracted society'). Based on the structural-functional approach, it delineates societies according to different social structures.

The three ideal-typical categories of societies are thus constructed on the basis of the extent to which rules in various organizations are exclusive or overlapping. The fused society has almost no specialization of rules, whereas the refracted society is at a high level of structural differentiation. The prismatic society forms the intermediate category. In the prismatic society, a high degree of formalism – discrepancies between norms and realities – overlapping and heterogeneity exist. Riggs has argued, therefore, that in a prismatic environment, institutional or formal structural analysis is likely to produce a disappointing outcome, since what might normally be expected to result from a particular administrative system on organizational patterns, fails to appear because of the big gap between formally prescribed norms and effective action.

These models emphasize ecology and Riggs is primarily concerned with examining how public administrative functions are performed by different types of structures. His approach emphasizes an open system perspective that has had increasing influence elsewhere in the social sciences. However, his systems' models lack the dynamic qualities developed in many other open system models, for in them he has not analyzed the process of refraction from a developmental perspective. He also does not appear to have worked out fully the implications of his theory on public administration. This is not, however, to underestimate the value of his theory, which, as Chapman believes, 'deepens our insight into some of the underlying problems of administrative development in transitional societies' (Chapman 1966: 423). His prismatic theory may perhaps be especially valuable for understanding the pathology of public administration, and it may be useful for diagnosis in the same way that principles help in the diagnosis of certain administrative malfunctions. What is noteworthy in Riggs' provocative suggestions is that he is attempting to place the administrative subsystem into a larger system, and to show both its functional relationship thereto and its conceptual consequences. To the extent that Riggs and others sharing his assumptions have provided a framework for further undertaking in the field, the study of comparative public administration has moved further to date than have the other subfields of comparative political systems.

In a recent debate and dialogue on comparative public administration published in two consecutive volumes (2000:66 and 2001:67) of the *International Review of Administrative Sciences,* V. Subramaniam (2000, 2001) of Carleton University criticized

> Riggs' concept of prismatic society with its accompanying vocabulary as being of limited use for two reasons: (a) the manufacture of numerous new categories by Western social scientists leads more to confusion than understanding; and (b) that it is heavily influenced by researches in East and South East Asian countries, in particular the Philippines, Thailand and Korea. There is practically no significant input from other sources and areas, such as from Latin America. As a result, the prismatic model, which claims to regard all public administration study as universally comparative, was in practice focused on two or three South East Asian societies, whose confrontation with the West was significantly different from that of most Afro-Asian countries under direct colonial occupation. (Subramaniam 2001: 336–37)

Despite this criticism, Subramaniam believes that the field of CPA is still wide open for exploration from a political economy approach. He suggests we regard public administration as the major link between state and society so as to explore it comparatively at the three interfaces of recruitment, policy demand and implementation. This comes closest to the stand of political economy, which is most likely to rescue CPA from its self-imposed confinement.

Commenting on Subramaniam's statement on CPA, Evans and Shields suggest that his analysis is particularly helpful in charting the historical course and marking the achievements and theoretical blockages which it has encountered on its path. However, his suggestion that the insular approach should give way to a deeper consideration of other social, economic and political forces and how these impact upon the administrative apparatus of the state remains essentially institutional in focus. His proposed research agenda continues to be state-centered in that it is not explicitly directed at the impact of societal forces on public administration. CPA, more generically, is a conservative discipline (Evans and Shields 2001: 329–334).

Replying to Subramaniam's criticism of his prismatic theory, Fred Riggs maintains that

> Viewing public administration in a comparative and historical framework will help us understand and influence the economic forces which elevated nationalism and ethnic consciousness in the minds of millions around the world where, traditionally, marginalized communities had accepted their unhappy lot as fated and irresistible. Globalization now provides both incentives and resources to support demands for equality of opportunity and social justice. [...] Unfortunately we have been trapped by the redundancy of the term 'comparative public administration', as it evolved in America. Until we recognize that fact and change our way of talking about it, we will remain prisoners of our terminology.

Riggs also believes that

> The only way to develop a widely relevant discipline of public administration involves using data on different countries to generate and test theories and explanations [...] Naturally, most specialists will want to focus on administration in their own countries, but they will be able to do so more usefully to the degree that they are informed by general theories of public administration that are indeed comparative. In fact, any good theory of public administration must be comparative. The phrase 'comparative public administration' is actually an oxymoron. (Riggs 2001: 323–328)

Riggs concedes that the essay by Subramanian contains important and useful information, and although he agrees with many of its positions, yet he feels that it is rather superficial (ibid. 327).

THE DEVELOPMENTAL MODEL

Closely related to the study of comparative public administration is the study of developmental administration. Developmental administration, an indispensable tool in the attainment of the goals of the 'good' society, has attracted the mainstream of comparative administrators who were seeking ways and means to improve administrative performance and to strengthen the planning and execution of development programs in developing societies. The idea had its origins in the desire of some of the wealthier countries to aid poorer countries and, more especially, in the obvious needs of the newly emerging nation-states to transform their colonial bureaucracies into more responsible instruments of socioeconomic change.

Developmental administration thus encompasses the organization of new agencies such as planning organizations and development corporations; the reorientation of established agencies such as departments of agriculture; the delegation of administrative powers to development agencies; and the creation of a cadre of administrators that can provide leadership in stimulating and supporting programs of socioeconomic improvement. It has the purpose of making change as attractive as possible (Gant 1966: 200). Strictly speaking, it may not be referred to as the 'applied side' of comparative public administration as there is no sharp distinction in intent, concepts and involved personnel between the two. Those interested in developmental administration are interested in and draw on many sources other than comparative public administration; and some of them are trained in and also identify themselves with disciplines other than political science or public administration (Montgomery & Siffin 1967; and Riggs 1970).

'Comparative administration' and 'development administration' are often used interchangeably. Although 25 years ago such usage would have been merely appropriate, now a distinction between them is useful. Comparative administration has largely fallen by the wayside. It gives an image of political scientists interested in variants among legal and political systems and who also describe and explain cross-national differences among bureaucratic practices.

On the other hand, developmental administration has come to mean the study and practice of induced socioeconomic change in developing countries. The image is transformational, directive and cross-cultural. In the field of developmental administration, three shifts in perspective have occurred during the last two-and-a-half decades. Developmental administration has moved away from the concept of induced development to planned and administered development and now to sustainable development. In the process, while developmental administration remains an important subfield of comparative public administration research, as was the case during the 1950s and 60s, by contrast the normative nature of much of this research – the notion that the West should export its administrative systems to the third-world countries – has become almost redundant (Pierre 1995: 9).

CPA AND THE 'NEW PUBLIC MANAGEMENT' (NPM)

The emergence of the New Public Management (NPM) movement in the 1990s both reinforced the status of public administration as a conservative discipline and introduced, implicitly at any rate, a theoretical/ideological orientation to the understanding of public management. Where CPA attempted to become universal and failed, the NPM came close to being universal, though with very different outcomes in wealthy as opposed to impoverished states. The component elements of NPM were based upon the supremacy of market and contractual mechanisms, the transformation of citizens into customers, management's right to manage, continuous improvement and alternative service-delivery. While many of the protagonists of NPM consider these as simply innovative management techniques and principles, they are in fact value-laden. 'This is a system of governance which demands that the public service be shrunk to a small core and that regulation and social welfare regimes be dismantled and replaced by a state with significantly narrowed scope for management of social and economic life in favor of market regulation'. The global dissemination of NPM has been greatly facilitated by transnational organizations like the OECD, the World Bank and the International Monetary Fund, and by such international consulting corporations as KPMG and Andersen Consulting. The NPM is institutionalizing a new culture and machinery of administration, which looks remarkably alike from state to state. State/society relations are indeed being reconstructed. 'Thus CPA would be a natural location for the critical analysis of the NPM from a global and comparative perspective' and would enrich in a significant way the research agenda set out by Subramaniam in his essay discussed above (Evans & Shields 2001: 332–34).

THE DECLINE OF GRAND THEORIES

Riggs' theory of prismatic society epitomized the search within the academic community to build comprehensive theories which can explain the irrational, pre-scientific and introductive bureaucratic behavior that was prevalent in developing countries (Riggs 1964). Those who were interested in inducing change translated theorizing into an enclave mentality which focused on the introduction of new institutions into environments dominated by old social forms. The question was how to plant an enclave of modern practices into a traditional environment and ensure that it would survive. This search was conducted under the title of 'institution building' (see for example Eston 1972).

In the early 1960s, practitioners of developmental administration also followed an enclave approach. The establishment of local universities, institutes of public administration and administrative staff colleges followed this pattern, as did the focus on civil service structures, position classification and similar concerns of Central Government (Esman & Montgomery 1980). Administrative modernization was regarded as an export of Western administrative methods and practices into the newly emerging independent nations. The Marshall Plan provided the model.

The international situation was changing and by the mid-1960s new concerns were emerging. Major donor agencies, like the World Bank and USAID, adopted a project-by-project approach to development. With the realization and recognition of the importance of the agricultural sector, projects became area-based and were placed within semi-autonomous implementation units with a life span coterminous with the end of project funding. This introduced a focus on smaller-scale, more immediate issues surrounding the many obstacles to the implementation and management of projects.

SOME PROBLEMS IN THE APPLICATION OF MODELS

The foregoing brief review of some of the models constructed by American public administrationists for the study of public administration specialists on a comparative basis raises a number of questions about their application in understanding the administrative systems in the developing world.

Which particular model is most appropriate and for what purpose, and where should it be applied? The central problem in the study of comparative public administration is that it is large enough to embrace all the phenomena that should be embraced without being too unwieldy, in spite of its large dimensions. The second problem is that of relating the universal and the particular in one system. The idea of the universal runs through administrative study from the assertions of the 'founding fathers' to the most sophisticated of our contemporaries in the field. However, to make comparisons implies not only to identify universals but also to discover the criteria of differentiation.

Accordingly, the choice of models is intimately related to the choice of a research strategy and to the most effective employment of limited resources. None of the models listed previously may present a perfect analysis of contemporary administrative scenes in diverse cultural settings. But if carefully used, they do serve as a framework for analyzing different aspects of administrative phenomena in a comparative perspective. These models may be useful in revealing more clearly the social, economic and political basis on which administrative institutions depend. In public administration they are impressionistic and non-quantitative; it is only when we understand their limitations that we can use models intelligently and safely to help us achieve an understanding of administrative behavior.

INDIAN STUDIES IN COMPARATIVE PUBLIC ADMINISTRATION

The study of public administration through the comparative method opens up immense possibilities of fruitful and meaningful research. However, in contrast to the historical method, it has been utilized only on a very small scale by researchers in India. The reason is that the significance of comparative methods of research has not been fully understood by many students of public administration. Much of the work that has been published in the name of comparative studies is no more than a juxtaposition of the account of one institution in a particular country against the account of the same institution in another country. Most other works in the field give an account of a foreign institution or practice that concludes with a small comment comparing it with some similar institution in India, without adequately taking into consideration the range of variables and the cross-cultural patterns which make such analysis difficult, if not impossible.

A brief survey of the literature on comparative public administration, undertaken by the present author some time back, indicates a very limited use of the comparative method by Indian scholars to interpret public administration phenomena in a scientific and comprehensive manner. (For a detailed analysis see Jain 1971 and ICSSR 1975.) It seems that only the bureaucratic model has been used in the study of public administration in India. The three dimensions of comparative research – namely, the *vertical* comparison (between the national administrative system and regional or local administrative systems), the *horizontal* comparison (analysis of administrative processes over a period of time), and the study of administrative institutions and processes *across national boundaries* with a new orientation and approach – have yet to be explored fully by Indian scholars of comparative public administration (Jain 1978: 260).

It is fitting to mention here the findings of some of the research studies that have used the bureaucratic model to understand the dynamics of the Indian bureaucratic system. This is an example of how the Weberian model of bureaucracy can be fruitfully employed to interpret bureaucratic phenomena in a cross-national perspective.

A basic conclusion emerging from one of the pioneering studies in this direction, undertaken by V.A. Pai Panandikar and S.S. Kshirsagar (1978), is that the general constructs of bureaucratic theory as evolved by Weber and others provide a useful basis for both practical and broader theoretical and comparative purposes. To the extent that the study identifies the universality of structural characteristics of bureaucracy, it supports Heady's thesis that for comparative purposes bureaucratic structures present a meaningful starting point (Heady 1984).

However, the study reveals that structural and behavioral characteristics in the Indian bureaucracy are only moderately related, that the functional content of the bureaucracy, the type of office and its level of mass contact to meet programmatic needs, together with the level of its skill composition, have a significant bearing on the behavioral characteristics. This finding has theoretical as well as practical implications.

Theoretically, it implies that bureaucracy is not a static phenomenon with certain standard structural and behavioral characteristics in more or less comparable proportion. Bureaucracy is a far more dynamic phenomenon, in that its functional content and the mass contact inherent in its objective, and several other factors, influence its behavioral characteristics. What is more, the behavioral characteristics appear, in turn, to modify or alter the bureaucratic structure itself. The study revealed the limitations of the existing theory of bureaucracy for understanding the bureaucratic phenomenon in developing countries like India. The Weberian model, accordingly, serves at best as a starting point in the study of these civil service systems.

BEHAVIORAL ORIENTATION OF DEVELOPMENTAL BUREAUCRACY: A COMPARATIVE ANALYSIS

In the past four decades, many public administration scholars in India have attempted to study the behavioral aspects of development bureaucracy in different socioeconomic or urban/rural set-ups. While the dominant trend in the 1950s was to study the socioeconomic background of India's higher administrative and other functional services (Subramaniam 1971; Rao 1963; Trivedi & Rao 1968; Bhamhri 1965), the later years saw a number of studies on different aspects of the perceptions, orientations, attitudes and practices of the bureaucrats engaged in developmental activities.

Such studies used systematic sampling and survey techniques to learn about the social backgrounds of politicians and administrators, their perceptions of and attitude towards each other and perceptions of their role in policy-making and politics. Although these studies are valuable in themselves, 'these are essentially historical. They cannot explore effectively questions of where such attitudes and perceptions come from and how or why such political administrators have come to hold them' (Potter 1986: 11–12). While it is not possible for the present author to attempt a detailed survey of all such studies, it is appropriate to describe the methods and framework used by one of my former colleagues, Kuldeep Mathur, to identify the 'self-images' of developmental bureaucrats and to 'evaluate their perceptions of the outstanding behaviors and practices of their public administration system' (Mathur 1972).

In his comparative analysis of the perceptions of the same level of officers in the two adjoining Hindi-speaking states of North India, viz., Rajasthan and Uttar Pradesh, the author at the outset identified certain geographical, socioeconomic and political factors which present a different background for the officials of the two states. Keeping such differences in mind, the author used the factor-analysis technique in an attempt to develop the major dimensions of bureaucratic thinking and perceptions so as to establish an empirical pattern of the reactions of the bureaucrats to the changing environment. He further attempted to develop a typology of differences in the perceptions and reactions of the bureaucrats of both states *vis-à-vis* one another and to correlate such differences, if any, to differences in the socioeconomic and political background of the officials. For such an analysis, the author used the techniques of survey research and computer data-processing to develop the profiles of the bureaucrats and employed the discriminant analysis method to find out whether the orientations of the Block Development Officers (BDOs), who are at the base of the hierarchy in implementing development plans, differ in the two states along the perception dimensions.

His findings sustained the hypothesis that states may be different in bureaucratic orientation. Sufficient answers could not be given as to why the bureaucrats differed. However, for further investigation it may be very fruitful to develop the particular features of each state or cultural region to discover which ecological influences go in to mold the behavioral orientations of bureaucrats. For example, the characteristic of political interference in administration has come out in many studies on North Indian states. It may be useful to carry out such a type of analysis in other states of India, to establish the generality of the phenomenon.

The findings of many studies on the bureaucratic role in development that have been conducted by various scholars, in different settings and ecological frameworks, seem to have firmly established the theory that the band of officials brought up in the traditional administrative culture and wedded to the Weberian model of bureaucracy is totally unfit to perform the responsibilities of development administration. It has been argued again and again that development administrators have to be quite flexible in their approach, shed current formalism, be amiable in nature, outgoing and people-oriented, and that they should be willing to take risks and on-the-spot decisions without worrying about procedures and existing rules, regulations notwithstanding.

In the same vein, a study entitled *Bureaucratic Values in Development* by R.B. Jain & P.N. Chaudhuri (1984) made use of comparative and empirical research methodology. It does not attempt to rebut this theory, nor do its findings indicate that such an attitude on the part of the officials would not be conducive to attaining developmental goals. The study does point out certain limitations to a blanket acceptance of the above premises, and in the process seeks to answer some questions that have certain theoretical implications.

The Jain & Chaudhuri comparative study clearly demonstrates that the values imparted by the colonial bureaucratic system, so far as its structural organization is concerned, do not necessarily stand in the way of the developmental process. The agricultural and industrial progress that has taken place in the state of Punjab since independence was attained through a hierarchical organization with a system of rules, prescribed individual responsibilities and the observation of impersonality on the part of the officials. These are not always impediments to development. Indeed, they provide a framework for the operation of the officials, without which the accomplishment of developmental goals would be difficult if not altogether impossible. However, the same characteristics tend to become dysfunctional when greater emphasis is placed on their observance than on making use of them as a tool toward the accomplishment of the tasks. The very fact that the state of Punjab in India has moved into a position of rapid development and that, with all the structural characteristics of bureaucracy, the government in the state of Madhya Pradesh has embarked on a program of development, shows that the bureaucratic system *per se* is not inimical to development.

It can also be inferred from the findings of this study that pre-independence bureaucratic traditions train officials to respect their political masters. To observe a system of rules and to maintain a high standard of integrity is not necessarily a stumbling block in the way of development. These qualities are as necessary, in the public services of a democratic developmental framework, as they are supposed to have been the traits of bureaucracy in India in pre-independence days. For one thing, adhering to the rules gives officials the chance to defend themselves against unwarranted criticisms or attacks; for another, it enables them to maintain impartiality in the face of enormous political and other pressures and to apply a modicum of egalitarian treatment in making the fruits of development available to people.

At the same time, the study does not suggest that the attributes of capability and honesty are irrelevant to development. In fact, the findings show a gap between the officials' own perception of their capabilities and the perceptions by citizens of their capabilities for development. Thus it appears that the most desirable attribute of a development administrator would be an inherent capacity to perform his development tasks. Here the study certainly reveals the weakness of officials' capacity to face developmental challenges.

TEACHING CPA IN INDIA

A recent survey of the offering of public administration courses undertaken by a Study Team of the Curriculum Development Center in Political Science of the University Grants Commission, New Delhi, noted that the relatively marginal status of the discipline of public administration in a wide range of universities is puzzling (University Grants Commission 1990: 174), given its pronounced period of growth in the country. In fact, so coextensive has been its scope that it has been organized within departments totally dissociated from departments of political science. The most beneficial aspect of such autonomy – greater disciplinary rigor, if it indeed materialized – does not seem to have appreciably, or perhaps even marginally, helped in enlarging the range of public administration core and optional courses, quite apart from enhancing the disciplinary quality or originality of existing courses in departments of political science. It would appear that the more adherent aspects of autonomous development are more prominent. Political science departments seem to have left public administration to 'autonomous development' and seem only too relieved to gain the necessary academic space for intensive study of other areas and concerns. This may not be justified in many cases, and it would be of the essence of any curriculum development program to bring the study of public administration back into the mainstream of a study of politics within political science departments (ibid.: 175–76).

The same survey noted that teaching in Indian universities on comparative public administration is mostly done through a few optional courses at the graduate level (M.A. in Political Science of Public Administration), under the titles of (a) Comparative Administrative Systems in Developing Countries, (b) Comparative Administrative Systems in Socialist Countries, (c) Administrative Systems in Western Democracies, as well as (a) Comparative Public Policy and (b) Theories of Bureaucracy at the M. Phil. level. In the case of Comparative Administrative Systems in Developing Countries, the courses evaluate critically the viability of the various models for comparative analysis of administrative systems, and help appraise the concept of development administration with a view to theorizing on administrative practices and institution-making in developing countries. In the case of Comparative Administrative Systems in Socialist Countries, the courses attempt an appraisal of Marxist-Leninist ideas of social management and their situational variations when these are implemented in different community systems of Asia and Africa. In the comparative study of Administrative Systems in Western Democracies, the courses endeavor to examine the issue involved in the theory and practice of administrative institutions/structures in some western democracies such as the USA, UK and France. The University of Delhi has introduced comparative public administration courses, including the study of the US, UK, Canadian, French and German administrative systems. In the M. Phil. program of Comparative Public Policy and Theories of Bureaucracy, core emphasis is placed on theories of public policy and bureaucracy in the light of practical experiences of some developed and developing countries, particularly India.

The two surveys on Research in Public Administration commissioned by the Indian Council of Social Science Research, the first covering the period until 1969 and the second covering the period 1970–79, have both lamented the lack of buoyancy or achievements either in the academic or practical worlds of public administration's continuing relevance to the needs of the country. Reporting on the progress of research in the second survey (1970–79), Kuldeep Mathur pointed out distortions in the discipline created by an inordinate research emphasis on the 'institutional view of public administration'. In his view, the researchers in India were failing 'to offer conceptual frameworks relevant to the Indian situation'. Acceptance of the 'instrumentality paradigm', so he argued, led to an overemphasis on techniques and skills and blurring of distinction between public and private administration. He observed that the general trend in public administration research was to accept bureaucracy as an impersonal apparatus, and to ignore the sociopolitical context within which public administration is situated. Calling for a shift in emphasis with a view to developing public administration as a social science discipline, Mathur recommended adoption of policy analysis orientation in public administration research under which public administration would be viewed 'as the implementation strategy of Public Policy' (Mathur, 1986). Mathur's general remarks are also applicable to the teaching of and research in CPA in India. Now is the time to accept the inadequacy of bureaucracy, which has been thus far the main focus of concern in many studies in comparative public administration in India, and to switch to a policy-analysis perspective on public administration. This would see public administration from a problem-solving perspective and establish a relationship between policy design and implementation strategies in a comparative framework, including an analysis of the various socioeconomic and political processes that influence its courses. It might help to understand why one policy rather than another one gets implemented in different societies and even within the same society. It would also make the public administration discipline more 'socially relevant', situating it within the socioeconomic and political context that shapes it and gives meaning to it.

PROBLEMS IN CPA RESEARCH: THE INDIAN CONTEXT

Evidently, the study of comparative public administration is fraught with many difficulties. The basic problem is one of competence in comparative research methodology. But that is not the only problem. Even if it is assumed that a researcher knows the techniques of comparative methods of study, there is always the difficulty of 'models-building', that is, the need to choose between various concepts and models of comparative research, or to develop a theory or hypothesis around which a generalization applicable to many administrative systems can be built and tested.

Aberbach and Rockman have explored three theoretical and methodological problems in the comparative study of public administration: (a) the relation of parts of the administrative system (usually the focus of enquiry) to the administrative system as a whole (usually the object of theoretical inference); (b) the connection between universals of organization theory and variables in the environment of organizations and administrative systems; and (c) the link between distinctive levels of analytic focus – structure (organizations), actors (officials) and actions (behavior), which are formidable. These broad theoretical and methodological problems anchor a more specific analysis of: (a) links between bureaucracies, bureaucrats and politics; (b) the ideas of centralization, planning and coordination; and (c) the notions of bargaining, mediation and subgovernments leading to conceptual ambiguities. Such problems make it tempting to abandon the comparative study of administration. Admittedly, the comparative analysis of administrative systems is an inherently difficult undertaking, but at the same time it stimulates clarity and understanding. Not only do we understand our own system better when we compare, we gain a better understanding of the methods, concepts and theories we employ (Aberbach and Rockman 1987: 473–506). The muddle of comparative administrative study may well be a hell, but not one whose suggested motto is 'abandon hope all ye who enter here' (ibid. 503).

An Indian scholar, in particular, faces difficulties due to the unavailability of data and material, particularly across national frontiers. The prohibitive cost and time involved may deter a researcher from venturing in this direction. Further difficulties arise from the nature of the data which some governments may consider confidential and which, therefore, may not be easily available to a researcher. Other difficulties arise from the range and nature of the variables that must be used in the study of comparative administration. Some variables simply cannot be measured precisely. A researcher may use certain general or cross-national variables (e.g., psychological or socioeconomic variables), but the unique character of each administrative policy and organization must in some form be measured if comparisons are realistically to account for the presence of a particular type of administrative phenomenon. Difficulties also arise from the interplays and interrelationships among the norms, structures and behavior of the administrative systems. Models and theories must take into account all these factors. Furthermore, any meaningful comparative research must attempt the study of societies as wholes if they are to be subjected to comparative analysis. Obviously, this requires an interdisciplinary approach to the study of administrative phenomena. In India, the study of public administration through an interdisciplinary approach has yet to begin on a serious footing. Models are difficult to build, and researchers have found the comparative method of research more difficult than the empirical or behavioral techniques that have to some extent been perfected.

EMERGING FRONTIERS OF CPA RESEARCH IN INDIA

The list of difficulties just presented does not mean that comparative research in India is impossible, or that there are no avenues open to research on a comparative basis. Indeed, the national frontiers of India enclose a veritable paradise for research in comparative administration.

In the first place, there is ample scope for comparative research in various administrations of the states and the union territories in India. The socioeconomic and cultural factors, which have both similar and dissimilar features in various regions of the country, present a challenge to a researcher eager to make a scientific inquiry into administrative institutions, program administration and policy implementation on a regional basis. An inquiry into the causes of the dynamism with which the same institutions work in a particular union territory or state, and the slow pace at which they work in other regions, would be a worthwhile area for study as a means of improving administrative organizations in various regions. More often the states or union territories are included in the survey, creating possibilities of 'administrative theory-building through empirically tested generalizations about Indian administration'. Such research, if undertaken by Indian scholars, would also obviate the subjective element that is likely to creep into research that has been exposed to the scholars' own political culture, for example, of the Western type. With some imaginative and concentrated efforts on the part of professional institutions and universities, a unified program to study various administrative phenomena on cross-regional bases could perhaps be drawn up. This would help build up a substantial amount of literature on the basis of which future researchers might develop improved research models for comparative study.

Secondly, there is considerable scope for researchers using a comparative approach with respect to policy and program administration in public and private settings. This will be especially fruitful in comparing the performances of public and private enterprises, particularly with reference to the same industry. The development of the public sector on an unprecedented scale has confronted the government with the problem of running those enterprises so that they would generate sufficient dividends necessary to establish a socialist welfare state. Horizontal studies of nationalized industries over a period of time would be logical and meaningful. For instance, it would be interesting to compare the performance of the banking industry before nationalization and after nationalization over a period of time, along with a comparison of, say, consumer satisfaction with banks in the private and public sectors.

Thirdly, vertical comparisons of various aspects of functional administration among the national, regional and local governments open an extensive field for researchers. It is generally admitted that administration at regional and local levels is weak when compared with that at the national level. This may perhaps be a universal phenomenon. In the Indian context, however, it would be beneficial to undertake such exercises with a view toward locating the factors that hamper the growth of sound administrative practices in many areas. The combination of comparative methods and empirical analysis will, it may be hoped, open up many bottlenecks of administrative processes.

Fourthly, given the recent changes in organizational environments all over the world due to the forces of globalization and the consequent pressures on administrative systems, there has lately been a powerful drive toward (a) increasing the efficiency of public administration coupled with the challenges from market-based actors and, sometimes, also (b) enabling private actors to deliver public services. Coupled with that process there has been a global shift toward opening up public administration to civil society at large. Also, the 1980s and 90s have seen strong political efforts to reaffirm the position of the citizen in relationship with public administration in a number of countries. For example, there was the Citizens' Charter in Britain and India, the Charter of Rights and Freedoms in Canada, a new chapter in the Constitution of Human Rights, the new Public Administration Act in Sweden and increasing cooperation between public administration and the private sector which gives credence to 'shared governance' in the process of public service delivery. All these developments have made the boundary between the political system and civil society (where public administration relates intimately to both spheres) highly dynamic and flexible. It would be interesting to know what processes of organizational adaptation have taken place in different countries, and how these experiences could be successfully replicated in the Indian situation. Thus CPA opens up a number of new vistas of study, research and analysis in the Indian context.

Finally, comparative studies on a cross-national basis provide vast possibilities for meaningful scientific research toward the identification of a universal administrative plane. Admittedly, such studies would have to be undertaken with considerable planning and insight, and with an adequate knowledge of the unlimited range of variables that are involved in the interplay of administrative processes across national frontiers. However, the difficulties are not altogether insurmountable. To begin with, cross-cultural studies can be undertaken on a regional basis (e.g., with respect to administrative phenomena in South Asian countries) with a little systematic effort. For instance, a common theme for a comparative analysis could be the impact of public administration on the developmental process with reference to South Asian countries, or with reference to Latin American countries or East African countries. Another theme for comparative and historical exposition could be the impact of the British Administration on the development of public administration in various former colonies. Yet another comparative study could be the analysis of the planning, policy-making and decision-making processes in various countries.

ANTICORRUPTION STRATEGIES AND 'GOOD GOVERNANCE': NEW CHALLENGES FOR STUDY IN CPA

Two terms that are very often used these days are *governance* and *corruption*. Not only do these terms remain largely undefined, but even the relationship between the two is either not properly understood or not well defined. While corruption is commonly defined as the abuse of public office for private gain, governance is a broader concept which can be defined as the exercise of authority through formal and informal processes and institutions for the common good. Governance encompasses the process of selecting, monitoring and replacing governments. It includes the capacity to formulate and implement sound policies and it assumes respect for citizens. From this framework, governance can be construed as consisting of six different elements. These are: (a) voice and accountability, which includes civil liberties and freedom of the press; (b) political stability; (c) government effectiveness, which includes the quality of policy-making and public service delivery; (d) quality of regulations; (e) rule of law, which includes protection of property rights and an independent judiciary; and (f) control of corruption. Thus, controlling corruption emerges as just one of the closely intertwined elements of governance. Combating corruption leads to improved governance. The key question therefore is: which strategies are needed to lower corruption and strengthen governance (Kaufman 2001:1–3)?

Improving governance requires a system of checks and balances in a society that restrains arbitrary action and harassment by politicians or bureaucrats, promotes participation by the population, reduces incentives for the corporate elite to engage in state captures and fosters the rule of law. A meritocratic and service-oriented public administration is a salient feature of such a strategy. However, synthesizing the strategy of key reforms for improving governance and combating corruption is a particularly daunting challenge, as is the task of detailing and adapting a strategy to each country-specific reality. Good governance is more than fighting corruption. Improving governance should be seen as a process that integrates three vital components: (a) knowledge, with rigorous data and empirical analysis, including in-country diagnostics and dissemination, utilizing the latest information technology tools; (b) leadership in the political and civil society and in the international arena; and (c) collective action via systematic participatory and consensus-building approaches with key stakeholders in society (here the technology revolution is also of help). No two countries arrive at the same strategy, but to maximize the prospects of success, any country that is serious about improving governance must involve all key stakeholders, guarantee a flow of information to them and lock in the commitment of the leadership (ibid.: 6).

It is evident from the above that combating corruption for sustainable development calls for the reduction of opportunities and incentives for corrupt behavior, thus increasing the sense of accountability on the part of public officials, and the effective implementation of anticorruption strategies. This would imply that measures should be logically consistent with regard to the phasing of a timetable for speedy investigation and conviction; a strong political commitment to implement the strategies and enforce anticorruption measures; and people's active participation from below in enforcement of administrative, legal and judicial measures, thus mobilizing the public against corruption in public life.

Apart from the above-mentioned fundamental conditions, it must be emphasized that fighting corruption requires (a) a national coordinating body responsible for devising and following up a strategy against corruption, along with a citizen board to oversee progress against corruption; (b) a high-powered independent prosecuting body to investigate and prosecute all known cases of corruption; (c) special courts for trying such cases at a stretch, so that the cases come to their legitimate conclusion without delay; (d) thorough overhauling and reform of the system of electoral laws and economic regulations to minimize the temptation to indulge in corrupt practices; (e) enactment of appropriate legislation to limit the number of ministries and departments both at the central and state levels, so that the temptation of expanding ministries for political gains could be minimized; and (f) providing specialized technical assistance to anticorruption agencies, organizing high-level anticorruption workshops or strategic consulting and hiring international investigators to track down ill-gotten deposits overseas.

Corruption-free governance calls for devising new strategies and innovations in politico-administrative reforms to meet the challenges posed by it. The numerous new reform measures in terms of enactment include the Prohibition of Unnamed (Benami) Transactions Act, a law providing for confiscation of illegally acquired assets of public servants, enactment of a Public Interest Disclosures Act and a Freedom of Information Act. Enacting the Ombudsman Act and strengthening the criminal justice system are also important strategies for reducing the incidence of corruption in public life. These have been tried in many countries, especially in the developing world. The question of which packages of reform measures that have been adopted in different countries would be most appropriate in a particular context reinforces the need for extensive and rigorous comparative research across nations to meet the challenges of corruption-free governance.

At the same time, it is also important that international institutions should take steps to encourage participatory approaches in developing countries to build a consensus for anticorruption drives and associated reforms. Civil society is likely to be a major ally in resisting corruption. More and more, it is this ally that seeks concrete support from more developed Western countries and international agencies (Kaufman 1997: 130). International cooperation can help national leaders develop political resolve, while international action can convey the useful truth that we are all touched by the problem of corruption and must find solutions together.

These are some of the emerging paradigms of corruption-free governance on which the strategies for a corruption-free sustainable development can be built and operationalized. They pose the formidable challenge to scholars of CPA to build appropriate strategies which may be of universal replication in most countries. It is heartening that people in almost all countries have recognized their importance, and it is likely that the growing concern about fighting corruption and devising innovations for 'good governance' may turn out to be a concerted international movement, one not confined to the realm of academics but one that takes constructive action for positive results while transcending national jurisdictions. This is the only hope to achieve universally good corruption-free governance and, ultimately, the very survival of humanity toward which we must all strive. (For a detailed analysis of these issues, see Jain 2004: ch. 1.)

RESEARCH AGENDA IN CPA IN THE INDIAN CONTEXT

From the above discussion, it is evident that public administration in India provides a veritable and extensive scope for research in CPA. Comparisons can be made between various aspects of administrative processes in India and in developed countries such as the USA, the UK, France and the Scandinavian countries, with a view to testing the validity of administrative generalizations evolved through regional comparisons and for the purposes of determining the overall performance of an administrative system in terms of goal achievement. Similar comparisons could also be established among the nations of the developing world. For instance, a common framework in this context can be an analysis of the administration of social services and welfare activities, the relationship between administration and civil society or total policy analysis with respect to as many systems as possible.

Some other suggested topics include (a) the impact of social structure on the evolution of bureaucracy and its procedures; (b) natural calamities/disasters and the administration's response; (c) technological developments and public administration; (d) public administration and political development; (e) social and economic systems and administration (ecology); (f) imperial traditions and their impact on administration; (g) political agitation and administrative response; (h) administrative load and popular demand; (i) international bureaucracies and world organizations such as the IMF, World Bank, OECD; (j) methods and strategies of organizational change and development; (k) bureaucratization and debureaucratization: experiences in downsizing public services; (l) comparative study of public enterprise reforms and privatization; (m) comparative national planning; (n) comparative economic policy and regulation; (o) comparative foreign policy administration; and (p) comparative policy analysis.

Such a research agenda for CPA in the Indian context can result in meaningful conclusions for practical adoption by policy-makers and practitioners of public administration. In addition, a number of reform measures which have been discerned through a recent survey in commonwealth countries can form the framework for comparative analysis with a view to finding out the most appropriate course for adoption in India. These reform areas are financial management and budgetary reforms, human resources management reforms, organization structure reforms, service-delivery reforms, performance management and accountability, increased focus on ethics and values, and increased use of information and communication technology (ICT) which should focus on the development of strategic frameworks within which reforms could be managed (Draper 2003:1–10).

Comparative studies lead to cross-national learning. In one of his recent essays, Bjorkman emphasizes that 'there is much to be learned from the experiences of different countries about the balance of advantages and disadvantages in trying to introduce carefully crafted new models, with every detail fully worked out, as against designing framework institutions that evolve over time'. A cautious approach to the import of foreign models might even suggest it is preferable to wait until several countries have tried out a particular policy or program model in order to test its robustness and its sensitivity to different institutional environments (Bjorkman 2004: 398–99).

However, all these suggestions are based on the assumption that research will be undertaken within a common framework to point out similarities and dissimilarities and to account for them, or at least to test the validity of certain generalizations through empirical studies of as many systems as possible. Only then can comparative studies be scientific and meaningful.

CONCLUSION: THE FUTURE OF COMPARATIVE PUBLIC ADMINISTRATION?

Since the end of World War II, trends in comparative public administration have been continually analyzed and illustrated. Therefore, we cannot really conclude the survey of public administration, and less so of CPA. In the contemporary developments of the discipline, nothing has really been concluded. There is still vagueness as to the claim of public administration to be a self-contained academic discipline. Interest in CPA continues, although sporadically. In the mid-1970s, the November/December 1976 issue of the *Public Administration Review* featured a series of articles about the field of CPA,

> ...which sounded like impressive eulogies at best, and at worst, sounded like the pre-sentence comments from a hanging judge [...] The major criticism was that the field was too involved in the quest for a comprehensive paradigm or meta-theory, not empirical enough, and that it was too self-absorbed in academic concerns to be sufficiently relevant. (Wart & Cayer 1990: 238)

A content analysis of research in CPA undertaken by Wart & Cayer a few years ago found that CPA research

> ...is indeed substantial, characteristics of which include a significant practitioner component, a substantial orientation toward policy recommendations, a

> relative paucity of theory-testing studies, wide and mature coverage of a range of topics, and methodological practices that seem slightly better than in the past but still far from ideal. However, the field as a whole lacks features that give it a clear identity (e.g. state-of-the-art-critiques, methodological pieces, and broader middle-range theorizing). Thus the overall status of comparative public administration remains ambiguous. (ibid.: 238)

Despite these shortcomings in the evolution of CPA as an independent 'self-conscious identity as a field of inquiry', at this point we can only say that the study of comparative public administration in spite of its many vagaries has reached at least a new consensus upon concepts, methods and analytical approaches capable of yielding a broad and precise science of administrative institutions:

> New criticism of the ongoing work of the field, no matter whether it is seen as well-placed methodological criticism or excessive purism, is likely to have a beneficial effect in kindling new interest and in challenging the lassitude that has typified comparative administration in the 1990s. (ibid.: 246)

It is possible that we will be able to develop better research strategies for comparative public administration once we have been able to gather enough empirical data about administrative behavior in as many systems as possible, particularly in the developing world, which has very few empirical data to offer for any meaningful comparative study leading to theory construction.

The need of the time is, therefore, not to strive for restoration of autonomy to the discipline of comparative public administration but to incorporate a comparative perspective into traditional, national study and research in public administration. By looking at the problems from a comparative perspective, public administration will widen its horizon of interest and will be in a much better position to offer relevant and practical solutions to the problems which humanity is facing. The Caidens have foreseen that, since

> Public administration of the early twenty-first century will look different, behave differently and perform differently from that of the mid-twentieth century, the need and potential for future comparative analyses of public administration thus appears to be tremendous. (Caiden & Caiden 1990: 384)

In this sense, comparative public administration is much more relevant today than many scholars think. With respect to the oft-repeated question whether CPA has a future, one cannot agree more with what Caiden & Caiden maintained already in 1990: 'One thing certain about the future of comparative public administration is that it has one' (ibid.). As has been demonstrated above, public administration in India would be greatly enriched in its theoretical, methodological and substantive indigenous paradigms if, notwithstanding the inherent difficulties, research in India were increasingly oriented towards CPA.

REFERENCES

Aberbach, J.D., & Rockman, B.A. (1987). 'Comparative Administration: Methods, Muddles and Models'. *Administration & Society* 18 (4).

Batley, R., & Larbi, G. (2004). *The Changing Role of Government: The Reform of Public Service in Developing Countries*. Houndmills: Palgrave Macmillan.

Bhambhri, C.P. (1965). 'The Administrative Elite and Political Modernization in India'. *Indian Journal of Public Administration* (11) 1.

Bjorkman, J.W. (2004). 'Comparative Policy Analysis: Learning from Others'. In P.L.S. Reddy, J. Singh & R.K. Tiwari (Eds), *Democracy, Governance and Globalization: Essays in Honor of Paul H. Appleby*. New Delhi: Indian Institute of Public Administration.

Caiden, G.E., & Caiden, N. (1990). 'Towards the Future of Comparative Public Administration'. In O.P. Dwivedi & K.M. Henderson (Eds), *Public Administration in World Perspective* (pp. 363–399). Ames: Iowa State University Press.

Caldwell, L. (1968). 'Conjectures on Comparative Public Administration'. In R. Martin (Ed), *Public Administration and Democracy: Essays in Honor of Paul H. Appleby*. Syracuse, NY; Syracuse University Press.

Chapman, R.A. (1966). 'Prismatic Theory in Public Administration: A Review of the Theories of Fred W. Riggs'. *Public Administration* 423.

Dahl, R.A. (1947). 'The Science of Public Administration: Three Problems'. *Public Administration Review* 7.

Draper, G.M. (2003). 'Public Service Reform: Strategies and Challenges'. In *Commonwealth Secretariat: Commonwealth Public Administration Reform 2004*. London: Commonwealth Secretariat.

Dunn, W.N., & Fozouni, B. (1976). *Toward a Critical Administrative Theory*. Beverly Hills, CA: SAGE.

Esman, M.J., & Montgomery, J.D. (1980). 'The Administration of Development'. In P.T. Knight (Ed), *Implementing Programs of Human Development*. Washington, DC: World Bank Staff Working Paper No. 403.

Eston, J.W. (Ed) (1972). *Institution Building and Development*. London, SAGE.

Evans, B.M, & Shields, J. (2001). 'The Poverty of Comparative Public Administration in a Neo-Liberal Era: A Commentary on Subramaniam'. *International Review of Administrative Sciences* 67, pp. 329–334.

Gant, G.F. (1966). 'A Note on Applications of Development Administration'. *Public Policy* 15, p.200 ff.

Heady, F. (1984). *Public Administration: A Comparative Perspective* (3rd ed). New York: Marcel Dekker.

Heady, F., & Stokes, S.L. (1962) (Eds). *Papers in Comparative Public Administration.* Ann Arbor, MI: Institute of Public Administration.

Indian Council of Social Science Research (1975). *A Survey of Research in Public Administration* (pp. 509–520) (vol. 2). Bombay: Allied Publishers.

Jain, R.B. (1971). 'Research Methods in Public Administration: A Critical Study of Important Works in Historical and Comparative Methodology'. *Indian Journal of Public Administration* 17 (4).

Jain, R.B. (1978). 'Comparative Aspects of Public Administration'. In R.W. Winks (Ed), *Other Voices, Other Views* (pp. 260ff.). Westport, CT: Greenwood Press.

Jain, R.B. (Ed) (2004). *Corruption-free Sustainable Development: Challenges and Strategies for Good Governance.* New Delhi: Mittal Publications.

Jain, R.B., & Chaudhuri, P.N. (1984). *Bureaucratic Values in Development.* New Delhi: Centre for Policy Research & Uppal Publishing House.

Kaufman, D. (1997). 'Corruption: The Facts'. *Foreign Policy.*

Kaufman, D. (2001). 'New Empirical Frontiers in Fighting Corruption and Improving Governance – Selected Issues'. Paper presented at the OSCE Economic Forum in Brussels.

Mathur, K. (1972). *Bureaucratic Response to Development.* Delhi: National Publishing House.

Mathur, K. (1986). 'Whither Public Administration?' In K. Mathur (Ed), *A Survey of Research in Public Administration.* New Delhi: Concept Publishing House.

Montgomery, J.D., & Siffin, W.J. (1967) (Eds). *Approaches to Development Politics, Administration and Change.* New York: McGraw Hill.

Panandikar, V.A.P., & Kshirsagar, S.S. (1978). *Bureaucracy and Development Administration.* New Delhi: Centre for Policy Research.

Pierre, J. (1995). 'Comparative Public Administration: The State of the Art'. In J. Pierre (Ed), *Bureaucracy in the Modern State: An Introduction to Comparative Public Administration.* Cornwall: Hartnolls.

Potter, D.C. (1986). *India's Political Administrators 1919–1983.* Oxford: Clarendon Press.

Rao, D.N. (1963). 'Disparities of Representation among the District Recruits in the IAS'. *Indian Journal of Public Administration* 9 (1).

Riggs, F.W. (1962). 'The "Sala" Model: An Ecological Approach to the Study of Comparative Public Administration'. *Philippine Journal of Public Administration* 6, pp. 3–16.

Riggs, F.W. (1964). *Administration in Developing Countries: The Theory of Prismatic Society.* Boston: Houghton Mifflin.

Riggs, F.W. (1970) (Ed). *Frontiers of Development Administration.* Durham,

NC: Duke University Press.

Riggs, F.W. (2001). 'Comments on V. Subramaniam: Comparative Public Administration'. *International Review of Administrative Sciences* 67, pp. 323–328.

Subramaniam, V. (1971). *Social Background of India's Administrators*. New Delhi: Ministry of Information and Broadcasting.

Subramaniam, V. (2000). 'Comparative Public Administration: From Failed Universal Theory to Raw Empiricism'. *International Review of Administrative Sciences* 66 (4).

Subramaniam, V. (2001). 'Comparative Public Administration'. *International Review of Administrative Sciences* 67 (2), pp. 336–337.

Trivedi, R.N., & Rao, D.N. (1968). 'Regular Recruit to the IAS: A Study'. *Journal of the National Academy of Administration* 5, pp. 50–80.

University Grants Commission (1990). Report of the Curriculum Development Center in Political Science. New Delhi: University Grants Commission (mimeo).

Waldo, D. (1963). 'Comparative Public Administration: Prologue, Performance, Problems and Promise' (pp. 11–12, mimeo). Symposium on Business Policy, 8–11 April. Graduate School of Business Administration, Harvard University.

Waldo, D. (1968). 'Public Administration'. In D.I. Sills (Ed), *International Encyclopedia of Social Sciences* 13. New York: Macmillan and the Free Press.

Wart, M., & Cayer, N.J. (1990). 'Comparative Public Administration: Defunct, Dispersed, or Redefined?' *Public Administration Review* 50 (2).

Wollmann, H. (2004). 'Local Government Reforms in Great Britain, Sweden, Germany and France: Between Multi-Functional and Single-Purpose Organizations'. *Local Government Studies* 30 (4), pp. 639–665.

Wood, D.M. (1970). 'Comparative Government and Politics'. In S.L. Wasby, *Political Science: The Discipline and its Dimensions: An Introduction*. Calcutta: Scientific Book Agency.

5

Public Administration Reform in Bangladesh: Incremental Changes, Reform Resistance and Lack of Political Will

MOHAMMAD MOHABBAT KHAN

INTRODUCTION

Even after three decades of independence, Bangladesh retains the characteristics of an administrative state. The assassination of elected political leaders, successive military governments, mass upsurge and holding national parliamentary elections under a 'non-party' caretaker government all exemplify political instability, the prominence of the military in affairs of state and failure to institutionalize a truly democratic governance system in the country. In the midst of all these trials and tribulations one institution, the civil service, though affected, still continues to function with minor changes as in the days of the British Raj and later Pakistani rulers. This chapter analyzes the reasons for the present state of affairs in the civil service from three interrelated perspectives. These are: the historical development of the civil service and the related failure of major administrative reforms, the impact of corruption on governance and public administration, and the impact of globalization and persistent governance crisis.

THE HISTORICAL DEVELOPMENT OF THE CIVIL SERVICE AND THE FAILURE OF MAJOR CIVIL SERVICE REFORMS

British Period

The present civil service is the remnant of a system introduced by the British throughout the Indian subcontinent. The genesis of a permanent civil service can be seen in the recommendations of the Macaulay Committee in 1854 (Das 1998: 117). After 1855, recruitment in the ICS was based exclusively on merit. This is significant, as the ICS has been described in such eloquent terms as the 'most distinguished civil service in the world' and the 'steel frame' of administration. Although there were other services both at the central and provincial levels in British India, the administration revolved around the ICS.

Now it is pertinent to enquire how and why the ICS became such a dominant civil service. The ICS was created to sustain and further the colonial interests in India. To rule as vast a country as India, the British crown needed a competent yet compact civil service whose performance could be observed, monitored, corrected and relied upon.

Besides the merit system, the ICS had other notable features. Promotions were based on seniority and given on a regular basis. The pay and other benefits of ICS officers were fabulous. As has been shown by Potter (1996), top ICS posts in 1935 carried much higher monthly salaries than those of the Governor of the State of New York, cabinet ministers in the UK and even the Chief Justice of the Supreme Court of the USA. Corruption was nonexistent and the ICS established a great reputation for being a most efficient and incorruptible organ of government (Sinha 1991: 98). In size, the ICS was small. Even at its peak, its number barely exceeded 1,000 and accounted for only .001% of the entire government personnel in British India (Das 1998: 122). By contrast, the number of government personnel in 1931 was one million, for an Indian population of 353 million (Potter 1996: 21). Entry into the service was only at the lowest level with no provision for lateral entry.

ICS officers occupied all key and controlling positions in the field, in the provincial secretariat as well as in the center. This reservation policy was crucial for maintaining the imperial interests and overall British strategy in India (Das 1998: 122; Khan 1980: 71). The majority of ICS officers worked in the district, because the district was the basic unit of administration in the then India. As the head of district administration, an ICS officer performed a number of functions in such areas as revenue, law and order, magistracy, general administration and local affairs. Some ICS officers worked as secretaries to the provincial governments and headed important field departments (Punjabi 1965). Still fewer ICS officers worked in the central government secretariat handling questions of policy.

Over the years, as a result of innovations and reforms, the ICS earned the respect of the population-at-large for a number of reasons. Firstly, the competitive and merit-based recruitment led to the induction of the best brains into the ICS. Secondly, the unquestioned probity of ICS officers as demonstrated in their work ensured the impartial nature of all decisions which affected the citizens. Thirdly, a clear-cut chain of command, based on a rigorous system of reporting, linked the junior-most ICS officer working in the field to the collectors, commissioners, secretaries, viceroy and government of India and, finally, to the parliament in the UK (Dewey 1996). This hierarchical and highly centralized system enabled ICS officers in the district to maintain constant supervision over a thousand or more subordinate officials and employees. The supervision was such as to ensure that the state apparatus performed its functions effectively (Potter 1996). Fourthly, a complex and explicit set of rules was in place enabling ICS officers to maintain effective control over the decision-making powers of a vast array of Indian subordinates who differed among themselves in terms of education and training (Das 1998: 125). Consequently, 'codification was extended to practically every branch of administration in the form of manuals which [contained] the law on the subject, as well as rules and regulations, e.g. on land acquisition, police, jails, registration, stamps, excise, etc' (O'Malley 1931: 97). Fifthly, another innovation was the institution of a number of checks – legal, financial and administrative – by the ICS. To these all officers of the government, from the lowest to the highest, had to adhere (Das 1998: 125). These various types of checks were meant to energize the administration. Subordinate officials had to file statements and returns specifying the work done and the decisions taken. All business had to be conducted in writing so that records were kept. ICS officers ensured the centralization of decision-making, as native subordinates could not be trusted and hence all their decisions were subject to approval. The administrative reforms undertaken during British rule, revolving around the ICS, were in perfect harmony with the colonial objectives of the Raj. ICS officers were the key instruments of imperial rule but, at the same time, were respected by the citizens. Still, the members of the ICS remained aloof from people and were mostly disdainful of local-level politicians (Khan 1989: 302).

Pakistan Period

When Pakistan gained independence on 14 August 1947, it inherited a well-developed bureaucratic system. The Civil Service of Pakistan (CSP), the premier service of Pakistan, was truly derivative in structure and ethos from the ICS (Braibanti 1966: 97). The CSP had been developed, influenced and conditioned largely by its administrative heritage. This was unmistakably British, and its elitist character ensured a monopoly over key policy-making and policy-implementing positions in the realm of public service (Khan 1979: 134).

A number of reform bodies were appointed periodically by successive governments to study and suggest reform measures pertaining to the public service, especially the CSP. None of the major reform bodies (Egger, Gladieux and Pay and Service Commission) found a justification for retaining an administrative system which had lost its usefulness and only encouraged inequality (Khan 1980: 128). They recommended far-reaching reform measures that included (1) the unification of all services; (2) restructuring of the district and secretarial administration; (3) merit-based recruitment and promotion; (4) an enhanced role for specialists; and (5) abolition of the reservation of posts in favor of the CSP (Khan 1989: 302).

Not surprisingly, none of the recommendations were implemented. Members of the CSP showed remarkable resilience through reservoirs of power in convincing Pakistan's political rulers that major changes in the administrative system were not only uncalled-for but would be detrimental to the interests of the country (Khan 1989: 302).

The failure of major administrative reform efforts in the CSP can be attributed, among other things, to (1) the strong ideological commitment on the part of the members of the CSP to preserve the colonial administrative heritage; (2) chronic political instability resulting in the disproportionate influence of the CSP on affairs of the state; (3) the military's assumption and retention of state power and its consequent dependence on senior members of the CSP to govern the country; and (4) the CSP's success in maintaining its position as a well-organized, entrenched, privileged and powerful interest group within Pakistan (Khan 1989: 302).

Bangladesh Period

Since the independence of Bangladesh 35 years ago, there have been several efforts by both successive governments and donors of technical aid to discern the flaws of the civil service system. Reform bodies studied the civil service systematically and recommended a number of fundamental changes in its structure, functions and ethos. Many of these recommendations intended to free the civil service of its colonial and neocolonial heritage and prepare it to better face the challenges of the modern era (for details see Khan 1989; Khan 1998).

GOVERNMENT REFORM EFFORTS

Almost every government, whether democratic or military, has appointed committees and commissions to 'reform' the civil service. So far, 17 major administrative reform and pay commissions and committees have been appointed and, with the exception of the National Pay Commission (NPC-IV), all have submitted recommendations. The NPC has yet to complete its work. Of these reform bodies, only seven dealt with the entire civil service and therefore had broad coverage. Six bodies dealt with matters of micro-restructuring within the civil service. Of these again, three bodies examined exclusively the pay structure of civil servants. The rest analyzed specific aspects of the civil service, such as recruitment and promotion.

Significant recommendations of seven major reform bodies and their fate are analyzed below. In 1972, two high-powered reform bodies – the Administrative and Services Reorganization Committee (ASRC) and the National Pay Commission (NPC-1) – were appointed. The ASRC recommended a single, classless and unified grading structure with an appropriate number of pay scales matching levels of qualifications, skills and responsibilities (Khan, 1989: 303). The committee recommended several measures for developing an integrated public personnel management system encompassing a rational selection process based on merit, long-term career planning, the formulation of a general training policy, the coordination of institutionalized training and a promotion procedure based on merit-cum-seniority (Khan and Zafarullah 1982: 164). The government, however, did not implement the 'radical' recommendations of the ASRC. The recommendations of NPC-1 for ten scales of pay instead of the then 2,200 pay scales were only partially implemented.

The Pay and Services Commission (P&SC), appointed in 1976, recommended the creation of an all-purpose civil service to include all functions within the traditional government sector. It emphasized the merit principle for recruitment and promotion, a new apex cadre with talented, efficient and experienced officers drawn from all cadres through appropriately designed tests for providing administrative leadership and a high level of coordination, the adoption of the cadre concept in the civil service structure, and the organization of cadre services at the top tier to constitute the nucleus of the civil service structure. It further proposed 52 scales of pay to reduce the multiplicity that had prevailed in the past.

Some of the major recommendations were implemented in modified form. Such implementation resulted in the creation of 28 services within 14 main cadres, the constitution of the Senior Services Pool (SSP) and the introduction of New National Grades and Scales of Pay [NNGSP] (Khan 1989: 304). Between 1982 and 1984, two major reform bodies were appointed: a Martial Law Committee (MLC) and a civilian one. The MLC recommended a reduction in the number of ministries, cutting the number of civil servants (mostly at lower levels), restructuring the role of the secretariat and other executive organizations and delegating financial and administrative powers down the hierarchy (Khan 1987: 352).

The implementation of the major recommendations of the MLC initially resulted in the reduction of the number of ministries and lower-level public employees. However, after some time the number of ministries increased again to the earlier level, and the number of lower-level employees also went up as a result of new and mostly unnecessary recruitment.

The Committee for Administrative Reorganization/Reform (CARR) is a civilian body that made significant recommendations in favor of devolving administrative, financial and judicial powers to the elected people's representatives at successive subnational levels (Khan 1988). Implementation of these recommendations led to the elevation of the lowest administrative tier with rather limited administrative and financial powers. However, real control remained in the hands of the national government.

The last important reform initiative came with the appointment of the Public Administration Reform Commission (PARC) in January 1997. The PARC submitted its recommendations in June 2000. Influenced by the New Public Management (NPM) concept, the Commission made a number of recommendations relating to (1) the improvement of service delivery; (2) the creation of functional clusters of ministries; (3) developing professionalism and a Senior Management Pool (SMP); (4) overcoming inter-cadre rivalries and facilitating fast-track promotion; (5) introducing strictly merit-based recruitment and promotion in public service; (6) decentralization and devolution of governmental authority allied to the reorganization of local government bodies; (7) rationalization of institutions and manpower; (8) creation of a powerful and independent anticorruption commission; (9) effective parliamentary oversight of administration; and (10) creation of a public administration reform and monitoring commission [PARMOC] (PARC, 2000: iii). In sum, PARC made as many as 137 recommendations. Of these, 30 were interim, 70 short-term and 37 long-term. However, only some of its recommendations have so far been implemented.

Donor Reform Initiatives

The donors' interest in administrative reform has been noticeable ever since the late 1970s. Such donors as the World Bank, the United States Agency for International Development (USAID), the United Nations Development Program (UNDP), the Department of International Development (DFID) and the Asian Development Bank (ADB) all invested considerable resources to make the civil service system more efficient, productive, effective and accountable. Donor-sponsored reform initiatives covered a number of important areas. However, only a few touched on all the key aspects of civil service structure and management. The discussion which follows is confined to those reform initiatives which recommended major reform measures. If these prescriptions had been accepted and implemented, radical changes would have occurred in the civil service.

The Public Administration Efficiency Study (PAES) was funded by USAID. The study was the first comprehensive donor effort to reform and redesign the civil service. The study was conducted from May 1984 to November 1989. The significant recommendations of PAES included (1) strengthening supervision through training and management support; (2) reducing the secretariat's operational activities through delegation of routine personnel and financial matters to departments, corporations and subordinate bodies; (3) reducing layers in decision-making; (4) introducing a two-tier career system with a view to raising the quality of the senior civil service; (5) increasing incentives for high performance including wider use of merit as a criterion for promotion; and (6) expanding practical, problem-solving training based on the assessment of organizational needs (USAID 1989: 1–3).

The major recommendations of PAES were not implemented due to (1) the enormity and complexity of the task involved; (2) poor manpower and insufficient financial resources available to the Ministry of Establishment (the implementing agency); (3) strong bureaucratic inertia; and (4) a lack of conviction among senior civil servants as to the commitment of the government to carry reform measures to their logical conclusion (Khan 1998: 134).

The Public Administration Sector Study (PASS) was funded by the

UNDP and was conducted between February and July 1993. The study made as many as 52 recommendations, the most significant of which included (1) establishing results-oriented management systems through setting up objectives and measures of outputs and impacts throughout the government; (2) establishing units in each ministry responsible for developing and applying performance criteria and measures, and developing internal performance audit capability; (3) streamlining government structure by reducing the number of ministries and divisions; (4) reviewing government rules and regulations to eliminate red tape and redundant functions; (5) selecting and promoting officers on merit and through transparent processes; (6) strengthening the Public Service Commission; (7) replacing the cadres and class system with a personnel management system based on a position classification system and grades; and (8) appointing a reform-implementation commission (UNDP 1993: 103–110). Not surprisingly, none of the major recommendations of PASS have been implemented.

The World Bank sponsored and financed a study entitled *Government that Works: Reforming the Public Sector (RPS)*. The wide-ranging study was conducted between 1994 and 1995 in several phases and aimed at delineating core-functions of the government and the essential services provided to the citizens (Khan, 1998: 138). The study recommended (1) redefining frontiers of the public sector – which meant rightsizing the central government; (2) enlarging the role of nongovernmental affiliations as well as local government and the private sector; (3) enhancing the level and nature of the accountability and responsiveness of public organizations to their owners (i.e., parliament, citizens and consumers); (4) streamlining regulations, level and process to ensure transparency, fairness and accountability of legal and regulatory institutions, policies and practices; (5) overhauling the rules and process by which government conducts its policy- and decision-making functions; and (6) maintaining an efficient, committed and professional public service (World Bank 1996: xvi).

The study understood the difficulty of implementing major administrative reforms but rightly warned that the cost of doing nothing would be lower growth, continued poverty and citizens continuing to receive less for more (World Bank 1996: xix). Still, the government implemented none of the major recommendations. The latest donor initiative to reform governance in Bangladesh materialized with the publication of *Taming the Leviathan* by the World Bank (2002). The report offered a broad-based strategy to ensure better governance. The strategy to promote good governance had five critical dimensions: (1) strengthening the core institutions of accountability; (2) building civil society; (3) decentralizing to bring government closer to people; (4) making public administration more effective and efficient; and (5) mobilizing national efforts to bring about the needed reforms (World Bank 2002: IX). We focus below only on public administration, as it is not possible due to space constraints to discuss other dimensions of the study.

To 'energize' administrative reform, the report made a number of recommendations. Firstly, there should be a strong correlation between performance and incentives. Competent and productive civil servants should be given adequate pay and benefits to retain them and keep them honest. Secondly, promotions and recruitment should be based on merit. To encourage meritocracy, a number of interrelated decisions need to be taken. Open competitive examinations should be held to select public servants for overseas training. Greater staff mobility between the private and public sectors must be encouraged in order to facilitate mutual understanding. Thirdly, there is a clear need to establish a credible oversight system to make the public service delivery system results-oriented. An Ombudsman, as provided in the constitution, should be appointed to limit the abuses suffered by citizens from public officials. Fourthly, systematic and open monitoring of the public administration should be undertaken as this can be a powerful instrument to increase efficiency and customer satisfaction. Greater transparency is needed in all spheres. To make the government accountable, freedom of information must be enacted. Fifthly, adhering to relevant guidelines and rules should ensure delegation of administrative and financial powers from ministries to corporations, executive departments and subordinates. Sixthly, the potential of information and communication technologies (ICT) ought to be tapped so that the country can move toward e-government. The ICT techniques can be productivity tools and a platform for improved service quality. They could strengthen the government information flows both within and without.

Though successive governments have repeatedly promised to take the donor-sponsored bodies' recommendations seriously, in reality, the opposite has happened. None of the major recommendations have been implemented.

It should be pointed out that the recommendations of government-appointed administrative reform (AR) bodies, like the key recommendations of donor bodies, went through the same old routines intended to delay and lessen their impact, and ultimately ensuring their place in cold-storage. High-powered committees were appointed, repeated consultations were held and ultimately old excuses were offered to the effect that these recommendations were nebulous, insufficiently specific, irrelevant and inappropriate, and that they put too heavy a burden on the national exchequer. The fate of the reform was thus sealed.

THE IMPACT OF CORRUPTION ON GOVERNANCE AND PUBLIC ADMINISTRATION

In Bangladesh, corruption is all-encompassing and touches every aspect of public life. This wide-ranging nature of corruption is understood by all and sundry. Corruption in public affairs is nothing new in this part of the world.

It existed under the Hindu, Muslim and British rule of the Indian subcontinent. It engulfed the civil administration, the judiciary and trade. There was no let-up of corruption during the Pakistan period (Khan 2003a).

Corruption in Bangladesh is both *systemic* and *endemic*. Petty, middling and grand corruptions are common in this country. The impact of all three variants of corruption on the country as a whole has been devastating. Petty corruption has prevented the poor from receiving education and health services from the public sector. This type of corruption has infected 'a broad range of commercial activities and by imposing needless costs, acts as an expensive, cumulative drain on development' (World Bank 2000: 7). Middling corruption, a widely reported practice in Bangladesh, affects rational patterns for the allocation of scarce public goods and encourages 'special payments' that inevitably lead to inefficient allocation (Khan 2004a). In the process, the nation as a whole suffers huge losses in equity, efficiency and development momentum (World Bank 2000: 7). Grand corruption, widely prevalent in Bangladesh, costs the impoverished country between US$300 million and $450 million a year (World Bank, 2000: 8). It eats up 10 to 15% of official procurement resources meant for purchasing goods at competitive prices abroad (Khan 2004b).

It is not surprising that governance in general and public administration in particular have been affected by corruption. A number of surveys undertaken during the last decade have demonstrated the prevalence of massive corruption in the public sector.

A 1992 survey of households in Dhaka city indicated that over 68% of residents were forced to pay bribes to members of the police force and to income tax and customs officials (Aminuzzaman 1996). Another opinion survey of 2,197 randomly selected individuals from 60 districts (main subnational administrative tier) found that the police was most corrupt, followed by customs and taxation officials (BUP 1997). A Transparency International Bangladesh (TIB) baseline survey of 2,500 households covering ten sectors found that widespread corruption existed in education, health, the judiciary, police, land administration, banks, utility-providing institutions and municipalities (TIB 1997). Another TIB survey, undertaken seven years ago, found large-scale losses of public revenues through corruption in the customs department and power sector (TIB 2000).

Other studies have indicated the nature of corruption in the public sector. Payment of speed-money, common to expedite the valuation and release of imports, implies collusion between customs officials and importers over assessment of duty (Laking 2001: 40). In the Power Development Board (PWD) and Dhaka Electric Supply Authority (DESA), the principal form of corruption results in system loss, mostly related to theft of power by illegal connections or underbilling; the theft requires the active participation of employees (Laking 2001: 40).

There are major instances of corruption in the Road and Highways

Department (R&HD), epitomized by kickbacks and managed tendering in the awarding of contracts, over-invoicing of materials, equipment and work done, and completion to below specification or not at all (Laking 2001: 40–41). The incidence of corruption in the banking sector is also high, as indicated earlier. One study found that a majority of loan defaulters used political connections to get loans approved, and bribes for loan approval ranged from 1 to 5% of the amount of the loan (TIB 2000).

Corruption in most ministries and departments is on the increase (Khan 2003b: 399). During the first six months of 2000, a total of TK.115.3 billion (60 Taka equivalent to 1US$) had been lost in the public sector due to 1,345 corruption incidents in various government agencies (*Daily Star*, 26 September 2000). Between 1994 and 2001, the Comptroller and Auditor-General's Office (CAGO) detected misappropriation and irregularities to the tune of US$2,570 million in 24 ministries and government agencies (*Daily Star*, 4 February 2002). The CAGO's 73 audit reports found cases of embezzlement, theft, wastage, non-deduction of value added tax (VAT) and income taxes, and non-compliance with financial rules and regulations (*Daily Star*, 4 February 2002).

Corruption is also pervasive in the private sector. Private sector corruption involves paying bribes to public servants and politicians in power (Khan, 2004b). A recent survey of 1,001 manufacturing firms in the private sector jointly undertaken by the World Bank and Bangladesh Enterprise Institute (BEI) showed that firms paid an average TK.70,000 in bribes to public officials (World Bank and BEI 2003:30–31). The corrupt officials belonged to a number of government agencies including customs, taxation, environment, labor, social welfare, telephone and telegraph, electricity and gas. An unholy alliance exists between public officials and businessmen, resulting in the increasing incidence of corruption throughout the country (Khan 2004b).

Leading political figures in the country have allegedly been involved in grand corruption. Former Army Chief of Staff and President Ershad was sentenced to five years' imprisonment, banned from contesting elections for five years and fined TK.50 million for misuse of office and corruption (Shah 2001: 43). During her first stint as prime minister between 1991 and 1996, Khaleda Zia, the BNP chairperson and present Prime Minister, was charged along with two ministerial colleagues and seven senior public servants with receiving kickbacks to the tune of TK.1.7 billion for the purchase of two Airbus passenger jets (Shah 2001: 43). In January 2002 when Khaleda Zia came to power for the second time, it was alleged in a white paper that Sheikh Hasina, Awami League President, former Prime Minister and now the opposition leader in Parliament, along with others pocketed US$123 million from the sale of eight Russian MiG 29s and a further US$3 million through the employment of foreign consultants in an export promotion scam (Singh 2003: 156).

There is little doubt about the negative impact of corruption on

Bangladeshi society. Naturally, governance and public administration have also been adversely affected by the spread of the ever-growing tentacles of corruption. In spite of the injection of billions of dollars by major international agencies for development assistance over the years, Bangladesh has remained one of the poorest countries (Zafarullah & Siddiquee 2001: 471). Bureaucratic corruption and inefficiency are taking a heavy toll on the country's economy, causing hundreds of millions of dollars worth of losses in terms of unrealized investment and income (*Financial Express*, 31 July 1997). More specifically, citizens have lost faith in public sector organizations in the face of increasing harassment, poor service delivery and constant demands for bribes. The credibility of public officials is at its lowest ebb. This is related to the ever-increasing incidence of corruption. Lower-level recruitment in the public sector is not based on merit. Hence it creates opportunities for corruption of various kinds. The situation is slightly better for Class I and Class II officers. Still, even their selection is susceptible to influence peddling and bribing, resulting in inappropriate selection in many cases. The transfer and promotion of civil servants at all levels is prone to undue political interference and bribing. One of the unfortunate consequences of the situation is the annihilation of moral and ethical values among civil servants.

Corruption among ruling party politicians has further undermined, and thereby made ineffective, all governance institutions including public administration. Political corruption is directly linked to the election of 'businessmen' and individuals with black money and muscle power to Parliament. An unholy alliance of corrupt politicians, civil servants and businessmen has resulted in wasteful expenditure, adversely affected macroeconomic stability and growth, contributed to excessive debt and led to a situation where governance in general and public administration in particular lack direction, dynamism and vitality.

THE IMPACT OF GLOBALIZATION AND THE GOVERNANCE CRISIS

Globalization has assumed a multidimensional character encompassing economic, social, political and cultural facets (Khan 2003c: 110). The importance of globalization is understood from the fact that it is considered an irresistible new force that will either save or wreck the planet (Lindsey, 2000). Naturally, there are both defenders and critics of globalization. For defenders it will bring a new civilization with qualitative changes (Farazmand 1999). By contrast, for critics (whose numbers grow by the day) globalization is a fad (Chase-Dunn 1994); a fashionable concept in the social sciences (Hirst and Thompson 1999); and little more than furtherance of the imperialist and capitalist world system under a different guise (Jin 2003). The critics of globalization accuse Western countries of 'hypocrisy and the critics are right' (Stiglitz 2002: 6):

> The Western countries have pushed poor countries to eliminate trade barriers but kept their own barriers, preventing developing countries from exporting their agricultural products and so depriving them of desperately needed export income. (ibid.)

Criticisms aside, there are disagreements as to the meaning of the term, as 'globalization incorporates a bundle of different economic, technological, political and ecological processes' (Vayrynen 1999). Globalization, for us, is 'increased and intensified flows between countries of goods, services, capital, ideas, transformation and people, which produce national cross-border integration of a number of economic, social and cultural activities' (UN 2001). This definition points out not only the changed role of the state but also a radically different type of public service. The public service needs to be equipped to handle the challenges of globalization, and also prepared to benefit from it. But the governance crisis that is now being witnessed in Bangladesh will make it extremely difficult for the country to successfully face the onslaught of globalization.

Bangladesh has recently been termed 'a state of disgrace' by *Time* magazine (12 April 2004). The *Time* reporter talked to a cross-section of the population and also witnessed the state of misgovernment in the country. His conclusion is a devastating indictment of the state of governance. For him, Bangladesh is the 'most dysfunctional country in Asia and is reeling from violence, corruption and political turmoil'. These are the symptoms of poor governance. But why has the situation reached such a pass? The reasons are not far to seek.

Democracy has not been institutionalized. Corrupt, incompetent and ill-qualified people are getting themselves 'elected' to Parliament because of their black money and influence, rather than by popular support. Checks and balances between different organs of the government do not exist. A dominant executive allows little freedom for a weak legislature and hapless judiciary to perform their designated roles. This is strange because a parliamentary system of government is operational in this country. The prime minister behaves more like an executive president and is blindly supported in all her actions by the cabinet. It is also widely held that a non-elected coterie both within the Prime Minister's Office (PMO) and outside actually make all the important decisions, while the majority members belonging to the ruling coalition in Parliament legitimate these with meek approval.

The public service is increasingly becoming nonfunctional. Resistance to reform, politicization and failure to induct the best and the brightest have created a situation where public servants are at best capable of taking routine decisions. Corruption has engulfed the entire society, with the most powerful elements having a field day and sharing the loot. The consequences of such widespread, systemic corruption are borne by the majority of the population in the form of poor services, the constant extortion of protection money and a total sense of insecurity.

The question that is frequently asked is how, in the midst of such misgovernment, is it possible for Bangladesh to face the challenges of globalization? To obtain the benefits of globalization, Bangladesh is required to take a number of actions like many other poor countries (Islam 2004: 3). Firstly, the domestic market needs to be liberalized, decentralized and deregulated. Secondly, specific rules and regulations are essential as these govern international transactions in commodities and factors. But the reality in Bangladesh indicates that many of the essential ingredients that would make integration with the world economy feasible are either missing or in a weakened state. Relevant policy reforms at the macro-, micro- and sector-levels leave much to be desired. Coordination among different policies for their effective implementation remains an unfinished job. Also, conflicting goals of policies at several levels make their implementation difficult. Considerable deficiencies exist within several agencies in the government formed to analyze and monitor trends and developments in the world economy and to respond appropriately. The civil service suffers from a lack of professional competence at the middle and top levels, thus handicapping the government in negotiating and bargaining at international fora. Lastly, ministers are largely indifferent to international scenarios, being preoccupied with local partisan politics and thus not in a position to provide the requisite leadership to senior civil servants in order to obtain the maximum benefit of globalization for Bangladesh.

CONCLUSION

Public administration reform (PAR) in Bangladesh is in an unsatisfactory state. Reform bodies have made detailed reform prescriptions after a meticulous examination of the deficiencies prevailing in the civil service system of the country. Minor and inconsequential modifications have been made to methods and procedures from time to time, but a thorough overhaul of the civil service has been resisted under one pretext or another. Significant administrative reform recommendations in most cases have been stalled or manipulated. As a consequence, change has been thwarted in the civil service. Inefficiency, ineffectiveness, lack of discipline, procrastination and malpractices pervade the entire civil service system.

It is no wonder that the civil service, as a key component of the governance system, has contributed so significantly to the phenomenal growth of corruption and to the crisis of governance. The country has earned notoriety as the most corrupt country in the world for the fourth time in succession. Governance institutions like Parliament and the judiciary continue to play a subservient role to the all-powerful executive. Absence of effective checks on the executive has emboldened civil servants to become more arrogant, abusive and corrupt.

The state of governance and the extent and level of corruption are ultimately related to the failure of political and other societal institutions, but also to the nature of public administration reforms (PARs) in Bangladesh. PARs have suffered because of a number of factors including incremental changes, resistance to major reforms by civil servants and lack of political will.

What has been the impact of major PAR failure in Bangladesh? Simply stated, the public service has not responded to the needs of society and has failed to meet the aspirations of the people. The public service is viewed with distrust by citizens. Public servants are becoming increasingly marginalized as they are unable to respond adequately to the challenges that confront them. The public service continues to depend on traditional modes of authority in order to get work done. In the process, the voices of stakeholders in the decision-making process go unheard. Finally, public servants are ill-equipped to respond effectively to the challenges of globalization in such areas as trade laws, investment, corporate governance and competition policies and customs regulation.

Public administration reform (PAR) efforts in Bangladesh are characterized by incrementalism, bureaucratic resistance and lack of political will.

REFERENCES

Aminuzzaman, S.M. (1996). 'Accountability and Promotion of Ethics and Standard of Behavior of the Public Bureaucracy in Bangladesh'. *Asian Review of Public Administration* 8 (2), pp. 13–27.

Braibanti, R. (1996). *Research on the Bureaucracy of Pakistan*. Durham, NC: Duke University Press.

BUP (1997). *Opinion Survey, 1997*. Dhaka: Bangladesh Unnayan Parishad.

Chase-Dunn, C. (1994). 'Technology and the Logic of World Systems'. In R. Palam & B.K. Gills (Eds), *Transcending State-Global Divide: A Non-Structuralist Agenda in International Relations*. Boulder, CO: Lynne Reiner.

Daily Star (2002). 4 February.

Daily Star (2000). 26 September.

Das, S.K. (1998). *Civil Service Reform and Structural Adjustment*. Delhi: Oxford University Press.

Dewey, C. (1996). *The Mind of the Indian Civil Service*. Delhi: Oxford University Press.

Farazmand, A. (1999). 'Globalization and Public Administration'. *Public Administration Review* 59 (6), pp. 509–522.

Financial Express (1997). 31 July.

Hirst, P., & Thompson, G. (1999). *Globalization Question*. Oxford: Polity Press.

Islam, N. (2004). *Looking Outward: Bangladesh in the World Economy*. Dhaka: UP Ltd.

Jin, K.K. (2003). In K.S. Jomo & K.K. Jin (Eds). *Globalization and its Discontents Revisited*. Delhi: Tulika Books.

Khan, M.M. (1979). 'Civil Service of Pakistan as an Institution: Reasons for Resistance to Change'. *The Indian Political Science Review* 13 (2), pp. 133–153.

Khan, M.M. (1980). *Bureaucratic Self-Preservation: Failure of Major Administrative Reform Efforts in the Civil Service of Pakistan*. Dhaka: University of Dhaka.

Khan, M.M. (1985). 'Major Administrative Reform and Reorganization Efforts in Bangladesh: An Overview'. *Indian Journal of Public Administration* 30 (3), pp. 1016–1041.

Khan, M.M. (1987). 'Politics of Administrative Reform and Reorganization in Bangladesh'. *Public Administration and Development* 7 (4), pp. 351–362.

Khan, M.M. (1988). 'Major Administrative Reform and Reorganization in Bangladesh, 1971–1985'. In C. Campbell & B.G. Peters (Eds), *Organizing Governance: Governing Organizations* (pp. 357–381). Pittsburgh: University of Pittsburgh.

Khan, M.M. (1989). 'Resistance to Administrative Reform in Bangladesh, 1972–1987'. *Public Administration and Development* 9 (3), pp. 301–314.

Khan, M.M. (1998). *Administrative Reforms in Bangladesh*. New Delhi: South Asian Publishers Private Ltd.

Khan, M.M. (2003a). 'Political and Administrative Corruption: Concepts, Comparative Experience and Bangladesh Case'. *Asian Affairs* 25 (1), pp. 5–33.

Khan, M.M. (2003b). 'State of Governance in Bangladesh'. *Round Table* 370, pp. 391–405.

Khan, M.M. (2003c). 'Changing Trends in Public Administration: The Globalization Context'. In A. Dhameja (Ed), *Contemporary Debates in Public Administration* (pp. 110–123). New Delhi: Prentice-Hall of India Private Ltd.

Khan, M.M. (2004a). 'Corruption in Bangladesh: A Critical Overview'. (Unpublished paper.)

Khan, M.M. (2004b). 'Enhancing Institutional Capacity of Public Administration in Bangladesh: Present State and Future Direction'. (Unpublished paper.)

Khan, M.M., & Zafarullah, H. (1982). 'Public Bureaucracy in Bangladesh'. In K.K. Tummala (Ed) *Administrative Systems Abroad* (pp. 158–187). Washington, DC: UP of America.

Laking, R. (2001). 'Bangladesh: The State of Governance'. Report prepared for Asian Development Bank (ADB). Dhaka: ADB.

Lindsey, B. (2000). *Against the Dead Hand: The Uncertain Struggle for Global Capitalism*. New York: John Wiley.

O'Malley, L.S.S. (1931). *The Indian Civil Service 1601–1930*. London: John Murray.

PARC (2000). *Public Administration for the 21st Century: Report of the Public Administration Reform Commission*. Vol. 1. Dhaka: Public Administration Reform Commission (Ministry of Establishment, Government of Bangladesh).

Potter, D.C. (1996). *India's Political Administrators: From ICS to IAS*. Delhi: Oxford University Press.

Punjabi, K.L. (1965) (Ed). *The Civil Servant in India*. Bombay: Bharatiya Vidya Bhavan.

Shah, A. (2001). 'South Asia'. In *Global Corruption Report 2001* (pp. 39–52). Berlin: Transparency International.

Singh, G. (2003). 'South Asia'. In *Global Corruption Report 2003* (pp. 153–164). Berlin: Transparency International.

Sinha, N. (1991). 'Role and Rationale of All-India Services'. *Indian Journal of Public Administration* 37 (1).

Stiglitz, J.E. (2002). *Globalization and its Discontents*. London: Allen Lane.

TIB (1997). 'Survey on Corruption in Bangladesh, Phase 2' at http://www.ti-bangladesh.org/docs/survey/phase 2.htm.

TIB (2000). 'Corruption in Public Sector Departments' at http://www.ti-bangladesh.org/docs/misc/overview1.htm.

Time (2004). 12 April.

UN (2001). *World Public Sector Report: Globalization and the State 2001*. New York: UN.

UNDP (1993). *Report on Public Administration Sector Study in Bangladesh*. New York: UN.

USAID (1989). *Report of the Public Administration Efficiency Study*. 5 vols. Washington, DC: USAID.

Vayrynen, R. (1999). Preface. In R. Vayrynen (Ed). *Globalization and Global Governance* (pp. 11–14). New York: Rowan & Littlefield.

World Bank (1996). *Bangladesh: Governance that Works: Reforming the Public Sector*. Washington, DC: World Bank.

World Bank (2000). *Corruption in Bangladesh: Costs and Cures*. Washington, DC: World Bank.

World Bank (2002). *Taming the Leviathan: Reforming Governance in Bangladesh*. Washington, DC: World Bank.

World Bank, & BEI (2003). *Improving Investment Climate in Bangladesh*. Washington, DC: The World Bank and Bangladesh Enterprise Institute.

Zafarullah, H., & Siddiquee, N.A. (2001). 'Dissecting Public Sector Corruption in Bangladesh: Issues and Problems of Control'. *Public Organization Review: A Global Journal* 1, pp. 465–486.

6

Public Ethics in China: Toward a More Transparent Government and More State Capacity to Confront Corruption

STEPHEN K. MA

INTRODUCTION

Public administration is always in a state of flux. As the pace of life accelerates and changes in public affairs come suddenly and fast, many portraits of phenomena in public administration become outdated. Qualifications required of public servants in order to deal with the challenges of society and the behavior expected of government officials are no longer the same. Administrative ethics is no exception. In 1979, Gerald Caiden wrote that

> Corruption is a particularly viral form of organizational cancer [...] we may catch it here and there, but it reappears in some other forms as soon as we relax our vigilance. We do not eliminate it, we merely drive it underground. We can make the corrupt suspend operation temporarily. We can dissuade the tempted. But it lingers, hovering always in the background for the next opportunity. (Caiden 1979: 494).

More than two decades have elapsed since 1979. Though corruption remains a critical issue in daily life, the environment in which anticorruption campaigns are being conducted has changed noticeably.

In 2001, Gerald Caiden and O.P. Dwivedi observed three recent trends in official and public service ethics reform. These included publicity and transparency, institutional capacity and confronting corruption (Caiden & Dwivedi 2001: 248–9). The shocking images on CBS's *60 Minutes* II and the human rights abuse at the US-run Abu Ghraib prison in Iraq, followed by the Congressional hearing and Defense Secretary Rumsfeld's apology, served as telling evidence of increasing sensitivity and, hopefully, transparency in the public service and an institutional capacity to confront corruption.

These trends can be detected in other administrative systems as well. This chapter will review the latest developments in China, as a younger generation is taking the lead in the world's most populous country where unethical behavior has been regularly among the most vexing pathologies authorities have had to cope with. It is fair to say that public administration in the post-

Deng/post-Jiang era has become more transparent, that it has gained institutional capacity to confront corruption. Nevertheless, the questions that merit attention remain: what has contributed to a more transparent administration there; how have authorities managed to obtain more institutional capacity to confront corruption; and does the case of China offer useful lessons about the arduous mission that institutionalization of accountability represents in the drive to elevate government officials above self-interest by placing collective good above private gain and greed?

TRANSPARENCY OF GOVERNMENT

The Chinese administrative system has become less closed to the public as the nation began to open itself to the outside world since the late 1970s and early 80s. Several factors have contributed to a more transparent government. Firstly, there was the emergence of a 'citizenship culture'. Gabriel A. Almond and G. Bingham Powell, Jr. have identified three roles played by average people, namely subjects, participants and parochials (Almond & Powell 1988: 42). China was largely a 'subject culture' in the past decades. The average Chinese was expected to obey and follow rather than participate, let alone to 'watch' his government. A transition to the 'citizen culture' has begun. Pressure for more participation has been gaining momentum. The cries for public involvement have led to public hearings that were held to receive public input on pending policy and/or programs. A July 2001 State Planning Commission decision stipulated that certain prices must be decided upon after public hearings. The term 'public hearing' gained such popularity that it became one of the nation's 21 hottest terms in 2001 (http://www.peopledaily.com.cn/GB/shenghuo/76/123/20020116/649280.html).

Meanwhile, open meetings have been experimented with in the municipal government of Xiamen, a coastal city of Fujian Province, in order to open up the decision-making process of government to the public and to help the public retain control over those who are supposed to be their servants (*World Journal*, 30 June 2003). China's electorate is no longer obedient and passive. Nearly half a million average citizens have taken government officials to court in the past five years. The percentage of lost cases declined from 36% in 1992 to 29% in 2001 (http://www.peopledaily.com.cn/GB/shehui/46/20030215/923792.html).

To safeguard a citizen's right to information, Dr. Jiang Yanyong, a retired medical doctor in a military hospital, decided to blow the whistle when the government claimed that SARS was not spreading dangerously in the country (Beech 2003: 63). His brave action shocked the world, brought down the nation's Minister of Health and the Mayor of Beijing and, more importantly, led to changes in bureaucratic behavior and administrative culture (Ratnesar

& Beech 2003: 54–56). Professor Jiao Guobiao of Journalism and Communications in Beijing University, which is considered China's top-ranking institute of higher education, published an article in which he charged that the government 'censorship orders are totally groundless, absolutely arbitrary, at odds with the basic standards of civilization and as counter to scientific common sense as witches and wizardry'. He mocked the ten 'forbiddens' and three 'musts' style used in propaganda orders and described 'fourteen diseases' and 'four cures', one of which is abolishing censorship (*New York Times*, 3 May 2004).

News media began to play a watchdog role in April 1994, when a twelve-minute-long daily TV program entitled *Interview with a Focus* (*Jiaodian Fangtan*) started reporting on a variety of problems that should have been addressed properly by the government. *Bynowit* has become one of the most influential media watchdogs in China (http://news.sina.com.cn/o/2004-03-30/14132179995s.shtml). Another program, entitled *Weekly Report on Quality* and broadcast by CCTV, has since April 2004 investigated the quality of certain consumer products. It has now become one of the most popular TV programs and is considered to be an important means of exercising 'supervision over the state by society media' (*World Journal*, 24 July 2004). In May 2004, a tragedy resulting from use of a phony baby formula was disclosed. Officially, 13 babies died and more than 170 suffered serious malnutrition in Fuyang, a city in the impoverished eastern province of Anhui, as a result of drinking the fake milk powder (*Los Angeles Times*, 3 May 2004). The malnutrition deaths stirred a public outcry, led to the arrests of government officials for attempting to cover-up and prompted an investigation and promise of a crackdown (*Los Angeles Times*, 26 May 2004).

These cases have had several implications. Firstly, external pressure from the media did have an impact. Secondly, internal professional standards encouraged people like Dr. Jiang and Professor Jiao to follow the guidelines in fighting against bureaucratic abuse of power. Thirdly, the political will of the leadership, namely the active involvement of the new generation of China's leadership headed by Party General Secretary Hu Jintao and Prime Minister Wen Jiabao, could be considered essential in facilitating change toward a healthy and honest administrative culture (Pomfret 2003).

The widespread application of new information technology and the resultant use of the Internet brought about new hope for more transparent government. For instance, though it was quickly banned by the Communist Party's propaganda department, Professor Jiao's treatise was widely circulated on the Internet. The Internet also led to the exposure of corrupt government officials. Mr. Li Xin, a deputy mayor of the city of Jining, Shandong Province, was arrested in July 2004 for soliciting and accepting bribes after disclosure of his abuse of power on the website 'Web on Media Supervision in China' (*Zhongguo Yulun Jiandu Wang*; http://www.yuluncn.com). Months later, *Renmin Ribao* (*People's Daily*) published an article applauding the 'watchdog' function performed by the website (20 September 2004; see also http://www.people.com.cn/GB/14677/ 21966/36358/2795504.html).

THE 'SECOND REVOLUTION' AND DEBUREAUCRATIZATION

The government's repeated failure to combat and curb administrative corruption made more transparent government an option in the anticorruption campaign. Ideological indoctrination used to be a powerful weapon against administrative corruption in the hands of the Chinese government. For decades, China's bureaucratic machine was placed under the Chinese Communist Party's (CCP) close supervision. Ideology, together with organization, was instrumental in achieving this goal (Schurmann, 1968). The de-Maoization which followed the Cultural Revolution of 1966–76 rendered the tool impotent. As Deng Xiaoping inaugurated China's 'second revolution' featuring policies of reform and opening China to the outside world, his post-Mao leadership condemned the use of both ideological indoctrination and political campaigns, depriving it of previous mechanisms to constrain bureaucratic behavior. Rampant corruption among government officials forced the Chinese authorities to search for other options in dealing with corruption. One of them was the establishment of ethical codes. A series of codes of ethics designed to set guidelines for Party and state bureaucracies have been enacted since 1993. Unfortunately, they have not yielded the expected results. Rather than ebbing, corruption has escalated and proliferated among high-ranking cadres. According to Jia Chunwang, Chief Procurator of China's Supreme People's Procuratorate, eleven senior administrators at the gubernatorial/ministerial level were investigated for involvement in crime in 2004 alone (http://www.chinanews.com.cn/news/2005/2005-03-09/26/548428.shtml).

Disciplinary measures and punishment have been employed to serve the purpose of 'killing the chicken to frighten the monkey'. For example, Cheng Kejie, once Governor of the Guangxi Autonomous Region, was sentenced to death for accepting a bribe in September 2000. He is the highest-ranking official to have been executed for corruption in the history of the People's Republic of China (http://news.bbc.co.uk/chinese/simp/hi/newsid_920000/newsid_924400/924452.stm). However, the warning seems to have fallen on deaf ears. As shown by the number of senior administrators suspected of corruption mentioned above, even capital punishment did not stop them from coasting into the abyss of crime.

A more transparent government would mean more access to information about government which could add to the legitimacy of the ruling elite. For example, in explaining why the Chinese state is allowing ever more freedoms to develop, Jean C. Oi suggests that 'exposing corrupt or inept cadres can help the state's case. Exposure does not absolve the central authorities of responsibility, but it redirects blame away from the state' (2004: 279–280). Will a transparent government work as an option in an anticorruption campaign? While this remains to be seen, a positive development in several areas would definitely make this option an effective one. To ensure administrative transparency, open meetings and 'sunshine laws' must be institutionalized. Access to information in the public sector must be assured. Supervision by the public of the behavior of government officials must be encouraged. Whistleblowers must be protected. All these steps require that the nation's leaders be resolute in moving toward transparent government as they challenge China's traditional Confucian culture of obedience to authority and the Party's supremacy in governance. The lack of a civic culture among the populace is a long-term problem which may need the efforts of several generations and must be dealt with patiently and persistently.

From the point of view of Western values, a multiparty system would be viewed as consistent with a transparent government, thereby curbing and constraining administrative corruption. Ironically, not only has the CCP shown little interest in the concept, which would probably threaten the ruling Party's monopoly of power, but also, the bulk of the public does not seem to be ready to accept it. As pointed out by Suzanne Ogden, people in China tend to believe that a multiparty system which would require national elections might spawn even greater corruption. Known as 'black and gold politics' (black for crime, gold for money), corruption is notoriously undermining Taiwan's efforts to democratize. The CCP would love to 'present this widely publicized situation to China's people as reason enough for prohibiting new political parties' (Ogden 2002: 278).

Nongovernmental organizations in China can contribute to a transparent government by checking over the Party and state bureaucracies. Indeed, they seem to be growing in number and influence in recent years. However, these Chinese associations

> …pursue public interests through the aggregation and articulation of their needs, ideas, and concerns, but they are simultaneously satisfying private interests by relying on personalistic ties and are frequently motivated by opportunities for profit-making, if not outright corruption. (Ogden 2002: 315)

Therefore, the move toward transparent government is unlikely to be eased or accelerated simply by following Western models.

STATE CAPACITY TO CONFRONT CORRUPTION

Official efforts to reinforce the state capacity to confront corruption were apparent in recent years. On the legislative front, the National People's

Congress (NPC) is 'not necessarily a "rubber stamp"', as Western observers used to believe (Wang 2002: 92). China's legislature, in Kevin O'Brien's opinion, is no longer a 'forum for policy review' since Deng inaugurated the reformist policies (O'Brien 1990: 37). More actions have been taken by the legislature in order to hold the reins of state bureaucracy. For example, in June 2002 the NPC's Standing Committee passed the Government Procurement Act, which regulates public procurement and which includes guidelines for preventing corruption. In August 2003, the Standing Committee also passed a law on administrative licensing designed to streamline and introduce transparency into the issuance of administrative permits (Transparency International 2004: 177–178).

Meanwhile, the legislature's supervisory capacity leaves much to be desired. This was shown in an article in a 2004 September issue of *Liaowang*, a weekly news magazine. The article observes that many legislators are lacking in either courage or capability when it comes to exercising their role in checking government bureaucrats. Therefore, the article urges the NPC to review and revise a bill on supervision in order to enable the nation's legislatures to become more effective in performing their oversight function. To achieve this goal, a legislature must ensure that the constitution and laws are upheld to the full; supervisory institutions are reinforced; investigative procedures are institutionalized; authority and procedures on conducting investigations are reinstalled and respected; government is kept accountable to the legislature, and procedures to recall and remove administrators are put into effect (http://www.china.org.cn/chinese/law/ 660148.htm). Pressures were building up for the legislature to shed its image of a 'rubber stamp' and to show its muscle as a capable and competent institution that keeps the state bureaucracy in check.

Within the executive branch, the National Audit Office under the State Council has played an increasingly important role in reining in government bureaucracy. In June 2004, Li Jinhua, Auditor-General of the National Audit Office, disclosed to the Tenth Plenum of the Standing Committee of the Tenth National People's Congress (NPC) the following disturbing facts, namely that 24 departments under the State Council submitted in 2003 either false or irregular final accounts of revenue and expenditure, totaling more than 4 billion Yuan; 788 enterprises had been caught in tax evasion amounting to more than 2.5 billion Yuan; the leadership of the former State Electricity Company had lost 4.5 billion Yuan in state funds; the Industrial and Commercial Bank of China and its 21 branches had failed to grant loans according to established rules; the former China Life Insurance Company had conducted rigged competitive bidding involving a total amount of nearly 2.4 billion Yuan; and the tax bureaus had failed to collect over 10 billion Yuan in taxes (http://www.people.com.cn/GB/jingji/1037/2598513.html). Li's report ushered in the so-called 'Auditing Storm' that would sweep across the entire nation, not only shocking the public but also scaring many government bureaucrats involved in corruption.

On the other hand, the establishment of anticorruption bureaus did not seem to add greatly to the state capacity to confront corruption. Since the first anticorruption bureau came into existence in Guangdong province in 1989, the agency's image has been tarnished again and again as an increasing number of the bureau chiefs themselves were arrested for corruption. It started in June 1998 when Luo Ji, Chief of the General Anticorruption Bureau under the nation's Supreme People's Procuratorate, was removed from office for withholding for himself and others more than 87 million Yuan. These funds had been confiscated through handling other corruption cases (http://members.fortunecity.com/tiannu/top10.htm). Other officials of anticorruption bureaus followed suit. In October 2003, Xie Jianzhuo, Vice-Chief of the Anticorruption Bureau of Xinhui County in Guangdong Province, was executed for absconding with over 16 million Yuan embezzled from state coffers (http://www.southcn.com/news/dishi/jiangmen/shizheng/200311010115.htm). In January 2004, Liu Guoqing, Chief of the Anticorruption Bureau in Guizhou Province, was sentenced to 13 years in prison for accepting more than 400,000 Yuan in bribes (http://www.epochtimes.com/gb/4/1/19/n451471.htm). In June 2004, Han Jianlin, Chief of the Anticorruption Bureau of Jiansu Province, stepped down as a result of involvement in a corruption scandal (http://www.xzjj.gov.cn/lzjy/alxd040623-1.htm). In September 2004, Jia Junying, Chief of the Anticorruption Bureau of Taiyuan City of Shanxi Province, was sentenced to life in prison for accepting a bribe and for assisting criminals in escaping punishment (http://www.southcn.com/news/china/cnzf/zfdaodu/200409200275.htm). The list of anticorruption officials convicted on corruption charges seems to be growing. This has raised a serious question about the effectiveness of China's state capacity to confront corruption.

Gerald Caiden has stressed the importance of maintaining clean and honest agencies of law enforcement in anticorruption campaigns:

> Public misconduct is uneven. Some areas of government are more prone to it than others simply because they exercise the greatest influence over public decisions [...] Temptations also are great for any officials who handle large sums of money, have dealings with private businesses, or tackle illegal goods and services. Possibly the prime target is law enforcement.

Only when the public eventually trusts and identifies with enforcement agencies shall we be able to 'do much to clean up the rest of government and keep all other public officials honest' (Caiden 1993: 25).

More importantly, anticorruption agencies alone are not sufficient in combating corruption. Anticorruption campaigns must involve the whole of society. This will require serious efforts on the part of both the rulers and the ruled. Firstly, political leaders 'must be committed to the eradication of corruption by setting a good example themselves'. Are they willing to live a humble life yet uphold high standards of conduct and honesty, so that they may deserve the respect and confidence people place in governance? Secondly, the public must be educated on what constitutes unacceptable public behavior and where to go for assistance in combating it. Apathy must be discouraged while voluntary associations devoted to clean and honest government must be encouraged. Thirdly, efforts to combat corruption must be focused on the prime target, namely law enforcement, so that the rule of law is upheld, equal access to the law ensured, unprejudiced enforcement achieved and public trust restored. Fourthly, codes of official ethics cannot remain merely paper. They must be enforced as a matter of both professional pride and personal self-discipline. To achieve this goal the public service not only needs to recruit able and honest officers but also to offer salaries and compensation commensurate with their status and rank. Finally, forces making for corruption must be curbed and contained. Such countervailing factors as ideological transformation, moral revolution, economic redistribution, political reform, sociocultural change, legal reform and administrative modernization need to receive support (Caiden 2001a: 33–35).

INSTITUTIONALIZATION OF ACCOUNTABILITY

As the Chinese government started combating corruption on various fronts, did the nation's bureaucrats demonstrate a more developed sense of duty? Are they now more accountable for their behavior? Will a culture of accountability be nurtured in the years to come? Some government officials who were held responsible for their misconduct took the blame and were forced to resign. As mentioned earlier in this chapter, both the Minister of Health and the Mayor of Beijing lost their jobs in disgrace for failing to fulfill their duties properly. However, one should not read into such cases any convincing proof of a culture of public accountability. Large numbers of Chinese bureaucrats still lack a sense of accountability and use state power 'solely for personal gain and self-promotion, without advancing the collective benefits, the common weal, and the public interest'. They are still alien to a culture of public accountability which suggests that 'power holders must remember that they personify the state; they must honor and dignify the state; and they must devote themselves to the public's business. Should they fail, they are removable and replaceable' (Caiden 2001b: 447). Much needs to be done in China before this level can be reached.

Whether the administrative bureaucrats like it or not, the public feels that government officials should be held accountable for their actions or inactions. A survey in April 2004, conducted among over four hundred people residing in twelve cities in China, revealed that nearly 70% of all respondents knew leading government officials who neglected their duties, committed grave errors, caused the state to sustain heavy losses or made such a bad impression on the public that they should take the blame and resign. Indeed, three leading officers did lose their jobs after a natural gas explosion, deaths in a lantern festival and a fire in a department store earlier that month. About half of the respondents believed that the resignations exemplified a step toward administrative accountability. However, it remains to be seen whether the measure would be institutionalized in the near future (*World Journal*, 30 May 2004).

In exploring how South Korea could institutionalize effective accountability mechanisms, Gerard Caiden & Jung H. Kim offered a list of suggestions. These include establishing an independent anticorruption agency, enacting stronger anticorruption legislation, building up more open government, facilitating investigatory mass media, encouraging 'citizen watchdogs', strengthening the audit function within the administration and protecting whistleblowers (Caiden 1993: 141–144). In the Chinese case, autonomy for an anticorruption agency is limited. Luo Ji, who served as first Chief of the nation's General Anticorruption Bureau, was discharged from his position in 1998. He admitted that, in comparison with the Independent Anticorruption Commission in Hong Kong, its counterpart on the mainland enjoys a lower status and less autonomy, its ability often falling short of its ambitions (http://news.163.com/2004w03/12482/2004w03_1078456738210.html). An independent anticorruption agency is unlikely to be enthusiastically welcomed by the Chinese authorities, as the ruling elite has shown little desire to give up its monopoly of power and share its privileged position in the administration with another institution.

As described earlier in the chapter, some anticorruption legislation has been introduced and passed by the NPC. However, the ruling party's support for effective legislative supervision has seemed rather lukewarm. The warning by Wu Bangguo, Chairman of the NPC's Standing Committee, is alarming. He claimed that the legislative supervision 'overstepped the bounds', 'exceeded its authority' and 'overrode' the CCP's power of government (Guan Jie 2004: 12). This raised the serious question whether, in the years to come, stronger anticorruption legislation would be likely to develop or whether China's anticorruption campaign might end up as an empty promise about which much was said but little was accomplished.

Some of the steps aimed at making government more transparent have been half-hearted. For example, government officials are required to reveal their personal financial assets. The General Office of the Party's Central Committee and the General Office of the State Council issued in 1995 'Rules on Filing an Income Disclosure by Leading Party and Government Cadres at the County/Division Level'. The rules require, *inter alia*, the semi-annual disclosure of salaries, bonuses, subsidies, welfare benefits; honoraria for consultation, lecturing, writing, reviewing manuscripts, and doing calligraphy or painting; and lastly, income from contracted business (*Renmin Ribao*, Overseas Edition, 25 May 1995). The disclosed information is confidential and is kept in the safe at the state personnel departments at different levels. There is no public access to the contents of the disclosure. Clearly, confidential disclosure can hardly contribute to a transparent government.

The fledgling investigatory mass media in China have undoubtedly encouraged a culture of accountability, yet at a price. The news reporters working for the ten-year long TV program series *Interview with a Focus* ran the risk of being kidnapped and detained illegally as they were conducting investigations. Their cars were broken into. Their lives were threatened. Although the nation's three recent prime ministers including Li Peng, Zhu Rongji, and Wen Jiabao all visited the reporters' office, professing their support for the program's role in media supervision over government, it was hard to predict whether a less hostile environment for investigatory media would emerge soon (http://news.sina.com.cn/o/2004-03-30/14132179995s.shtml).

It requires determination, perseverance and defiance of danger to step forward. Few, therefore, become watchdogs and whistleblowers. Three bureaucrats who offered first-hand information to state auditors and who assisted in an investigation of corruption found themselves harrassed and persecuted for 15 months soon after their whistleblowing (http://news.sohu.com/20041210/n223428740.shtml). Jiang, who broke the news about SARS in 2003, sent an appeal to the Chinese government in 2004 requesting that the official verdict on the 1989 student demonstration be redressed. After being kept under house arrest for more than eight months, he was released in March 2005 (*World Journal*, 24 March 2005). Examining whistleblowing in China, Ting Gong observes that 'It is practically not easy for whistleblowing to serve as an effective bottom-up social control channel. As everywhere else, there is always a high probability of reprisal. No matter what may have motivated them, whistleblowers risk losing everything' (2000: 1913).

Jiang's case was leaked and so became well-known to the outside world. How many similar cases of whistleblowing have taken place in China but remain unreported is anyone's guess.

CONCLUSION

Several factors have contributed to more transparent government in post-Mao China. These include the emergence of a citizenship culture, the widespread application of new information technology and the government's repeated failure to combat and curb administrative corruption. Meanwhile, there have apparently been official efforts to reinforce the state capacity to confront corruption. The legislature took more action to keep the state administration under control. The National Audit Office under the State Council has played an increasingly active and aggressive role in reining in the government bureaucracy. Anticorruption Bureaus have been established within the judicial branch. However, more needs to be done in order to institutionalize a culture of accountability.

Melanie Manion has asked: 'assuming Chinese leaders are sincere anti-corruption reformers, why not choose a constitutional design for clean government?' A constitutional design would certainly facilitate the institutionalization of a culture of accountability. However, 'top Chinese leaders have tied their claims of political legitimacy to the sustained health and growth of the Chinese economy' (Manion 2004: 208). Therefore, 'institutional designs that constrain the abuse of public power are not a winning bet'. It may take years or even decades before the dream of an institutionalized culture of accountability takes root in China.

However, this does not imply that corruption in China will remain unchallenged and unchecked and that corrupt officials will continue to prevail. In the long run, unethical people will have a harder time. That is because, to paraphrase the Caidens, the hunt for people alleged to have committed crimes against humanity will intensify and a new doctrine of administrative responsibility will be enforced in many other ways, buttressed by a host of new public accountability mechanisms. The public will grow more vigilant and mass media will grasp every opportunity to reveal and expose what is scandalous (G. Caiden & N. Caiden 2003: 331–333).

REFERENCES

Almond, G.A., & Powell, G.B., Jr. (1988). *Comparative Politics Today: A World View* (4th ed) (p. 42). Glenview, IL: Scott, Foresman & Co.

Beech, H. (2003). 'Unmasking a Crisis'. *Time* (21 April), p. 63.

Caiden, G.E. (1979). 'Coping with Administrative Corruption: An Academic Perspective'. In S.K. Sharma (Ed), *Dynamics of Development – An International Perspective*. Concept Publishing Co.

Caiden, G.E. (1993). 'Abuse of Public Trust: Fact or Way of Life?' *Annual Editions: Public Administration* (3rd ed). Dushkin Publishing Group.

Caiden, G.E., & Kim, J.H. (1993). 'A New Anticorruption Strategy for Korea'. *Asian Journal of Political Science* 1 (1), pp. 141–144.

Caiden, G.E. (2001a). 'Corruption and Governance'. In G.E. Caiden, O.P. Dwivedi, & J. Jabbra, *Where Corruption Lives* (pp. 33–35). Bloomfield, CT: Kumarian Press.

Caiden, G.E. (2001b). 'Dealing with Administrative Corruption'. In T.L. Cooper (Ed), *Handbook of Administrative Ethics*. New York: Marcel Dekker.

Caiden, G.E., & Caiden, N. (2003). 'Public Ethics and the Role of Bureaucracy: The Trend to Universality and Moral Conformity?' In *Gerald Caiden on Administrative Ethics* (pp. 331–333). Fudan University Press.

Caiden, G.E., & Dwivedi, O.P. (2001). 'Official Ethics and Corruption'. In G.E. Caiden, O.P. Dwivedi, & J. Jabbra. *Where Corruption Lives* (pp. 248–9). Bloomfield, CT: Kumarian Press.

Gong, T. (2000). 'Whistleblowing: What Does it Mean in China?' *International Journal of Public Administration* 23 (11), p. 1913.

Guan, J. (2004). *Wu Bangguo Jinghu Renda Jiandu Chugui* (Wu Bangguo Cries Out in Alarm that the NPC's Supervision Has Overstepped the Bounds). *The Trend Magazine*, September 12.

Manion, M. (2004). *Corruption by Design: Building Clean Government in Mainland China and Hong Kong*. Harvard University Press.

O'Brien, K.J. (1990). *Reform without Liberalization: China's National People's Congress and the Politics of Institutional Change*. Cambridge University Press.

Ogden, S. (2002). *Inklings of Democracy in China*. Harvard University Press.

Oi, J.C. (2004). 'Realms of Freedom in Post-Mao China'. In W.C. Kirby, *Realms of Freedom in Modern China* (pp. 279–280). Stanford University Press.

Pomfret, R. (2003). *Central Asia since 1991: The Experience of the New Independent States*. Paris: OECD.

Ratnesar, R., & Beech, H. (2003). 'Tale of Two Countries: A Time Investigation into What Went Wrong'. *Time* (5 May), pp. 54–56.

Schurmann, F. (1968). *Ideology and Organization in Communist China* (2nd ed). University of California Press.

Transparency International (2004). *Global Corruption Report 2004* (pp. 177–178). Berlin: Pluto Press.

Wang, J.C.F. (2002). *Contemporary Chinese Politics: An Introduction* (7th ed). Pearson Education Inc.

7

The Challenges of Public Administration Reforms in Japan and South Korea

YONG-DUCK JUNG

INTRODUCTION

Since the early 1980s, most OECD countries have experienced transition in governance in one way or another. Through numerous attempts, they have sought to improve their administrative systems by transforming a traditionally hierarchical bureaucracy into a more flexible and accountable public administration. The English-speaking OECD member states in Australasia, North America and the UK led this transition. These advanced democracies, 'considered among the best governed and administered', have tended to 'reject radical ideologies in favor of pragmatic centrist policies termed "The Third Way" – promising to strengthen their democratic ethos' (Caiden & Caiden 2000: 1).

Since the late twentieth century, the Northeast Asian countries, which include China, Japan and South Korea, have been no exception to this trend of governance transition. They have undertaken a series of administrative reforms in order to respond effectively to the rapidly changing international and local environments. Among these Northeast Asian countries, Japan and South Korea are OECD member states which have devoted their efforts to modernizing their 'developmental state', an Asian form of administrative state. They institutionalized the governance system that paved the way for the state-led industrialization during the twentieth century. Since the late 1970s however, the rapidly changing external and internal environments have forced them to seek new approaches to sustainable development. To this end, they tried to adopt many elements of the models first applied by the English-speaking OECD countries. Nevertheless, to date the resulting forms of governance are not so much Anglo-Saxon as they really are Asiatic. This chapter analyzes and compares the initiatives and achievements in Japan and South Korea since the early 1980s and compares their reform efforts and performance.

BACKGROUND AND ATTEMPTS AT ADMINISTRATIVE REFORM

Historical Developments in Public Administration in Northeast Asia

The neighboring three countries in Northeast Asia – China, Japan and South Korea – nearly one fourth of the world population, two thirds of the total GDP of the 25 EU countries, and almost the same trade as that of the three NAFTA member states. Their geographical proximity contributed to common sociopolitical institutions influenced by Confucianism which date back as far as 200 BC.

This Confucian form of governance 'placed a heavy reliance on a meritocratic, centralized, more or less autonomous, paternalistic bureaucracy' (Painter 2005: 335). Still, each country also developed distinctive governance systems, as can be inferred by comparing their respective ceramics, porcelains and architecture.

After the late nineteenth century, the three countries pursued different paths toward modernization. In the wake of the Meiji restoration, Japan led the process of Westernization and joined the 'late industrializers' (Thompson 1996). The Meiji public administration combined the traditional governance system that remained from pre-modern era Japan with the Prussian bureaucracy model. Subsequently, in the first half of the twentieth century the country became an imperial garrison state. Both Korea and China tried to modernize without outside assistance but were largely unsuccessful. Japan colonized Korea as well as part of China and imposed its governance system on Korea, Manchuria and Taiwan.

After World War II, the governance systems of China, Japan and Korea diverged even further. The conclusion of the war ended colonization in Korea and the occupied parts of China. Both countries started to move toward modernization but adopted different strategies and ideologies. In 1949, China followed the Soviet Union's lead in establishing a socialist society. This included rooting out the traditional bureaucracy and creating a radically egalitarian governance system. The process reached its zenith during the Cultural Revolution from 1962 to 1978 (Hood 1999: 129; 142).

At the end of World War II, Korea was divided into two states with radically different ideologies and governance systems: South Korea (a US occupation zone) adopted a system of free market democracy and North Korea (a USSR occupation zone) was a socialist people's republic. South Korea began by maintaining most of the institutions of the former centralized colonial bureaucracy. North Korea, by contrast, successfully removed the old colonial legacy and established a Stalinist state.

Japan evolved under the influence of democratization pursued by the American military. It undertook an array of reforms to deconstruct the imperial garrison state. These measures included the strengthening of representative institutions and decentralizing government. This led to the elimination of the Ministry of Interior, which had been a pilot central agency of the centralized governance system before the end of World War II. Nevertheless, the post-war governance system, called the System of 1955, retained some vestiges of the Meiji administrative system (McCubbins & Noble 1995: 56–80; Nishikawa 2004).

More recently, in the late twentieth century, China, Japan and South Korea have undertaken additional reforms to respond to the rapidly changing global environment. Since 1978, China, under the leadership of Chairman Deng Xiaoping, adopted a series of measures for 'reforming and opening-up' as part of its attempts to promote a free-market economy in tandem with its politics of socialism. In 1998, the country under the leadership of President Jiang Jemin conducted a series of administrative reforms deemed an 'administrative revolution' or the 'largest-scale dramatic reforms in its history' (Saich 2001: 52–79; Bai 2005).

China's reform reflects an attempt to build a modern state by inducing a bureaucratization of its public administration while sustaining a socialist political system.[1] For example, for the first time since the founding of the People's Republic, China established a system of administrative law and legislated the Civil Service Act in the name of 'limited government and rule-of-law administration' (Bai 2005). It reduced the size of government, consistent with the principle of 'small government and big society'. As a result, the number of the central administrative apparatuses under the State Council decreased. For example, the cabinet-level organizations declined from 52 in 1983 to 40 in 1998 and then to 28 in 2003; the number of agencies of the State Council diminished from 100 in 1981 to 62 in 2003; and 200 bureaus and divisions were eliminated during the period (National School of Administration 1999; Chinese Public Administration Society 2003). Concurrently, the staff of the central cabinet ministries was reduced from 51,000 in 1978 to 39,000 in 1982, 31,000 in 1998 and 15,000 in 2001 (Li 2000; Kim 2004; Bai 2005). China is continuing to reduce the size of government by means of a variety of measures. These include privatization of state-run enterprises and deregulation of private enterprises.

Nevertheless, the government of so-called socialist but market economy-oriented China remains large, centralized and hierarchical in comparison with free-market democracies such as South Korea and Japan. Furthermore, the Communist Party still 'acts as a substitute for the state apparatus' and politicizes public administration as indicated by the new Civil Service Act, which includes a clause for the 'removal of political neutrality' of civil servants (Balme 2004; Bai 2005).

Compared with socialist China, South Korea and Japan have conducted more and similar administrative reform efforts since the late twentieth century. The two countries institutionalized similar governance systems and paved the way for successful state-led industrialization. However, the rapidly changing external and internal environments that have arisen since the late 1970s have made both countries search for and institutionalize new governance models for sustainable development.

Reform Efforts in Japan and South Korea since the Late Twentieth Century

Since the early 1980s, public policy-makers in Japan and South Korea have deemed it necessary to conduct aggressive administrative reforms in order to respond to the new international environment. This new environment included the end of the Cold War followed by the expansion of globalization and the resultant unlimited economic competition in the global market. Since the early 1980s, both countries have also deemed it necessary to conduct administrative reforms in response to domestic political and economic pressures. There has been widespread distrust in the efficiency and accountability of the administrative system. This public distrust was exacerbated by maladministration during the oil shocks and financial deficit in Japan and by the democratization and foreign liquidity crises in the case of South Korea.

There have also been symbolic implications associated with the closing of one century and the ushering in of another. In both countries, the drive in preparation for the twenty-first century (or for a new millennium) was replete with a symbolism for the drive in political activities since the late 1980s. The movement of ideas in the advanced democracies stimulated an interest in government reform in Japan and South Korea. In fact, both countries' governments have invested considerable effort in public administration reform. In order to conduct these reforms effectively, they have established a number of ad hoc steering committees (see Table 1). The reform goals and attempts conducted in Japan and South Korea will be outlined in the remainder of this section.

One of the most affluent countries in the world, Japan has paradoxically continually faced fiscal failure since the late 1970s (Kumon 1984: 147–151). During the period of economic expansion, a continuing increase in government expenditures was built into the budget structure. Consequently, however, revenues fell far short of expenditures. After the second oil crisis of 1979, Japanese economic growth fell to 3% and revenues from corporate and personal taxes dropped. The government had to cover the shortfall between increasing expenditures and decreasing revenues by issuing public bonds. Between 1974 and 1979, the deficit rose from 1.6% to 6.1% of GNP. In the 1979 general election, the Ohira administration's attempt to introduce a general consumption tax met with strong public opposition, and the ruling Liberal Democratic Party suffered a setback in the 1979 Diet election. Business leaders called for administrative reforms before any tax increases and demanded a streamlined, efficient government.

Table 1 *Ad hoc* steering committees for administrative reforms (year launched)

Japan	Korea
Second Provisional Commission for Administrative Reform (1981);	Administrative Reform Committee (1980);
Provisional Councils for the Promotion of Administrative Reform (1981);	Presidential Committee of Administrative Reform (1988);
Administrative Reform Promotion Headquarters (1994);	Joint Council for Decentralization (1991);
Administrative Reform Committee (1994);	Presidential Committee of Administrative Innovation (1993);
Decentralization Promotion Commission (1995);	Government Reorganization Committee (1997);
Administrative Reform Conference (1996)	Managerial Diagnosis and Steering Committee (1999);
	Decentralization Promotion Committee (1999);
	Government Reform Committee (2000);
	Presidential Committee for Government Innovation and Decentralization (2003)

Policy diffusion from the Anglo-Saxon countries also played a part in sustaining the momentum for neo-liberal administrative reform. The public policy-makers introduced the concept of 'government failure', an idea largely alien to the Japanese people. They then initiated a series of measures directed at both a smaller government and the debureaucratization of government.

To meet this demand, in the 1980s the Second Provisional Commission for Administrative Reform (Second PCAR) and the Provisional Council for the Promotion of Administrative Reform were established within the Office of the Prime Minister to review overall administrative and financial policies. The Second PCAR aimed at the 'rehabilitation and reconstruction of public finance through the far-reaching rationalization of administrative functions and systems'. It sought a medium-sized government for Japan (Second PCAR 1984; Muramatsu 1987: 36).

In addition to building smaller government and reducing the financial debt, the Japanese government also wanted to respond to the rapidly changing international environment in light of such developments as the end of

Cold War and the expansion of globalization. First, the government deemed it necessary to improve the prime minister's policy-making and coordination capabilities. Policy-makers believed that the more complex and specialized public affairs became, the greater the need for policy coordination. In 1990, the Third Administrative Reform Promotion Committee under Prime Minister Kaifu stressed 'fostering internationalization' as one of its main objectives. The Committee emphasized that 'reinforcement of cabinet-level coordination function' was an important administrative reform. The goal of strengthening the prime minister's policy coordinating power was further underscored by the government of Prime Minister Hashimoto, which was elected in 1996 (Agata 2003). In establishing the Administrative Reform Conference right after the election, the Hashimoto government conducted aggressive measures to enhance its policy coordination capability, as well as to reduce and recast the size and process of government (Muramatsu 2001).

As a developing country founded in 1948, South Korea has continuously undertaken administrative reforms in order to respond effectively to the changing international and domestic environment, which affected national goals. The principal objectives of administrative reform of earlier periods were nation-building in the 1940s; restoring social order and reconstruction in the post-Korean War era of the 1950s; and facilitating rapid industrialization in the 1960s and 70s. The reform goals of that period reflected an ideology of 'administered development' (Caiden & Jung 1981). By contrast, the reforms initiated since the early 1980s have pushed for different goals. It all started with reconsideration of what the appropriate role of government is. As the nation was successful with the development of the heavy and chemical industries in the late 1970s, a number of policy-makers and experts began to think that the Korean economy no longer needed to rely on aggressive government interventions, which included the five-year economic development planning that had been a staple since 1962.

Such reconsideration of the appropriate role of government was further stimulated by the 'small government' idea prevalent in Anglo-Saxon countries. In 1980, the Chun Doo-hwan government adopted the idea of a market-oriented government. This was partially introduced through the 1981 Administrative Reform of 15 October, which in one move dismissed about 12% of the higher-ranking, central government civil servants (Jung 1997). From that time and at least until 2003 with the inauguration of the Roh Moo-hyun government, small government has been the norm in undertaking serious administrative reform in South Korea.

Since the democratic transition in 1987, the democratization of public administration has been another objective of public administration reform. In 1988, the Presidential Committee on Administrative Reform (PCAR), which initially consisted primarily of civilian experts, proposed as the most important reform goal a 'small and efficient government that would contribute to the formation of a democracy' (Jung 1997). Reducing the plethora of government regulations and decentralizing power, both between the central and local governments and within the bureaucracy, were among the major goals of the PCAR. The final proposal of the PCAR (PCAR, 1989) well reflects these reform goals. However, implementation was feeble. During the five years of the Rho Tae-woo government, the civil service increased by 180,000 at an average annual increase rate of 4.7% (Korean Institute of Public Administration 1996). In addition, the government did not effectively implement the reform goals of deregulation and decentralization. The Presidential Committee of Administrative Innovation (PCAI) which was formed in 1993 under the leadership of President Kim Young-sam and which again consisted primarily of civilian experts, publicized reform goals such as reforming 'the presently prevailing bureaucratic-minded institutions and practices', establishing a democratic and efficient administration, and building 'a lean, clean and strong government' (PCAI 1995: 14). By the end of 1997, however, the Kim government failed to manage a lack of foreign currency liquidity and had to request a rescue loan from the International Monetary Fund (IMF).

The government of Kim Dae-jung, inaugurated in February 1998, had to start its term by overcoming the foreign exchange crisis and the resultant economic difficulties. Korea's economic growth rate decreased from an average 7% since the 1960s to -6.5% in 1998. The unemployment rate, which had remained below 2.5% throughout the 1990s, increased to 8% in 1998. Under the supervision of the IMF, the Kim government aggressively conducted a series of structural adjustments in the financial, corporate, labor and public sectors. The IMF's guidelines for public sector restructuring devolved from the market-oriented reform model of 'New Public Management' (NPM). Unlike the previous four governments since the early 1980s, the incumbent Roh Moo-hyun government, inaugurated in 2003, did not adopt a small government policy. Instead, it proposed an 'efficient and capable government' as one of its most important reform goals. Other administrative reform objectives included 'making the government more open, transparent and closer to the people; improving the quality of life for people; and introducing simplified and uniform procedures' (PCGID 2003).

ACHIEVEMENTS

Administrative reform in Japan and South Korea since the early 1980s has resulted in meaningful changes in government size, administrative processes, policy coordination capacity and decentralization.

Downsizing Government and Deregulation

Both Japan and South Korea have kept their governments comparatively small. As Figures 1–3 show, the number of government employees as a percentage of the total workforce, the amount of public expenditures on wages as a percentage of GDP and total government expenditures as a percentage of GDP are the lowest among OECD countries. It needs to be stated that some of the main reasons include the low level of defense expenditures, in the case of Japan, and the equally low level of welfare expenditures in the case of South Korea. Still, since the early 1980s, both countries have promoted a small government as an important goal of administrative reform.

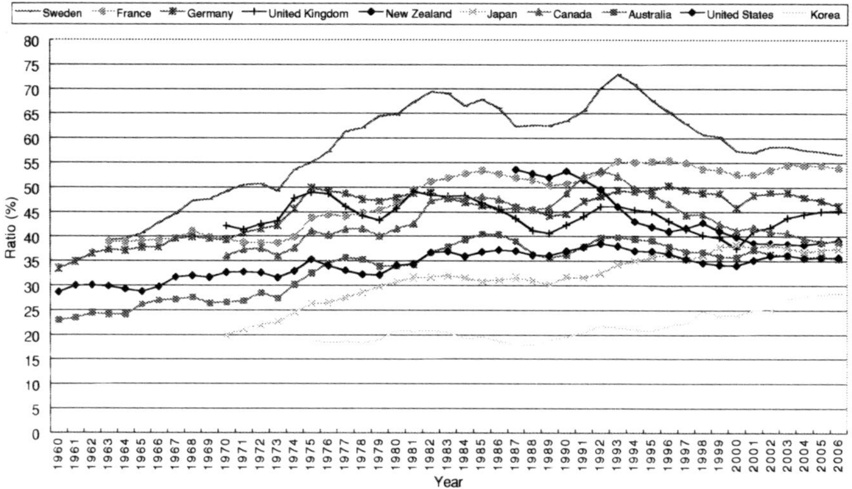

Source: Figures based on OECD Economic Outlook Database (http://new.sourceoecd.org).

Figure 1 Changes in Government Expenditures in Selected OECD Countries (Percentage of GDP)

Japan has had several successes in downsizing government. In the late 1980s, Japan privatized public corporations, which included the so-called Big Three: the National Railways, the Nippon Telegraph and Telephone, and the Japanese Tobacco and Salt Corporation, which together employed more than 90% of the public enterprises' workforce. Since then, the government has also privatized other public services such as nursing care services, postal services, highways, the Tokyo subways and sewer constructions. It has reformed the subsidies for public pensions, health care and rice. It has further eliminated dependence on deficit bond financing budget (Agata 2003). The government also conducted intra-organizational restructuring to reduce the number of divisions by 10%: this had eliminated 240 divisions by 1986 (Institute of Administrative Management 1995). Beginning in 1984, downsizing decreased government expenditures as a percentage of GDP; however, since 1992, this trend has been reversed (see Figure 1).

In 1968, the Japanese government introduced the Total Staff Number Control System to regulate the number of civil servants. Beginning in the early 1980s, the government opted for a more aggressive step by requiring all agencies to reduce the number of civil servants annually by specific percentages (Jung & Kim 1997). Since 1982, these measures resulted in decreased government employment as a percentage of total employment even with the decrease in the absolute number of public staff during the late 1980s. However, the absolute number and ratio of government employees to total employment levels have continually increased since the early 1990s (see Figure 2).

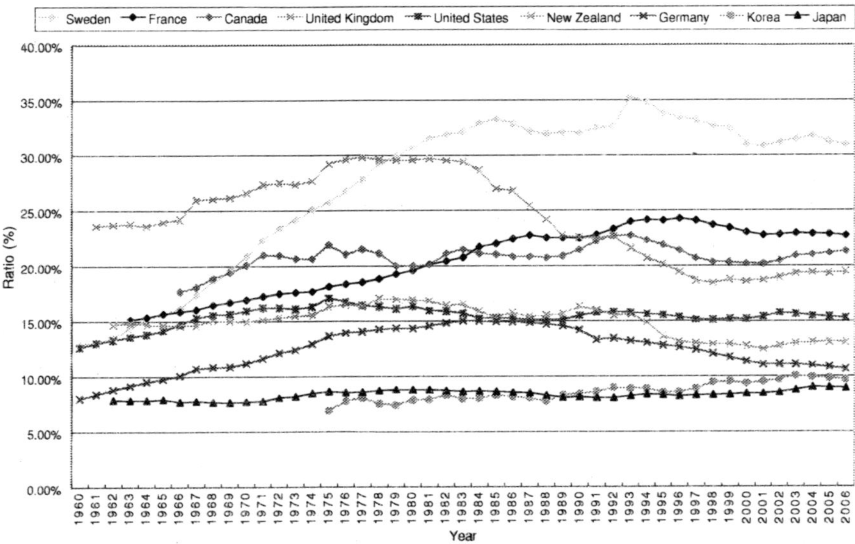

Figure 2 Changes in Government Employees in Selected OECD Countries (Percentage of Total Employees)

As noted above, the Chun government first applied the idea of small government in South Korea in 1981 with the reduction of 599 employees at the upper-division director level and 35,890 employees below that rank – altogether about 5% of the central government. This downsizing, however, focused mainly on reducing the number of civil servants without reducing the number of functions or positions of the central government. Consequently, the number of government employees increased again by about 1.7% in the following year. The Kim Young-sam government conducted reorganizations in 1993–94, which abolished a substantial number of positions in the central bureaucracy but failed to reduce the total number of public service employees. One reason for this was the National Public Service Act, which protected public servants from dismissal and created so-called 'satellite' personnel. With the exception of the years from 1998 to 2002 – immediately after the foreign exchange crisis – the total number of civil servants has continued to increase. The foreign exchange crisis of 1997 forced the Kim Dae-jung government to make structural adjustments and to adopt the New Public Management model in order to comply with the IMF recovery guidelines. However, since its inauguration in 2003, the Roh Moo-hyun government added about 50,000 civil servants to the workforce. From 1983 to 1988, the ratio of government to total employment decreased. By contrast, it has risen continually since then (Figure 2).

As one of its small government strategies, the South Korean government announced a privatization policy for public enterprises. Targeted for privatization by 1997 were 13 public enterprises, including the Big Four: the Korean Telecommunication Corporation, the Tobacco and Ginseng Corporation, the Korea Heavy Industry, and the Korea Gas Corporation. Because of fluctuating stock markets, however, the privatization plan was implemented slowly and incrementally. Another constraint was the reluctant compliance of the powerful Ministry of Finance and Economy, which has been a stakeholder in public enterprises. One of the major reasons for this reluctance may have been the practice of some higher-ranking officials in the economic bureaucracy of transferring to a high position in a related public enterprise after retiring from public service. This 'parachute staffing' was a thorn in the flesh of the public sector unions, who held a veto over the privatization of the public enterprises.

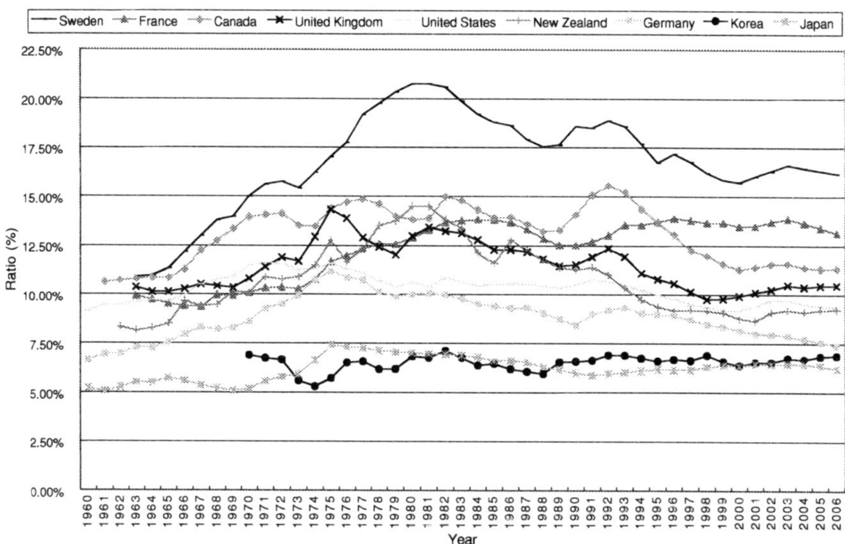

Figure 3 Changes in Government Consumption of Wages in Selected OECD Countries (Percentage of GDP)

In the 1980s, South Korea's government expenditure as a percentage of GDP was among the lowest of the OECD countries at about 20% with no financial deficit. Consequently, the government did not take seriously the issue of budget size and did not present a specific expenditure reduction plan. Since 1988, public expenditure has continually expanded by nearly 10% during the 2000s (Figure 1).

The process of political democratization can explain this continuous growth of the South Korean government. Since 1987, the democratic transition has intensified the demands for services, especially in favor of the poor, disabled or aged, of women and the young. The new political environment with a more competitive electoral process has forced the policy-makers to comply with such demands.

Although Japan and South Korea have not been as successful at downsizing government as they planned, their governments remain the smallest among OECD countries. In addition to the aforementioned, the underdevelopment of welfare state policies in South Korea and the restrained buildup of military power in Japan, as well as great reliance on regulatory policies, helped explain why governments were able to remain small in both countries. Both governments have made use of a wide variety of regulatory policies, including the so-called administrative guidance, which allows for discretionary administrative intervention without legislative approval. In general, regulatory policies contribute to keeping a government quantitatively small by transferring the implementation costs to the regulated.

Since the early 1980s, both governments have invested considerably in regulatory reforms in order to revitalize business. Based on a series of recommendations by the administrative reform committees, the Japanese government has consistently implemented wide-ranging deregulation policies. These include the Emergency Economic Measures of September 1993 (94 items), the Midterm Administrative Reform Program of February 1994 (250 items) and the abolition or simplification of 151 reporting requirements. In June 1994, 279 items were deregulated, some in priority areas such as the expanding domestic demand and the promotion of imports, which led to narrowing price differentials between Japan and the rest of the world. However, the total number of regulations increased by 527 items from 10,054 in 1985 to 10,581 in 1990. To tighten regulations, 344 new regulatory items were also added although the nature of regulation has changed from strong to weak (Institute of Administrative Management 1995).

The South Korean government also initiated a wide variety of deregulations by establishing the PCAR (1993–1998), the Economic Deregulation Commission (1993–1997) and the Regulatory Reform Council (1998–). According to the official annual reports, a number of administrative procedures and regulations have been improved. For example, 1,880 among the 2,177 regulatory reform cases filed in 1993–96 were settled (Jung 2001). However, 70% of the cases settled by the PCAR were procedural rationalizations, while merely 10% involved the abolition of regulatory functions. Under the Roh administration, the number of government regulations has tended to increase. During the first year of government, the regulatory practice increased from 7,575 cases to 7,797 cases. The 'sunset law' was applied to only 0.58% of total government regulations (Kwon 2005).

Reorganizations and Enhancement of Policy Coordination Capacity

The South Korean and Japanese governments also aimed at improving the policy coordination mechanism of the core executive. The Second PCAR initiated in 1981 in Japan under the leadership of Prime Minister Nakasone proposed a series of measures to strengthen the prime minister's and the cabinet's capacities in policy-making and coordination. In 1986, the Second PCAR's recommendation succeeded in reorganizing the Prime Minister's Office by establishing six new sections in charge of domestic and foreign affairs, and the National Security Council as an improved organization of the former Defense Council. Furthermore, in 1984 the Nakasone government integrated the Administrative Management Agency and related sections of the Prime Minister's Office into the newly created Management and Coordination Agency. This new central agency became responsible for ensuring that central government management was 'efficient, responsive and well coordinated' (Abe, Shindo & Kawato 1994). By contrast, it failed to create a General Planning Council under the Prime Minister's Office (Muramatsu 1987).

In the late 1990s, additional aggressive measures enhanced the powers of the prime minister and the cabinet. In 1996, Prime Minister Hashimoto established the Administrative Reform Conference (ARC), which proposed several measures to strengthen the core executive's policy-making capabilities. These included the establishment of a new Cabinet Office (replacing the Prime Minister's Office) to empower the Cabinet Secretariat. It has also created the Ministers for Special Missions, the Council on Economic and Fiscal Policy (an 'amalgam organization' modeled on the British Public Service and Public Expenditure Cabinet Meeting and the American Council of Economic Advisors), the Council on Science and Technology Policy, and other councils for information technology, social security, specialized zones and tourism (Shiroyama 2005). Another institutional achievement was the elevation of the former Management and Coordination Agency (upgraded in 1984) to become the Ministry of General Affairs.

In order to realize these proposals, in 1998 the Hashimoto government enacted the Basic Law for Central Government Reform and in 2001 inaugurated the new administrative system. Under this law, the government introduced a new super-ministry system, which encompassed one office and 12 ministries, to replace the former one office and 22 ministries that had been in existence since the early 1950s (see Table 2). This radical reorgani-

Table 2 Central Government Reorganizations Conducted in 2001 in Japan

Before January 2001	After January 2001
Prime Minister's Office	
Economic Planning Agency	
Development Agency, Okinawa	Cabinet Office
Ministry of Finance	Financial Security Agency Ministry of Finance
Defense Agency	Defense Agency
National Public Safety Commission	National Public Safety Commission
Agency of General Affairs	
Ministry of Home Affairs	Ministry of Public Management
Ministry of Post and Telecommunications	
Ministry of Justice	Ministry of Justice
Ministry of Foreign Affairs	Ministry of Foreign Affairs
Ministry of Education	Ministry of Education, Culture, Sports, Science and Technology
Agency of Science and Technology	
Ministry of Health	Ministry of Health, Labor and Welfare
Ministry of Labor	
Ministry of Agriculture, Forestry and Fisheries	Ministry of Agriculture, Forestry and Fisheries
Ministry of International Trade and Industry	Ministry of Economy, Trade and Industry
Ministry of Construction	Ministry of Land, Infrastructure and Transport
Ministry of Transport	
Land Agency	
Development Agency, Hokkaido	
Environment Agency	Ministry of Environment

Source: Agata 2003.

zation of the central ministries was designed to strengthen the core executive's coordinating power between ministries, by reducing the span of control and entrenched departmentalism.

The South Korean government also conducted a series of reorganizations designed to improve the policy coordination mechanism and to reduce the size of government. Policy coordination among agencies was difficult because of the incremental growth of the administrative apparatus during the years of rapid industrialization; this led to a number of functional overlaps among government ministries and agencies. To improve policy coordination and streamline the policy process, the reform committees proposed a super-ministry system that would merge the related organizations and functions of different agencies. The Kim Young-sam government succeeded in reorganizing the central government dramatically by abolishing three ministries, one agency and one outer-bureau (Jung 1997). At this point, the powerful pilot agency of South Korea's developmental state, the Economic Planning Board, merged with the Ministry of Finance to establish the new Ministry of Finance and Economy. The 1993 reorganization eliminated four ministers, five vice-ministers, five deputy vice-ministers, 34 bureau directors general, 127 division directors and 966 staff below the rank of division director. However, the Kim Young-sam government was probably less than consistent because in 1996 it established a new Ministry of Oceanography and Marine Resources. Since that time, the super-ministry system, as a strategy for enhancing policy coordination capacity and for reducing government size, has lain dormant.

In fact, the South Korean government has established a number of new institutions in response to post-industrialization and post-democratic transition issues (Table 3). The former includes the establishment of the Ministry of Labor (1981), the Ministry of Environment (1990), the Fair Trade

Table 3 Central Government Organizations Created in Korea since 1980

Agencies	Year	Agencies	Year
Ministry of Labor	1981	Presidential Truth Commission on Suspicious Deaths	2000
Constitutional Court	1988	Ministry of Gender Equality	2001
National Economic Advisory Council	1990	National Human Rights Commission	2001
Ministry of Environment	1990	Korea Independent Commission Against Corruption	2002
Fair Trade Commission	1994	National Assembly Budget Office	2004
Presidential Advisory Council on Science and Technology	1994	National Emergency Management Agency	2004
Ombudsman of Korea	1994	Defense Procurement Agency	2005
Korea Food and Drug Administration	1998	Higher Officials Maladministration Investigation Agency	2005
Financial Supervisory Commission	1998		
Ministry of Planning and Budget	1998		
Civil Service Commission	1999		
Government Information Agency	1999		

Commission (1994) and the Financial Supervisory Commission (1998). The latter includes the Constitutional Court (1988), the National Ombudsman (1994), the Ministry of Gender Equality (2001) and the Higher Officials Maladministration Investigation Agency (2005). These new institutions have resulted in greater democratization of public administration. They have improved the checks and balances within the government and provided citizens and interest groups with greater access to government. Such accretions and the resultant pluralized system have made the tasks of policy coordination more difficult. Nevertheless, when compared to Japan, the South Korean core executive has maintained a high level of policy coordination capacity with such effective institutional support mechanisms as the powerful Presidential Secretariat, the Prime Minister's Policy Coordination Office and central agencies.

Process Reengineering and Decentralization

The Japanese and South Korean governments have publicized as one of their reform goals the reengineering of administrative processes to overcome bureaucratic inefficiencies. These reforms include empowering lower levels of administration, institutionalizing a performance evaluation system, creating British-style executive agencies and developing e-Government.

Both governments have delegated decision-making power to lower levels of public administration. The Japanese government initiated measures to 'make administrative organizations flat' and to 'make the managers manage' (Agata 2003; Shiroyama 2005). To realize the goal of 'making the managers manage', the government introduced the Policy Evaluation System (PES) in January 2001. The PES is composed of three levels of evaluation: self-evaluation by each ministry and agency, interministerial evaluations and recommendations by the Administrative Evaluation Bureau of the Ministry of General Affairs (MGA), and meta-evaluation by the Commission on Policy Evaluation (www.soumu.go.jp). These are expected to enhance administrative flexibility within bureaucracy.

Significantly, these measures have also strengthened the core executive's policy coordination capability. For example, the MGA, the central agency upgraded in 2001, has effectively contributed to enhancing the core executive's power to control ministries by performing administrative inspection and policy evaluation functions. Public personnel administration is another telling example. The personnel policy of the core executive is, since 2001, more effectively supported by the upgraded central agency MGA. Under the new system, moreover, public personnel administration within a ministry has been under the leadership of its newly created and politically appointed senior vice-minister, who ranks above the existing political and administrative vice-ministers. Previously, the administrative vice-minister, who was an appointed career bureaucrat, was the de facto decision-maker in charge of personnel administration with respect to standard operating procedures within the ministry (Onishi 1998).

Compared to Japan, South Korea has been more aggressive in seeking decentralization. Policy coordination among the ministries and agencies has been hierarchical, stemming from the Presidential Secretariat at the Blue House and the powerful central agencies such as the Economic Planning Board (the Ministry of Planning and Budget since 1998). Since the democratic transition of 1987, presidents have promised to decentralize the administrative system. However, to this day, no government has effectively implemented those promises. Instead, they have maintained about ten Senior Secretary Offices that have been a de facto inner cabinet, along with about six central agencies. Even the government of former opposition leader Kim Dae-jung strengthened the president's policy coordination powers, albeit in the name of conducting the structural adjustment plans effectively.

Still, the Roh Moo-hyun government has conducted a series of structural adjustments of the core executive. Upon assuming office, President Roh reorganized the presidential secretariat into two Policy Secretary Offices to deal with macro-policy issues, and delegated detailed policy coordination functions to the Prime Minister's Policy Coordination Office. The central agencies have also delegated some of their administrative control functions to line ministries. These include delegation of the detailed budget reviewing functions of the Ministry of Planning and Budget; the detailed organizing and staff number controlling functions of the Ministry of Government Administration and Home Affairs; the personnel administration controlling functions of the Civil Service Commission; and the legality-oriented auditing functions of the Board of Audit and Inspection. These reform measures should improve administrative flexibility by reducing the regulations imposed on the line ministries and agencies by the central agencies.

The Roh government has also initiated a more 'open, contract-based, performance-based personnel management system' by establishing the Senior Executive Service for all 1,400 G1 to G3 level civil servants; by 'swapping' director-general level staff between ministries; and by the imposition of a 'total salary cost system'. These new personnel administration systems will, it is expected, make the administrative bureaucracy more flexible by partially deconstructing the career civil service system. The new system will also enhance the core executive's administrative power over ministries on personnel policy. In addition, the Comprehensive Performance Evaluation System will enhance the core executive's control over the bureaucracy, which will guarantee administrative accountability in line with decentralization.

Since the late 1990s, both Japan and South Korea have introduced the executive agency system. However, their agencification attempts are limited by comparison to the UK, Australia and New Zealand. Most importantly, the number of agencies involved is limited. Since 2000, the Korean government has established 23 Administrative Executive Agencies (AEA) that implement routine policy functions such as issuing driver's licenses and operating national theaters. Since 2001, the Japanese government has created 197 Independent Administrative Institutions (IAI) that include such research and training institutions as the National Environmental Research Institute and 99 national universities such as Tokyo University.

The Japanese and South Korean executive agencies differ also from those of the British Commonwealth countries in terms of their operations. Although the CEOs are appointed by an open competition, the staff retain their civil servant status with the exception of Japanese national universities. More importantly, it is uncertain that the new system has overcome the hierarchical relationships between the ministry and the agencies. In both countries, the agencies' personnel and budget administration are not flexible enough to secure independence from the ministries. The Japanese government intended to grant the IAIs a limited autonomy from the ministries by introducing the self-evaluation system and the third-party evaluation systems of the Evaluation Committee for IAIs. However, these evaluation systems have not worked because of inadequate resources and personnel, and ambiguous policy objectives (Shiroyama 2005).

E-Government projects are another attempt at debureaucratization. The Japanese government introduced three systems of networks: among government organizations (e.g., the LGWAN), between governments and market 'e-Procurement', and between governments and citizens (Agata 2003). The South Korean government has even achieved the world's highest level of e-Government and ranks within the top ten countries in terms of PC supplies (with 26 million), development of the super-rapid cable networks, digitalization of all government documents and the number of internet users (with 32 million) (NCA 2005). Paradoxically, the level of information-sharing between the administrative units remains low, indicating strong resilience of the bureaucratic bottlenecks. The South Korean government is at the fourth step of e-Government ('e-Transaction'), yet has not attained the fifth step ('seamless integration') (United Nations 2002). According to a United Nations report published in 2004, South Korea and Japan rank 5th and 18th respectively among 178 counties in an e-Government Readiness Index, and 6th and 21st respectively among the UN member states in an e-Participation Index (United Nations 2004).

Since the late 1990s, Japan and South Korea have considered decentralization between the central and local governments an important strategy towards a flexible and efficient administration. Both countries fostered autonomous local government systems immediately after World War II. Japan enacted the New Constitution of 1947 to establish autonomous local governments; the Local Autonomy Law was based on that provision. The same year, local councils were formed and the local chief executives were elected by universal suffrage. Autonomous local government systems have remained relatively stable since then (Muramatsu 1987). South Korea enshrined the principle of local autonomy in the constitution of the First Republic of 1948 and enacted the Local Autonomy Law based on that provision. In 1952, local councils were established for the first time and local chief executives were elected through universal suffrage. After 1961, however, the military dictatorship suspended local autonomy and so it remained dormant for 30 years (Jung 1987). As the transition toward democracy gained momentum in the late 1980s, the South Korean government instituted a series of reforms to prepare for the resurrection of local autonomy. It reformed the local councils in 1991 and began electing the local chief executives by popular vote in 1995.

Despite these differences in the institutionalization of local autonomy, South Korea and Japan have a number of similar, centralized intergovernmental institutions. Following the postwar reforms and the emergence of autonomous local governments, it was expected that some central government functions – particularly policy implementation functions – would be transferred to local governments. However, rather than transfer those functions to local governments, the central governments both in Japan and in South Korea retained conventional control by various institutional arrangements. For example, the central government of both countries organized Special Local Administrative Agencies designed to implement public policies directly at the local level. Currently, the Korean central government ministries have 316 such special local administrative agencies; the Japanese government has 189 (Jung 2002; Abe, Shindo & Kawato 1994).

Another typical example of this attempt to retain control in the central governments' agency delegation, is the practice of delegating administrative tasks to local governments without corresponding jurisdictional changes. In the 1990s in Korea, 48% of all local governments' tasks were tasks of agency delegation from the central government; in Japan, the figures were 80% of all first-tier tasks and 50% of all second-tier tasks of local governments (Jung 2002; Abe, Shindo & Kawato 1994; Muramatsu 2001). Furthermore, the Korean and the Japanese central governments retained a number of control mechanisms over local governments' personnel management, public finance and budgeting, and reorganization.

Since the mid-1990s, both governments have invested considerably in decentralization. In Japan, these efforts resulted first in the passage of the Decentralization Promotion Act of 1995 which established the Decentralization Promotion Commission (1995–2000), and then in the Comprehensive Law for Local Decentralization of 1999 which was to revise 475 laws related to decentralization (Muramatsu 2001). In this process of devolutionary reforms, the Japanese government publicized its intention to apply the principle of subsidiarity, which the European Union developed into a general principle for all its member states (Endo 2005).

Since the late 1990s, the South Korean government, too, has instituted a series of devolutionary reforms. Pursuant to the recommendations of the Local Transformation Promotion Committee (1999–), 917 administrative functions of the central government were devolved to first- and second-tier local governments. Following the recommendations of the Presidential Committee for Government Innovation and Decentralization (2003–), the Roh government passed the Special Law for Decentralization and the Comprehensive Law for Local Transfer, and adopted principles such as 'decentralization first and establishment later' and 'subsidiarity' (PCGID 2003). Additionally, decentralized systems for police and education administration are now in the process of legislation.

CONCLUSION

The above discussion illustrates similarities and differences among the goals, concerns, efforts and results of the administrative reform efforts conducted in Japan and South Korea since the early 1980s. Both countries have pursued a small government policy but with different motives and results. Japan initiated a small government policy principally in order to solve the deficit problem that the country has confronted since the 1970s, whereas Korea's major motivation for a small government policy was related to the desire for political and administrative democratization and a free market economy. Japan has been relatively successful in implementing small government initiatives by reducing the public staff and public sector budget. By contrast, with the exception of the five years of post-IMF structural adjustments, South Korea has not achieved its announced intention of downsizing government; government staff and budgets have increased continually. Political democratization since the late 1980s has caused an expansion of public service demands in addition to policy-makers' compliance with those demands. In spite of these differences in goals and performances, the two countries share a desire to keep their staff and budgets at the lowest level of the OECD countries.

Japan and South Korea's unsuccessful attempts at regulatory reform can partially explain their maintaining small governments. Both countries institutionalized highly effective regulatory systems that include administrative guidance, which is a discretionary administrative power by which administrative agencies exercise an influence on decision-making by civil society. In general, government regulation as a policy tool contributes to keeping governments small by transferring the implementation costs to the regulated. Consequently, Japan and South Korea share another commonality. Both retain the characteristics of strong states largely thanks to their regulatory mechanisms – regardless of their comparatively small governments.

The two countries have different reform agendas for the core executive's policy leadership. The Japanese government has intended to augment the prime minister's policy capabilities, while the South Korean government announced that it intended to decrease the president's power. Japan has been relatively successful at increasing the core executive's policy coordination capabilities by institutionalizing some central agencies, strengthening ministerial leadership on personnel policy and reducing the number of ministries and agencies. These institutional changes have improved the coordination and bureaucracy nexus in the policy process. In South Korea, by contrast, the policy coordination capabilities of the core executive have decreased somewhat with the incumbent Roh government, because of delegation of decision-making powers to the lower-level administrative units on the one hand and the enlarged 'span of control' caused by the newly established ministries and organizations on the other. Nevertheless, the president has retained significant powers of control over the core executive and the bureaucracy because of the central agencies' new tools such as performance-based audit and personnel and budgetary management. Therefore, regardless of their differing goals, in neither country have the core executive reforms resulted in a significant reduction of the strong central government leadership that states enjoyed during the twentieth century.

Finally, both countries have pursued or have at least announced their intention to pursue debureaucratization. South Korea has been more successful in this than Japan because it has pushed ahead with process reengineering, by delegating administrative functions to lower-level administrative units and by establishing e-Government at the higher level. Nevertheless, neither government has devolved significant administrative authority to lower-level administrators. The issue of debureaucratization seems to be a difficult one in both countries, whose institutional traditions are steeped in the typical 'machine bureaucracy'. The 'pass-the-word-down' control mechanism embedded in the 'machine bureaucracy' has also contributed to maintaining a strong authoritarian tradition in both countries.

Overall, by adopting the reform models of the English-speaking OECD countries, Japan and South Korea have invested considerable effort in administrative reforms with some significant achievements. However, the outcome to date displays the Asiatic administrative state model rather than pointing to the Anglo-American model. This suggests that the policy guidelines and implementation of administrative reforms are selectively adopted in a manner and direction that maintains and sometimes reinforces the previously established institutional structure of the state.

REFERENCES

Abe, H., Shindo, M., & Kawato, S. (1994). *The Government and Politics of Japan*. Tokyo: University of Tokyo Press.

Agata, A. (2003). 'Administrative Modernization in Japan since 1980s'. Paper presented at the International Conference on the Alexander von Humboldt Foundation's 50th Anniversary (The Public Sector in Transition: East Asia and the European Union Compared). Berlin, 7–10 December.

Bai, Z. (2005). 'The Acceptance of "PA" in China and the School of Government at Peking University'. Paper presented at the International Workshop on Government Reform and the Role of Public Policy and Administration Schools. Tokyo University, 16 February.

Balme, R. (2004). 'Institutional Change in Comparative Perspective: A European View on State Reform in China'. Paper presented at the Alexander von Humboldt Foundation–International Institute of Advanced Studies Conference. Kyoto, 14–16 October.

Caiden, G., & Jung, Y. (1981). 'The Political Economy of Korean Development under the Park Government'. *Journal of Public and International Affairs* 2 (2), pp. 173–83.

Caiden, G., & Caiden, N. (2000). 'Toward More Democratic Governance: Modernizing the Administrative State in Australia, North America, and the United Kingdom'. *Korean Journal of Policy Studies* 15 (1), pp. 1–24.

Chinese Public Administration Society (2003). *Public Administration Innovation in China*. Beijing: Chinese Review of Public Administration. (In Chinese.)

Endo, K. (2005). 'A Political Thought for the Age of Globalization? "Subsidiarity" in the Post-National Governance in Europe and Japan'. Paper presented at the IPSA R-17 International Conference (Globalization and the Governance Model Types). Berkeley, CA: UC, 26–27 February.

Hood, C. (1999). *The Art of the State: Culture, Rhetoric and Public Management*. Oxford: Oxford University Press.

Institute of Administrative Management (1995). *The Management and Reform of Japanese Government*. Tokyo: IAM.

Jung, Y. (1987). 'The Territorial Dimension of the Developing Capitalist State: Measuring and Explaining Centralization in Korea'. *International Review of Administrative Sciences* 53, pp. 128–53.

Jung, Y. (1997). 'Administrative Reorganization in the Strong State'. In Y. Cho & G. Frederickson (Eds), *The White House and the Blue House: Government Reform in the United States and Korea* (pp. 89–110). Lanham, Maryland: UP of America.

Jung, Y. (2001). 'Globalization and the Institutional Persistence of the Developmental State in Korea'. *Korean Journal of Policy Studies* 15 (2), pp. 27–40.

Jung, Y. (2002). *The State Apparatus in Korea and Japan*. Seoul: Daeyoung. (In Korean.)

Jung, Y. (2005). 'Stateness in Transition: The Korean Case in a Comparative Perspective'. *Zeitschrift für Staats- und Europawissenschaften* 3 (3), pp. 1–22.

Jung, Y. & Kim, K. (1997). 'The State Institutions and Policy Capabilities: A Comparative Analysis of the Administrative Reforms in Japan and Korea'. Paper presented at the XVII World Congress of the International Political Science Association (Conflict and Order). Seoul, 17–21 August.

Kim, Y. (2004). 'The Institutional Changes of the State Administration'. Unpublished Doctoral Dissertation, Seoul National University.

Korean Institute of Public Administration (1996). *Statistical Data of Public Administration.* Seoul: KIPA.

Kumon, S. (1984). 'Japan Faces Its Future: The Political-Economics of Administrative Reform'. *Journal of Japanese Studies* 10 (1), pp. 143–65.

Kwon, H. (2005). 'A Critical Review on the Administrative Reform of the "Participatory Government"'. *Korean Society and Public Administration* 16 (1), 35–56.

Li, S. (2000). 'Institutional Characteristics of Administrative System and the Administrative Reforms in China'. MPA Thesis, Seoul National University.

McCubbins, M. & Noble, G. (1995). 'The Appearance of Power: Legislators, Bureaucrats and the Budget Process in the United States and Japan'. In P. Cowhey & M. McCubbins (Eds), *Structure and Policy in Japan and the United States* (pp. 56–80). Cambridge: Cambridge University Press.

Muramatsu, M. (1987). 'In Search of National Identity: The Politics and Policies of the Nakasone Administration'. *Journal of Japanese Studies* 13, pp. 307–42.

Muramatsu, M. (2001). 'The Sudden Emergence of NPM Reforms in Japan'. Paper presented at the International Conference of the Korean Association for Public Administration (The State, Governance, and Civil Service: Transition and Continuity in Comparative Perspectives). Seoul, 13–16 October.

National School of Administration (1999). *Reorganization of the Administrative Apparatuses in China.* Beijing: National School of Administration Press. (In Chinese.)

NCA (2005). *National Informatization White Paper.* Seoul: National Computerization Agency. (In Korean.)

Nishikawa, Y. (2004). 'Visions of Public Administration in Modern Japan between East and West: A Historical and Comparative Analysis'. Paper presented at the Alexander von Humboldt Foundation-IIAS Conference. Kyoto, 14–16 October.

Onishi, Y. (1998). 'A Comparative Study on the Ministerial Reorganization in Japan and Korea'. *Leviathan* 23, pp. 126–50. (In Japanese.)

Painter, M. (2005). 'Transforming the Administrative State: Reform in Hong Kong and the Future of the Developmental State'. *Public Administration Review* 65 (3), pp. 335–46.

PCAI (1995). *Administrative Innovation in Korea: In Search of New*

Paradigms. Seoul: Presidential Committee for Administrative Innovation. (In Korean.)

PCAR (1989). *Proposal for Administrative Reform*. Seoul: Presidential Committee for Administrative Reform.

PCGID (2003). *Roadmap for Government Innovation and Decentralization*. Seoul. Presidential Committee for Government Innovation and Decentralization. (Also available at www.innovation.go.kr.)

Saich, T. (2001). *Governance and Politics in China*. New York: Palgrave.

Second PCAR (1984). *The Final Report on Administrative Reform*. Tokyo: Institute of Administrative Management. (In Japanese.)

Shiroyama, H. (2005). 'Public Sector Reform in Japan'. Paper presented at the International Workshop on Government Reform and the Role of Public Policy and Administration Schools. Tokyo University, 16 February.

Thompson, M. (1996). 'Late Industrializers, Late Democratizers: Developmental States in the Asian Pacific'. *Third World Quarterly* 17 (4), pp. 625–47.

United Nations (2002). *Benchmarking E-Government: A Global Perspective. Assessing the Progress of the UN Member States*. NY: UNDPEPA/ASPA.

United Nations (2004). *Global e-Government Report: Towards Access for Opportunity* (www.unpan.org/egovernment4.asp).

NOTES

1 Interestingly, since the early 1980s, public administration has been resurrected as an academic discipline in China. The Chinese government now allows universities and government training institutions to offer public administration courses and has established the Chinese Public Administration Society. Before 1949, public administration was taught in universities and civil service training institutions, but in 1952 the University Department Reform Act abolished all public administration courses and programs (Bai 2005).

8

The Australian Public Service in Transition, 1972–2004

DENISE K. CONROY

INTRODUCTION

Few textbooks on Australian public administration provide an historical context, but Caiden's two early studies *Career Service* (1965) and *The Commonwealth Bureaucracy* (1967) are exceptions. He accepted the premise that the historiography of administrative history could not be understood if not explicitly linked to the political, social and economic environment in which it occurs.

To some extent, the monographs on governments produced by the Centre for Research in Public Sector Management, by the Institute of Public Administration Australia (since 1983) and more recently the administrative essays published in the *Australian Journal of Public Administration* fill a gap in changes to Australian Commonwealth Administration – as do some of the key references in this chapter. However, Caiden's scholarship and early historical writings referred to above as well as his other contributions to the Australian discipline and its practice are exemplars for those interested in the administrative history of Australian Public Service (APS).[1]

It is a privilege to be invited to honor Gerald Elliot Caiden in this *Festschrift*, because he has exerted considerable influence, both directly and indirectly, on public administration in Australia from the time when he completed his 1959 doctoral dissertation (titled 'A Comparative Study of the Commonwealth Public Service of Australia and the Federal Civil Service of Canada') to the present.

In 2001, the federal Australian Public Service celebrated its centenary. Public administration commenced under colonial rule (first settlement in New South Wales in 1788) and at the federal level in January 1901, upon the establishment of the Commonwealth of Australia. Ours is a relatively recent history compared to public administration in the USA and in most Western European countries. From early times, Australian colonies embodied their structures for public service management in legislation and their principles of public service in British civil service reforms of the nineteenth century, particularly the Northcote & Trevelyan Report. There have been three Public Service Acts governing Australian public service (1902, 1922 and 1999).

This chapter provides a brief overview of federal Australian public administration in transition – particularly from the 1970s onwards. The major focus is on reforms affecting the Portfolio Departments of the Australian Public Service. It is not possible, given the length allocated to this chapter, to cover comprehensively all reforms of the period under discussion, so the major changes are discussed by political period: the government ministries (see Appendix A). The major changes to the public service will be presented first with the social, economic and political conditions identified, which will be followed by an analysis of the major trends and influences which the reforms reflect.

HISTORICAL BACKGROUND

On the establishment of a federal system of government on 1 January 1901, Australia's first Governor General through Executive Council created the first seven departments of the Commonwealth. This structure lasted for ten years until the creation of a separate Prime Minister's Office (previously External Affairs). The Postmaster-General's Department was the largest, making up 89% of the service on its inception (post, telegraph and telephone services were transferred from the states on Federation) and remained so until it became two statutory authorities in 1975 (PSMPC 2001a: chapter 1). It was not until World War II that the number of departments increased significantly from nine in 1916, ten in 1921 and 13 in 1931 to 25 in 1941 (Caiden 1965: 450). This number of departments remained fairly constant until 1987 although there were a number of changes through amalgamations, new departments, cessations and 'splits' (see Appendix A).

The APS from its inception to the 1960s has been well covered by Caiden (1965; 1967). In *The Commonwealth Bureaucracy*, Caiden suggested that, given Australia's transplanted culture, 'it could not be expected to evolve a distinctive administrative style of its own, particularly when its derived political institutions have experienced universal tendencies in their development' (1967: 3). However, he found that in public personnel administration, Australia was in some respects ahead of other countries.

During the 1960s, Australia experienced relative economic prosperity, full employment and low inflation. The public sector at that time was responsible for 40% of capital expenditure, 25% of the labor force and 20% of gross national expenditure. The labor movement was highly organized with three unions represented in the APS (Caiden 1967: 6–26). In the post-war period 1949–1972, Australia experienced a stretch of 23 years of liberal/conservative rule with 12 successive governments (Menzies to McMahon; see Appendix A). Menzies followed the Chifley government's initiatives but a significant development was the 'grab for power' in matters relevant to trade by the Trade Department, so much so that it challenged the authority of the Treasury on commercial matters (Whitwell in PSMPC 2001a: 52). Through the 1960s and 70s, the central offices of almost all departments moved to Canberra, involving 4,700 staff from 18 departments and agencies (PSMPC 2001a: 90). Under the Menzies government, Aboriginals became eligible for the first time for social security/welfare benefits and they were given the right to vote in national and state elections. In a successful 1967 referendum (Constitutional Amendment), the Commonwealth was able to make laws on Aboriginal affairs and they were to be included in population censuses (PSMPC 2001a: 54).

The conservative governments under Menzies favored a professional and apolitical public service – a true 'career service' notion where merit is based solely on the ability to perform in the job. However, Menzies did not support the recommendation of the 1958 Boyer Committee that Second Division public servants be selected by an entrance exam similar to the British Administrative Class at that time. The major thrusts of the Committee's recommendations were subsequently implemented by a new Public Service Board Chairman (Frederick Wheeler) through reviews of occupational categories (PSMPC 2001a: 157).

Menzies' return to government in 1949 (he had previously served from 1939 to 1941) took place when the preceding Chifley government's economic reforms were beginning to bear fruit. There was also an economic stimulus from Australia's involvement in the Korean War and the post-World War II mass-migration program. In 1951, Menzies instructed that public service staff be reduced by 10,000, but this was achieved by reducing temporary and exempt staff (Castleman 1992: 202).

After his 1955 election, Menzies introduced further reforms to improve cabinet efficiency. In 1951, he had already streamlined the way in which cabinet submissions were presented and dealt with. In 1955, he created an 'inner' and an 'outer' cabinet to distinguish the ministers concerned with policy-making from those concerned with administration. His acceleration of the relocation of public servants and departments to Canberra was also aimed at achieving efficiency. The development of the national capital Canberra had been slowed by the 1930s depression and by World War II. Relocated public servants from Melbourne began arriving in 1958 and Canberra's population grew from 28,000 in 1954 to 93,000 when Menzies retired in 1966 (*Australia's Prime Ministers – Robert Menzies* [n.d.]).

The coalition governments which followed Menzies – Holt, Gorton and McMahon – made minor changes to the machinery of government as it affected the public service. The number of departments fluctuated little between 1966 and 1972 and there were no significant changes to the APS during this period other than those associated with departmental changes. The beginning of a 'new' era in public sector reforms started with the Whitlam government in 1972.

GOUGH WHITLAM (1972–75)

The Whitlam government was elected in December 1972 following 23 years of conservative rule. The economic environment of the 1950s and 60s had been one of unprecedented economic growth, full employment and low inflation. Australia's trade balance was favorable and there had been a high level of foreign investment which offset an overall current-account deficit. The Australian dollar was 10–12% above the US dollar during this period. However, by the early 1970s this situation was changing. The Australian dollar was 'sliding' with wage rises, and an increased money supply was contributing to a rapid increase in inflation. In 1971–72, the unemployment rate went up to 2.5% and the annual CPI change was 6.8% (Matthews & Grewal 1995: 1–30).

Against this economic background, the Whitlam government came to power with a swag of reforms based on a social-democratic ideology coupled with inexperience because of 23 years on the opposition benches. Much of the 'vision' came from Whitlam himself and was hastily put into action during a 14-day *duumvirate* where Whitlam (Prime Minister) and Barnard (Deputy Prime Minister) held 27 portfolios between them, pending the appointment of ministers (*Australia's Prime Ministers – Gough Whitlam* [n.d.]).

The scope of change attempted by the Whitlam government is perhaps best depicted by the 120 inquiries it established (Prasser 1985: 10–12). In part, this was due to distrust of the public service, although Whitlam claimed it was to seek some new ideas (Whitlam 1973). He adapted the machinery of government changes to his vision for reform. On assuming government Whitlam abolished six existing departments, created 16 new ones and renamed two others. This resulted in movement of personnel (particularly heads of departments) and staff increases (Walter 1980: 55). Full-time staff increased each year of Whitlam's government from 244,361 in 1972, to 254,367 in 1973, to 266,752 in 1974 and 277,455 in 1975 – a 13.6% overall increase (Australian Public Service Board 1977: Table 100). Whitlam also institutionalized the role of personal advisors.

Committees of note during Whitlam's period of government were the Commission of Enquiry into the Australian Post Office (1974), and the Committee on Administrative Discretions chaired by Sir Henry Bland. The Royal Commission on Australian Government Administration, set up in 1974, was the second major inquiry into the public service (and statutory agencies) since the McLachlan Royal Commission in 1918–1920.

Interestingly, most of the major changes to the public service which resulted from these inquiries did not take place during Whitlam's terms of government, but he did set in train major policy reforms in 'new' areas such as a national health scheme (Medibank), urban and regional development, social welfare (childcare, family law, maternity leave), human rights (racial discrimination, equal pay), education, the environment and heritage – most of which had been the preserve of the states under Australia's Constitution (Section 51). The public service had become actively engaged in federal/state relations, and, where state governments would not cooperate, the federal government bypassed them by giving direct grants.

The Whitlam government was determined to be a pacesetter in public service pay and conditions of service. Public servants were granted an extra week's leave (Public Service Act of 1973); new maternity provisions in line with ILO Conventions and equal pay for women were introduced. In 1973, the government ratified the ILO Convention on Discrimination, Employment and Occupation (Mackerras 1978).

The social as well as urban reconstruction reform focus benefited women significantly, and a number of schemes and payments were set up which added tasks to the bureaucracy. A Women's Advisor was appointed and Australia was recognized as world leader in gender-equity reforms at the 1975 United Nations Conference on the occasion of the International Women's Year, in Mexico (Emy, Hughes & Matthews 1993: 16–31, 86–96). However, the Whitlam legacy in women's policy and machinery, and other reforms, left much unfinished business when he was dismissed from government in 1975. The public service had undergone a major shift from a 'classic' career service to the direct imposition of political will on staffing and changed conditions of service.

MALCOLM FRASER (1975–83)

Malcolm Fraser's election to office, although a sound win politically, was met with great apprehension by senior public servants. His first action was to review the APS in order to identify overlap and redundancy and to effect economies in departments and agencies in ways that countered the 'excesses' of the Whitlam period. However, in his efforts to effect improvements, there were fluctuations in the number of ministries and departments entailing some 1,100 reallocations of Acts (Castleman 1992: 368). He split the Treasury into two departments in 1976, and in 1978 there was a major change to the Commonwealth Employment Service in order to address rising unemployment.

Significant changes during Fraser's period were administrative reforms aimed at improving the relationship between citizens and the public service. New legislation from 1975 to 1982 covered the introduction of an Ombudsman institution, freedom of information and administrative review processes, and conduct of public servants. Also, there were reviews of government functions (1975, 1981 and 1983) which improved the efficiency and accountability of the APS. Fraser increased the powers of the Department of Prime Minister and Cabinet and, like Whitlam, he used a number of personal advisors to ensure his dominance over the public service (Thompson 1989: 213). Introduction of legislation which enabled the government to terminate public service employment (CERR Act of 1981) added to a relationship of mistrust and hostility with the bureaucracy.

Other reforms were aimed at achieving greater efficiency and at reducing costs. The Royal Commission on Australian Government Administration (RCAGA) Report (1976) recommended that the Auditor General be given extended functions and powers to conduct efficiency audits. The Fraser government set up a working party to examine the RCAGA recommendations and this culminated in the Audit Amendment Act of 1979. The use of inquiries by the Fraser government (some 80 over the period) again reflected the frustration of the government with public service advice. Although Fraser initially rejected the need to increase the number of public servants, he was forced to do so due to demands for action.

From 1976 to 1980, Fraser's approach to inflation had reduced the budget deficit. But inflation continued to rise and reached 10% in mid-1980. Unemployment had risen to over 6%. The 1982–83 budgets were expansionary with tax cuts, increased spending on infrastructure (roads, civil aviation), welfare housing and increased family allowances but resulted in a deficit. The economy was in recession and effects worsened due to a severe drought. However, the reduction in the numbers of public servants through 'staff ceilings' failed to appease the electorate and it further alienated public servants. The Fraser government was defeated before the Reid Report recommendations could be implemented (*Australia's Prime Ministers – Malcolm Fraser* [n.d.]).

ROBERT HAWKE (1983–91)

The Hawke government came to office with reform proposals already drawn up. The Public Service Reform Act of 1984 brought about significant changes: a Senior Executive Service (SES); capacity for increased use of consultants; ability of ministers to employ own staff; devolution of creation/abolition of positions or reclassifications to secretaries of departments; enactment of the merit principle and equal employment opportunity; provision of permanent part-time employment; departmental industrial democracy plans; and establishment of a Merit Protection and Review Agency (*Australia's Prime Ministers – Robert Hawke* [n.d.]).

Public service responsiveness had been a problem for the Whitlam and Fraser governments and Hawke was determined that the only way to achieve the desired relationship with the bureaucracy was to undertake long-term reforms. The above-mentioned changes were accompanied by reforms to financial management, resulting from a budget deficit in mid-1986. The Block Efficiency Scrutiny Unit (ESU) was set up. The Public Service

Legislation (Streamlining) Act of 1986 repealed the CERR Act of 1979 but allowed the government to dismiss public servants on the basis of redundancy or inefficiency (Thompson 1991: 129–131).

The first Hawke government term introduced the SES as a way of broadening commitment to a professional service rather than narrow loyalty to a department. The top echelon of the public service was to be 'mobile', thus allowing ineffective bureaucrats to be moved and, if found unable to perform set tasks, dismissed or made redundant. Union resistance was overcome by public appeal for support of cutbacks in a time of economic crisis.

The Financial Management Improvement Program (FMIP) focused on efficiency. This led to a priority of managerialism over policy analysis for public services and was reinforced through the parliamentary committees system. The theme of FMIP was that management systems should be drawn by clearly-stated, publicly-defined objectives at a program level. Program-management and budgeting was introduced in 1987 but was slow to be introduced into departments (Auditor General, 1992; Department of Finance, 1987). An evaluation in 1990 revealed many deficiencies and recommended the establishment of a Task Force on Management Improvement (House of Representatives Standing Committee on Finance and Public Administration, 1990).

Hawke's initial terms of government, 1983 to 1984 and 1984 to 1987, saw only modest changes to the machinery of government, but there were 28 departments. Prior to the 1987 election, the ESU reported and the prime minister released a statement on major changes to the structure of the APS – reducing the number of departments from 28 to 18. Among potential benefits of the changes were listed: enhanced ministerial control; better coordination and decision-making processes; greater coherence in policy advice and program development; greater scope for delegation to portfolios; reduction in overlap and duplication; and greater flexibility in portfolio operations and potential stability in machinery of government (Castleman 1995; Kouzmin, Nethercote & Wettenhall 1984; Nethercote, Kouzmin & Wettenhall 1986; Wettenhall & Nethercote 1988).

One of the influential advisors on this change was Peter Wilenski (1988: 31–33) who had served Whitlam as an advisor, had overseen the RCAGA and had held several posts as departmental secretary while also conducting public service inquiries in New South Wales. He had appreciated the need for 'flatter structures' in working with McKinsey as well as the benefits of 'horizontal' links between functional units.

The 'managerial' reforms were accompanied by marketization: privatization, outsourcing and outcontracting. Government business enterprises were sold off to achieve a reduction in foreign debt in pursuit of budgetary goals. There were claims of gains in economic efficiency from competition, but the bottom line was to reduce government expenditure and the size of the public sector. When Hawke took office in 1983, there were 159,190 public servants. When Paul Keating succeeded him after a successful challenge in 1991, there were 161,303, but the gender composition had changed from 100,542 males in 1983 to 86,589 males in 1991 and from 58,648 females in 1983 to 77,496 females in 1991. Despite the legislative gains made in EEO in the public service and the passage of the Affirmative Action (Equal Opportunity for Women) Act of 1986, women remained concentrated in the lower echelons of the public service and were poorly represented in the SES at 12% (APSC 2004: Table 5).

PAUL KEATING (1991–96)

Paul Keating's first term in government focused on domestic economic problems. He had been Treasurer in the period of the Hawke government and had first-hand experience of Australia's prolonged economic recession. His priorities were an Australian republic, economic improvement by expanding trade in the Asia-Pacific region, and 'One Nation': an economic program for the creation of 800,000 jobs by 1996 (*Australia's Prime Ministers – Paul Keating* [n.d.]).

His leadership contest with Hawke revealed a division of opinion as to the way forward to stem the discontent with the government. Keating promised a new approach to leadership and this was evident in the changes made to the public service. The Secretary of the Department of Prime Minister and Cabinet (PM&C) resigned at the change of political leadership and was replaced by someone with a different style. Keating relied on ministerial colleagues and personal advisors in his early period, many of whom were advisors when he was Treasurer. He diminished the role of PM&C, particularly its Economic Division (Halligan 1995: 2).

A few machinery-of-government changes occurred without increasing the number of portfolio departments. Though logically sensible in 1987, the major restructuring in addition to other reforms was extremely disruptive and delayed other aspects of the reform program (Halligan 1995: 9). However, Keating's lack of interest in the public service was due to 'electoralism' being given the premier status in determining policy (Singleton 1997: 2).

In 1994, the Public Service Act of 1922 was amended to provide for fixed-term statutory appointments of secretaries. Together with the emphasis on managerialism, this facilitated Keating's desire to politicize the top echelons of the public service so that those who were not responsive to the government's needs could be redeployed or retrenched. The Report of the Task Force on Management Improvement (1993) was subjected to scrutiny in August 1994 shortly after a task force had been set up to review the Public Service Act (May). The McLeod Report was tabled in December 1994; it contained few surprises. Many of the proposals dated back to the late 1970s

(O'Brien in Singleton 1997: 185). The accountability of the public service was enhanced during the Hawke–Keating periods of government, with particular improvements to the role of scrutinizing departmental estimates.

Keating's second term of government (1993–1996) was troublesome. He continued to promote economic development as the way to address social development yet, despite a slightly lower unemployment rate and interest rate than in 1993, in 1996 foreign debt was increasing. He also lost senior ministers and the Working Nation plan to expand employment for young people was not delivering results. The government was defeated in 1996 by a landslide victory (a 40-seat majority) of the Liberal–National Party coalition led by John Howard.

JOHN HOWARD (1996–)

On winning the election in 1996, the Howard government put in place sweeping economic reforms which included cost-cutting in the public service and the privatization of Telstra. Also on the agenda were industrial relations reform, tax reform and Asia-Pacific trade and diplomatic relations (*Australia's Prime Ministers – John Howard* [n.d.]).

Howard's vision for the APS was to decrease its size and the role of unions; decrease reliance on ongoing staff; increase labor market access to APS employment; and increase staff mobility (Turner 2001). Two early reports by the National Commission of Audit (June 1996) and the Korak-Kakabadse report on leadership (August 1996) highlighted the cultural and structural changes needed by the APS. Two MAB/MIAC reports identified cost and effective work inefficiencies.[2]

From 18 major departments in 1987, the number of departments rose to 20 under Keating's period of government but was cut to 17 during Howard's first term. They currently stand at 18 (Nethercote 1999). The public sector reform momentum from 1983 focused on results and Howard acknowledged the contribution of these effects in his 'Sir Robert Garran Oration' in 1997 (Howard 1998). However, he believed that there could be further cost reductions; that the APS employment and industrial relations framework should closely resemble the rest of the workforce; and that the public service should focus more on managing contracts, developing policy, and administering legislation and regulating frameworks, and less on direct service delivery and managing staff (Turner 2001: 7).

To achieve such outcomes, the government introduced the Workplace Relations Act in 1996, service charters in 1997, Centrelink in 1997, outcontracted Job Network in 1998 and introduced a new Public Service Act in 1999. The Public Service Act of 1999 and the Parliamentary Service Act of 1999 established the separation of parliamentary departments from public service departments. They enshrined such features as values and codes of conduct (included for the first time in the Public Service Act), protection for whistleblowers, employment equity, prohibition on patronage and favoritism, and streamlining of employment powers of departmental secretaries. Furthermore, they provided for departmental secretaries to enter into collective and/or individual contracts and agreements (Verspaandonk 2003: 14–15).

Accountability improvements are to be achieved through various Acts (Financial Management and Accountability, Charter of Budget Honesty, Public Service Act) as well as parliamentary scrutiny and an independent Auditor-General. The government inherited a deficit of $8 billion when it took office in 1996, but major tax reforms introduced in 1998 have created budget surpluses, the first since 1989–90. Expenditure cuts and privatization contributed to a reduction of 10,000 public servants in 1996 and another 16,000 in 1997 (Manne 2004: 8–9).

One interesting feature during Howard's term has been the significant increase in the number of women in the SES: from 329 in 1996 (19%) to 597 (or 31.6%) in 2004. Some part of this increase is a result of the reduction of male SES numbers due to retirement (a trend from 1992), but may also be due to the fact that in 2001 women comprised 50% of public servants for the first time. The three largest agencies comprise 50.4% of total public service numbers, a constant situation over the last five years from 1999 to 2004 (APSC 2004: 3).

MAJOR PUBLIC SERVICE REFORMS (1972–2004)

Most writers on reforms in the APS agree that they cover a number of key dimensions: marketization, regulation, political control, privatization, decentralization and corporate management (Davis & Rhodes 2000; Halligan 2001; Hughes 2003; Podger 2001; Singleton 1997, 2000). There is less agreement, however, about how to characterize the changes resulting from the reforms. The foci of the changes from 1972 to 2004 are on openness, equity and welfare within the APS and on achieving efficiency and effectiveness. These have been driven mainly by: significant administrative law reform in the 1970s; merit and equity changes from the 1974 RCAGA review and 1980s EEO emphasis; the economic situation facing governments where constituents demanded smaller government; financial management reforms of the 1980s and 90s; and close scrutiny by the Auditor-General, parliamentary committees and coordinating agencies (to the current Public Service Act of 1999, under which departmental secretaries have assumed this responsibility). The media also play a scrutiny role in that 'scandals' or deficiencies are detected and publicly pursued. The rationale for reform, as depicted in each prime-ministerial period, was based primarily on economic performance, budget deficits, a rethinking of the role of the state, economic theory and the separation of policy from implementation.

Since 1972, there have been two periods of Labor governments (1972–75 and 1983–1996) and two periods of Liberal/National Coalition governments (1975–1983 and 1996 to date). The agendas of governments were quite different and, apart from the Whitlam government, reflected changes which addressed the economic conditions prevailing at the time as much as they did any ideological commitment to public service. The Whitlam government had a major focus on social reform but it did change structures, improve conditions of service for public servants and set up a comprehensive inquiry into government administration. It changed a federal public service which had become inflexible and overly conservative. It also increased the number of public servants. In Wilenski's terms, this was to be 'reform as distinct from incremental change' (Wilenski 1986: 171).

Malcolm Fraser's period as prime minister was troublesome due to his poor relationship with the bureaucracy, but his was the first Western government to make significant cuts in public expenditure. He did not adopt free-market reforms to tackle the economic crisis of the time but he focused on social issues such as immigration, and he established land-rights legislation and a human rights commission. Such social justice reforms also extended to opening up administrative decisions to public scrutiny through an Ombudsman, FOI legislation and administrative review processes, and thus may appear at odds with liberalism.

The Hawke and Keating Labor governments pursued the economic rationalist approaches of other governments (particularly the UK, USA and New Zealand) as well as major civil service reforms in the UK, USA and Canada, which resulted in the introduction of the SES, merit principle, human resource and structural changes, financial management improvement changes, corporatization and outsourcing. The focus in the 1980s and 90s was on better management, transparency, increased accountability and performance. Driving forces for this change were the economy, technological advances, uncertainty and a trend toward the primacy accorded to 'clients' of public sector agencies.

In the federal public sector during the 1980s and 90s, there were significant management reforms as a result of the adoption of the principle of equal employment opportunity (EEO) for women and other disadvantaged groups, 'commercial' reforms such as outcontracting, industrial relations (IR) reforms as well as administrative reforms and a changing management focus which included strategic planning, downsizing, total quality management, customer orientation and benchmarking. These were part of the social agenda of Labor governments but also reflected the global trends towards economic rationalism and managerialism.

When it came to office in 1996, the Howard government introduced the second wave of performance-related pay (PRP), boosted by the concurrent introduction of the Workplace Relations Act of 1996 which allowed for individual employment agreements, and a change to make agency heads responsible and accountable for the application of PRP rather than a central agency. The 'first wave' PRP was hastily introduced in 1983 and was assessed by the Australian National Audit Office in 1993 as a failure (Turberville and Barrett 1999: 8). This latest reform of industrial relations in the public service has decentralized management and freed up staffing arrangements providing that agencies stay within budget allocations. In part, these IR reforms allow for great flexibility, efficiency and accountability, yet they are also part of a political strategy by the government to reduce the influence of trade unions, i.e., of organized labor which historically has provided a significant base of support for the Australian Labor Party. It is, by far, the most contentious reform in recent APS history and is seen as essentially politically motivated.

Overall, the reforms of the 1990s and 2000s have been influenced by experiments in the UK (Next Steps), the USA (Reinventing Government), Canada (Public Service 2000) and New Zealand (output-based budgeting). Australia's contribution is its Financial Management Improvement Program (FMIP), which emphasises outcomes, not just efficiency. The 'levers for change', as described by Wilenski (1986: 179–182), were used by all governments from Whitlam to Howard: enactment of new legislation, creation of new institutions, recruitment/appointment of new personnel, changes to formal processes and changes to formal organizational structure. There were unprecedented changes in the machinery of government from 1976 to 1991 as a result of pressures to create a more responsive public service and to deliver government objectives (Codd 1991). Political appointments and staff movements were facilitated by changes to appointment conditions of departmental secretaries and the introduction of the SES in 1984 to improve staff flexibility.

If there is one 'failure' in the reform period, it relates to the scarcity of women in senior positions in comparison to their numbers in the APS. The EEO agenda was strongly promoted by the Labor governments (from 1984 on), yet more women remained in the lower levels relative to the corresponding numbers of men, despite the fact that the marriage bar, the major 'hurdle' for women, had been removed in 1966. From 1990 to 2000, women comprised 49.6% of all staff and 26.1% of the SES (PSMPC 2001b).

Women have not been well represented in some APS departments over the years. From 1984 to 1992, women's representation in the SES ranged from 3.9% to 13.3% (Conroy 1989, 1994). In 2004, the departments with the largest staff were Centrelink (19.3% of total APS staff), Australian Tax office (ATO, 16.5%) and Defence (14.6%). More than 50% of Centrelink and ATO staff was female.

The number of women in the SES has been increasing gradually over the last eight years (1996 to 2004), but this has been largely the result of the declining number of males, a trend since 1993. A 2003 report by the Management Advisory Committee (MAC) found that the APS will lose fully one quarter of its current staff between 2003 and 2008 as 42% of SES staff and 27% of executive level staff reach retirement age (MAC 2003). Questions about the ongoing capability of the public service to deliver successful policy implementation have resulted from a review of the qualities of current staff and an attempt to develop a comprehensive approach on management skills for the government. This will be a significant challenge over the next two decades. The major challenges in managing the economy will remain regardless of the politics of the government of the day. It will require a modern, well-resourced public service to implement government policies and to provide advice and guidelines on such policies.

Much of what Gerald Caiden noted as deficiencies in the APS in the 1960s has been addressed during the period from 1972 to 2004: administrative law reforms, overspecialization and departmentalism, the career-service concept and the need for a comprehensive inquiry into the APS (Caiden 1967). One review of *The Commonwealth Bureaucracy* suggested that

> Caiden's tendency to rush into attack is perhaps best explainable in terms of his basic thesis. One of his major themes [in the book] is that Australians in general, and the bureaucracy in particular, object to anyone rocking the boat. Dr. Caiden is essentially a boat rocker! (Lyall 1967: 383)

Caiden's observations on reform, 13 years later, are also relevant with respect to a reform model. For Caiden,

> Contemporary administrative problems require new approaches, new organisational designs, new laws, new commitments, new relationships, new attitudes, new techniques, and new inventions. (Caiden 1980: 453)

There are a number of ways by which public service transition can be judged, and there are a number of Australian scholars cited in this chapter who have made such judgments on the Australian experience. Their work examines those elements of a reform model which are espoused by Caiden and they provide an interesting contrast as to their assessment of benefits or improvements, as well as an alternative to that which has been presented in official documents and reports.

To celebrate the centenary of the Australian Public Service, a 'potted' history of its development was produced (PSMPC 2001a). However, those responsible for its production admitted that it was not intended as either a narrative or an institutional history, since many departments and agencies had produced their own. It is, nevertheless, an invaluable contribution because it draws together the major references on the APS and provides an excellent start for scholars interested in undertaking an in-depth analysis of changes to personnel administration and/or the changes to the composition of the workforce in the APS.

What has become evident over the last three decades is that there were – still are – some 'boat-rockers' inside the public service who have contributed to the reform process. There has also been considerable parliamentary and public scrutiny of the major changes undertaken. Structural and procedural reform has been constant and pervasive, like the experiences with reform in the public services of New Zealand, Canada, the United Kingdom and the United States. In many cases, Australia has followed the trends of reform in other countries but has adapted them to the prevailing social and economic conditions of the country tempered by the political ideology of the government in power. In some other cases, the driving force was a leader.

The public service reforms under the current Howard government reflect not only the political ideology of the government (liberalism/conservatism) but also the acceptance of the need for any government to demand output and outcome performance as well as accountability from its bureaucracy. For the past 15 years or so, the APS performance has been measured by plans, targets and reviews, it has been subjected to contestability through outcontracting, and it has been required to meet consumer-service obligations.

At the time of writing, there appears to be a move back toward administration-through-line-departments to improve and to make transparent the lines of accountability – a tenet of good governance. This is a move away from the fragmentation among some 960 federal government bodies towards a reinvigorated 'department of state'. It will be interesting, indeed, to review 'the transitions' over the next twenty years.

APPENDIX A: MINISTRIES AND PORTFOLIO DEPARTMENTS, 1901–2004

	Government[1]	Dates[1]	No. of Depts[2]		Government[1]	Dates[1]	No. of Depts[2]
1	Barton	1.1.1901– 24.9.1903	7	31	Menzies	11.1.1956– 10.12.1958	) 25) 24
2	Deakin	24.9.1903– 27.4.1904	7	32	Menzies	10.12.1958– 18.12.1963	24
3	Watson	27.4.1904– 17.8.1904	7	33	Menzies	18.12.1963– 26.1.1966	25
4	Reid-McLean	18.8.1904– 5.7.1905	7	34	Holt	26.1.1966– 14.12.1966	25
5	Deakin	5.7.1905– 13.11.1908	7	35	Holt	14.12.1966– 19.12.1967	26
6	Fisher	13.11.1908– 2.6.1909	7	36	McEwen	19.12.1967– 10.1.1968	26
7	Deakin	2.6.1909– 29.4.1910	7	37	Gorton	10.1.1968– 28.2.1968	26
8	Fisher	29.4.1910– 24.6.1913	) 7) 8	38	Gorton	28.2.1968– 12.11.1969	) 26) 27

	Government[1]	Dates[1]	No. of Depts[2]
9	Cook	24.6.1913– 17.9.1914	8
10	Fisher	17.9.1914– 27.10.1915	) 8) 9
11	Hughes	27.10.1915– 14.11.1916	9
12	Hughes	14.11.1916– 17.2.1917	9
13	Hughes	17.2.1917– 8.1.1918	) 9) 10
14	Hughes	10.1.1918– 9.2.1923	) 10) 11
15	Bruce-Page	9.2.1923– 22.10.1929	) 12) 13
16	Scullin	22.10.1929– 6.1.1932	) 13) 14
17	Lyons	6.1.1932– 7.11.1938	12
18	Lyons	7.11.1938– 7.4.1939	) 12) 14
19	Page	7.4.1939– 26.4.1939	14
20	Menzies	26.4.1939– 14.3.1940	) 15) 16) 19
21	Menzies	14.3.1940– 28.10.1940	20
22	Menzies	28.10.1940– 29.8.1941	) 20) 25
23	Fadden	29.8.1941– 7.10.1941	25
24	Curtin	7.10.1941– 21.9.1943	) 25) 26
25	Curtin	21.9.1943– 6.7.1945	) 26) 27
26	Forde	6.7.1945– 13.7.1945	27
27	Chifley	13.7.1945– 1.11.1946	) 27) 26
28	Chifley	1.11.1946– 19.12.1949	25

	Government[1]	Dates[1]	No. of Depts[2]
39	Gorton	12.11.1969– 10.3.1971	27
40	McMahon	10.3.1971– 5.12.1972	27
41	Whitlam	5.12.1972– 19.12.1972	27
42	Whitlam	19.12.1972– 12.6.1974	) 37) 31
43	Whitlam	12.6.1974– 11.11.1975	) 29) 28
44	Fraser	11.11.1975– 22.12.1975	28
45	Fraser	22.12.1975– 20.12.1977	) 25) 26) 27) 28
46	Fraser	20.12.1977– 3.11.1980	) 29) 28
47	Fraser	3.11.1980– 7.5.1982	26
48	Fraser	7.5.1982– 11.3.1983	26
49	Hawke	11.3.1983– 13.12.1984	28
50	Hawke	13.12.1984– 24.7.1987	28
51	Hawke	24.7.1987– 4.4.1990	) 18) 17
52	Hawke	4.4.1990– 20.12.1991	17
53	Keating	20.12.1991– 27.12.1991	17
54	Keating	27.12.1991– 24.3.1993	18
55	Keating	24.3.1993– 11.3.1996	) 19) 20) 19) 20
56	Howard	11.3.1996– 21.10.1998	) 18) 17
57	Howard	21.10.1998– 26.11.2001	) 17) 18) 17

	Government[1]	Dates[1]	No. of Depts[2]		Government[1]	Dates[1]	No. of Depts[2]
29	Menzies	19.12.1949– 11.5.1951	) 25) 23	58	Howard[3]	26.11.2001– 31.8.2004	17
30	Menzies	11.5.1951– 11.1.1956	24	59	Howard[4]	26.10.2004–	18

Sources:

1. Parliament of Australia (2005), *Ministries*
2. Compiled by Rob Lundie, Parliamentary Library, Canberra, from PSMPC *Serving the Nation* (2001a: 211–213)
3. APSC *Statistical Bulletin 2003–2004* (2004)
4. *Administrative Arrangements Order* (2004)

REFERENCES

Administrative Arrangements Order 2004.

Auditor–General (1992). *Efficiency Audit. Program Evaluation in the Department of Social Security and Primary Industries and Energy*. Audit Report No. 26, 1991–92. Canberra: Australian Government Publishing Service.

Australian Public Service Board (1977). *Statistical Yearbook*. Canberra: Australian Government Publishing Service.

APSC – Australian Public Service Commission (2004). *Statistical Bulletin 2003–04*. State of the Service Series 2003–04. Retrieved 20 February 2005 (http://www.apsc.gov.au).

Australia's Prime Ministers – Malcolm Fraser (n.d.). Retrieved 24 February 2005 (http://primeministers.naa.gov.au).

Australia's Prime Ministers – Robert Hawke (n.d.). Retrieved 24 February 2005 (http://primeministers.naa.gov.au).

Australia's Prime Ministers – John Howard (n.d.). Retrieved 24 February 2005 (http://primeministers.naa.gov.au).

Australia's Prime Ministers – Paul Keating (n.d.). Retrieved 24 February 2005 (http://primeministers.naa.gov.au).

Australia's Prime Ministers – Robert Menzies (n.d.). Retrieved 24 February 2005 (http://primeministers.naa.gov.au).

Australia's Prime Ministers – Gough Whitlam (n.d.). Retrieved 24 February 2005 (http://primeministers.naa.gov.au).

Caiden, G.E. (1959). 'A Comparative Study of the Commonwealth Public Service of Australia and the Federal Civil Service of Canada'. PhD Thesis, London: University of London.

Caiden, G.E. (1963). *The Study of Australian Administrative History*. Canberra: Department of Political Science, Research School of Social

Sciences, Australian National University.

Caiden, G.E. (1965). *Career Service: An Introduction to the History of Personnel Administration in the Commonwealth Public Service 1901–1961*. Carlton, Victoria: Melbourne University Press.

Caiden, G.E. (1966). *The ACPTA: A Study of White Collar Public Service Unionism in the Commonwealth of Australia, 1885–1922*. Occasional Paper No. 2. Canberra: Department of Political Science, Research School of Social Sciences, Australian National University.

Caiden, G.E. (1967). *The Commonwealth Bureaucracy*. Carlton, Victoria: Melbourne University Press.

Caiden, G.E. (1971). *Public Employment and Compulsory Arbitration in Australia*. Ann Arbor, MI: Institute of Labor and Industrial Relations.

Caiden, G.E. (1975). *Toward a More Efficient Australian Government Administration: First Report* (RCAGA Task Force on Efficiency). Canberra: Australian Government Publishing Service.

Caiden, G.E. (1980). 'Administrative Reform'. *Australian Journal of Public Administration* 39 (3/4), pp. 437–453.

Caiden, G.E. (1981). 'Recent Administrative Changes in Australasia'. *International Review of Administrative Sciences* 57 (1), pp. 9–23.

Caiden, G.E. (1990). 'Australia's Changing Administrative Ethos'. In A. Kouzmin and N. Scott (Eds), *Dynamics in Australian Public Management: Selected Essays*. Melbourne: Macmillan.

Castleman, B. (1992). 'Changes in the Australian Commonwealth Departmental Machinery of Government: 1928–1982'. PhD Thesis, Melbourne: Faculty of Social Sciences, Deakin University.

Castleman, B. (1995). *The Hawke and Keating Departmental Machinery of Government Changes: Patterns and Prospects*. Parliamentary Research Service, Research Paper No. 18, 1994/1995. Canberra: Department of the Parliamentary Library.

Codd, M. (1991). *Federal Public Sector Management Reform – Recent History and Current Priorities*. Public Service Commission, Senior Executive Staffing Unit. Canberra: Australian Government Publishing Service.

Conroy, D. (1989). 'Opportunities and Barriers to Career Development in Management: The Senior Executive Service in the Australian Public Service'. Paper presented at the International Association of Schools and Institutes of Administration Annual Conference, Marrakesh.

Conroy, D. (1994). 'The Glass Ceiling: Illusory or Real?' *Canberra Bulletin of Public Administration* 76, pp. 91–103.

Davis, G., & Rhodes, R. (2000). 'From Hierarchy to Contracts and Back Again: Reforming the Australian Public Service'. London: Paper presented to the Political Studies Association UK 50th Annual Conference, 10–13 April.

Department of Finance (1987). *Evaluating Government Programs – A Handbook*. Canberra: Australian Government Publishing Service.

Emy, H., Hughes O., & Matthews, R. (1993) (Eds). *Whitlam Revisited. Policy Development, Policies and Outcomes.* Leichhardt, NSW: Pluto Press Australia.

Halligan, J. (1995). 'The Process of Reform: Balancing Principle and Pragmatism'. In J. Stewart (Ed), *From Hawke to Keating. Australian Commonwealth Administration 1990–1993.* Centre for Research in Public Sector Management and Institute of Public Administration Australia. Canberra: University of Canberra.

Halligan, J. (2001). 'Contribution of the Australian Public Service to Public Administration and Management'. *Canberra Bulletin of Public Administration* 101, pp. 20–25.

House of Representatives Standing Committee on Finance and Public Administration (1990). *Not Dollars Alone! Review of the Financial Management Improvement Program, Report.* Canberra: Australian Government Publishing Service.

Howard, J. (1998). 'A Healthy Public Service is a Vital Part of Australia's Democratic System of Government'. The Sir Robert Garran Oration, 19 November 1997. *Australian Journal of Public Administration* 57 (1), pp. 3–11.

Hughes, O. (2003). *Public Management and Administration: An Introduction* (3rd ed). New York: Palgrave Macmillan.

Korak-Kakabadse, A., & N. (1996). *The Leadership Challenges for the Australian Public Service (APS): An Internationally Comparative Benchmarking Analysis.* Retrieved 18 January 2005. (http://www.apsc.gov.au/publications96/kakabadse.htm).

Kouzmin, A., Nethercote, J., & Wettenhall, R. (1984) (Eds). *Australian Commonwealth Administration 1983.* Canberra: Canberra College of Advanced Education.

Lyall, E. (1967). 'Dr Caiden's Views on the Commonwealth Bureaucracy'. *Public Administration* 24 (4), pp. 377–383.

MAB/MIAC (1995). *Achieving Cost Effective Personnel Services.* Report No. 18, July. Canberra: Australian Government Publishing Service.

MAB/MIAC (1996). *2 + 2 = 5: Innovative Ways of Organising People.* Report No. 20, August. Canberra: Australian Government Publishing Service.

Mackerras, M. (1978). *The Whitlam Years. Australia's Labor Legislation 1972–1975.* Special Volume of the New Legislation of the Australian Parliament Series, Limited Edition. Canberra: Parliament of Australia.

(MAC) Management Advisory Committee (2003). *Organization Renewal.* Canberra: Commonwealth of Australia. Retrieved 12 November 2004 (http://www.aspc.gov.au/mac/organisationrenewal.pdf).

Manne, R. (2004) (Ed). *The Howard Years.* Melbourne: Black Inc. Agenda.

Matthews, R. and Grewal, B. (1995). *Fiscal Federalism in Australia: From Whitlam to Keating.* CSES Working Paper No. 1. Melbourne: Committee for Strategic Economic Studies.

McLeod, D. (1994). *Report of the Review of the Public Service Act.* Canberra: Australian Government Publishing Service.

National Commission of Audit (1996). *Report to the Commonwealth Government.* Canberra: Australian Government Publishing Service.

Nethercote, J. (1999). *Departmental Machinery of Government Since 1987.* Canberra: Parliamentary Library, Parliament of Australia. Retrieved 13 February 2005 (http://www.aph.gov.au/library/pubs/rp/1998-99/99rp24.htm).

Nethercote, J., Kouzmin, A., & Wettenhall, R. (1986) (Eds.). *Australian Commonwealth Administration 1984: Essays in Review.* Canberra: School of Administrative Studies, Royal Australian Institute of Public Administration, ACT Division, & Canberra College of Advanced Education.

Parliament of Australia (2005). *Historical Information on the Australian Parliament: Ministries.* Retrieved 13 February 2005 (http://www.aph.gov.au/library/handbook/historical/ministries.htm).

Podger, A. (2001). 'Reforms and Their Significance'. *Canberra Bulletin of Public Administration* 99, pp. 14–20.

Prasser, S. (1985). 'Public Inquiries in Australia: An Overview'. *Australian Journal of Public Administration* 44 (1), pp. 1–15.

PSMPC Public Service and Merit Protection Commission (2001a). *Serving the Nation. 100 Years of Public Service.* Canberra: Commonwealth of Australia.

PSMPC Public Service and Merit Protection Commission (2001b). *Statistical Bulletin 2000–2001.* Retrieved 11 July 2004 (http://www.apsc.gov.au).

Singleton, G. (1997) (Ed). *The Second Keating Government. Australian Commonwealth Administration 1993–1996.* Centre for Research in Public Sector Management and Institute of Public Administration Australia. Canberra: University of Canberra.

Singleton, G. (2000) (Ed). *The Howard Government. Australian Government Administration 1996–1998.* Sydney: University of New South Wales Press.

Thompson, E. (1989). 'The Public Service'. In B. Head & A. Patience (Eds), *From Fraser to Hawke: Australian Public Policy in the 1980s* (ch. 9). Melbourne: Longman Cheshire.

Thompson, E. (1991). 'Democracy Undermined: Reforms to the Australian Public Service from Whitlam to Hawke'. *The Australian Quarterly* 63 (2), pp. 127–142.

Turner, A. (2001). *An Analysis of Changes to the Australian Public Service Under the Coalition Government 1996–2001.* Discussion Paper No. 89. Canberra: Australian National University. Retrieved 20 January 2005 (http://www.anu.edu.au/pubpol/Discussion% 20 Papers/No89Turner.pdf).

Turberville, S. & Barrett, R. (1999). *Managed Decentralism: Performance Related Pay in the Australian Public Service.* Working Paper 32/99.

Department of Management, Monash University. Victoria, Australia.
Verspaandonk, R. (2003). *Changes in the Australian Public Service 1975–2003*. Canberra: Parliamentary Library, Parliament of Australia. Retrieved 13 February 2005 (http://www:aph.gov.au/library/pubs/chron/2002-03/03chr01.htm).
Walter, J. (1980). *The Leader: A Political Biography of Gough Whitlam*. St Lucia, Queensland: University of Queensland Press.
Wettenhall, R. & Nethercote, J. (1988) (Eds). *Hawke's Second Government. Australian Commonwealth Administration 1984–1987*. School of Management, Canberra CAE, and Royal Australian Institute of Public Administration, ACT Division. Canberra: Canberra College of Advanced Education.
Whitlam, G. (1973). 'Australian Public Administration under a Labor Government', *Garran Memorial Oration*. Canberra: Royal Australian Institute of Public Administration.
Wilenski, P. (1986). *Public Power and Public Administration*. Sydney, NSW: Hale & Iremonger.
Wilenski, P. (1988). 'Making the New Machinery of Government Work'. *Canberra Bulletin of Public Administration* 54, pp. 31–33.

NOTES

1. Major works by Gerald Elliot Caiden on Australian public administration include:

Books:
(1963) *The Study of Australian Administrative History.*
(1965) *Career Service: An Introduction to the History of Personnel Administration in the Commonwealth Public Service 1901–1961.*
(1966) *The ACPTA: A Study of White Collar Public Service Unionism in the Commonwealth of Australia, 1885–1922.*
(1967) *The Commonwealth Bureaucracy.*
(1971) *Public Employment and Compulsory Arbitration in Australia.*
(1975) *Toward a More Efficient Australian Government Administration: First Report.* (RCAGA Task Force on Efficiency.)

Chapter in book:
(1990) 'Australia's Changing Administrative Ethos'. In A. Kouzmin and N. Scott (Eds), *Dynamics in Australian Public Management: Selected Essays*. Melbourne: Macmillan.

Articles in journals:
(1980) 'Administrative Reform'. *Australian Journal of Public Administration* 34 (3/4), pp. 437–453.
(1981) 'Recent Administrative Changes in Australasia'. *International Review of Administrative Sciences* 57 (1), pp. 9–23.

2. MAB/MIAC (1995), *Achieving Cost Effective Personnel Services*, Report No. 18.
MAB/MIAC (1996), *2 + 2 = 5: Innovative Ways of Organising People*, Report No. 20.

9

Administrative Reform in Singapore: An Evaluation of Public Service 21 (1995–2004)

JON S.T. QUAH

INTRODUCTION

In May 1995, the Singapore Civil Service (SCS) launched 'Public Service for the 21st Century' (PS21) for two principal reasons: (1) to nurture an attitude of service excellence in meeting the needs of the public with high standards of quality, courtesy and responsiveness; and (2) to foster an environment which induces and welcomes continuous change for greater efficiency and effectiveness, by employing modern management tools and techniques while paying attention to the morale and welfare of public officers ('About PS21: Challenges and Objectives', 1).

PS21 is not the first administrative reform introduced by the People's Action Party (PAP) government. However, it is the most comprehensive administrative reform to be introduced in Singapore as it represents 'an extension of existing schemes and campaigns', namely: the Work Improvement Teams (WITs), Suggestions, Service Improvement, Staff Welfare, Organizational Review, Public Contact Improvement, Courtesy, Healthy Lifestyle, Zero Manpower Growth and Productivity (Prime Minister's Office 1995: 2).

Apart from being the most comprehensive reform, PS21 is also the most ambitious in terms of its second objective of creating an environment that encourages and welcomes continuous change. What has been the impact of PS21 on the SCS and its members? More specifically, the purpose of this chapter is to evaluate PS21 in terms of its twin objectives. In other words, has the introduction of PS21 improved service in the SCS and its members' attitude towards change? The main thesis of this chapter is that, while PS21 has succeeded in improving the quality of service provided by the SCS and in enhancing the emphasis given to training, it has not been able to foster an environment that encourages and welcomes continuous change in the SCS. To evaluate the impact of PS21 on the SCS, it is necessary to provide background information on the SCS, a brief history of administrative reforms in Singapore from 1960 to 1994, and the major components of PS21.

Before proceeding further, let me attempt to define administrative reform. The concept has been viewed in various ways. Gerald E. Caiden replaced his original definition of administrative reform as 'the artificial inducement of administrative transformation against resistance' (1969: 1) with 'the induced systemic improvement of public sector operational performance' (1991: 1). However, Caiden's 1991 definition of administrative reform did not address the two weaknesses of his 1969 definition, namely the failure to distinguish between the *institutional* and *attitudinal* aspects of administrative reform, and the failure to answer the question: *administrative reform for what?* (Quah 1976: 52–55). Accordingly, for this chapter, administrative reform will refer to

> A deliberate attempt to change both (a) the structure and procedures of the public bureaucracy (i.e., reorganization of the institutional aspect) and (b) the attitudes and behavior of the public bureaucrats involved (i.e., the attitudinal aspect), in order to promote organizational effectiveness and attain national development goals. (Quah 1976: 58)

Clearly, administrative reform consists of two aspects: institutional and attitudinal reform. Both aspects must be addressed for administrative reform to be successful.

THE SINGAPORE CIVIL SERVICE

The SCS today consists of the Prime Minister's Office and 14 ministries. These encompass community development, youth and sports, defense, education, environment, finance, foreign affairs, health, home affairs, information, communications and the arts, law, manpower, national development, trade and industry, and transport (*Singapore 2004*: 42). It has grown in size by more than two times from 28,253 employees in June 1959 to 61,516 employees in 2004. Table 1 below provides details on the size of the SCS from 1985 to 2004.

In 1947, the Trusted Commission recommended that the SCS be reorganized into four divisions according to the duties and salaries of its members. Division I comprised those in the administrative and professional grades; Division II the executive grades; Division III the clerical and technical grades; and Division IV those performing manual tasks (Quah 1978: 417). This reform was the first introduced by the British colonial government and it has been retained during the past 58 years as the basis for determining the entry points into the SCS for salary scales and fringe benefits.

Apart from its four divisions, the SCS has two types of employees: those belonging to the departmental services and those belonging to the non-departmental or general services. Thus, civil servants in the first category are attached to a department of a ministry, while their non-departmental coun-

Table 1 Employees in the Singapore Civil Service by Division, 1985–2004

Division	**1985 (a)**	**1990**	**1995**	**2000**	**2002**	**2004 (b)**	**Change (b-a)**
I	10,158	12,348	16,952	24,400	25,783	28,638	+18,480
II	22,915	21,095	18,249	18,939	17,605	16,608	-6,307
III	22,369	20,150	17,941	14,993	12,843	12,250	-10,119
IV	14,188	9,799	6,881	4,984	4,009	4,020	-10,168
Total	69,630	63,392	60,023	63,316	60,240	61,516	-8,114

Source: Singapore 1996: 44, Table 4.10; and Singapore 2005: 61, Table 4.9

terparts are usually based at the ministerial headquarters or temporarily attached or seconded to a department or a ministry. For the general services, Division I officers make up the Administrative Service, which had 294 officers in 2001 in senior policy-making and administrative positions (Jones 2002: 72). Division II grades are occupied by executive officers with varying levels of seniority while Division III grades consist of clerical and technical officers. Division IV grades are manual workers, office attendants, cooks and drivers.

Division I grades in the departmental and non-departmental services can be divided into super-scale and time-scale. Examples of super-scale officers in the Administrative Service are the permanent secretaries and deputy secretaries; their departmental counterparts are the directors and deputy directors. The time-scale officers in the Administrative Service are the principal assistant secretaries, assistant secretaries, and administrative assistants. Division I officers on the time-scale include professional personnel working in the departmental divisions or sections responsible to section heads (Quah 2003a: 168).

While the SCS had grown by two and a half times between 1959 and 1985, Table 1 above shows that it has declined in size by 8,114 members during 1985 to 2004. More specifically, during this period, only the number of Division I officers has increased by 18,480, while the other three divisions were reduced in size by 6,307, 10,119, and 10,168 employees respectively. The size of the SCS is an important factor influencing the success of administrative reform efforts for, other things being equal, it is easier to implement reforms in Singapore than in Indonesia, which had 4,135,000 employees in 1999 (Manning et al. 2000: 10).

ADMINISTRATIVE REFORMS IN SINGAPORE, 1959–94

Administrative reform was neglected during the colonial period. The British introduced only two reforms: the reorganization of the SCS into four divisions in 1947 and the establishment of the Public Service Commission (PSC) in January 1951, which laid the foundation for meritocracy in the SCS by promoting localization and ensuring its political neutrality (Quah 1996a: 63–64).

In contrast, the PAP government which assumed power in June 1959 was compelled to transform the colonial bureaucracy it inherited from the British in order to ensure the effective implementation of its socioeconomic development programs. To rectify the bureaucratic weaknesses which had accumulated during the 140 years of British colonial rule, the PAP leaders initiated a comprehensive reform of the SCS in 1959.

Between 1959 and the introduction of PS21 in May 1995, the PAP government introduced a plethora of administrative reforms.

Comprehensive Reform of the Public Bureaucracy, 1959

- Structural reorganization of the SCS resulting in the formation of the Ministry of Culture to promote nation-building, and the Ministry of National Development to ensure socioeconomic development.
- Dissolution of ineffective statutory boards (Singapore Improvement Trust and Singapore Harbor Board) and their replacement by the Housing and Development Board and the Port of Singapore Authority, respectively, to promote efficiency and effectiveness.
- Reduction of the salaries of senior civil servants by discontinuing their variable allowances in order to promote economy and reduce the budget deficit.
- Creation of the Political Study Center to change and reshape the attitudes of the civil servants (Quah 1991: 86).

Reform of Anticorruption Measures, 1960

- Strengthening legislation against corruption through the enactment of the Prevention of Corruption Act (POCA).
- Impartial implementation of the POCA by the Corrupt Practices Investigation Bureau (Quah 1989: 844–846).

Budgetary Reforms, 1978 and 1989

- Replacement of the line-item budgeting system with a limited version of the program and performance budgeting system (PPBS) in 1978.
- The PPBS was replaced by the block-vote budget allocation system (BVBAS) in 1989 (Quah 1991: 91–94).

Reforms in Personnel Management, 1982 and 1986

- The SCS changed its personnel management philosophy from a task-centered to an employee-centered one in 1982.
- In January 1983, the Public Service Division was formed within the Ministry of Finance to formulate and review policies and to reduce PSC workload.
- Introduction of the Shell System of potential appraisal in the SCS.
- A manpower-reduction exercise was launched in 1986 to reduce staff levels in the SCS (Quah 1991: 94–96).

Decentralization of PSC Functions, 1990 and 1995

- PSC workload was reduced in 1990 with the formation of the Education Service Commission (ESC) and the Police and Civil Defense Services Commission (PCDSC) to recruit and promote teachers, police officers and civil defense officers.
- In 1995, the recruitment and promotion functions of the PSC, ESC and PCDSC were devolved to a system of 31 personnel boards (Quah 1996b: 497–502).

Competing for Talent through Salary Revisions, January 1972–September 1994

- To stem the brain-drain from the SCS to the private sector, the PAP government accepted the recommendation of the National Wages Council to pay an Annual Wage Supplement (or 13th month pay) to all civil servants from 1972 on.
- Civil service salaries were periodically revised in 1973, 1979, 1982, 1989 and 1993 to minimize the gap between wages in the public and private sectors (Quah 2003b: 149–153).

Service Improvement Unit, April 1991

- The Service Improvement Unit (SIU) was formed in April 1991 for two reasons: 'to monitor and improve upon the standard of public administration' and 'to maintain the highest possible standards in our public services' by obtaining feedback from citizens to improve the service provided by the SCS and statutory boards (Quah 1994: 214).
- To assist the SIU in performing its duties, 90 senior civil servants were appointed as Quality Service Managers (QSMs) in the SCS and statutory boards. Senior officers were selected as QSMs to ensure that the public could get direct and immediate access to decision-makers who could deal effectively with complaints or channel these to the relevant ministries or departments (Quah 1994: 214).

Benchmarking Salaries to Institutionalize Salary Revision, October 1994

- On 21 October 1994, a White Paper on *Competitive Salaries for a Competent and Honest Government* was presented to Parliament to justify the pegging of the salaries of ministers and senior civil servants to the average salaries of the top-four earners in six private sector professions.
- The White Paper recommended the introduction of formal salary benchmarks for ministers and senior bureaucrats, additional salary grades for political appointments and annual salary reviews for the SCS.
- Adoption of the long-term formula proposed in the White Paper had two advantages: it eliminated the need to justify 'from scratch' every revision of the salaries of ministers and senior civil servants, and it targeted the building of 'an efficient public service and a competent and honest political leadership, which have been vital for Singapore's prosperity and success' (Republic of Singapore 1994: 18).

Having identified the major administrative reforms in the SCS from 1959–1994, we can proceed to account for the introduction of PS21 in May 1995 and analyze its major components before providing an assessment of its impact on the SCS.

RATIONALE FOR PS21

Why was PS21 introduced? When the permanent secretaries initiated PS21 on 5 May 1995 to prepare the SCS for the twenty-first century, Lim Siong Guan, who was then Permanent Secretary in the Prime Minister's Office and the prime mover behind PS21, described PS21 as 'the label we have given to the stance the Public Service must take in the face of an unpredictable future'. More specifically: 'PS21 is basically a change about change – not a change to a specific final state but an acceptance of the need for change as a permanent state' (Lim 1998: 125). On the other hand, a scholar has described PS21 as 'a detailed mission statement and program of action which maps out the future of the Singapore Public Service' (Jones, 1997: 76). The PS21 website describes PS21 as 'the Singapore Public Service's commitment to Anticipate, Welcome and Execute change, influencing developments in order to provide Singapore with the right conditions for success' (http://app.ps21.gov.sg/newps21/default.asp?id=1).

In his paper 'The Public Service' which was presented at 'The Year in Review 1995' annual conference organized by the Institute of Policy Studies on 22 January 1996, Lim Siong Guan noted that the SCS had to be responsive to 'a public that is increasingly demanding higher standards of service' and an 'increasingly outward-oriented' economy. Accordingly, the

> Public Service must not only change in step with developments in Singapore society and the international development, but also move ahead to point and lead the way forward, create and facilitate programs for national growth, and be a model for efficiency, innovation and service quality. (Lim 1996: 36)

In the past, civil servants served as regulators, provided the services and set the standards. As such, members of the public had no choice but to tolerate the standards that the SCS had set if they wanted the services. Now, however, according to David K.L. Ma (2000: 137), former Director of the Institute of Public Administration and Management, the situation has changed because of 'a higher educated and a more demanding public' and 'the advent of a knowledge-based economy'. Furthermore, the demand for quality services can be attributed to three factors: firstly, rising affluence and the spread of education which contribute to higher public expectations; secondly, the need to compete for talent and investment, pressuring the SCS to enhance Singapore's competitiveness by 'simplifying rules and procedures and by reducing business costs'; and thirdly, sensitivity to the need to uphold the SCS's reputation as an efficient and effective service provider, where a 'strong internal desire to excel has become the most important driving force for quality service' (Ma 2000: 137–138).

In the same paper, Lim elaborated on the rationale of PS21 by discussing 'some of the more fundamental concepts behind PS21'. Firstly, the intent of PS21 is for the SCS to be at the forefront or 'at the head of the pack in seeking continuous empowerment and innovation'. This means that the SCS should be transformed by PS21 to be 'a catalyst for change, a standard bearer and pace setter'. Secondly, 'to be in time for the future', PS21 must enable the SCS to welcome, anticipate and execute change. According to Lim,

> Welcoming change is opening mental windows to see change as opportunity rather than threat, with PS21 adopting the approach of making everyone an 'activist' for change and improvement. Anticipating change is accepting the unpredictability of the future but being prepared for alternative landscapes, the instrument PS21 uses being scenario-based planning [...]. And executing change is superior management of people and resources, of hope and fear, of penalty and reward. (Lim 1996: 39)

Finally, Lim stressed that the PS21 approach is 'one of evolution in execution but revolution in results'. He further admitted that 'there is some way yet to go in internalizing the demands of PS21 in public servants' as 'changes are quietly, possibly even subconsciously, taking place'. Another obstacle is that 'some people find it difficult to see the sense or value of programs that deal with processes rather than with specific tangible end goals'. Teaching civil servants to 'fish' is 'obviously superior to giving them fish' but some observers 'have difficulty appreciating the point of teaching "fishing" in the Public Service through PS21' (Lim 1996: 39–40).

COMPONENTS OF PS21

The permanent secretaries identified four priority areas, namely, Staff Well-being, Work Improvement Teams (WITs) and Staff Suggestion Schemes (SSSs), Quality Service, and Organizational Review. For staff well-being, emphasis has been given to the personal needs of the civil servants in order to enhance their psychological and physical welfare and improve their motivation and morale. The aim of WITs and the SSSs is to encourage innovation and learning among civil servants by providing them with opportunities to introduce changes into their working environments. The commitment to quality service is manifested in the introduction of measures to improve counter services and the performance of counter staff in the SCS. Finally, organizational structures and procedures will be constantly reviewed to ensure efficiency, reduce red tape and maximize effectiveness (Jones 1997: 77–79).

To implement and manage PS21, there is the Central PS21 Committee, which consists of all the permanent secretaries and which is chaired by the Head of the SCS. Below the Central PS21 Committee, there are four functional committees, each of which is chaired by a permanent secretary and includes representatives from all the ministries. Table 2 below provides details of the four PS21 functional committees and their specific terms of reference. The Public Service Division (PSD) has a PS21 Office to provide secretariat support to the Central PS21 Committee. The four functional committees have developed measurements in their respective areas. Periodic surveys have also been conducted to assess the effectiveness of PS21 in changing attitudes among civil servants and the public perception of the SCS (Prime Minister's Office 1995: 6–7).

Table 2 Terms of Reference for the PS21 Functional Committees

Functional Committee	**Terms of Reference**
PS21 Staff Well-being Committee	To promote policies and programs that provide for the well-being of public servants
PS21 Quality Service Committee	To promote quality service in meeting the needs of the public as well as of the internal customers
PS21 WITs and Suggestions Committee	To foster positive attitudes towards change and an environment which seeks continuous improvement
PS21 Organizational Review Committee	To examine organizational structures and procedures for greater effectiveness and efficiency

Source: Prime Minister's Office 1995: 6

IMPACT OF PS21

The immediate impact of PS21 is the plethora of quality service initiatives undertaken by the SCS to meet the needs of citizens and the business community. These initiatives are characterized by the overall quality-service framework of **CARE**, an acronym for **C**ourtesy, **A**ccessibility, **R**esponsiveness, and **E**ffectiveness (Ma 2000: 138). More specifically, these four features are defined thus:

Courtesy: providing e-Government services in the most user-friendly, speedy and convenient way that minimizes the effort to obtain the services;
Accessibility: providing convenient and easy access to e-Government service, 'anytime-anywhere' if possible;
Responsiveness: delivering services promptly with minimal bureaucracy;
Effectiveness: effectively meeting the public need in a secure and reliable manner without creating complexity in the process (Tan and Yong 2003: 218).

SETTING SERVICE STANDARDS IN THE SCS

With PS21, all government agencies have *pledged* to provide excellent service by setting and publishing their performance standards. For example, the Singapore Police Force (SPF) has pledged to answer emergency calls within 10 seconds at least 90% of the time, to arrive at urgent incident sites within 15 minutes and non-urgent ones within 30 minutes at least 85% of the time, to respond to letters from the public within five working days at least 90% of the time and to update victims of crime on the outcome of cases within 28 days at least 90% of the time (Singapore Police Force 1999: 38) Table 3 below shows that the SPF has exceeded the targets for these indicators between 1997 and 2002.

In his assessment of the SPF service standards, Paul Lim (2004: 44–46) concluded that 'there is no doubt that the SPF has to a large extent achieved the first objective of Public Service for the 21st Century (PS21), that is, to provide quality service and nurture an attitude of service excellence among its members'. He pointed out, however, that between 1997 and 2002, the SPF had received 1,379 complaints and 189 compliments even after the implementation of the Service Pledge in 1997 (Lim 2004: 33). More importantly, he found that while the SPF performance in providing services to the public is good it is nonetheless 'trailing behind the Hong Kong Police Force (HKPF) in the provision of services to its customers, although it has been doing better than the New Zealand Police Force (NZPF)' (Lim 2004: 46).

A second example is provided by the Singapore Immigration and Registration Department, which has promised to issue identity cards within

Table 3 SPF's Service Pledge Statistics, 1997–2002

	Answering '999' calls	Responding to urgent incidents	Responding to non-urgent incidents	Replying to letters from the public	Updating crime victims on outcome of cases
Target	90%	85%	85%	90%	90%
1997 results	94.8%	92%	94%	99.6%	94.6%
1998 results	92.5%	87.5%	91.8%	99.2%	98.8%
1999 results	91.6%	88.9%	94.7%	99.7%	99.1%
2000 results	92.4%	94.1%	97.1%	99.8%	99.5%
2001 results	98.7%	94.4%	96.8%	99.5%	99.9%
2002 results	97.9%	80.3%	94.8%	99.8%	99.9%
Target exceeded	4.65%	4.53%	9.86%	9.60%	8.63%

Source: Compiled from data provided in Singapore Police Force 1999 and Singapore Police Force 2004.

seven working days upon request and make a change of address within 10 minutes. Finally, the Registry of Companies and Businesses has pledged to process 98% of the applications for registration of new companies within 10 minutes (Ma 2000: 138).

The exercise of setting service standards has enhanced quality control and encouraged the public to provide feedback 'when the standards are not met or when they feel that the standards are too low'. Civil servants are required to review the way they work in order to raise their service standards. Thus, through a review process, the Ministry of Manpower has shortened the time it needed to process the claims for workmen's compensation from five months to one month. Similarly, by centralizing all the applications for factory registration instead of processing them according to industries, the Department of Industrial Safety has reduced the registration process from two months to two weeks (Ma 2000: 138–139).

INTEGRATING THE SCS

To improve the delivery of services to the public the SCS has introduced the following projects and initiatives:

- *e-Citizen Center*

In April 1999, the SCS launched the e-Citizen Center, which is a 'one-stop, non-stop virtual Public Services Center focused on the needs of citizens' that is accessible on the Internet (*Challenge* 1999a: 12). Designed for every citizen, the e-Citizen Center focuses on important transitions in a person's life journey like birth, education, marriage and unemployment, during which a citizen has to interact with the SCS. The advantages of the e-Citizen Center are manifold: apart from saving citizens the inconvenience of dealing with many agencies, they are not required to know which agency to contact, they simply can access the website to select the services needed (Ma 2000: 139).

The e-Citizen Center was originally organized in terms of nine towns or groupings: Business, Defense, Education, Employment, Family, Health, Housing, Law and Order, and Transport. In the case of a citizen wishing to purchase a house or apartment, all the relevant information is provided into the Housing town. More specifically, detailed instructions are provided on the procedures to be followed and the documents required. Answers are also given to frequently asked questions and application forms can be downloaded and submitted online. More than 30 government agencies participated in the e-Citizen Center, either as town-owners or as service or information providers. They offered more than 100 services online.

The e-Citizen Center or Portal was reorganized on 17 October 2001 into 14 towns and the number of e-services was increased from 380 to 540 (*Challenge* 2002a : 10). By May 2002, more than 70% of all the public services that could be delivered electronically were already online (*Challenge* 2002b: 9). Currently, the e-Citizen Portal is organized according to these seven categories: Culture, Recreation and Sports; Defense and Security; Education, Learning and Employment; Family and Community Development; Health and Environment; Housing; and Transport and Travel (see http://www.ecitizen.gov.sg).

The e-Citizen Portal initially received an average of 100,000 visitors a month (Ma 2000: 139). The feedback on the enhanced e-Citizen Portal was positive as 'visitors have found it comprehensive, convenient, well-designed and user-friendly' (*Challenge* 2002b: 9). Hence, it is not surprising that the average number of hits per month has increased from 1.2 million in May 2002 to 4.2 million in September 2002 and to 8.7 million in February 2003 (*Challenge* 2002b: 9; Tan & Yong 2003: 225; Yong & Koon 2003: 307).

• *MARINET*

MARINET was introduced by the Maritime and Port Authority of Singapore in April 1999 to provide ships calling at the port of Singapore with these four services: sending statutory declarations to the Port Authority online; shipping agents can use the system to order pilot and towage services; port-users can access MARINET for information on the arrival, departure and location of vessels; and bunker suppliers can send their monthly returns to the Port Authority. MARINET, which has more than 1,600 subscribers from over 400 companies in the shipping industry, handles an average of 350,000 such transactions each month (Ma 2000: 140).

- *Using information technology to improve service*

The SCS has been relying on information technology to improve services to the public. For example, the use of e-Filing for income tax returns by the Internal Revenue Authority of Singapore from 1998 and e-Flat for the purchase of public housing apartments from 2000 have saved citizens time and effort in their interactions with the SCS. They can now conduct their transactions anytime, even when they are abroad, without the inconvenience of queuing or physically reporting to multiple agencies. By 2002, 808,000 taxpayers or 52% of all taxpayers in Singapore had used e-Filing for their income tax returns (Tan & Yong 2003: 224). Applicants for public housing apartments who use the e-Flat system are informed within a week of the outcome of their applications. Hence, it is not surprising that soon after its introduction, about 20% of new flat applications received by the Housing and Development Board were submitted through e-Flat (*Challenge* 2000a: 8). In short, the strategic use of information technology has enabled government agencies in Singapore to provide a higher quality and more efficient service to the public, and has also resulted in savings in costs to these agencies (Ma 2000: 140).

- *The Home Team*

In 1995 the Minister for Home Affairs, Wong Kan Seng, introduced the concept of 'the Home Team' to provide an integrated and seamless service among its nine agencies: its headquarters, the Internal Security Department, the SPF, the Singapore Civil Defense Force, the Singapore Prisons Service, the Central Narcotics Bureau, the Singapore Immigration and Registration, the Commercial and Industrial Security Corporation, and the Singapore Corporation of Rehabilitative Enterprises. Wong elaborated on the Home Team concept in the following way:

> The competence of each department is high. By themselves, they do very well, whether in fighting fires or dealing with crime or drug traffickers or illegal immigrants. But I thought that more synergy will lead to greater strength with the common objective of keeping Singapore safe and secure. This is the same mission for all departments. The Home Team concept brings together different departments, different traditions, built at different times. It took some time, but the various departments have come to understand the importance and usefulness of working together. There is a comfort level in working together now. (Quoted in Soh 2003: 15)

By moving away from the traditional approach of each agency emphasizing its own roles and responsibilities, the Home Team officers focus on the outcome to be achieved as a team and perform many functions so that citizens do not have to deal with numerous agencies. In other words, the nine agencies in the Home Team improve the quality of services provided to the public by working together as a team (Ma 2000: 140).

- *Customer Service Center*

The SCS has also provided integrated services through the establishment of customer service centers. For example, the Ministry of Education set up a customer service center known as eduMALL in July 1998 to provide teachers and members of the public with a one-stop access to educational resources and services. More specifically, eduMALL consists of four components: (1) Lobby provides reviews of the latest educational software; (2) Teachers' Network enables teachers to support each other through collaboration and professional dialogue; (3) eduLibrary provides members of the public with details of the approved list of textbooks and program schedules for the Educational Television program. Teachers can find sample lesson plans, check the availability of specific learning resources, source educational software or check useful websites; (4) eduPlex enables principals and teachers to review materials on workshops conducted for implementing the Masterplan for Informational Technology in Education (*Challenge* 1999b: 9).

A second example is provided by the Central Provident Fund (CPF) Board, which has set up e-Customer Counters at its main office and two branch offices to enable its members to check their CPF accounts or other services. Alternatively, CPF members can also access the CPF website from their home or office to perform various transactions online (*Challenge* 1999c: 13).

WORKING WITH THE GROUND

While strong leadership is important for enhancing its effectiveness, the SCS realizes the need to shift away from a top-down approach by ensuring that citizens can provide feedback on 'what they want and what needs to be done'. Such feedback is important because as customers, members of the public know their needs better; and as citizens, they are expected to have a sense of ownership by providing suggestions for improvement (Ma 2000: 141). The following schemes provide members of the public with ample opportunities for making suggestions.

- *Excellence in Public Suggestions Award*

The SCS initiated a nationwide public suggestion scheme known as the Excellence in Public Suggestions Award in September 1997. The aim of this scheme was to recognize and reward members of the public who provided suggestions for improving the SCS. Awards are given every year to the best suggestions considered to be worthy of adoption (Ma 2000: 141).

- *The Enterprise Challenge*

This scheme was launched in March 2000 with the assistance of the Ministry of Finance, which provided a sum of S$10 million as seed money. Anyone with good ideas on improving public services could apply to a panel of members from the public and private sectors for funding. During its first three months, the panel received more than 120 proposals and awarded S$1 million for the development of three proposals (Ma 2000: 141).

- *Community Safety and Security Program*

The Home Team of the Ministry of Home Affairs introduced the Community Safety and Security Program (CSSP) in October 1997 to mobilize the residents, grassroots leaders and Home Team officers in order to identify and address the safety and security concerns of various neighborhood precincts in Singapore. The CSSP has provided the community with the ownership of solutions to its problems and has enhanced its sense of safety and security. More than 450 grassroots organizations had participated in the CSSP by May 2000 (Ma 2000: 141).

- *Regular dialogues*

As part of Singapore 21, citizens are encouraged to participate actively in the conduct of public affairs (Singapore 21 Committee 1999). Accordingly, government agencies have organized regular dialogues with their constituents. A survey of the ministries has shown that they have met regularly with more than 300 groups of customers. Some ministries have also conducted focus group discussions to gauge the public response to proposed new services before launching these services. David Ma has argued that these 'proactive efforts, together with the regular review of rules and regulations, ensure that the services provided to the public are relevant' (2000: 142).

- *Work Improvement Teams (WITs) and Staff Suggestion Scheme (SSS)*

In 1981, the Committee on Productivity recommended, among other things, the introduction of quality control circles (QCCs) in the SCS so that their benefits could be enjoyed by civil servants. The acronym WITs was suggested as QCCs had industrial implications and was inappropriate for the SCS. Thus, WITs is the SCS's adaptation of the QCC concept and their birth can be traced to the first meeting of the Central Productivity Steering Committee on 28 September 1981 (Ng 1990: 184). The WITs movement in the SCS was launched on 7 October 1981 with the creation of a WITs Development Unit to promote, monitor and provide training for WITs facilitators, leaders and members.

WITs consist of small voluntary groups of civil servants of different ranks from the same work units. They have been formed for three reasons: (1) to enhance the quality of work life in the SCS, by improving job satisfaction and the work environment, and promoting teamwork and human relations among civil servants; (2) to increase the SCS's performance, by improving its quality of service, productivity and teamwork; and (3) to motivate civil servants by making their work more meaningful through giving recognition, providing challenges, having more open and effective communications and developing more positive work attitudes (Ng 1990: 188).

From September 1981 to July 1990, 7,800 WITs were formed in the SCS, with 23,000 projects completed. Training was also provided for 2,000 WITs facilitators and 1,700 WITs leaders (Tan 1991). From April to December 1999, the 11,691 WITs in the SCS completed 14,228 projects and saved the SCS more than S$84 million. During the same period, civil servants contributed more than 520,000 suggestions to the SSS. Implementation of 60% of these resulted in savings of S$115 million to the SCS. Thus, in addition to cost savings, these improvements have enhanced the standard of service to the public (Ma 2000: 142).

TRAINING AND RECOGNITION OF CIVIL SERVANTS

PS21 has improved training in the SCS with the implementation of a new training policy in November 1996. This has entitled every civil servant to a minimum of 100 hours of training per year or 12.5 days (with eight hours of training daily) by 2000. This policy gave a tremendous boost to training in the SCS as only 40 hours or five days were devoted to training in 1996 (*Challenge* 1996: 1). Furthermore, a Counter Allowance Scheme was introduced in August 1995 to encourage counter staff to provide good customer service and to recognize those civil servants who have given superior customer service. To qualify for this allowance, which ranges from 5% to 10% of a civil servant's monthly salary, civil servants are required to attend the prescribed training program, to pass the requisite test and to obtain a positive evaluation of their performance from their supervisors and customers (Ma 2000: 142–143). Surveys conducted have indicated that the Counter Allowance Scheme has been successful in 'giving greater recognition to the difficulties counter staff faced in dealing with the public, in equipping them with the necessary skills and knowledge and, above all, in providing better services to the public' (Ma 2000: 143).

PROBLEMS IN IMPLEMENTING WITS

The SCS has not encountered any problems in the various PS21 initiatives to improve customer service. However, unlike the first objective of nurturing an attitude of service excellence in the SCS, the second objective of PS21, which is the creation of an environment which induces and welcomes continuous change in the SCS, has met with some resistance, especially in the implementation of the WITs.

In her excellent analysis of the implementation of WITs in the SCS, Nancy Ng, the Head of the WITs Development Unit in the Civil Service Institute, identified a total of seven 'people problems' and 13 'operational problems' (Ng 1990: 198–205). She found that the response to WITs was clearly related to management support and commitment in as much as 'ministries with strong management support and encouragement tend to be more active in the formation of WITs' (Ng 1990: 197). On the other hand, if management support is lacking, the implementation of WITs will encounter 'people problems – their attitudes, their behavior, their fears and their expectations, and their excuses – all symptoms of the very human response to change – avoidance, resistance, indifference, fear of inability to cope, fear of failure, fear of commitment, and above all, fear of loss of power and authority, and fear of "exposure" of "weaknesses"' (Ng 1990: 198). Indeed, where managers were critical and not supportive, the implementation of WITs has been difficult. For example, a manager compelled his supervisor to form a WIT and when he did so, the manager criticized the exercise as a waste of time. Civil servants who are critical of WITs have referred derisively to the acronym as "Wasting an Individual's Time". Indeed, five years after the implementation of PS21, Lim Siong Guan, the then-Head of SCS, admitted that 'a number of people have told me WITs stands for "Wasting Important Time". This is because they think WIT meetings are a waste of time' (*Challenge* 2000b: 3). Another manifestation of inadequate management support for WITs activities is the delay by managers in reading the WITs reports and implementing useful recommendations (Ng 1990: 203).

Initially, civil servants were informed that their participation in WITs would be taken into account in their performance evaluation. However, this was not done and many civil servants were discouraged from participating in WITs since they had to do so in addition to their regular duties. For example, even though the SPF WITs teams have performed well at the annual PS21 WITs Convention, there is low participation among some WITs teams in the SPF because of the following problems: (1) some participants felt that they had been obliged to undertake the projects; (2) most of them had other more important priorities than the WITs projects; (3) most could not afford the time outside their jobs to meet and discuss issues; and (4) the teams viewed WITs as ends rather than as a tool to use in their daily work (Chan 1999).

Resistance to WITs among junior police officers is manifest in their negative attitude towards WITs projects. According to Chia Tong Seng of the SPF Public Affairs Department, the main problem of WITs is the 'negative attitude' of police officers who did not believe in WITs but rather took the view that WITs were 'wasting an individual's time', did not acknowledge that WITs would lighten their workloads and mostly refused to acknowledge that WITs could increase job satisfaction (Chia 1999).

In its progress report for 2001, the SPF's Service Development and Inspectorate Department highlighted the Criminal Investigation Department (CID) as one of the departments with both a low WITs project ratio of 0.2 and the lowest SSS suggestion ratio, of 2.12 (Farouk 2002: 70). This finding is not surprising for two reasons. Firstly, in view of their heavy workload, CID officers accord higher priority to their operational demands than to WITs or SSS which they consider 'peripheral to the assessment of the department' (Farouk 2002: 49–50). Secondly, while 'there are no serious repercussions for not complying with the requirement of completing two WITs projects per year', there are also no incentives for participating in WITs or SSS (Farouk 2002: 51). Thus, CID officers are neither punished for not performing as desired nor rewarded for performing as desired. In other words, performance does not matter for CID officers as far as their participation in WITs and SSS is concerned.

The negative attitude of junior police officers towards WITs is because they are expected to participate in WITs projects in addition to performing their regular duties. Such participation is not rewarded by promotion or other incentives, and is therefore often considered as a waste of time. Why should they participate in WITs if such desired performance is punishing (Mager & Pipe 1997: 43–59)? As the SPF is an uniformed organization with a clear hierarchy of authority and emphasis on discipline, it is surprising that there is still resistance to WITs. The implication is that in other government departments or statutory boards where discipline is not emphasized so greatly, there will probably be greater resistance to WITs, unless participation in WITs is linked to incentives. For example, WITs have been very successful in the Central Provident Fund Board because of its General Manager's recognition of the importance of staff participation in WITs projects.

Finally, the Cut Waste Panel (CWP) was formed on 1 September 2003 'to receive suggestions from the public on where the government can cut waste, remove frills and make savings in the delivery of public services'. More specifically, the CWP:

> Will ensure that the suggestions are properly considered and appropriate solutions implemented. When a suggestion is received, the Panel will send it to the relevant agency for study without revealing the identity of the suggestor. The secretariat of the Cut Waste Panel will contact the suggestor for more details on the suggestion if needed. The suggestions and agencies' responses will be published on the Cut Waste website without identifying the contributors.

The Panel can ask that costs be adjusted, rules removed, programs stopped, and fees and charges reviewed, if it finds them unnecessary. It will help the government get good value for money in the delivery of services which meet the needs of the public at an acceptable standard (Ministry of Finance 2003a).

The CWP was originally chaired by Lim Siong Guan, the then-Head of the SCS, and consisted of seven other members including two members of parliament, two journalists, a grassroots leader, an accountant and a consumer advocate. The response to the CWP was good, as it received 1,263 suggestions by November 2003 and the various government agencies had agreed with 87% or 700 of the 805 suggestions processed (Ministry of Finance 2003b).

Among the many suggestions received by the CWP, I wish to highlight the four suggestions received in November 2003 and January 2004 concerning WITs as further evidence of the problems encountered in implementing WITs in the SCS.

Subject: Wasteful WITs program
Suggestion: Currently, all government departments are required to take part in WITs program and competition. Staff is assigned in teams to come up with ideas to produce a comprehensive report which take extensive man hours. […] In this economic situation, I deem this WITs is wasteful of resources, manpower and budget and should be scrapped totally. […] Resources wasted are stationery, man hours, energy and miscellaneous and invisible costs. Please check with any government department to confirm my suggestion (Prime Minister's Office 2003a).

Subject: WITs program
Suggestion: All government departments are subjecting their staff to take part in WITs program. The percentage of WITs ideas [that] are adopted and cost-saving are minuscule when compared to wastage incurred overall. […] It has become ridiculous to an extent that staff is [*sic*] taking part under duress just to produce a submission representing his/her department. Nonsensical and impractical ideas are submitted just for showcase. […] This WITs program is a national wastage in manpower, resources and cost to the country and not benefiting the country greatly (Prime Minister's Office 2003b).

Joyce Chia, Assistant Director for Public Affairs and Administration in the Public Service Division, replied to the above suggestions on 11 and 24 November 2003 with the same 'canned' answer:

> The Public Service needs to anticipate change and continually improve to continue to serve Singapore well. The Work Improvement Team Scheme (WITs) Movement is an essential part of this process. It encourages public officers to continuously look for new ways to improve the quality of their work. It provides a means by which public officers can work as a team to solve work-related problems. Through WITs, public officers are given the opportunity to exercise ownership and responsibility for making improvements to their work. They are the ones who really know the problems within their respective work areas and are best suited to find the right solutions.

> The topics proposed for WITs must be work-related and are endorsed by the organization's management before the Work Improvement Teams commence their projects. This ensures that the topics chosen are relevant to the organization's mission and purpose. Participation in WITs is considered part and parcel of every officer's work and is not an extracurricular activity, nor a waste of time.
>
> We monitor the overall cost savings and benefits from the WITs Movement every year. The total cost savings from the WITs Programme for Fiscal Year 2002 was substantial – about S$165 million dollars. This does not include the intangible value added from WITs projects which enhance service delivery.
>
> We recognize that the WITs Movement can be improved in the way it is implemented. The necessary changes are being made. For instance, the WITs judging criteria have been reviewed to place more emphasis on results, and less on process and strict adherence to WITs tools. We have also introduced a wider variety of and greater flexibility in the use of tools for WITs. We also want to balance the quantitative indicators with qualitative indicators (Prime Minister's Office 2003a and 2003b).

The third suggestion received by the CWP concerned a review of the reward structure for WITs and the SSS. As WITs was 'incentive driven', the suggestor recommended that the CWP should check whether the ministries and statutory boards have spent a great deal of money on WITs and SSS. On 26 November 2003, Joyce Chia replied that as the SSS was introduced for civil servants to improve productivity in the SCS, 'good ideas that are accepted are awarded a small token amount' of S$2 and 'higher-quality suggestions that result in higher savings or value created are awarded more, but not excessively so'. The token award is meant to encourage civil servants to participate in the SSS, and 'the amount that an officer gets out of SSS will not enrich him' (Prime Minister's Office 2003c).

The final suggestion recommended the removal of WITs:

> ...as most civil servants find WITs [to be] a big headache. They tend to keep ideas they have for any work improvement year after year so that they have projects to meet the target. WITs actually slows down any improvement that they may already have in mind. The presentation of WITs is another big waste of resources and time and achieves little purpose. Suggest to remove WITs. (Prime Minister's Office 2004)

In her reply on 27 January 2004, Joyce Chia reiterated her earlier statement on the aim of WITs, rejected this suggestion and defended the retention of WITs thus:

> In the latest survey on WITs, many public officers indicated that they understand and are aware of WITs. A majority also indicated that they enjoy taking part in WITs, and will participate voluntarily. [Specific details on this survey like sample size and who conducted it were not provided.]
>
> The targets that are set for WITs are a means of encouraging and motivating officers to participate and are not quotas that have to be met. If there are

> government agencies where WITs is practiced wrongly, then it is for these agencies to change and implement WITs in the right spirit and manner. Incorrect implementation of the idea should not mean that the idea itself should be abandoned. (Prime Minister's Office 2004)

Unfortunately, Ms Chia's rejection of the suggestion to remove WITs is a reflection of the government's refusal to acknowledge the widespread resistance to WITs. In contrast to the survey findings reported by Ms Chia above, a 2003 survey of civil servants found that nearly half of them, if given a choice, would not participate in WITs. This finding was similar to that of a 1998 survey of civil servants (*Straits Times* 2003). Ironically, the continued retention of WITs, in spite of its unpopularity, contradicts the second objective of welcoming 'continuous change for greater efficiency and effectiveness by employing modern management tools and techniques while paying attention to the morale and welfare of public officers'. It seems that WITs is 'here to stay', even if it undermines the morale of many civil servants.

CONCLUSION

The problems encountered in implementing WITs in the SCS illustrate the difficulties involved in changing the mindset of civil servants, especially in changing their attitudes toward change. In a recent interview, Ngiam Tong Dow, who retired from the SCS as Permanent Secretary (Finance) in 1999, astutely observed that 'it takes a certain temperament and mindset to be a civil servant. The former head of the civil service, Sim Kee Boon, once said that joining the administrative service is like entering a royal priesthood. Not all of us have the temperament to be priests' (Long 2003: 39). In the same interview, he expressed his concern about the SCS as follows:

> The greatest danger [to the SCS] is we are flying on autopilot. What was once a great policy, we just carry on with more of the same, until reality intervenes [...] We have been flying on autopilot for too long [...] I suspect we have started to believe our own propaganda. There is also a particular brand of Singapore elite-arrogance creeping in. Some civil servants behave like they have a mandate from the emperor. We think we are little Lee Kuan Yews. (Long 2003: 39)

Ngiam's assessment of the SCS should be taken seriously. He was a senior civil servant for 40 years (1959–1999) and became the youngest Permanent Secretary at the Ministry of Communications at the age of 33. His subsequent postings as permanent secretary were in the Ministries of Finance, Trade and Industry, National Development and the Prime Minister's Office. Ngiam's remarks are instructive. His criticism of the SCS as 'flying on autopilot' implies that the PS21 second objective of transforming the civil servants' attitudes towards change has been neglected or not attained so far. The continued retention of the WITs program in the face of widespread resistance is another good illustration of the SCS 'flying on autopilot'.

One of the major strengths of public administration in Singapore is its reliance on policy diffusion, or the willingness to learn from the experiences of other countries in order to avoid making the same mistakes (Quah 2003a: 176). Thus, instead of 'reinventing the wheel', it would be instructive to examine briefly Canada's ambitious but unsuccessful project Public Service 2000 (PS2000). This might help identify relevant lessons for the implementation of PS21 in the SCS. PS2000 was launched in December 1989 by Prime Minister Brian Mulroney who was anxious to 'revitalize the Canadian public service and prepare it for the twenty-first century' (Caiden, Halley & Maltais 1995: 86). This was followed in early 1990 by the formation of ten task forces, which produced over 300 recommendations and 80 policy decisions on various themes (Dwivedi 1993: 51–54).

Caiden, Halley and Maltais identified five lessons from Canada's PS2000, which should be noted by the PS21 Office and those responsible for implementing PS21 in the SCS in order to avoid making the same mistakes as the Canadian reformers. These are the five lessons. Firstly, it was recognized too late that political support was only nominal during the design of Public Service 2000 and inadequate during its implementation. Secondly, greater focus and candor were needed throughout PS2000. Impressive as it was, PS2000 covered too much and involved too many changes at the same time. It promised too much and raised many expectations. It was not clear what its priorities were, thereby creating perhaps unnecessary confusion as to where the real effort should be made. Thirdly, cultural changes require tools that the reformers did not have or know how to use. The reformers did not know how to overcome middle-management resistance. They did not do enough to change the reward system and provide incentives that might have produced the needed changes. Fourthly, monitoring was quite inadequate and original expectations could not be modified on the basis of feedback. And fifthly, the time-frame for implementing PS2000 was underestimated. Reforms need time to take effect. Although PS2000 allowed itself ten years, it was already being judged within two years and found wanting (Caiden, Halley & Maltais 1995: 99–100).

In short, to ensure the effective implementation of PS21 in the SCS, there must be consistent support from the political leadership, greater focus and realistic expectations. Reformers must be given tools to overcome middle-management resistance and modify the incentive system to produce the needed changes, and there must be adequate monitoring and a longer time-frame for gauging the effectiveness of the reforms. For PS21 to succeed, it must be supported by *everyone* in the SCS and not just by the permanent secretaries who were responsible for its genesis. Interviews with some civil servants have revealed that support for PS21 today varies among the ministries depending on the permanent secretary concerned. For example, Bilahari Kausikan, the second Permanent Secretary of the Ministry of Foreign Affairs, was critical of the time, effort and money spent on the elaborate presentations at the annual WITs convention. He also added that 'WITs and SSS are widely perceived as a numbers game, an extracurricular activity and an additional burden, not an integral part of work' (*Straits Times* 2003). These civil servants have also expressed the view that support for PS21 was much stronger when Lim Siong Guan, former Head of the SCS, was Permanent Secretary of the Ministry of Finance and responsible for implementing PS21. Indeed, it appears that support for PS21 will decline even further under Peter Ho, the current Head of the SCS.

Unlike previous administrative reforms, PS21 does not appear to have the support of the political leaders as it was formulated by the permanent secretaries themselves. While the political leaders have not explicitly objected to PS21, it is also significant that neither the prime minister nor any minister has made a speech on PS21 during the past ten years. However, this is not surprising as PS21 is an in-house effort to 'reinvent' and prepare the SCS for the twenty-first century. Thus, while PS21 has improved the quality of service and training in the SCS which benefits citizens directly in terms of the provision of services, the impact on citizens of the second objective, i.e., preparing civil servants to accept and welcome change, is indirect and long-term and so far has not been achieved, even after a decade.

The successful implementation of PS21 in the SCS also presupposes high morale and little or no resistance to PS21 among civil servants. The aim of the Staff Well-Being Subcommittee is to formulate policies and programs to enhance the well-being of all civil servants. Indeed, the SCS has initiated many schemes to assist civil servants and their families. For example, the SPF won the Singapore Health Gold Award in 2001 for its efforts in improving the well-being of its officers. However, the 'emphasis on the high-flyers or scholars at the expense of the low-flyers and non-scholars' in the SCS has resulted in serious morale problems among civil servants which PS21, for all its concern with staff well-being, does not address (Quah 1996a: 63–64). For example, in the case of the SPF, Mohamed Farouk (2002: 39) found that there was 'a wide disparity in the treatment of scholars and non-scholars', the scholars being promoted more rapidly than non-scholars. Thus, for PS21 to be implemented successfully in the SCS, the Public Service Division must take steps to improve the morale of those disgruntled civil servants and to provide the permanent secretaries and other senior civil servants with guidelines for dealing with resistance to PS21 and WITs.

In sum, what has been the impact of PS21 on the SCS? The first benefit that PS21 has provided to the SCS is the improvement of service standards and the acceptance of the importance of ensuring good quality service among the various government agencies. In other words, PS21's first objective of developing an attitude of service excellence in the SCS has been attained through various PS21 initiatives which have improved the service provided by government.

In addition to improving service quality, PS21 has also enhanced the importance of training in the SCS. A significant consequence of the British colonial legacy is the emphasis on on-the-job training in the SCS and its resistance to conducting off-the-job training programs (Quah 1996c: 52). For example, in 1987 Singapore's per capita expenditure on formal off-the-job training was only S$100, which was much lower than the corresponding amounts of S$300 in West Germany, S$750 in the USA and S$3,000 in Japan (Cox 1987: 40). In April 1988, the Ministry of Finance announced that 'out of a total of 200 working days each year, at least 10 days will be spent on staff training' (*Straits Times* 1987: 32). With the introduction of PS21 to the SCS in May 1995, the number of days devoted to training has been increased to 12.5 per year or 100 hours for each civil servant.

Finally, the second objective of PS21 cannot be measured accurately because of its intangible nature. Was it realistic to expect civil servants in Singapore to 'induce and welcome continuous change' after the introduction of PS21 in May 1995? The answer is probably 'no', judging from Ngiam Tong Dow's criticism that the SCS is 'flying on autopilot' and from the resistance shown by many junior civil servants toward WITs. Indeed, it is as unrealistic to ask Singapore civil servants to initiate and accept continuous change as it is asking a leopard to change its spots. In sum, PS21's contribution to the SCS so far is the improvement of service standards and training. Moreover, these standards would not be eroded even if PS21 were to be abandoned tomorrow, because of the acceptance by the SCS and Singaporeans of the importance of providing good customer service and training. Indeed, as I concluded in my assessment of the impact of PS21 on the SPF,

> PS21 has certainly reinforced the SPF's commitment to service and organizational excellence. However, in my view, if PS21 were to be abandoned tomorrow, no one in the SPF (or the SCS) would shed any tears, as they would not be adversely affected in any significant way. (Quah 2005: 103)

In order to avoid the same fate as Canada's PS2000, the objective of inducing and welcoming continuous change by civil servants should be abandoned as unrealistic and unattainable.

REFERENCES

About PS21: Challenges and Objectives (2005). Singapore: PS21 Office, Public Service Division. Retrieved 25 February 2005 (http://www.ps21.gov.sg/about_challenges.htm).

Caiden, G.E. (1969). *Administrative Reform.* London: Penguin.
Caiden, G.E. (1991). *Administrative Reform Comes of Age.* Berlin: de Gruyter.
Caiden, G.E., Halley, A.A., & Maltais, D. (1995). 'Results and Lessons from Canada's PS2000'. *Public Administration and Development* 15, pp. 85–102.
Challenge (1996). 'Training gets Premium Treatment'. 1, p. 1.
Challenge (1999a). 'e-Citizen Center Answers All Your Questions'. 5, pp. 12–13.
Challenge (1999b). 'Visit EDUMALL: Teaching Resources Under One Roof'. 5, p. 9.
Challenge (1999c). 'E-Customer Service @ CPF'. 5, p. 13.
Challenge (2000a). 'HDB Launches e-Flat System'. 6, p. 8.
Challenge (2000b). 'Wasting Important Time?' 6, p. 1.
Challenge (2002a). 'Towards Citizen-centered Services – e-Government and You'. 8, p. 10.
Challenge (2002b). 'More services with e-Citizen portal revamp'. 8, p. 9.
Chan, Y. Fun (1999). Interview on May 20. Quoted in Panirsilvam & Tan (1999).
Chia, T.S. (1999). Interview on May 28. Quoted in Panirsilvam & Tan (1999).
Cox, N. (1987). 'Singapore lagging in off-the-job training'. *Asian Business* 23, pp. 39–40.
Dwivedi, O.P. (1993). 'Public Service Reforms in Canada for the 21st Century'. *Indian Journal of Public Administration* 39, pp. 46–66.
Jones, D.S. (1997). 'Public Service for the 21st Century – PS21'. In F.K. Chua & T.L. Thaver (Eds), *Everyday Life, Everyday People* (pp. 76–80). Singapore: Gifted Education Branch, Ministry of Education and Faculty of Arts and Social Sciences, National University of Singapore.
Jones, D.S. (2002). 'Recent Reforms in Singapore's Administrative Elite: Responding to the Challenges of a Rapidly Changing Economy and Society'. *Asian Journal of Political Science* 10, pp. 70–93.
Lim, P.C.C. (2004). 'Improving Singapore Police Force's Service Standards'. B.Soc.Sc. Honours Thesis, Department of Political Science, National University of Singapore, Singapore.
Lim, S.G. (1996). 'The Public Service'. In L.H. Yeo (Ed), *Singapore: The Year in Review 1995* (pp. 35–48). Singapore: Institute of Policy Studies.
Lim, S.G. (1998). 'PS21: Gearing up the Public Service for the 21st Century'. In A. Mahiznan & T.Y. Lee (Eds), *Singapore Re-engineering Success* (pp. 124–131). Singapore: Oxford University Press.
Long, S. (2003). 'S'pore bigger than PAP'. *Sunday Times.* 28 September, p. 39.
Ma, D.K.L. (2000). 'Delivering Results on the Ground: Improving Service to Citizens in Singapore'. *Asian Journal of Political Science* 8, pp. 137–144.

Mager, R.F., and Pipe, P. (1997). *Analyzing Performance Problems or You Really Oughta Wanna* (3rd ed). Atlanta: Center for Effective Performance.

Manning, N., et al. (2000). *Pay and Patronage in the Core Civil Service in Indonesia.* Washington, DC: World Bank.

Ministry of Finance (2003a). 'Government Sets Up Cut Waste Panel'. Singapore: Press Release, 4 September. Retrieved 26 February 2005 (http://app.mof.gov.sg/cutwaste/pressreleasedetails.asp?pressID=109).

Ministry of Finance (2003b). '87% of Cut Waste Suggestions Agreed With'. Singapore: Press Release, 12 November. Retrieved 26 February 2005. (http://app.mof.gov.sg/cutwaste/pressreleasedetails.asp?pressID=120).

Mohamed Farouk bin Mohamed Ismail (2002). 'Implementing PS21 in the Singapore Police Force (1995–2001): An Evaluation'. B.Soc.Sc. Honours Thesis, Department of Political Science, National University of Singapore, Singapore.

Ng, N. (1990). 'The Implementation of Work Improvement Teams in the Singapore Civil Service'. In C.T. Foo & C.H. Chan (Eds), *Productivity in Transition* (pp. 179–206). Singapore: McGraw-Hill.

Panirsilvam, S.D., & Tan, A. (1999). *Business Process Re-engineering and Work Improvement Teams.* Singapore: Report prepared for the Ministry of Home Affairs.

Prime Minister's Office (1995). 'The Case for PS21: Public Service for the 21st Century'. Singapore: PS21 Office, Public Service Division.

Prime Minister's Office (2003a). 'Wasteful WITs program'. Singapore: Reply of 11 November. Retrieved 26 February 2005 (http://app.mof.gov.sg/cutwaste/suggestionview.asp?id=211).

Prime Minister's Office (2003b). 'WITs Program'. Singapore: Reply of 24 November. Retrieved 26 February 2005 (http://app.mof.gov.sg/cutwaste/suggestionview.asp?id=255).

Prime Minister's Office (2003c). 'Review of reward structure for WITs and SSS'. Singapore: Reply of 26 November. Retrieved 26 February 2005 (http://app.mof.gov.sg/cutwaste/suggestionview.asp?id=301).

Prime Minister's Office (2004). 'Remove WITs (work improvement team)'. Singapore: Reply of 27 January. Retrieved 26 February 2005 (http://app.mof.gov.sg/cutwaste/suggestionview.asp?id=298).

Quah, J.S.T. (1976). 'Administrative Reform: A Conceptual Analysis'. *Philippine Journal of Public Administration* 20, pp. 50–67.

Quah, J.S.T. (1978). 'The Origins of the Public Bureaucracies in the ASEAN Countries'. *Indian Journal of Public Administration* 24, pp. 400–429.

Quah, J.S.T. (1989). 'Singapore's Experience in Curbing Corruption'. In A.J. Heidenheimer, M. Johnston, & V.T. LeVine (Eds), *Political Corruption: A Handbook* (pp. 841–853). New Brunswick: Transaction Publishers.

Quah, J.S.T. (1991). 'Administrative Reform: Singapore Style'. *International Review of Administrative Sciences* 57, pp. 85–100.

Quah, J.S.T. (1994). 'Culture Change in the Singapore Civil Service'. In S.A. Chaudhry, et al. (Eds), *Civil Service Reform in Latin America and the Caribbean: Proceedings of a Conference* (pp. 205–216). Washington, DC: World Bank.

Quah, J.S.T. (1996a). 'Public Administration in Singapore: Managing Success in a Multi-Racial City-State'. In A.S. Huque, J.T.M. Lam, & J.C.Y. Lee (Eds), *Public Administration in the NICs: Challenges and Accomplishments* (pp. 59–89). Basingstoke: Macmillan Press.

Quah, J.S.T. (1996b). 'Decentralizing Public Personnel Management: The Case of the Public Service Commission in Singapore'. In S. Kurosawa, T. Fujiwara, & M.A. Reforma (Eds), *New Trends in Public Administration for the Asia-Pacific Region: Decentralization* (pp. 492–506). Tokyo: Local Autonomy College.

Quah, J.S.T. (1996c). 'Commentary on the Public Service'. In L.H. Yeo (Ed), *Singapore: The Year in Review 1995* (pp. 49–57). Singapore: Institute of Policy Studies.

Quah, J.S.T. (2003a). 'Public Administration in Singapore: The Role of the Public Bureaucracy in a One-Party Dominant System'. In K.K. Tummala (Ed), *Comparative Bureaucratic Systems* (pp. 165–183). Lanham: Lexington Books.

Quah, J.S.T. (2003b.) 'Paying for the "Best and Brightest": Rewards for High Public Office in Singapore'. In C. Hood, B.G Peters, & G.O.M. Lee (Eds), *Reward for High Public Office: Asian and Pacific Rim States* (pp. 145–162). London: Routledge.

Quah, J.S.T. (2005). 'Implementing PS21 in the Singapore Police Force, 1995–2002: A Case Study of Civil Service Reform'. In A.B.L. Cheung (Ed), *Public Service Reform in East Asia: Reform Issues and Challenges in Japan, Korea, Singapore and Hong Kong* (pp. 83–104). Hong Kong: Chinese University Press.

Republic of Singapore (1994). *Competitive Salaries for Competent and Honest Government: Benchmarks for Ministers and Senior Public Officers.* White Paper presented to Parliament on 21 October. Command 13 of 1994.

Singapore (1996). *Yearbook of Statistics, 1995.* Singapore: Department of Statistics.

Singapore (2005). *Yearbook of Statistics, 2005.* Singapore: Department of Statistics.

Singapore Police Force (1999). *Annual Report 1998/99.* Singapore: SPF Headquarters.

Singapore Police Force (2004). *Annual Report 2003.* Singapore: SPF Headquarters.

Singapore 21 Committee (1999). *Singapore 21: Together, We Make the Difference.* Singapore: Prime Minister's Office.

Singapore (2004). Singapore: Ministry of Information, Communications and the Arts.

Soh, F. (2003). *Phoenix: The Story of the Home Team.* Singapore: Times Editions for the Ministry of Home Affairs.

Straits Times (Singapore) (1987). 'Civil Servants may soon get at least 10 days' training a year'. 19 August, p. 32.

Straits Times (Singapore) (2003). 'Civil Service Ideas Need Revamp: Changes on the way as too much time, effort and money go towards preparing for elaborate annual WITs convention'. 14 November.

Tan, C. (1991). Interview on 22 February at the Civil Service Institute in Singapore. Quoted in J.S.T. Quah (1994). 'Improving the Efficiency and Productivity of the Singapore Civil Service'. In J.P. Burns (Ed), *Asian Civil Systems: Improving Efficiency and Productivity* (pp. 152–185). Singapore: Times Academic Press.

Tan, J.B.H., & Yong, J.S.L. (2003). 'Many Agencies, One Government – Singapore's Approach to Public Services Delivery'. In J.S.L. Yong (Ed), *Enabling Public Service Innovation in the 21st Century: E-Government in Asia* (pp. 204–240). Singapore: Times Media.

Yong, J.S.L., & Koon, L.H. (2003). 'The e-Services Portal – Doorway to e-Government'. In J.S.L. Yong (Ed), *Enabling Public Service Innovation in the 21st Century: E-Government in Asia* (pp. 301–320). Singapore: Times Media.

10

Balancing Tensions between Personal and Public Obligations: A Context for Public Ethics and Corruption

STEVEN E. AUFRECHT

INTRODUCTION

Precisely defining corruption has proven very difficult. Heidenheimer et al., in their 1989 handbook on political corruption, devote the first five chapters to discussions of this subject. Perry (1997), introducing political corruption into political geography, spends one chapter discussing the difficulty of defining corruption and another mapping out several possible definitions. Caiden and Dwivedi (2001) devote much of their first two chapters to defining corruption.

In this essay, I am not overly concerned with specific definitions of corruption. Rather, I work on describing the context for a class of activities including ethical misconduct and corruption. I develop a model that describes all public officials as subject to a basic tension between their personal, private obligations and their public obligations. Because this tension exists for every public official, I argue that conflicts of interest are not inherently bad but rather simply a fact of life. To understand corruption and other unethical behaviors and to decrease the likelihood of corruption, we need to understand the nature of this tension in different settings and for different individuals. The model developed in this essay is intended to be descriptive rather than prescriptive. Most definitions of corruption focus on acts that deviate from the accepted norms for public officials. In this essay, I use the term to cover elected officials, public administrators and other public employees. Some writers such as Heidenheimer et al. (1989) have raised the question 'Whose Norms Set the Criteria?' (11). The model developed here acknowledges that public officials have obligations to other sets of norms besides those governing their public offices, which it would be unreasonable to expect them to ignore. The dilemma for public officials is to balance these conflicting obligations, so that the inherent conflict does not lead to abuse and that their personal obligations do not compromise their public obligations. The two most common negative outcomes of such a compromise are undue gain and improper influence, or a combination of the two.

This premise that corruption and other ethical problems of public officials arise from the conflicts between their personal and public obligations leads directly to the question: under what conditions do officials pursue personal goals over their public obligations? I offer four conditions that increase the likelihood of this: (1) when their personal needs cannot be met legitimately; (2) when their personal needs can be met illegitimately; (3) when the societal controls are weak enough that violations are unlikely to be apprehended; and (4) when apprehended, the cost is less than the benefit. These conditions lead to the next basic question: under what conditions would a particular individual perceive that those conditions were met to a degree that he would be likely to breach his public obligations?

Finally the model leads me to the question: what strategies can organizations and societies use to keep the tension between personal and public obligations in balance? Those who have studied the literature on ethics and corruption will recognize many of the options I propose because other scholars have come up with similar conclusions. It is my hope that recognition of a familiar ground reached from a different theoretical path may yield a useful new understanding of the workings of corruption.

THE INHERENT CONFLICT OF INTEREST FOR ALL OFFICIALS WHO MUST BALANCE THE TENSION BETWEEN THEIR PUBLIC AND PRIVATE OBLIGATIONS

Conflicts of interest are commonly seen as *the* problem for public sector ethics. For example, the American Society for Public Administration (ASPA) *Code of Ethics*, Standard III.3, demands of a public official that he/she 'zealously guard against conflict of interest or its appearance: e.g. nepotism, improper outside employment, misuse of public resources or the acceptance of gifts' (American Society for Public Administration 2002). The problem with identifying conflict of interest as *the* problem is that it makes all public officials automatically corrupt, because they all have conflicts of interest. Public officials feel trapped. Furthermore, citing nepotism, misuse of public resources and gifts as examples of conflict of interest misses a subtle but important distinction between them.

Public officials are human beings who have taken on the additional role of a public official. Thus they are acting in at least two different roles. The core of ethical dilemmas for public officials is the tension between the individual official's personal and public obligations. All public officials fall somewhere on a continuum between what I will call potential conflict and egregious conflict for every issue they face every day (see Figure 1).

For example, minutes before an important public meeting, an official is informed that his child has been seriously injured in an accident. The conflict between family and office is so strong that a word exists in English

Point (1) clearly is a problem; Point (2) marks the appearance of a conflict of interest. (The problem points (1) and (2) cannot be placed at any exact point, but these are a very rough location.)

Figure 1 Conflict of Interest Continuum for Public Officials

for its abuse – nepotism. In organizational settings where the official's work can easily be delayed or covered by someone else, there is little question he should take care of his child. In situations where the official's absence would have grave consequences, the choice of which obligation to honor would be more difficult.

If everyone has at least a potential conflict of interest, when does a conflict of interest become a problem? There are two key points on the continuum. (1) A conflict of interest is clearly a problem when one's personal obligations negatively impact the manner in which one carries out one's public or professional obligations. This will occur at a different point on the line for different people, different organizations, different situations and different cultures. But even if an official is exceptionally self-aware, and exceptionally objective in her decision-making, there is always the possibility that to others there will be (2) the appearance of a conflict of interest. Again, this point will vary from place to place, time to time. This ambiguity is one of the great dilemmas for those promoting ethics as well as those officials unexpectedly caught by public outrage. The point at which one official's personal obligations affect her professional obligations is different for each public official.

When one's decisions are colored by one's personal interests, the public usually loses: inferior goods are purchased, inflated prices are paid, illegal behavior is rewarded, and less qualified applicants are chosen. But even if one's judgment is not affected, the appearance of conflict can erode public trust in government. When the public is convinced that decisions are made fairly and resources are spent equitably, efficiently and effectively, their compliance is greater. The greater the voluntary compliance with government is (whether obeying traffic laws or paying taxes), the less is the cost of enforcing the law. As trust and then compliance decline, the costs of enforcement go up, decreasing efficiency and further deteriorating trust.

When individual public officials begin to approach those problem points on the continuum, there appear to be three basic options. The first is disclosure. This is more appropriate for elected officials, whose voters can ultimately decide at the next election. But it also works for administrators whose supervisors can reassign a decision to another administrator. The second is to recuse oneself from the decision. This works if such conflicts are few and far between and there are other officials available to make the decision. There can still be the lingering concern that the colleagues may also be biased by their professional connections to the recused official. The third option is resignation. This is the option if the conflict is so widespread as to raise questions about all the decisions one might make. It is also the option after a decision has been made and public opinion clearly sees a serious conflict.

The Tension between Personal and Public Interests

Rose-Ackerman (1999: 2) has argued that 'there is one human motivator that is both universal and central to explaining the divergent experiences of different countries. That motivator is self-interest, including an interest in the well-being of one's family and peer group'.

Thus it is critical that there be a significant overlap between an administrator's personal and public obligations. The individual's obligations, ideally, will be met by the agency. Salary and perquisites should be sufficient to allow employees to take care of their family's basic needs. Ideally, colleagues can meet some of the employee's social needs. The opportunity to do good work toward noble ends should help meet esteem and, occasionally, actualization needs. Obviously, this is the ideal. But individuals need not meet, and generally should not have to meet, all those needs at work. They should have, at the minimum, adequate compensation to cover basic food, housing and health care, and should have work schedules that give them sufficient time to meet many of their needs away from work. And their job should not put them in positions that compromise their personal values and obligations.

But even in the best of situations, where an employee has the ideal job – say an air force pilot whose job gives him the opportunity to fly the powerful jet fighters he loves and would otherwise not have access to, or a doctor whose job allows her to provide life-giving treatment to her patients – there may come a time when the interests of the organization and the interests of the employee diverge. Organizations change. New leaders with different priorities appear. Financial strains change priorities. Even the best employees may find that the organization no longer meets their personal needs. Or family crises may distract individuals from their work duties. They may even consider ways to use their positions to help solve their personal problems. In the worst situations, employees may hate the organizations they work for, feeling coerced to stay by the necessity to earn a living. They share none of the organization's goals; they have no sense of public service.

This *tension* between personal and public obligations is what is usually known as a *conflict of interest*. However, the conflict itself is not inherently harmful. Rather it is inevitable, to some extent, because public employees are human beings with lives outside the organization. Some conflicts are accepted as normal. John Roberts, the new United States Supreme Court Chief Justice, argued many a case before the Supreme Court and then Chief Justice John Rehnquist. However, no one complained about a conflict of interest for Rehnquist because Roberts had earlier been his law clerk. The problems arise when the employee favors the private obligations over the public obligations, or when the public strongly perceives this to be the case. The two key problematic outcomes are undue gain and improper influence.

Undue gain is easier to understand if we first discuss due gain. For public employees, due gain is the salary and perquisites that they officially receive in return for the work they do. This is perhaps most explicitly spelled out when there is a union contract. In other situations the contract is unwritten. Undue gain, in contrast, includes payments, favors, and other advantages one receives in addition to those spelled out in one's contract, in exchange for one's official work. Such undue gain could include cash from a contractor to speed up approval of a building permit, promise of a future high-paying job in exchange for choosing a particular company for a government contract, or even the emotional satisfaction of thwarting an adversary's access to a deserved governmental service or position. In each case, the public official has gained something of personal value through the conduct of official business – something in addition to the official benefits of office, something to which the general public does not have access.

Improper influence relates directly to the way public officials and administrators make decisions. Proper influence occurs when an officer adheres to the rule of law, standard operating procedures, professional standards or other recognized and sanctioned criteria for making a decision. In those situations that the standards do not cover, the administrator should use administrative discretion that is firmly grounded on the intent of the relevant rules and is consistent with all such previous decisions. Improper influence occurs when a public administrator adds and/or substitutes criteria, in the decision-making, that sway the process away from what would have resulted using only the official standard criteria. This could happen when an official selects a route for a new road because it will increase the value of property owned by a friend, or when an applicant is rejected because of her skin color. Improper influence and undue gain often occur together, when some form of payment becomes the illegitimate, unadmitted criterion used to supplant the legitimate decision in favor of the most qualified applicant.

ASPA's examples of conflict of interest blur the distinction between conflict of interest, undue gain, and improper influence. The first is the source of the problem; the latter two are the effect. Not all officials who have a conflict of interest act improperly. The examples in the ASPA Code are not conflicts of interest, but examples of undue gain and/or improper influence. We have already mentioned that family ties present a well-recognized conflict; however, nepotism describes the acting on that conflict, not the conflict itself. Hiring a relative certainly has the appearance of improper influence. The job itself is a benefit to the family, clearly an undue gain if better applicants did not have equal access to apply or were not chosen. Even if the relative is the most qualified applicant, the constant presence of a close relative to the boss among the employees keeps improper influence as a constant danger. The close ties of family make this a (1) and most likely a (2) on the conflict of interest continuum presented earlier.

Improper outside employment sets up the employee to have conflicts between obligations to the other employer and his public employer. The employee will likely keep the interests of the outside employer in mind while making official decisions. If the outside job represented a reward for the decisions made as a public official, then this is clearly undue gain obtained for an improper influence. The use of public resources becomes *mis*use when applied to or used for undue gain. The acceptance of even token gifts is technically undue gain, and larger gifts are likely factors in improper influence. At the very least they raise issues of appearance of conflict of interest. The ASPA examples are the result of favoring private obligations over public ones, of falling to the temptation set up by the conflict of interest. They are not examples of conflict of interest.

CONDITIONS THAT LEAD TO UNDUE GAIN AND IMPROPER INFLUENCE

If unethical behavior – including corruption – stems from this conflict between personal and public obligations, we should be able to learn something about preventing unethical behavior and corruption by studying the conditions under which this tension leads to undue gain and improper influence.

The first basic question we would have to ask is: under what conditions do officials pursue personal obligations over their public obligations? While the focus here is on the individual, the decisions individuals make are strongly influenced by the institutional contexts in which the official lives. Caiden (2001) lists seven factors that contribute to corruption: (1) psychological, (2) ideological, (3) external, (4) economic, (5) political, (6) sociocultural and (7) technological. All of these can play a role, but I would point out that these factors can have positive as well as negative effects.

Addressing an Immanent Tension

The greater the overlap between personal and public obligations, the less likely it is that personal obligations will seriously interfere with public obligations. Public officials are more likely to let personal obligations interfere with public obligations when (1) they cannot meet their private obligations by following the legitimate government rules; (2) those obligations can be met by breaking the rules; (3) the chances of being caught are low; and (4) the cost from getting caught is lower than the potential gains from breaking the rules. These conditions work progressively. However, if any individual condition holds, it could be a weak link allowing corruption even though the others do not generally hold.

To understand how to increase the likelihood that public officials will be faithful to their public obligations, we have to understand why individuals make decisions to compromise their public obligations, and how to establish conditions that reduce the likelihood of that happening. While that is a much larger task than this chapter could handle, I can, at least, begin a quick look at a few of the paths stemming from this model. Let's turn the conditions above into questions.

Meeting Needs

What do people need? This question has been answered differentially by many people. I will try to answer that question here, but hope to offer a glimpse into a likely approach. On a macro-level, one of the most cited lists of human needs is Maslow's hierarchy of needs: survival, shelter, affection, self-esteem and self-actualization. It is useful because it is generic; these general needs are recognizable across cultures, though how a specific individual meets these needs is shaped largely by the environment – geography, family and society. Thus everyone eats, but the food they eat depends on where they live. People may or may not be born into a society that values their particular genetically inherited traits and abilities. The variety of combinations of genetic inheritance and of social, economic and political conditions leads to people who differ in their success at meeting the needs that Maslow and others describe.

Most obviously, public officials need enough compensation to cover their expenses. How much they 'need' depends on a variety of factors. Public employees must earn compensation that allows them to live at a standard of living that is reasonable for their position. This does not mean that an administrator at a particular level does not have aspirations above his position. This leads us to the second key point in this section – the rules. Can an employee live, and expect to reasonably better his situation, within the rules of the system?

Rules

Question 1 asks about meeting one's needs within the rules. One problem is that an individual lives in a world of many different overlapping systems with rules that may or may not be consistent. There are the rules of the government agency in which the employee works. If the agency has a set of rules that favor merit, but the society is one that requires loyalty to family and friends, which set of rules will the employee follow? Are there other systems – perhaps underworld organizations – that work outside the law and are strong enough to compel compliance through offers of rewards or threats of punishment? The interplay of all these rules is complex and ever-changing. Campbell (1989), for instance, discusses the linkages of friendships based on favors among Greek peasant villagers. If one friend gains a prominent position such as president of the municipality, the ability to offer favors becomes asymmetrical and develops into a form of patronage in exchange for votes. He tells of how a few members of an outside group 'sold' their votes for favors, and how other members of the outside group saw them as traitors but then slowly gave them grudging admiration for taking care of their families. These villagers had to choose between competing sets of rules. Some chose group loyalty, others broke the rules of group loyalty to take care of their families. Public officials face similar kinds of choices, and how they answer these questions depends both on their needs and their perception of those needs and values.

Breaking the Rules

If one's income is too low to meet, through the rules, the socially acceptable standard of living appropriate to one's position, what options are there beyond the rules to meet those needs? In some cases, the options are few or nonexistent. In other cases, the nature of one's position – particularly positions with approval power with significant consequences – may give rise to offers of extra payments for prompt and/or favorable decisions. Are there opportunities to create alternative, underground systems to provide what legal systems do not provide? There are, for example, various levels of legal and illegal systems for getting loans, for getting electricity, getting illegal substances and weapons. Rose-Ackerman, citing Gambetta, writes that the rise of the Sicilian Mafia resulted from the Italian state's lack of capacity to handle an increase in private property transactions (Rose-Ackerman1999: 97).

Can One Break the Rules without Getting Caught?

How effectively do the institutions of accountability – both legitimate and illegitimate – enforce the rules? If the police and the judges are overworked, incompetent or corrupt, the chances of breaking the rules with impunity are much higher. There may be rules reinforced by social structures that effectively keep most people of a community in line, or outlaw organizations may emerge whose enforcement powers are more effective than the government's.

Is the Price of Getting Caught Worth the Risk?

What are the benefits of breaking the rules compared to the costs of being caught? Again we have to consider the various systems – organizational, social, economic, political and moral. The calculation here will be different for each person. Gardiner & Lyman (1989), writing specifically about land-use regulation, suggest reducing the 'incentives and opportunities for corrupt behavior' and increasing 'incentives and opportunities for non-corrupt behavior and the costs of corrupt behavior' (827).

At first, this way of looking at it makes it seem simple. The basic issue before us is not that complex. However, the complexity of each individual official, combined with the complexity of different settings, makes application of the model in individual situations difficult. One could argue that this is a fault of the model. I would argue that the model is merely reflective of the complexity of the world. Part of the complexity stems from the relationship between human beings and bureaucracies.

The Role of Human Beings in Bureaucracy

Max Weber envisaged bureaucracy as the application of rationality to the human organization. Just as science applied to technology can produce creative inventions, bureaucracy can be viewed as a tool to apply rational principles to the task of organizing the collective efforts of human groups to achieve collective goals more effectively and efficiently. Humans using bureaucracies under the right circumstances are able to achieve amazing things – delivering mail to almost any address around the world in two weeks or less; creating an air transportation network that enables passengers to travel the world on a set schedule; sending human beings into space and bringing them back. Bureaucracy is the application of the scientific method to human organizations. In its ideal form, the organization is a rational machine. It is part of the modern world where science and rationality become the arbiters of truth and the good. Unfortunately for this vision, human beings often function in a pre-modern world. While they can be rational and scientific, the non-rational often seems to take over, especially at times of stress. Besides being members of rational bureaucracies, humans are also members of various other groupings or networks with conflicting rules of loyalty. Unfortunately, there are also humans who see the power of public bureaucracies primarily as a means of furthering their own personal interests rather than the public good.

Figuring out how any specific individual is going to answer the above-mentioned questions would require knowing how the individual conceives of his/her needs and his/her obligations toward the various networks to which he/she belongs. It would require knowing whether the organization met those needs, and what options there were for him to break the rules to meet the needs as well as one's assessment of the risks and level of risk-taking. However, the model also offers us ways that organizations and societies can minimize the likelihood that public officials will break the rules in general.

STRATEGIES FOR PREVENTING UNETHICAL BEHAVIOR AND CORRUPTION

From the questions and answers above, we may logically progress to the following strategies toward minimizing corruption.

A. Public officials and the citizens they serve must be able to follow the rules and still meet their basic needs.

A key step toward minimizing unethical behavior would be to develop relationships between public organizations and employees that maximize the overlap between the organizational obligations and the personal obligations of employees. Basically, this aims at making sure that the organization meets employees' key needs and gives employees the resources – including free time – to meet the rest of their needs outside of the organization. Some specific means for doing this include:

(1) Providing sufficient compensation for employees to meet their personal obligations. When, for example, police officers are paid excessively low salaries, they may be more susceptible to bribes.
(2) Establishing reasonable working hours that do not consume so much time that people cannot meet their personal obligations to family, friends, etc.
(3) Matching talent to the task so that the workers' values and the organization's are consistent.
(4) Developing clear and reasonable rules that are consistent with the cultural values of the society. Normal human courtesies should not be turned into crimes. Rose-Ackerman (1999) writes: 'If behavior labeled "corrupt" by some observers is, nevertheless, viewed as acceptable gift-giving or tipping in a country, it should simply be legalized and reported' (110). Financial disclosure laws should be sensibly developed so that they prevent abuse but also so that they do not discourage good citizens from taking positions requiring financial disclosure.

B. Public officials should not be able to meet their needs through illegal channels.

This calls for reinforcement of social, political and economic structures that minimize the opportunities for corruption and requires a society in which people can

(1) 'fulfill that society's version of "reasonably meeting their needs"',
(2) access material wealth or other socially valued goals in ways that are reasonably equitable and consistent with societal values,
(3) meet their respective needs via legitimate channels, and
(4) lack the incentives to resort to illegal means in order to meet their needs, or to misuse the public for illegal private gain.

While this model suggests cutting off opportunities to meet one's needs illegally, I would point out a potentially serious problem. If the society itself cannot meet the needs of the people, does it truly make sense to prevent meeting those needs through other means? Probably not. However, the better long-term strategy is to create a society that can meet those basic needs. Yet, some people may not be satisfied with meeting basic needs; they have wants that tempt them to go beyond the rules. Opportunities to meet such wants illegally – particularly when it means that outlaws live better than law-abiding citizens – should be minimized. Invariably, the best strategy is having a political and socioeconomic system that can allow individuals to meet their needs and wants through established, legitimate channels.

C. Public officials pursuing illegal channels should have a high probability of being caught.

The likelihood that corrupt public officials will be caught can be increased through a number of strategies that are reasonably well known. They include

(1) **transparency** (openness can be achieved through public records laws, open meetings laws, financial disclosure laws, meaningful citizen participation venues and other ways to make the concealment of unethical acts more difficult);
(2) **independent watchdogs** with adequate access and power to monitor, such as an active, independent and inquisitive press, independent audit agencies, ombudsman offices, independent justice systems, international monitoring systems, strong auditing agencies, citizen participation options, and protections for whistleblowers;
(3) **a political structure** in which power is *dispersed* among different branches and levels of government;
(4) **an economic and political system** in which wealth and power are *equitably* distributed among the population, so that opposition to corruption is widespread and no group has so much power that they are immune to enforcement of rules; and
(5) **a population sufficiently educated** to understand the dynamics of the economic, political and social systems in which they live is less susceptible to propaganda that supports the corrupt.

D. Punishments for corruption need to be greater than the rewards from corrupt practices.

This principle must be linked to the previous ones. Even if the punishment is death, if the likelihood of punishment is minimal, people may well pursue the illegal options. Even death, as suicide bombers demonstrate, may not be a deterrent if the perceived benefits are high. Thus it would be fruitless to identify possible sanctions, beyond the basic principle that they be greater than the rewards of corrupt behavior.

CONCLUDING REMARKS

The list of options for decreasing the likelihood of corruption is not unique. It mirrors those developed by scholars over the decades. Caiden and Dwivedi's list of ten prerequisites of good governance covers much the same ground (2001: 251–252). The way the options are tied together is what is new in this paper. Other scholars have also supplied much of the detail for implementing changes that I have necessarily had to leave out of this overview. Particularly helpful in this regard is Rose-Ackerman's (1999) detailed analysis of the structure of corruption in bureaucracy and structural ways to minimize corruption.

There is also recognition that conflicts of interest are inevitable and real. Rather than try to eliminate them, reformers should endeavor to understand the tensions public officials must balance and develop systems that maximize the overlap between personal and public obligations. The key implication is that trying to stop the leaks through various anti-corruption measures may prove to be less effective than helping develop societies in which people can reasonably meet their personal needs through legitimate channels. And while corruption often makes it more difficult to achieve the good governance that makes corruption less viable, there are signs of hope. New technologies, such as satellite television and the Internet, make it more difficult for corrupt states to conceal world standards and local conditions from their people. Globalization, along with its problems, can also put pressures on corrupt states by giving alternative options to citizens and raising expectations for equity, efficiency and effectiveness in host country institutions. Thus the often unspoken factor – power – can come from outside the country when there is a great imbalance of power inside the country. Ultimately, the most productive way to fight corruption is through improving people's chances of meeting their needs through legitimate means.

REFERENCES

American Society for Public Administration (2002). *Code of Ethics*. http://www.aspanet.org/scriptcontent/index_codeofethics.cfm.

Caiden, G.E. (2001). 'Corruption and Government'. In G.E. Caiden, O.P. Dwivedi, & J. Jabbra (Eds), *Where Corruption Lives* (pp. 17–37). Bloomfield, CT: Kumarian Press.

Caiden, G.E., & Dwivedi, O.P. (2001). 'Official Ethics and Corruption'. In G.E. Caiden, O.P. Dwivedi, & J. Jabbra (Eds), *Where Corruption Lives*. Bloomfield, CT: Kumarian Press.

Campbell, J.K. (1989). 'Village Friendship and Patronage'. In A.J. Heidenheimer, M. Johnston, & V.T. LeVine (Eds). *Political Corruption: A Handbook* (pp. 327–337). New Brunswick, NJ: Transaction Publishers.

Gardiner, J.A., & Lyman, T.R. (1989). 'The Logic of Corruption Control'. In A.J. Heidenheimer, M. Johnston, & V.T. LeVine (Eds), *Political Corruption: A Handbook*. New Brunswick, NJ: Transaction Publishers.

Heidenheimer, A.J., Johnston, M., & V.T. LeVine (1989). (Eds). *Political Corruption: A Handbook*. New Brunswick, NJ: Transaction Publishers.

Maslow, A.H. (1943; 2004). 'A Theory of Human Motivation'. In J.M. Shafritz, A.C. Hyde, & S. Parkes (Eds), *Classics of Public Administration* (5th ed) (pp. 123–131). Belmont, CA: Thomson-Wadsworth.

Perry, P.J. (1997). *Political Corruption and Political Geography*. Aldershot: Ashgate.

Rose-Ackerman, S. (1999). *Corruption and Government*. Cambridge, UK: Cambridge University Press.

11

Pathology of the State: Diagnosing in Terms of Corruption or Integrity

L.W.J.C. HUBERTS

INTRODUCTION

Everywhere in the world interest in corruption, ethics and integrity has been growing and many international organizations have become active in fighting corruption. I will illustrate the increasing involvement of the international community by presenting a brief sketch of the international policy-making arena. Two characteristics are important to note: the focus is on corruption, and corruption is widely recognized as a central problem for good governance and socioeconomic development.

I will then discuss corruption in the Western democratic country I know best: the Netherlands. Reputation research suggests that the Netherlands is comparatively corruption-free, but this conclusion has been criticized within the country. Critics point to a number of corruption and fraud scandals that have led to much publicity and debate both in parliament and in society at large.

The contradiction between the international reputation of the Netherlands for 'cleanliness' and the national debate about corruption and fraud has been the starting point for this essay. What are the extent and nature of corruption and integrity as phenomena in Western democratic societies? What characterizes the relevant problems of governance (politics and administration) in these countries; what types of violations can be distinguished? More clarity about the concepts is necessary in order to deal with those questions. Thus, conceptual clarification is the main goal and theme of this essay. I will use and discuss Gerald Caiden's innovative conceptual work in this field and combine it with the research we are currently conducting in the Netherlands. What I hope to show is that views on corruption and integrity in our societies may benefit from redefining the issue, possibly applying a new typology of integrity violations. Concepts other than the ones we are often using may be better suited in order to arrive at more realistic estimations of the pathology of Western democratic politics and public administration. Western societies may not be corrupt, but they are confronted with major integrity problems.

INCREASED INTEREST IN CORRUPTION POLICIES

Until approximately 1985, corruption and integrity issues attracted little attention from public administration practitioners or from researchers, even though there were important exceptions such as Heidenheimer (1970), Gardiner and Olson (1974), Sherman (1974) and Gerald & Naomi Caiden (1977). The first International Anticorruption Conference was in Washington in 1983, but it took until 1993 for the now famous nongovernmental organization Transparency International to be founded.

Since then, an enormous amount of attention has been paid to corruption and ethics in international fora. We have got used to anticorruption congresses with thousands of participants. Conventions and treaties have been prepared, signed and implemented; in international relations, conditions of good governance have become a salient topic. Governments are more aware of the importance of their national integrity systems. Many global and international initiatives are worth mentioning (Caiden, Dwivedi & Jabbra 2001; Huberts 2003).

The UN General Assembly Resolution on Corruption in 1997 reaffirmed its concern with the seriousness of the corruption problem and adopted the International Code of Conduct for Public Officials. The resolution recommended that member states use the code as a tool to guide their efforts against corruption (UNDP 1998). In 2001 the foundations for a UN Convention against Corruption were discussed in The Hague at the Second Global Forum on Fighting Corruption and Safeguarding Integrity (Fijnaut & Huberts 2002), and in October 2003 the Convention was approved by the UN General Assembly. Secretary-General Kofi Annan stated that

> Corruption is an insidious plague that has a wide range of corrosive effects on societies. It undermines democracy and the rule of law, leads to violations of human rights, distorts markets, erodes the quality of life, and allows organised crime, terrorism and other threats to human security to flourish [...] I am therefore very happy that we now have a new instrument to address this scourge at the global level. The adoption of the United Nations Convention against Corruption sends a clear message that the international community is determined to prevent and control corruption. It warns the corrupt that betrayal of the public trust will no longer be tolerated. And it reaffirms the importance of core values, such as honesty, respect for the rule of law, accountability and transparency, in promoting development and making the world a better place for all. (http://www.unodc.org/unodc/en/speech_2003-10-31_1.html)

Within the UN, the UN Development Program approaches the issue of corruption as a governance problem and it has made the minimization of corruption central to achieving the organization's overall purpose of alleviating poverty and attaining social and people-centered sustainable development (UNDP 1998).

In line with political developments, major international financial and economic institutions such as the World Bank and the International Monetary Fund have made corruption their topic. The World Bank changed its policies in 1996 and declared the cancer of corruption a crucial problem for economic development. Its 'Pillars of National Integrity' are interdependent and include the rule of law, sustainable development and quality of life. Corruption and fraud have become important topics within Bank-financed projects as well as in the country-assistance strategies and country-lending considerations (UNDP 1998; Pieth & Eigen 1999; Klein Haarhuis 2005).

The Organization for Economic Cooperation and Development (OECD) has 29 member states and represents the industrialized world. It has made anticorruption initiatives, ethics and integrity policies an important aspect of its work (OECD 2000a, 2000b). The concept of an 'Ethics Infrastructure' summarizes the position of the OECD. Its core elements comprise political commitment, workable codes of conduct, professional socialization and mechanisms to that effect, an ethics-coordinating body, supportive public service conditions (i.e., decent working conditions), an effective legal framework, efficient accountability mechanisms and an active civil society. The OECD supports its pleas with research and analysis on measures undertaken by its member countries. In the international arena, the OECD's main contribution has been the 1997 OECD Convention on Combating Bribery of Foreign Public Officials in International Business Transactions. The Convention was signed by all member states. It came into force in 1999. Its main achievement was that of making bribery of a foreign public official a criminal offence in many countries (while in the past this bribe was often tax-deductible in several OECD countries).

Based in Berlin, Transparency International (TI) is a nongovernmental international organization against corruption with chapters in roughly 85 countries. TI favors a holistic approach to a national integrity system (Pope 2000; Transparency International 2001). Although each country or region is unique in terms of history and culture, sociopolitical system and stage of economic development, similarities do exist, which make lessons often transferable. TI proposes a National Integrity System as a comprehensive method of fighting corruption. It comprises eight pillars: public awareness, public anticorruption strategies, public participation, watchdog agencies, the judiciary, the media, and the private sector and international cooperation which are interdependent. Every two years TI organizes the International Anticorruption Conference (IACC).

The initiatives mentioned are part of a more general trend towards anticorruption policies, as for example is also shown by the Organization of American States (Inter-American Convention Against Corruption), the European Union (Bossaert & Demmke 2005), the Council of Europe (and its Group of States Against Corruption GRECO), the Global Coalition for

Africa and the International Chamber of Commerce (UNDP 1998; Pieth & Eigen 1999; OECD 2000b; Caiden, Dwivedi & Jabbra 2001).

Even though corruption, ethics and integrity have become increasingly topical in national and international political, economic and social fora, this does not mean that there is an overall consensus on concepts, causes and policies. Criticism is still heard on a wide range of subjects. Among these subjects are questions about the interests being served, notably free market capitalism and globalization, but also the interests of the peoples of poor countries (Argyriades 2001). Other arguments encompass the idea that there is no 'one best way' to fight corruption, even though some international organizations seek to impose their analysis and views (Doig & Moran 2002; Johnston 2002). Most fundamentally, doubts regarding the universality of the message on political and administrative ethics have also surfaced lately (Cooper 2004). Such views point to the necessity to be clear about the concepts that we are using in the international debate.

CORRUPTION IN THE NETHERLANDS

Internationally, the Corruption Perception Index (CPI) of Transparency International and Göttingen University is a crucial and useful instrument for international debate and policy-making. The CPI summarizes the amount of corruption in the eyes of business people and risk analysts. It estimates a country's corruption on a scale 1–10, 10 being corruption-free. The Netherlands has a rather stable positive image, as Table 1 shows, an image that is confirmed for other democratic Western countries.

Table 1 Corruption reputation of some Western countries 1980–2004

	1985–88	1988–92	1996	1998	2000	2002	2003	2004
The Netherlands	8.4	9.0	8.7	9.0	8.9	9.0	8.9	8.7
Finland	8.1	8.9	9.1	9.6	10.0	9.7	9.7	9.7
Sweden	8.0	8.7	9.1	9.5	9.4	9.3	9.3	9.2
United Kingdom	8.0	8.3	8.4	8.7	8.7	8.7	8.7	8.6
Germany	8.1	8.1	8.3	7.9	7.6	7.3	7.7	8.2
France	8.4	7.5	7.0	6.7	6.7	6.3	6.9	7.1
Spain	6.8	5.1	4.3	6.1	7.0	7.1	6.9	7.1
Italy	4.9	4.3	3.4	4.6	4.6	5.2	5.3	4.8
USA	8.4	7.7	7.7	7.5	7.8	7.7	7.5	7.5
Canada	8.4	9.0	9.0	9.2	9.2	9.0	8.7	8.5
Australia	8.4	8.2	8.6	8.7	8.3	8.6	8.8	8.8

Source: Transparency International: http://www.icgg.org/overview-g.csv.

Even though the Corruption Perception Index has been very widely used, critics often state that it offers only a very limited picture of what is really happening in the fields of ethics and integrity in governance. Nevertheless, in the case of the Netherlands, there are other data that suggest that the level of corruption is low.

In 1991 and 2003 we surveyed local governments to collect data on the internal investigations on corruption and fraud undertaken during the past five years (Huberts et al. 2004). Table 2 provides the extrapolated mean results from the internal investigations for the 1991 and 2003 research. In approximately 500 municipalities, the total number of investigations amounted to 179 in 2003. Even though the number has risen, the total number is rather limited, certainly when viewed from an international perspective.

Table 2 Annual number of internal corruption and fraud investigations

Mean over the preceding years	1991	2003
Number of local internal corruption and (per year) fraud investigations in local government	102	179
Ratio Corruption	46%	34%
Fraud	54%	66%

Source: Huberts, Hulsebosch, Lasthuizen & Peeters 2004.

Such findings notwithstanding, local as well as national politicians and civil servants are convinced that the reputation of the Netherlands as a corruption-free country tells only part of the story. There are concerns over the integrity of governance, and a new ethics and integrity 'industry' is developing to protect that integrity (institutions, policies, laws, codes etc.). The possible contradiction between the optimistic view about corruption on the one hand and a degree of pessimism about integrity on the other cannot be separated – in my view – from a fundamental conceptual debate or the confusion that lies underneath the surface of the public, political and scientific debate.

CORRUPTION AND PATHOLOGIES

Conceptual clarity is important, especially when it concerns public debate, policy-making and theory development on an international level. The concept of corruption is often at the heart of the debate about the moral quality of government (Caiden 1988; Klitgaard 1988; Heywood 1997; Newburn

1999; Rose-Ackerman 1999; Crank & Caldero 2000; Caiden, Dwivedi & Jabbra 2001; Heidenheimer & Johnston 2002; Bull & Newell 2003). It is, therefore, imperative to be aware of at least three definitions of corruption.

Firstly, there is a more specific or narrow interpretation that we find in definitions of corruption or bribing in legal frameworks. In the Netherlands, for example, corruption in the penal law is equated with 'bribing' (i.e., giving or accepting a bribe). This presupposes that a functionary is acting in the interest of another actor because of advantages promised or given to him. Secondly, corruption is interpreted as 'behavior which deviates from the formal duties of a public post or role, because of private-regarding (i.e., personal, close family, private clique), pecuniary or status gains; or [which] violates the rules against the exercise of certain types of private-regarding influence' (Nye 1967: 419; see also Caiden 2001). The same elements can be found in the definition used in the work of international organizations against corruption: corruption as the abuse of office for private gain (Pope 2000). All of these definitions portray corruption as a breach of moral behavioral norms and values involving private interests, but the presence of a third party is not seen as a necessary condition.

The third and broadest definition views corruption as synonymous with all types of wrongdoing. In this broadest form, corruption is treated as synonymous with the vices, maladies and flaws of politics and bureaucracy. Referring to the bureaucracy, Caiden called these bureaupathologies (Caiden 1991: 490) and he distinguished 179 types, including corruption, deceit, discrimination, fraud, injustice, mediocrity, red-tape and waste.

The last view brings into focus a concept that has become prominent in contemporary discussions: integrity (Anechiarico & Jacobs 1996; Dobel 1999; Huberts & van den Heuvel 1999; Klockars et al. 2004; Montefiori & Vines 1999; Uhr 1999; Fijnaut & Huberts 2002). It needs to be emphasized that integrity is not the same as the absence of political or administrative pathologies. Let me first sketch different perspectives on integrity, and then come back to its present relationship with pathology and corruption. What exactly is integrity?

INTEGRITY

In the literature on ethics and integrity, a number of perspectives can be distinguished.

Under the first perspective, integrity is seen as 'wholeness' or completeness, consistency and coherence of principles and values (in line with one of the meanings of the Latin term *integer*, which means intact, whole, harmony). This view is predominant, based on an inventory of the literature: 'The association with wholeness seems to be dominant' (Montefiori 1999). He summarizes the perspective as 'persons of integrity may be taken to be those whose overall patterns of desire and working principle are fully integrated, as it were, and who are neither at conflict with themselves nor given to wayward departures from their normal patterns of conduct over the course of time' (1999: 9). Within this approach is the view that integrity approximates to professional wholeness or responsibility (van Luijk 1993, 2004): 'You do what you are expected to do as a professional and you stand for what you are doing' (Karssing 2001: 3).

A disadvantage of the interpretation in terms of wholeness and consistency is the lack of what Brenkert calls a moral filter:

> Integrity involves more than simply doing what one says; what one says and does must also pass through some moral filter. As such, integrity is closely bound up with business ethics and forms of social responsibility (Brenkert 2004: 4).

Both fictional and academic literature provides many examples in which a person shows high internal coherence and therefore high personal integrity, yet we would not grant him high integrity (McFall 1987).

The other perspectives amount to more than the consistency perspective, which refers to morals, and which is characterized by the relationship between integrity and what is right and wrong. The second perspective sees integrity as one specific value. This is often the case in codes of conduct with integrity forming one of the basic values. Then it usually means incorruptibility or righteousness. The official should not be guided by self-interest or group or party interest but should serve the general interest of the organization or of society as a whole.

Others view integrity as an umbrella concept combining sets of values that are relevant for the functionary who is judged. One such view is the legal or constitutional one, summarized by Rohr concerning the 'Ethics for Bureaucrats' (1989: 4–5):

> To the extent that formal, legal or institutional controls over the bureaucrat's behavior are either non-existent or ineffective, bureaucrats have an ethical obligation to respond to the values of the people in whose name they govern. The values in question are not popular whims of the moment, but rather constitutional or regime values.

The constitutional interpretation of the relevant norms and values is an attractive one because it is clear on the type of values and norms that matter and those that should be interpreted when we try to judge the integrity of a public official. The problem, however, is that the law itself may not provide a clear guiding principle in actual decision-making and implementation processes, whether in government or in the business sector. Indeed, sometimes the law is in conflict with the moral values and norms of the population.

As a consequence, a broader interpretation in terms of 'complying with the moral values and norms' seems more appropriate. In this view, integrity is a characteristic or quality of a public official, for instance, meaning that what the official does or does not do is in accordance with the relevant values and norms and the laws resulting therefrom (for example, Fijnaut & Huberts 2002; Thomas 2001; Uhr 1999). This, of course, comes close to 'a general way of acting morally' and 'morality' (Brenkert 2004: 5). The last view stresses integrity as something to strive for. Van Luijk for instance stated that 'integrity now stands for complying in an exemplary way with specific moral standards' (2004: 39). Or even stronger, integrity is the 'stuff of moral courage and even heroism' (Blenkert 2004: 5).

In our research on the integrity of governance, we define integrity as the quality of acting in accordance with relevant moral values, norms and rules. Integrity is a quality of individuals (Klockars et al. 1997; Solomon 1999) as well as of organizations (Kaptein & Wempe 2002). Additionally, ethics may be defined as the collection of values and norms that functions as standards or yardsticks for assessing the integrity of one's conduct (Benjamin 1990). The moral nature of these values and norms refers to what is judged as right, just or good conduct. Values are principles that carry a certain weight in one's choice of action (to do what is good or refrain from doing what is bad). Norms indicate morally correct behavior in certain situations. Values and norms guide actions and provide a moral basis by which to justify or evaluate what one does and who one is (Lawton 1998; Pollock 1998).

INTEGRITY VIOLATIONS

In our research, we use a typology of categories of integrity violations (Huberts et al. 1999). This typology was the outcome of an analysis of the literature on police integrity and corruption and was assessed against the results of empirical research on internal investigations in the police force. It was important, in developing the typology, that it include (1) all types of relevant behavior (behavior within the organization, the interaction with external actors and private time behavior as far as it is relevant for the organization); (2) all types of relevant norms and values (laws and rules, internal codes and procedures and the informal norms and values which are not written down); and (3) behavior contrary to the organization's interest but also behavior favoring the organization but harmful to relevant norms and values.

Table 3 summarizes the typology of integrity violations or forms of public misconduct. Nine types are distinguished. For every type of integrity violation, various forms of behavior can be distinguished depending on the distance to the norm and values. For corruption, such as bribing, the amount of private gain or money involved can vary from cents to billions of dollars. Furthermore, the weight of the decision can differ very widely, from doing

Table 3 Types of Integrity Violations

1. Corruption: bribery
   misuse of public power for private gain; asking, offering or accepting bribes
2. Corruption: nepotism, cronyism, patronage, clientelism
   misuse of public authority to favor friends, family, political party or club
3. Fraud and theft
   improper private gain acquired from the organization with no involvement of external actors
4. Conflict of private and public interest
   personal interest through assets, jobs or gifts that interferes or might interfere with public interest
5. Improper use of authority (for noble causes)
   to use illegal/improper methods in order to achieve organizational goals (within the police, for example recourse to illegal methods of investigation and the degrading or inhuman treatment of prisoners)
6. Misuse and manipulation of information
   lying, cheating, misrepresentation of facts, manipulating evidence, breaching confidentiality
7. Discrimination and sexual harassment
   misbehavior towards colleagues, citizens or customers
8. Waste and abuse of resources
   failure to comply with organizational standards, inadequate performance, incorrect or dysfunctional internal behavior
9. Private-time misconduct
   conduct in one's private time which harms the public's trust in administration/government.

Source: Huberts, Pijl & Steen 1999, pp. 449–451.

a friend a favor with a bit of information, to policies and projects likely to have disastrous consequences for the population. Even sexual harassment can vary from a passing sexist remark to rape.

The typology makes clear that integrity or morally appropriate behavior means more than not being corrupt, even though corruption is no doubt the crucial aspect of organizational integrity.

WHY COMPLEXITY INSTEAD OF SIMPLICITY?

In our work on the ethics of governance we have moved from 'corruption research' (in the more specific sense) towards 'integrity research'. It is important to understand the reasons and arguments for this development towards more 'diversity and complexity'.

The first and most obvious reason is that differentiation and specification add to our knowledge of the phenomenon under study. The description and analysis of the moral dimension of the behavior of individuals, organizations and even countries are enriched by the availability of a more extended conceptual framework. It is not only worthwhile to know more about the amount of bribery and favoritism in government and administration, but it is also important to find out more about waste, discrimination, improper use of authority, private-time misconduct etc. Therefore, it seems worthwhile to distinguish more clearly between subtypes of 'corrupt' or 'unethical' behavior (or integrity violations).

The second, more practical, reason has to do with the country we are working in. Where serious bribing, nepotism and patronage are rather exceptional, other types of unethical behavior take on greater salience for the legitimacy and credibility of the political and administrative system. Examples are conflict of interest through sideline activities, fraud and private-time misbehavior. Our research into internal investigations by governmental organizations shows that the number of investigations into corruption in a specific sense is very limited compared to other types of violations.

Table 4 illustrates this point. For the purpose of the study on police integrity, we used the typology to distinguish a total of twelve types of integrity violations. All Dutch regional police forces participated in the research, offering information about the number and character of internal integrity investigations. The table shows that six types of police integrity violations are more often subject to investigation (Lamboo et al. 2002; Punch et al. 2004). A clear number 1 is off-duty private-time misconduct. In 23.5% of the investigations, private-time misconduct was under scrutiny. This concerns a wide range of behavior (most prominent: contacts with criminals, theft and fraud, violence, driving under the influence of alcohol). The other types of behavior that were frequently under investigation are: improper use of force (17.1%), waste and abuse of organizational resources (14.3%), abuse of information (13.6%), improper manners (11.3%) and theft or fraud (together 14.7%). There were many fewer investigations on perjury in court, conflicts of interests through gifts and discounts, use of dubious investigative methods, corruption and moonlighting.

The third reason for choosing a broad and complex integrity framework has to do with our research agenda which includes questions about the causes of 'corruption' and the effectiveness of 'anticorruption' policies. A lesson we have learned is that umbrella concepts tend to limit the advancement of knowledge about unacceptable and unethical behavior. Patronage and favoritism might be caused by factors other than bribery, private-time misbehavior, fraud, or conflict of interest. The 'slippery slope' hypothesis

Table 4 Investigated types of integrity violation 1999–2000

	% of investigations
Private-time misconduct	23.5
Improper use of force	17.1
Waste and abuse of resources	14.3
Abuse of information	13.6
Improper manners (discrimination etc.)	11.3
Theft	11.0
Fraud	3.7
Moonlighting (sideline activities)	2.0
Corruption	1.5
Use of investigative methods	1.5
Gifts and discounts	0.1
Perjury	0.2
Other	3.1
Vague terms	4.0
No information available	2.3
Total	110.3%*
N	1569

*Exceeds 100% because an investigation can concern more than one form of misconduct.
Source: Lamboo, Naeyé, Nieuwendijk & Van der Steeg 2002.

suggests that serious corruption cases have started with minor offenses, conceivably in a culture without clear norm. Accordingly, we might learn more about the extent and character of corruption when the related phenomena are also studied and measured. Differentiation is also important because it is probable that organizations or governments will have to develop specific policies against different types of integrity violations, including corruption. When you want to fight fraud, it might be effective to be strict and tough in norms, leadership and policies, while this toughness might have a negative effect on the presence of intimidation and discrimination (Lasthuizen, Huberts & Kaptein 2002).

NEITHER TOO COMPLEX NOR TOO BROAD

Even though I am arguing in favor of broadening our perspective from corruption to integrity, I think we have to be careful not to broaden the scope excessively. Even when we limit ourselves to the behavior of public officials instead of incorporating all 'evil' (Adams & Balfour 2004), there are many bureaupathologies, as Caiden (1991) has convincingly stated. However, not all of these should be considered integrity violations. To put it simply: an employee can do something wrong, can make mistakes, even stupid mistakes, without committing an integrity violation. When this distinction is blurred too much, an organization loses sight of what is morally important and what is not. Such blurring can have very negative consequences. Employees become afraid to take any risk, for fear of doing something wrong; they are paralyzed, with good reason, by the idea that making a mistake might lead to an investigation questioning their integrity.

Accordingly, organizations need to define very clearly what their central moral values and norms are. The organizational ethics will clarify which type of value or norm violation is considered serious and calls for an integrity investigation. This is never an easy endeavor, but it is an important one for organizations that take ethics and integrity seriously. For government and public administration, Caiden (1999) reflected on values and norms in a paper called 'The Essence of Public Service Ethics and Professionalism'. He pointed at principles concerning public benefits, enforcing the rule of law, ensuring public responsibility and accountability, setting an example, improving professional performance and promoting democracy. For public organizations, this set of standards and values might offer a useful starting point for reflection on the crucial elements of their mission, goals and ethics. Always, a 'translation' of the general principles and standards will be necessary. For a police officer other standards apply than for the average civil servant.

One last implication of using a blanket concept for integrity (or corruptness) has to be mentioned. It is important to be precise about what we are analyzing and evaluating. An integrity violation means that a public servant or a politician does something which is contrary to existing relevant moral values and norms. The next question is whether this behavior is important enough to conclude that the functionary's integrity is in doubt, that is to say, the functionary is immoral, unethical or corrupt. We should be aware of the possibility of oversimplification and overgeneralization in our analysis in terms of integrity, ethics or corruption (Huberts 2005).

CONCLUSION

Departing from Caiden's sketch of bureaupathologies on the one hand and his work on corruption on the other, I have outlined a proposal for a conceptual framework that might be useful to reflect on corruption and integrity in Western democratic countries. Such corruption as misuse of a public position for private gain is rather exceptional, and not really indicative of the actual integrity level of government and administration in Western democratic countries. We need more differentiation and specification in our research and theorizing about their ethics of 'governance'. Bribery may indeed be rare, but that is not necessarily the case for other integrity violations.

The concept of pathology, on the other hand, misses the moral dimension which relates failures and mistakes to the relevant moral values and norms. Functionaries should be allowed to make mistakes but organizations should clarify what types of behavior are contrary to the organization's mission and values. These types are the integrity violations an organization should be concerned about, and policy development should concentrate on those violations.

REFERENCES

Adams, G., & Balfour, D. (2004). *Unmasking Administrative Evil.* Armonk, NY: M.E. Sharpe.

Anechiarico, F., & Jacobs, J.B. (1996). *The Pursuit of Absolute Integrity. How Corruption Control Makes Government Ineffective*. Chicago: University of Chicago Press.

Argyriades, D. (2001). 'The International Anticorruption Campaigns: Whose Ethics?' In G.E. Caiden, O.P. Dwivedi, & J. Jabbra (Eds), *Where Corruption Lives* (pp. 218–226). Bloomfield, CT: Kumarian Press.

Benjamin, M. (1990). *Splitting the Difference: Compromising and Integrity in Ethics and Politics*. Kansas: University Press of Kansas.

Bossaert, D., & Demmke C. (2005). *Main Challenges in the Field of Ethics and Integrity in the EU Member States.* Maastricht: EIPA.

Brenkert, G. (2004). 'The Need for Corporate Integrity'. In G. Blenkert (Ed), *Corporate Integrity & Accountability* (pp. 1–10). Thousand Oaks, CA: SAGE.

Bull, M.J., & Newell, J.L. (2003) (Eds). *Corruption in Contemporary Politics*. Houndsmill, Basingstoke: Palgrave Macmillan.

Caiden, G.E., & Caiden, N.J. (1977). 'Administrative Corruption'. *Public Administration Review* 37 (3), pp. 301–309.

Caiden, G.E. (1988). 'Toward a General Theory of Official Corruption'. *Asian Journal of Public Administration* 10 (1), pp. 3–26.

Caiden, G.E. (1991). 'What Really Is Public Maladministration?' *Public Administration Review* 51 (6), pp. 486–493.

Caiden, G.E. (1999). 'The Essence of Public Service Ethics and Professionalism'. In L.W.J.C. Huberts & J.H.J van den Heuvel (Eds). *Integrity at the Public–Private Interface* (pp. 21–44). Maastricht: Shaker.

Caiden, G.E. (2001). 'Corruption and Governance'. In G.E. Caiden, O.P. Dwivedi, & J. Jabbra (Eds), *Where Corruption Lives* (pp. 15–37). Bloomfield, CT: Kumarian Press.

Caiden, G.E., Dwivedi, O.P., & Jabbra, J. (2001) (Eds). *Where Corruption Lives.* Bloomfield, CT: Kumarian Press.

Cooper, T.L. (2002). *Handbook of Administrative Ethics.* New York: Marcel Decker.

Cooper, T.L. (2004). 'Big Questions in Administrative Ethics'. *Public Administration Review* 64 (4), pp. 395–407.

Crank, J.P., & Caldero, M.A. (2000). *Police Ethics: The Corruption of Noble Cause*. Cincinnati, OH: Anderson.

Dobel, J.P. (1999). *Public Integrity.* Baltimore: John Hopkins University Press.

Doig, A., & Moran, J. (2002). 'Anticorruption Agencies: The Importance of Independence for the Effectiveness of National Integrity Systems'. In C. Fijnaut & L.W.J.C. Huberts (Eds), *Corruption, Integrity and Law Enforcement* (pp. 229–251). Dordrecht: Kluwer Law International.

Fijnaut, C., & Huberts, L. (2002) (Eds). *Corruption, Integrity and Law Enforcement.* Dordrecht: Kluwer Law International.

Gardiner, J.A., & Olson, D.J. (1974). *Theft of the City: Readings on Corruption in Urban America.* Bloomington: Indiana University Press.

Heidenheimer, A.J. (1970). *Political Corruption: Readings in Comparative Analysis.* New York: Holt, Rinehart & Winston.

Heidenheimer, A.J., & Johnston, M. (2002) (Eds). *Political Corruption: Concepts & Contexts* (3rd ed). New Brunswick: Transaction Publishers.

Heywood, P. (1997) (Ed). *Political Corruption.* Oxford: Blackwell.

Huberts, L.W.J.C., & van den Heuvel, J.H.J. (1999) (Eds). *Integrity at the Public–Private Interface*. Maastricht: Shaker.

Huberts, L.W.J.C., Pijl, D., & Steen, A. (1999). 'Integriteit en corruptie'. In C. Fijnaut, E. Muller, & U. Rosenthal (Eds.), *Politie. Studies over haar werking en organisatie* (pp. 433–472). Alphen aan den Rijn: Samsom.

Huberts, L.W.J.C. (2001). *The Netherlands: Corruption and Anticorruption Policies in the Netherlands. An Evaluation.* Berlin: Transparency International.

Huberts, L.W.J.C. (2003). 'Global Ethics and Corruption'. In Jack Rabin (Ed.), *Encyclopedia of Public Administration and Public Policy* (pp. 546–551). New York: Marcel Dekker.

Huberts, L.W.J.C., Hulsebosch, H., Lasthuizen, K., & Peeters, C. (2004). *Nederland fraude- en corruptieland? De omvang, achtergronden en afwikkeling van corruptie- en fraudeonderzoeken in Nederlandse gemeenten in 1991 en 2003.* Amsterdam: Vrije Universiteit.

Huberts, L.W.J.C. (2005). 'Integriteit en Integritisme in Bestuur en Samenleving'. Address delivered at the Faculteit der Sociale Wetenschappen, Vrije Universiteit Amsterdam.

Johnston, M. (1986). 'Corruption and Democracy in America'. In J.B. McKinney & M. Johnston (Eds), *Fraud, Waste and Abuse in Government* (pp. 137–150). Philadelphia: ISHI.

Johnston, M. (2002). 'Independent Anticorruption Commissions: Success

Stories and Cautionary Tales'. In C. Fijnaut & L.W.J.C. Huberts (Eds), *Corruption, Integrity and Law Enforcement* (pp. 253–265). Dordrecht: Kluwer Law International.

Kaptein, M., & Wempe, J. (2002). *The Balanced Company: A Theory of Corporate Integrity.* New York: Oxford University Press.

Karssing, E.D. (2001). *Morele competentie in organisaties* (2nd ed). Assen: Van Gorcum.

Klein Haarhuis, C. (2005). *Promoting Anticorruption Reform: Evaluating the Implementation of a World Bank Anticorruption Program in Seven African Countries (1999–2001).* Utrecht: ICS Dissertation Series.

Klitgaard, R. (1988). *Controlling Corruption.* Berkeley: University of California Press.

Klockars, C.B., et al. (1997). *The Measurement of Police Integrity: Executive Summary. A Report to the National Institute of Justice.* Washington, DC: NIJ.

Klockars, C.B., Kutnjak Ivkovic, S., & Haberfeld, M.R. (2004) (Eds). *The Contours of Police Integrity.* Thousand Oaks, CA: SAGE.

Lamboo, M.E.D., Naeyé, J., Nieuwendijk, A., & van der Steeg, M. (2002). 'Politie neemt integriteitsschendingen serieus'. *Het Tijdschrift voor de Politie* 64 (10), pp. 4–11.

Lasthuizen, K, Huberts, L.W.J.C., & Kaptein, M. (2002). 'Integrity Problems in the Police Organization: Police Officers' Perceptions Reviewed'. In M. Pagon (Ed), *Policing in Central and Eastern Europe: Deviance, Violence and Victimization* (pp. 25–37). Leicester: Scarman Centre University of Leicester, & Ljubljana: College of Police and Security Studies.

Lawton, A. (1998). *Ethical Management for the Public Services.* Buckingham: Open University Press.

Luijk, H. van (1993). *Om redelijk gewin. Oefeningen in bedrijfsethiek.* Amsterdam: Boom.

Luijk, H. van (2004). 'Integrity in the Private, the Public and the Corporate Domain'. In G. Blenkert (Ed), *Corporate Integrity & Accountability* (pp. 38–54). Thousand Oaks, CA: SAGE

McFall, L. (1987). 'Integrity'. *Ethics* 98, pp. 5–20.

Menzel, D.C., & Carson, K.J. (1999). 'A Review and Assessment of Empirical Research on Public Administration Ethics: Implications for Scholars and Managers'. *Public Integrity* 1 (3), pp. 239–264.

Menzel, D.C. (2005). 'Research on Ethics and Integrity in Governance'. *Public Integrity* 7 (2), pp. 147–168.

Montefiori, A. (1999). 'Integrity: A Philosopher's Introduction'. In A. Montefiori and D. Vines (Eds), *Integrity in the Public and Private Domains* (pp. 3–18). London: Routledge.

Montefiori, A., & Vines, D. (1999) (Eds). *Integrity in the Public and Private Domains.* London: Routledge.

Newburn, T. (1999). *Understanding and Preventing Police Corruption: Lessons from the Literature*. Police Research Series, Paper 110. London: Home Office Policing and Reducing Crime Unit.

Nye, J.S. (1967). 'Corruption and Political Development: A Cost-Benefit Analysis'. *American Political Science Review* 61 (20), pp. 417–427.

Organization of Economic Cooperation and Development (2000a). *Trust in Government: Ethics Measures in OECD Countries*. Paris: OECD.

Organization of Economic Cooperation and Development (2000b). *No Longer Business as Usual: Fighting Bribery and Corruption*. Paris: OECD.

Pieth, M., & Eigen P. (1999) (Eds). *Korruption im internationalen Geschäftsverkehr. Bestandsaufnahme. Bekämpfung. Prävention.* Neuwied, Kriftel: Luchterhand.

Pollock, J.M. (1998). *Ethics in Crime and Justice: Dilemmas and Decisions*. New York: West/Wadsworth.

Pope, J. (2000). *Confronting Corruption: The Elements of a National Integrity System (TI Source Book 2000)*. Berlin: Transparency International. Also at http://www.transparency.org.

Punch, M., Kolthoff, E., van der Vijver, K., & van Vliet, B. (1993) (Eds). *Coping with Corruption in a Borderless World: Proceedings of the Fifth International Anticorruption Conference*. Deventer: Kluwer Law and Taxation Publishers.

Punch, M., Huberts, L.W.J.C., & Lamboo, M.E.D. (2004). 'Integrity Perceptions and Investigations in the Netherlands'. In C.B. Klockars, S. Kutnjak Ivkovic, & M.R. Haberfeld (Eds), *The Contours of Police Integrity* (pp. 161–174). Thousand Oaks, CA: SAGE.

Rohr, J.A. (1989). *Ethics for Bureaucrats: An Essay on Law and Values* (2nd ed). New York & Basel: Marcel Dekker.

Rose-Ackerman, S. (1999). *Corruption and Government: Causes, Consequences and Reform*. Cambridge: Cambridge University Press.

Sherman, L. (1974) (Ed). *Police Corruption: A Sociological Perspective*. New York: Anchor Press.

Solomon, B. (1999). *A Better Way to Think about Business: How Personal Integrity Leads to Corporate Success*. New York: Oxford University Press.

Transparency International (2001). 'The National Integrity System. Concept and Practice'. A Report by Transparency International (TI) for the Global Forum II on Fighting Corruption and Safeguarding Integrity (A Report Prepared by Alan Doig and Stephanie McIvor). Berlin: Transparency International.

Uhr, J. (1999). 'Institutions of Integrity, Balancing Values and Verification in Democratic Governance'. *Public Integrity* 1, pp. 94–106.

United Nations Development Program (1998). *Corruption & Integrity Improvement Initiatives in Developing Countries*. New York: UNDP.

12

'Justified Corruption' in State and Local Finances

JEFFREY I. CHAPMAN, S. COLLEEN BYRON AND MIN SU KIM

INTRODUCTION

Gerald Caiden's writings reflect a substantive and nuanced analysis of the issues of corruption and ethics that confront society (1988, 1994, 2001; Caiden, Dwivedi, & Jabbra 2001). His incisive analyses of political graft and ethical violations that must be contained so that they do not become endemic in society have resulted in a sturdy platform for further analysis. This chapter will extend this analysis further by applying his reasoning to the activities that local governments have undertaken because of the fiscal stress that they have encountered. In this context, the concept of justified corruption will be examined.

Although not all discussions of corruption revolve around some fiscal phenomena and governance issues, many do. For example, Caiden (2001) discusses the reduction of capital flight and laundered money as well as explanations of corruption related to scarcity and governance and the requirement of better governance in the reduction of corruption (Caiden, Dwivedi, & Jabbra 2001). However, historically, nearly all definitions of corruption relate to personal gain because of deviations from formal public rules which they entail (Caiden 2001). Corruption is sometimes divided into two categories: 'systematic corruption', which identifies concrete forms of political behavior and the deliberate creation of economic rents through selective granting of economic privileges, leading to the corruption of economics by politics; and 'venal corruption', which is the pursuit of private economic interests through the political process. Venal corruption occurs when economics corrupts politics (Wallis 2004: 2–3).

This chapter addresses a third type of ethical issue: the situation in which a government is fiscally starved because of voter actions, yet must undertake certain activities. In Nelson's words, 'there is a declining support for the public sector without a similar decline in the expectations for public sector response' (Nelson 2002). In order to maintain some of these responses, government may engage in activities which, while clearly being legal, corrupt the very systems they seek to promote. These activities may be called 'justified corruption' – truly an oxymoron yet descriptive of the actions undertaken in today's world.

Traditionally, definitions of corruption have required personal gain. 'A general definition of corruption is the use of public office for private gain. This includes bribery and extortion which necessarily involve at least two parties and other types of malfeasance which public officials can carry out alone, including fraud and embezzlement' (Grey & Kaufmann 1998). The corruption of entire systems by well-meaning individuals who did not personally gain from either illicitly acquired money or benefits (such as unearned, paid time off or lavish travel) was considered systemic breakdown but not corruption.[1] Corruption was limited to 'the abuse of public power for private benefit', and this definition is the current institutionalized definition used by such organizations as the World Bank that regularly confront corruption. The definition was widened to include benefits to 'one's party, class, tribe, friends, family, and so on' (Tanzi 1998). We suggest that benefit to one's agency or organization is the natural extension of this progressive widening of the definition of corruption. While government employees themselves may not be corrupt, they are corrupting government systems by hiding the decision-making and financing processes from citizens and justifying this behavior by accurately claiming that they have no other ways to fulfill citizen demands. In this case, their agency may benefit because it appears to provide a response without incurring corresponding costs.

In this context, it is important to note that we are looking at corruption through an institutional lens. We address not the corruption of individuals, but the corruption of government systems and the institutions that are made up of those systems by well-meaning public servants. These individuals have justified their actions through juxtaposing service demands with funding that is inadequate to meet those demands. It is the corruption of government systems through fiscal stress, not the corruption of government employees, which is of primary concern here.

The first section of this chapter will examine some of the reasons that fiscal stress appears to be increasing and then recount some of the deliberate state and local government responses to these stresses. The next sections will discuss the justified corruption issues that arise because of these responses. We shall conclude with some policy recommendations. Foreshadowing the conclusions, it may be fair to argue that almost all 'justified corruption' problems occur because of the desire of state and local governments to continue providing what most citizens agree to be necessary services, even though such local governments do not have the resources to provide these services straightforwardly.

FISCAL STRESS

Some Nuances

There is a rich literature that confronts the problems associated with defining local governments' fiscal stress (e.g., Bradbury 1982; Sokolow 1993).

However, underlying all of these is a fundamental constraint: not enough revenue is raised through the existing system and techniques to accommodate the existing level of demands for government goods and services. There are least three reasons for this.

1. Macroeconomy

Every revenue-raising system has a set of fixed parameters that apply to a variable base. By fixed, we mean that it takes a discrete action by the relevant government to change the parameter. By variable, we mean a base that can be varied without direct action by the governmental decision maker. For example, a property tax rate is fixed. The base of the property tax varies with the state of the economic environment. If there is an exogenous increase in property values caused by market fluctuations, then property tax revenues will increase.[2] Sales and income taxes work similarly, although they are far more cyclical since the business cycle affects income and sales much more quickly than property values. In general, for all levels of government, when the economy slows down, public sector revenues from taxes fall.

Simultaneously, expenditure demands typically increase during business-cycle slowdowns. As more workers lose their jobs, reliance on government health and welfare benefits typically increases; there is likely to be more crime, causing the demand for public safety expenditures to rise. Total expenditures are driven higher without changes in eligibility criteria. These two budgetary phenomena are beyond the immediate control of state and local government, and both are likely to occur simultaneously. This leads to periods of boom and bust. Fiscal stress from this factor comes during the bust cycle.

2. Political/Voter-Imposed Property Tax Limits and Mandated Expenditures

Fiscal stress also comes from the deliberate political activities of the populace. In particular, the citizenry as well as elected legislative bodies often appear to be schizophrenic. At times, they wish to constrain revenues directly, typically through property tax limits (e.g., California's Proposition 13 [Chapman 1998]) or limits on types of debt issuance (e.g., tax allocation bonds cannot be issued in Arizona). Sometimes, they accidentally constrain revenues through land-use controls that prohibit tax-generating retail establishments.

However, these same participants often mandate expenditures regardless of the fiscal implications. It is not unusual for states to lock into law specific support for education, welfare eligibility criteria or health benefits. These activities not only take away some of the autonomy of local governments but, in conjunction with the macroeconomic events described before, they can generate additional fiscal stress.

3. Cultural: The Appropriate Role of Government

A third set of reasons why fiscal stress can occur relates to the political culture and politics of the jurisdiction (Wildavsky & Caiden 2004). There are some state and local governments that take advantage of an expanding economy to cut taxes because the prevailing political ethos is that government interferes too much. Other jurisdictions, during the same times of economic expansion, increase services because they value education more than lower property tax rates. Though both may be legitimate political philosophies, they engender very different long-run levels of government and both of these activities increase the odds of fiscal stress occurring over time.

Fiscal Stress and the Tools Used to Respond

Fiscal stress, arising because of this diverse set of pressures, often causes governments to attempt to accomplish more (or at least the same) with a set of often diminishing resources. In public administration this has led to the use of a variety of tools, several of which are grouped under the rubric of the New Public Management (NPM) (Lane 2000; Jones & Thompson 1999; see also Salamon 2002). Although the NPM can justifiably be criticized because it fully ignores such issues as equity and justice and focuses instead on narrow management issues, it is considerably more robust than merely appealing to the public interest as a way of solving fiscal stress problems. If care is not used, the focus can be so much on the tool that the ethical issues associated with the tool, as well as the opportunities for corruption that are derived from the tool, are ignored. The rest of this chapter will attempt to fill this hole.

State and Local Responses to Fiscal Stress

Because most state and local governments by law must submit balanced budgets, they must directly confront means of dealing with fiscal stress. Although local governments have developed most of the responses, there are some indications that states can be quite innovative. In the following discussion, we will emphasize local responses but note state activities when important.[3] An additional caveat is that there are strong incentives for both the state and local governments to use complex disclosure techniques in their public documents. In particular, revenue sources can be scattered throughout the formal budget document and a good deal of careful inspection of the General Fund summary is required to track through the streams. Over time, this problem is likely to be solved because the public and the media will gain expertise in tracking the numbers. The following are generic examples of five state and local responses.

1. Revenue Shifts

State and local governments have developed unique ways of finding revenues. Often these involve complex revenue shifts both between levels of government and between revenue sources at a particular level. An example of the former is the 'triple-shift' that has gone on in California when that state attempted to find a way through its crushing constraints and responsibilities. In 2004–05, the state took money from local governments by forcing locals to lower their sales tax rate while the state increased its rate, leaving the total rate the same (the state has promised not to do this again). The state used this money to service newly issued debt. Then the state took money from school districts and gave it to local governments so that the latter suffered no revenue losses. Finally, the state then made school districts whole through a direct appropriation. Since the interest paid on the debt was less costly than the aid to the schools, in the short run, everyone came out whole.

2. Economic Development Issues

An attempt to increase economic development was also included in the set of activities used to avoid potential fiscal stress. Although most empirical work indicates that tax incentives work poorly across states to generate new activities (Wasylenko 1997), these tax abatements and incentives do work better in attracting industries once these industries have decided upon the general area in which they want to locate. This involves a detailed bargaining process, much of which is confidential and some of which is proprietary to the industry.

The goal for the local government is not to give too much away, especially if the firm was inclined to locate in the area (Chapman 2003). Some of these agreements can be quite complex. One city 'borrowed' another city's property classification of a foreign trade zone (which is assessed at 5% rather than 25% of the assessed value) to give to a firm. In exchange, the firm provided a large subsidy to the city library, improved the streets surrounding the area and installed a water purification plant with enough capacity to serve both the firm and the jurisdiction. Nevertheless, there are examples of very expensive subsidies to industries that create very few jobs or other benefits to the community (Chi & Leatherby 1997).[4]

3. New Debt

A third type of activity that state and local jurisdictions have undertaken relates to debt issuance. While not directly prohibited by tax limits, the restrictions on property taxes have made General Obligation bonds much more difficult to finance and led to debt instruments with convoluted characteristics.[5] The following three examples demonstrate two of these features.

They are so arcane that they are sometimes completely misunderstood by the enabling legislative body, and since they do not need formal voter approval, they can be enacted more easily.

(a) Tax-increment financing

Tax-increment financing predates the advent of the fiscal limits movement started by Proposition 13 by about twenty years. However, after the beginning of this movement, it rapidly grew and spread throughout the USA. Now, only Arizona, Washington and North Carolina do not allow the utilization of this technique.

Under this method of financing, the legislative body declares a specific section of the jurisdiction to be blighted. This is sometimes a controversial decision. Further, inherent in this declaration is the belief that the private sector will not redevelop the area unless government helps. Obviously, there are political games involved in this declaration and it would be unusual for any private developer to turn down the offer of free government help. Once this declaration of a blighted area is finalized, the value of the property taxes collected from this area is calculated. The jurisdiction establishes a nonprofit agency (in small cities the board of the nonprofit agency is identical to the city council; in larger cities it is often a different set of actors). This nonprofit agency issues tax-exempt debt to finance infrastructure improvement within the blighted area. In theory, developers rush in to take advantage of the available free improvements and property values increase. The increase in these property values is used to service the debt.

(b) Certificates of Participation

Certificates of Participation are debt instruments that are technically not debt. In their simplest form, the city again sets up a nonprofit agency that has the task of constructing a new public building. In brief, this agency issues bonds to garner enough funds to undertake the construction. The agency then leases the building back to the city and receives a lease payment large enough to service the debt. This lease payment is then distributed to the certificate holders, since they participate in financing the construction. This bears a measure of risk. The city council pays the lease out of General Fund revenues and must commit itself for the full maturity of the bonds. There are some legal technicalities associated with this long-term commitment, because a city council commits future city councils.

In more complex versions, the nonprofit agency can buy a city building, thus generating cash for the city; it can lease the existing building back to the city. In this case, the city receives a large immediate payment that must be serviced over a long-term time horizon, a 30-year contract, for example. A third case occurs when an existing building is used as security for the transaction, although the existing building is not sold.

(c) Community Facilities Districts

Community Facilities Districts (CFDs) are another way of avoiding the pressures of ensuring that people understand what they are paying for and what they are getting. These districts are formed by agreements among the landowners of vacant parcels. They vote to issue a debt and then impose a lien on the property which is passed on to the new landowners as they purchase property. The proceeds of the debt are used to finance the infrastructure of the undeveloped land. As houses are sold, there appears a line item on the property tax bill that earmarks a portion of the total tax to service the CFD debt. For commercial property, not only may part of the property tax be earmarked, but also part of the sales tax might be included. These payments are in addition to the normal taxes paid, which differentiates this process from the tax-increment financing process.

The CFD can be drawn with pockets of development excluded. In some states, until relatively recently, this CFD debt did not have to be disclosed to the property purchasers. Technically, debt issued under a CFD agreement is not local debt, so the jurisdiction can maintain a hands-free posture.

4. Soft-Budget Utilization

The concept of hard-bargaining over budgetary responsibilities between local governments on the one hand and the state on the other has long been part of American fiscal culture. A hard-budget constraint exists when it is known beforehand that the state will not be persuaded to contribute money to help local governments in times of fiscal constraints. Soft-budgeting occurs when the state is not vigilant in protecting its resources and local governments can successfully extort the state to provide extra funds (Inman 2003).

In typical soft-budgeting, local governments will deliberately overspend on services that citizens find necessary, or, conversely, deliberately cut back on those same services to unacceptably low levels. Included in this game are complex revenue shifts, promises of future repayments and complex discussions of bailouts versus buyouts. Again, much of this sleight of hand is not transparent to the citizen; it reflects powerful special interests bargaining among themselves and it leads to openings for sophisticated fiscal deals.

5. Use of Nongovernmental Tools

A final set of approaches can also be attributable to the onset of fiscal stress. Most recently discussed as the 'new governance' (Salamon 2002), this is an outgrowth of the New Public Management philosophy which, in turn, is a derivative of the 'reinventing government' movement (Osborne & Gaebler 1992). This differs from the classical public administration approach that can be generally described as being based on programs, hierarchy and management skills by focusing instead on tools, networks and enablement skills.[6] We argue that without this fiscal stress, the growth in the field would have been considerably slower.

However, this has not been an uncontroversial movement. The concept of the citizen as a simple 'consumer' of government programs has been quite justifiably criticized (Moore 2002). The role of the legal system has often been trivialized or ignored when privatization tools have been justified, and equity issues have often taken a back seat to efficiency concerns. With the inclusion of the private sector as a partner, there has been an increase in the odds of unethical behavior because incentive systems might well differ from the public, nonprofit and private sectors. In general, because of this complexity there are again the same sets of disconnects that came about because of the use of complex financial instruments which led to a separation of public participation and government.

This introduction to some of the techniques used to continue the government provision of services, while incomplete, is illustrative of the potential for the arcane and misunderstood methods that currently exist today. It is also illustrative of the potential arenas in which ethical questions can arise. The next section of this chapter examines some of these questions in a conceptual framework relating Klitgaard's (2004) analysis of corruption to these complex financial instruments.

ETHICS AND CORRUPTION ISSUES IN USING COMPLEX INSTRUMENTS TO FINANCE GOVERNMENT

The purpose of this section will be to scrutinize the use of complex financial instruments (CFIs) in the enabling of governmental operations. It will attempt to isolate some characteristics of CFIs that may facilitate corruption. While there is no universally accepted definition of corruption, Klitgaard's (2004) succinct equation: Corruption = Monopoly + Discretion – Transparency, serves as a good organizing model through which to examine the potential hazards to governance. While corruption may be difficult to eliminate, its causes can be understood and attempts can be made to mitigate its prevalence.

Monopoly

One of the problems with using complex instruments to finance public works is that complex financial instruments invite the aggregation of access-to-government monopoly power. Complex financial instruments such as those described above deteriorate social capital and contribute to subsequent declines in citizen involvement in the determination of the public interest. This creates a monopoly environment in government, in which organizational elites have an advantage in securing government benefits. The people who play roles in utilizing CFIs are expertise elites who have extremely specialized skills that are incomprehensible to most citizens and public employees. Complex financial instruments are access-exclusive, in both the expertise which is needed to negotiate their use, and in the physical resources required to co-create a market for instrument exploitation. There are some socially responsible trusts that utilize certificates of participation for generalized participation, but these are isolated and exceptional examples. By and large, Certificates of Participation, Community Facility District debt or complex public–private partnerships are purchased, sold or engaged in by institutional investors, investor pool consortia and large family trusts.

Furthermore, it has been argued that CFIs are actually used to produce outcomes that are counter to the public will. A large portion of CoP use is in arenas where the public debt has been specifically limited statutorily. Public administrators, faced with what amounted to mountains of unfunded mandates against comparatively low debt ceilings, reacted, understandably, with instruments that did not technically increase debt loads. In retrospect, the response was a natural reaction to unavoidable potential crises, but again it excluded citizens by demonstrating disregard for a clear and unequivocal budgetary mandate. We would argue that this further weakens social capital formation that is based, in part, on trust. Citizens do not trust governments that disregard their specific statutory instructions, nor do they trust governments that engage in transactions which they judge to be unintelligible. This cycle of decreasing social capital facilitates preferential government and is expensive in terms of increased transaction costs for oversight. The need for oversight increases as social capital decreases (Fukuyama 1995).

Finally, when the improper use of CFIs becomes known, community capacity is eroded to such an extent that confused, disillusioned and disenfranchised citizens withdraw their participation. It is difficult to assess the damage to the fabric of Orange County's community capacity from the bankruptcy caused by the misuse of CFIs. It is safe to say that government service and civic participation had been marginalized already without the fallout from high-risk investment losses.[7] If we accept the notion of stewardship promoted by Larry Terry, then one of the foundation responsibilities of government is to provide safe, predictable outcomes to a public that requires certainty and reliability as the bedrock of government authority (Terry 1995). There is no room for creative risk-taking in this conception of government, let alone active, widely misunderstood high-risk capital manipulation. From the stewardship perspective, it matters little if those responsible for mistakes in Orange County were deceitful in their development of investment strategies or not, because in either case they had violated their fiduciary responsibility to provide safe, reliable and predictable government. Everything that contributes to the downward spiral of decreasing social capital encourages corruption by creating monopoly power out of access to government.

Discretion

If necessity is the mother of invention, it is easy to see why creativity has come to be highly valued in government finance. Creativity has bought discretion for strained administrators facing the impossible task of financing statutorily required programs in the face of conflicting statutorily required budgetary restrictions. In private institutional investing, creativity can facilitate the development of a methodology for evaluating a new financial instrument that defines that very instrument. It is anticipated that this valuation method will create substantial profits for those who developed the method through judicious application of their valuation strategy. In government, the 'profit' mostly sought by administrators is discretion. Sometimes they seek discretion because they cannot do their statutorily mandated job without it. Sometimes they seek discretion because without it they cannot provide the level of service which they believe is appropriate. Sometimes they seek discretion for reasons of ego or power aggregation for power aggregation's sake. In any event, public administration is often a work of discretion, and creativity in the pursuit of discretion is rewarded in government systems.

It goes without saying that creativity should be rewarded, because government would be 'frozen solid' without discretion. However, it is unfortunate that one of the places in government where creativity is (at least monetarily) rewarded most highly is in the creation and successful use of CFIs. This is unfortunate because this is the place where danger in discretion grows. Discretion here is dangerous because, as Klitgaard (2004) points out, discretion in concert with monopoly power mediated by a lack of transparency is the recipe for corruption.

Transparency

Those who practice 'justified' corruption are attracted to the complexity that CFI use creates because complexity is an excellent place to obscure process. There are two reasons for this. Firstly, oversight of CFIs is more expensive, because the expertise required to exercise oversight on CFIs is a scarce resource. The number of people in government service who knew what a derivative was, let alone the potential risk associated with derivative use, was non-existent before the Orange County meltdown, and may still be negligible now. Wherever oversight expertise is at a premium, transparency is compromised. Secondly, with complexity comes the ease of obfuscation which further degrades transparency. Intricacies provide buffers between those who would take whatever steps they believe necessary to provide services and those who demand transparency. Between these two related issues – natural places to obscure process and oversight that is both expensive and scarce – a Petri dish for justified corruption calls out to well-meaning and intelligent, but constrained, public administrators to do what, in their opinion, is necessary for the public good.

Even in well-regulated systems operated by people of good will 'the problem of many hands' (Thompson 1980) creates a lack of transparency and, subsequently, an accountability issue in the use of CFIs. The expertise and distribution channels needed to negotiate the use of CFIs are simultaneously diverse and specialized. Municipalities typically tend to rely on a large group of private consultants, investment bankers and securities law specialists in their use of CFIs. In turn, these investment professionals either specialize in working with governmental agencies or have a division that specializes in working with governmental agencies. Even so, these professionals are not government employees. Their approaches to problem-solving are 'private-sector' in focus. While they will adjust their approach to the constraints of municipal responsibility, that is not their initial approach. In this environment, where many familiar consulting partners work together on a frequent, project-by-project basis, it is often hard to figure out whose idea it was to invest a large portion of the retirement account in a particular hedge fund. Accountability requires transparency and transparency is decidedly compromised by the many familiar hands that must touch the CFIs.

SPECIFIC INSTANCES OF POTENTIALLY JUSTIFIED CORRUPTION

This final section of the paper gives five specific examples of how these complex financial instruments, in the context of Klitgaard's definition, are specifically related to issues of justified corruption, and illustrate today's conundrum of modern public-sector financial management. In all of the following examples, every activity is legal, every activity is complex, every activity is based on the monopoly power of the jurisdiction concerned and every single activity demonstrates the ability of the jurisdiction to engage in discretionary activities. In many of these, the activities are done with the citizens' approval, although in many cases the actions are so arcane that citizens may either be perceiving the information inaccurately or be unaware of the full implications of the action.

Development Imbalances

Land-use decisions based on fiscal short-run revenue and expenditure problems can lead to potential corruption in the political arena. Developers may be influential decision-makers, often little interested in overall community welfare, congestion externalities or affordable housing. Their rent-seeking behavior could potentially lead to public-development decisions that do not make sense in the long run. State and local governments must focus on growth patterns and transit-oriented development solutions based on community-planning concerns as well as economic efficiency. Such 'fiscalization' of land-use policy affects retail location and creates incentives for more imbalanced development patterns (Lewis 2001).

While local jurisdictions with restrictions on property taxes have been diversifying their revenue base toward other forms of taxes and fees, there is a tendency for local governments to encourage retail development over other forms of development. Therefore, cities find themselves competing with one another in pursuing high-value, sales-tax generating projects only to discover later that they have ended up with imbalanced development. After California's post-Proposition 13 abandonment of property taxation, local jurisdictions, with their heavy reliance on sales taxation as a source of local discretionary revenue, began to pay more attention to the fiscal outcomes of land-use decisions that generated revenues in addition to property taxes (Chapman 1998; Fulton 1997; Innes & Booher 1999; Lewis 2001; Schrag 1998; Schwartz 1997; Wassmer 2002). Local governments that feel fiscal stress or that desire to maximize revenues compete for the generation of a large amount of sales-tax revenue from a small geographical area. These activities result in greater local retail development, such as 'big-box' retail and car dealerships in non-central metropolitan places (Chapman 1998; Fulton 1998). The enchantment with collecting other taxes such as license fees or other business taxes from retailers provides an additional motivation for these types of development over residential development.

Land-use decisions often favor big-box retail projects. This reflects the new planning philosophy that land-use decisions should be based on the sales- and property-tax values of a proposed project rather than other criteria, such as not degrading the environment, environmental justice or even jobs. This land-use orientation undermines the necessary cooperation and engagement among local jurisdictions required for the overall economic prosperity of the region. Meanwhile, housing and industrial sites may be in short supply because the 'fiscalization of land use' has hampered housing and other non-retail development.

In this process, as there are more approvals for retail proposals than for residential, industrial or other proposals, there is a serious urban sprawl or an imbalance in regional development patterns. These imbalanced development patterns and practices indirectly affect environmental quality. Urban form influences travel decisions and, therefore, land-use decisions may have a serious impact on transportation, environmental health and the general quality of life. The result is a job–housing imbalance, more traffic congestion, longer commutes for employees, more air pollution from increased vehicle use and a steady deterioration of the quality of life throughout a region. In addition, as new retail outlets proliferate, existing main streets, strip malls and older shopping centers battle vacancies because retail capacity exceeds the market demand. While the owners of big-box retail and car dealerships are attempting to obtain economic incentives for locating in a particular jurisdiction, local government efforts can be a public sector 'give-away' to retailers or developers.

Incorrect Price Signals Leading to Erroneous Policy Choices

Because of the restrictions attached to the local property tax as well as its unpopularity with voters, local governments may attempt to turn away from this tax source and use less-restricted revenue sources, particularly charges for enterprise activities and impact fees. Nearly every type of government levies a charge or fee on facilities and services. These fees and charges constitute a significant revenue source for local jurisdictions.

Fees and charges influence supply-and-demand decisions for services through altered cost–price relations. So long as charges or fees are based on the actual marginal costs of providing a service, they signal the users of services on the cost-efficiency of investing in devices to reduce unnecessary use or waste. Fees for services should be charged to those who benefit from the goods or services. User fees should not ordinarily be used merely as a revenue-enhancement device since, if they are set too high, they will cause a lower-than-efficient demand for services, thereby hurting the citizens' welfare. This is the analog of a private-sector monopolist who charges too high a price and produces not enough of the good. Since jurisdictions engage in this type of behavior in order to secure a large profit and to offset the lack of tax revenues, it also acts to conceal the real cost of government from the taxpayers and serves to evade limitations on the level of taxation voted by taxpayers.

Local jurisdictions intend to recover the full cost of providing goods and services. However, under some circumstances, the jurisdictions might set an impact fee on a developer at less than cost. Setting inappropriate fees or charges can lead to price signals that do not convey the true information on the cost of the service provided. Sometimes, public officials interested in expanding their budgets or the size of their jurisdiction through increased development can have an incentive to withhold or distort cost information. These incorrect price signals can result in economic inefficiencies and the sub-optimal allocation of resources. However, responding to incorrect price signals leads to bad decision-making in terms of both economic efficiency and deleterious equity results. It has been shown theoretically that too low an impact fee can lead to urban sprawl (Brueckner 2001).

Development fees (payments required to obtain approval for new construction) are important for local jurisdictions to internalize the costs of public capital and service for new development (Yinger 1998). Development fees are distinguished from taxes because they are voluntary, and are imposed only upon developing land, rather than on all landowners or taxpayers. Development fees are placed on developers because providing infrastructure for new developments benefits the new residents.

Development fees signal the price of housing and the quantity of new construction. It is likely that the price increase will be less than the fees. In this way, the developer may face a net burden and will supply less housing (Chapman 1998; Yinger 1998). Both the buyer and the developer share the burden of the tax. Furthermore, as the price of new homes increases, some buyers will shift to a purchase of an existing home. This will increase the price of existing homes, producing windfall gains to those homeowners.

However, the effects of fees on prices may change due to different economic conditions and lead to negative policy consequences. In particular, the degree of competition for new housing, the infrastructure that is financed by development fees and exaction, the market for land and the nature of competition in the building industry all affect the conventional results. If new housing prices do not rise with the imposition of fees landowners are likely to bear the burden of development fees, but if the building industry is noncompetitive, builders could shift some of the development-fee burden (Chapman 1998). In other words, the setting of optimal price signals is also constrained by the lack of information concerning consumer demands, while policy 'success' depends on the right price signals to cover the impact on a number of environmental, economic, political and practical factors.

Economic Development Waste

Local governments can attempt to stimulate private investment opportunities in order to create new jobs for their residents and provide a net tax increase. Local public fiscal stress increases the need for new economic development or for an increase in redevelopment activities (Man 1999). In these activities, local governments may try to invest in tax and financial incentive programs to attract business investment or enter into partnerships with private enterprises. An obvious question concerning this type of development activity is whether it works in stimulating economic development. Empirical research on taxes and business location suggests that state and local taxes have a statistically significant effect on business-location decisions, although this effect is typically between jurisdictions and is very small between states (Bartik 1989; Wasylenko 1997).

However, benefits in the form of jobs for residents and net benefits to the overall fiscal condition of these states and local governments are questionable (Fainstein, Fainstein, Hill, Judd & Smith 1983; Squires 1989). In other words, it is not certain that the tax revenue lost by the tax exemptions used to encourage development could potentially be more than replaced by the new tax revenue generated by employment and other income associated with development. Further, much of the analysis is short-run based and ignores such long-run problems as financing local public goods under reduced revenues or even reduced funds for infrastructure finance. These problems reinforce the potential for the use of CFIs.

Tax abatements and other incentives as a method of economic development may eventually weaken the revenue base and adversely affect property taxes on non-abated property. They place a heavier burden on homeowners and curtail the city's capacity to provide services (Stone 1987; Krumholz 1991). Sometimes subsidies and incentives of economic development tend to focus only on the benefits and ignore the costs of economic development policy, such as where the development occurs, regressive distribution of benefits and the opportunity cost of the subsidy. Many development strategies are really fiscal illusions, since the public does not know their true cost (Spindler & Forrester 1993). The cost of most economic development policies is invisible because the policies are supported with 'hidden' taxes or tax expenditures (Rubin & Rubin 1987). Tax abatements are relatively invisible to the public in terms of cost.

To stimulate development and reap the benefits of increased sales taxes, property taxes and employment, local government may also become a partner with a private developer or group of developers. Local jurisdictions may recognize a changing revenue flow based on the profitability of the development project. For a partnership with a private developer, the jurisdictions can provide certain services and help finance others. Local governments can provide some of the infrastructure and help change zoning restrictions for the needs of the developers. However, the profitability of the development project is questionable and, in some cases, it may not work out as originally intended. Clearly, therefore, local governments are taking risks.

In addition, the public–private partnerships doing local economic development have focused massive public subsidies on real-estate deals that provided tangible benefits to developers, landowners, politicians and development officials. Often, the private-sector balance sheets in these partnerships are confidential and are open only to selected public officials. Sometimes benefits in the form of jobs and net benefits to the overall fiscal condition of these cities are questionable (Fainstein, Fainstein, Hill, Judd & Smith 1983; Squires 1989).

Public officials have a potential for offering incentives that allow them to accomplish something concrete, thereby building a record of tangible achievements (even though they surrender a portion of their tax base and even though their economic development incentives limit the budget for essential public services). In general, it is agreed that many of these fiscal incentives are not good development policy. Very often they result in wasting public dollars, subsidizing shareholders and management for economic activities that they would have undertaken anyway and fostering unfair competition by selectively helping specific firms (Shafroth 2005). The potential for graft and unethical behavior is great. However, sometimes public officials need to gamble in their attempts to undertake economic development projects because of their jurisdiction's fiscal stress. These officials take advantage of the monopoly power and discretion of their position.

Although the public perceives transparency, this may not be an accurate perception.

Debt Misinformation to Voters

There are a variety of debt instruments that state and local governments can utilize to finance capital facilities. Although traditional General Obligation and Revenue bonds typically require voter approval, powerful debt instruments exist that can be operationalized without going public. In these cases, it is very likely that the public does not know that debt has been incurred. Often the elected officials have set up shell agencies to undertake the issuing process. Because the public may be unaware of these instruments, they are equally unaware of how their tax dollars are spent. This can cause alienation from government and lead to a deeply held suspicion of the public sector. These instruments are so arcane that often even the elected officials misunderstand them. Individual graft and corruption as well as systemic corruption can be the result. To give a measure of the magnitude of these CFIs, in 2003, suffice it to say that California jurisdictions issued $1.4 billion of (Mello-Roos) Community Facilities District debt, $4.3 billion of Certificates of Participation, both state and local, and $4.3 billion of redevelopment debt. All of this was done for what many consider to be legitimate public purposes. However, none was submitted to the voters.

SOME CONCLUSIONS AND POLICY RECOMMENDATIONS

Local governments often face the dilemma of choosing to be negligent in providing necessary services or utilizing methods that, while legal, are designed to obfuscate necessary information and are not always clear to the public. Local finance directors are constantly looking for revenue and service niches that allow them to improve their cities. However, the cumulative impact of the different ways in which complex financial instruments are used to create discretion (while inviting monopoly power and discouraging transparency) make them particularly vulnerable to justified corruption. It is this combination of discretion with monopoly power and opaque operational processes that makes us particularly wary of the potential for justified corruption with the use of complex financial instruments.

Two phenomena must occur before any progress can be made to diminish the proclivity to justified corruption. The first is that state and local governments need a revenue stream that is stable, predictable, dependable and controllable. Governments with very limited fiscal autonomy are less likely to be able to command resources and to spend those resources in ways that are consistent with citizen needs and preferences. At the same time, the public must understand how its money is spent. Citizens need to realize that quality public services cost money and, if they want quality services, they should insist on an observable revenue stream to their government. Likewise, citizens need to recognize that if they want low taxes they cannot expect high-quality government services.

Education of both the public and those charged with oversight is another key factor to diminishing justified corruption. If citizens need to understand how their money is being used, then they must be educated on the subject. If they are to understand the cost–benefit ratio of quality government service then they must be provided with the tools to do so. Furthermore, if oversight agencies are to provide effective evaluation of complex financial instrument use then their staffs must be trained in the intricacies and potential problems associated with CFIs. With the education of citizens and oversight agency staff, we believe that the tendency toward the monopolization of government by information elites and the unknowing dispensation of unintended discretion will diminish, while the demand for and the capability of providing transparency will increase.

As we break down the component parts of the equation for corruption through education, we diminish the opportunity for justified corruption. This is profoundly important because justified corruption erodes the fabric of government institutions and causes a decline of institutional legitimacy. The potential for progressive deterioration of legitimacy in government through 'justified corruption' is a concern that should not and, indeed, cannot be ignored.

REFERENCES

Bartik, T.J. (1989). 'Small Business Start-ups in the United States: Estimates of the Effects of Characteristics of States'. *Southern Economic Journal* 55, pp. 1004–1018.

Bradbury, K.L. (1982). 'Fiscal Distress in Large US Cities'. *New England Economic Journal*, November/December, pp. 33–44.

Brueckner, J.K. (2001). 'Property Taxation and Urban Sprawl'. In W.E. Oates (Ed), *Property Taxation and Local Government Finance* (pp. 153–172). Cambridge, MA: Lincoln Institute of Land Policy.

Caiden, G.E. (1988). 'Toward a General Theory of Official Corruption'. *Asian Journal of Public Administration* 10 (1), pp. 3–26.

Caiden, G.E. (1994). 'Administrative Reform'. In R. Baker (Ed), *Comparative Public Management*. Westport, CT: Praeger Publishers.

Caiden, G.E. (2001). 'Corruption and Governance'. In G.E. Caiden, O.P Dwivedi, & J. Jabbra (Eds), *Where Corruption Lives* (pp. 15–38). Bloomfield, CT: Kumarian Press.

Caiden, G.E., Dwivedi, O.P., & Jabbra, J. (2001). 'Introduction'. In G.E. Caiden, O.P. Dwivedi, & J. Jabbra (Eds), *Where Corruption Lives* (pp. 1–14). Bloomfield, CT: Kumarian Press.

Chapman, J.I. (1998). *Proposition 13: Some Unintended Consequences.* San Francisco: Public Policy Institute of California.

Chapman, J.I. (2003). 'The Impacts of Public Fiscal Tools on Private Development Decisions'. *National Tax Association Proceedings, 2002* (pp. 308–315). Washington DC: National Tax Association.

Chi, K., & Leatherby, D. (1997). *State Business Incentives: Trends and Options for the Future.* Lexington, KY: Council of State Governments.

Cuno, C., et al. versus Daimler-Chrysler, & al. 6th Circuit, decided and filed 19 October 2004.

Fainstein, S.S., Fainstein, N.I., Hill, R.C., Judd, D., & Smith, M.P. (1983). *Restructuring the City*. New York: Longman.

Fukuyama, F. (1995). *Trust: The Social Virtues and the Creation of Prosperity*. New York: Free Press.

Fulton, W. (1997). *The Reluctant Metropolis: The Politics of Urban Growth in Los Angeles.* Point Arena, CA: Solano.

Fulton, W. (1998). 'Twenty Years of Proposition 13'. *California Planning and Development Report* 13 (6), pp. 8–10.

Grey, C.W., & Kaufmann, D. (1998). 'Corruption and Development'. *Finance and Development* 35 (1), pp. 7–10.

Inman, R.P. (2003). 'Transfers and Bailouts: Enforcing Local Fiscal Discipline with Lessons from U.S. Federalism'. In J. Rodden, G.S. Eskeland, & J. Litvack (Eds), *Fiscal Decentralization and the Challenge of Hard Budget Constraints* (pp. 35–83). Cambridge, MA: MIT Press.

Innes, J.E., & Booher, D.E. (1999). 'Metropolitan Development as a Complex System: A New Approach to Sustainability'. *Economic Development Quarterly* 13, pp. 141–156.

Jones, L.R., & Thompson, F. (1999). *Public Management: Institutional Renewal for the Twenty-First Century.* Stamford, CT: Jai Press.

Klitgaard, R. (2004). 'Leadership under Systematic Corruption'. Mekong Summit Address. p. 3.

Krumholz, N. (1991). 'Equity and Local Economic Development'. *Economic Development Quarterly* 5 (4).

Lane, J.E. (2000). *New Public Management.* New York: Routledge.

Lewis, P.G. (2001). 'Retail Politics: Local Sales Taxes and the Fiscalization of Land Use'. *Economic Development Quarterly* 15 (1), pp. 21–35.

Man, J.Y. (1999). 'Fiscal Pressure, Tax Competition and the Adoption of Tax Increment Financing'. *Urban Studies* 37 (7).

Moore, M.H. (2002). 'Privatizing Public Management'. In J.D. Donahue & J.S. Nye (Eds), *Market-based Governance* (pp. 296–322). Washington, DC: Brookings Institution Press.

Nelson, B. (2002). 'Education For the Public Interest'. NASPAA Plenary Address. Los Angeles, CA, 17 October.

Osborne, D., & Gaebler, T. (1992). *Reinventing Government.* Reading, MA: Addison-Wesley.

Rubin, I.S., & Rubin, H.J. (1987). 'Economic Development Incentives: The Poor (Cities) Pay More'. *Urban Affairs Quarterly* 23 (1), pp. 37–62.

Salamon, L.M. (2002). 'The New Governance and the Tools of Public Action: An Introduction'. In L.M. Salamon, (Ed), *The Tools of Government: A Guide to the New Governance* (pp. 1–47). Oxford: Oxford University Press.

Schrag, P. (1998). *Paradise Lost: California's Experience, America's Future*. New York: New Press.

Schwartz, J. (1997). 'Prisoners of Proposition 13: Sales Taxes, Property Taxes, and the Fiscalization of Municipal Land Use Decisions'. *Southern California Review* 71, pp. 183–217.

Shafroth, F. (2005). 'What Could the State Economies of Tomorrow Be? Effective Economic Development in the States'. *State Tax Notes*, 3 January, pp. 915–920.

Sokolow, A.D. (1993). 'State–Local Relations in California: What Happens When They Take Away the Property Tax?' Working Paper, Department of Community Development, University of California–Davis.

Spindler, C.J., & Forrester, J.P. (1993). 'Economic Development Policy: Explaining Policy Preferences among Competing Models'. *Urban Affairs Quarterly* 29 (1), pp. 28–53.

Squires, G.D. (1989). *Unequal Partnerships*. New Brunswick, NJ: Rutgers University Press.

Stone, C.N. (1987). 'Summing up: Urban Regimes, Development Policy and Political Arrangements'. In C.N. Stone & H.T. Sanders (Eds), *The Politics of Urban Development* (pp. 269–290). Lawrence: University Press of Kansas.

Tanzi, V. (1998). 'Corruption Around the World: Causes, Consequences, Scope and Cures'. *IMF Staff Papers* (45) 4, pp. 559–594.

Terry, L. (1995). *Public Bureaucracies: The Administrator as Conservator*. Thousand Oaks, CA: SAGE.

Thompson, D.F. (1980). 'Moral Responsibility of Public Officials: The Problem of Many Hands'. *American Political Science Review* 74, pp. 905–916.

Wallis, J.J. (2004). 'The Concept of Systemic Corruption in American Political and Economic History'. National Bureau of Economic Research Working Paper, Number 10952 (December). http://www.nber.org/papers/w10952.

Wassmer, R.W. (2002). 'Fiscalization of Land Use, Urban Growth Boundaries and Non-Central Retail Sprawl in the Western United States'. *Urban Studies* 39 (8), pp. 1307–1327.

Wasylenko, M. (1997). 'Taxation and Economic Development: The State of the Economic Literature'. *New England Economic Review*, pp. 37–52.

Wildavsky, A. & Caiden, N. (2004). *New Politics of the Budgetary Process* (5th ed). Old Tappan, NJ: Longman.

Yinger, J. (1998). 'The Incidence of Development Fees and Special Assessments'. *National Tax Journal* 51 (1), pp. 23–42.

NOTES

1 For example, in the Orange County, California, bankruptcy event, none of the public officials personally profited by their intricate financial activities.
2 The timing of the assessment necessary to obtain the correct property value is also a political decision – the more active the assessor, the more accurate the assessment. Further, the number of types of property (called the property roll) is also a political decision. This becomes important because often jurisdictions convert the appraised value into an assessed value by applying a parameter to the particular type of roll. For example, California does not separate property into commercial, industrial and residential – all are assessed at the time of sale at the full sale price. Arizona, on the other hand, has eleven different property classifications, each of which is converted into assessed value by a particular factor – a household's assessed value is 10 percent of appraised value while business assessed value is 25 percent of appraised value.
3 Note that because of 'Dillion's Rule' most of the local responses need to be acceptable to the state, as indicated either by authorizing legislation or by precedent.
4 In 1993, for example, the State of Alabama offered incentives worth about $168,000 per job provided. The *Cuno v. Daimler Chrysler* judgment (2004) may be putting an end to competitive state subsidies.
5 For example, in some states there are two property taxes: one under the limit and one that can exceed the limit with voter approval.
6 Tools are quite complex and, as Salamon (2002) argues, consist of a package of goods, delivery vehicles, delivery systems and rules.
7 Note that no public official personally profited from the Orange County bankruptcy.

13

The Dilution and Distortion of the Ombudsman Concept

DONALD C. ROWAT

INTRODUCTION

When Gerald Caiden edited his well-regarded two-volume work on the ombudsman in 1983, the ombudsman institution had already begun its spread around the world as a standard part of the legislative machinery of democratic government for supervising the bureaucracy by investigating complaints from citizens. After its transplantation from Sweden and Finland to Denmark in 1955 and to Norway and New Zealand in 1962, it had spread so rapidly that, by 1983, 12 national plans had been adopted in the developed democracies and 11 in the developing countries (Rowat 1985: 134, 169). By then, there were also numerous adoptions at the state and local levels of government and for particular segments of administration, such as the army or prisons.

Few people then suspected that there would be such a vast growth in other types of ombudsmen – general executive, specialty executive, university, hospital, media and human rights ombudsmen, and also business corporation ombudsmen for internal dispute resolution and/or for customer complaints. Nor was it realized that their numbers would swamp the legislative ombudsmen, diluting and distorting the original concept and starting a controversy about the very nature and definition of an ombudsman.

The spread of the institution is an interesting case study in the international transfer of institutional reforms. As with the adoption of most reforms, this one turned out to be less difficult than its opponents predicted yet failed to accomplish as much as its advocates thought it would. At first, opponents said the institution could not be transplanted because the Swedish and Finnish systems of government were so unique. But the successful early adoptions elsewhere proved them wrong. The proponents became so enthusiastic that they insisted it would not only defend the vulnerable citizen against the bureaucratic dragon, but also cure political corruption as well as advance democracy in the developing countries. As with the transplantation of any political institution, especially where the receiving country was looking for international aid or approbation, there was the danger of transferring the form but not the substance or function. Yet the legislative ombudsman has turned out to be one of the most important institutional inventions of democracy, on a par with the secret ballot, the representative legislature, the public service commission, the legislative auditor and the public corporation. Hence the question became: how should the legislative ombudsman be defined so that the substance will be transferred along with the form?

It is said that a good definition of a word or phrase is one that includes all units that are the same, yet excludes all similar units that are not quite the same. Thus, one cannot define a chair simply as an item of furniture with four legs because that would include a table. One has to complete the definition with the function, by adding 'and whose purpose is for sitting upon' (rather than 'serving food upon'). Similarly, the office of ombudsman cannot be defined as only 'an institution to remedy citizens' grievances against administrative agencies', because this would include a court, especially an administrative court. So one must add something like this: 'which makes recommendations to remedy grievances, but not binding decisions like a court's'.

KEY FEATURES OF THE COURTS AND OMBUDSMAN INSTITUTIONS

The great advantage of making only recommendations is that the ombudsman institution cannot substitute its judgment on the substance of decisions for that of trained specialist administrators. Its specialty is to judge the fairness of the administrative process, not the substance, which often requires specialized knowledge. Thus, its great virtue is that it is not a gate across the administrative road, as the courts with their binding decisions can be, but rather a guiding fence along that road. Another great advantage of an ombudsman over a court is its informality. All the complainant has to do is phone or write the ombudsman's office; by contrast, a court is forbidding, cumbersome, slow and often prohibitively costly.

What is the key feature of the courts that makes them otherwise so acceptable for remedying administrative grievances? It is their neutrality, arising from their independence, as the third arm of government. How do ombudsmen achieve a similar degree of independence? By being agents of the legislature, created by the constitution or a law, which ensures independence by such devices as appointment by a special majority for a long term, dismissal only by a like majority, pegging their pay to that of the judges and giving them control of their own hiring. Creation by law also has the advantage that the office cannot be influenced, changed or abolished at the whim of the executive or an agency head.

However, in order to be effective, ombudsmen need strong powers as a substitute for not making binding decisions. So legislatures give them the power to investigate by subpoena, the power of persuasion through publicity and, at the same time, the power to keep confidential the name of a complainant who may fear retaliation. This means that they must be enabled to issue public reports and must be willing, thanks to the security of independence, to embarrass the administrative wrongdoer into providing a remedy or even to persuade the legislature that it should amend a law if it results in maladministration.

Another reason the legislative ombudsman cannot be defined only as an institution to remedy citizens' grievances is because this would include an ordinary complaint bureau within the department or agency being complained against. Such a bureau cannot be truly independent, and may not even have the appearance of neutrality to the complainant. So one must add to the definition: 'which is made independent by a law' that grants the above essential powers.

With the growing international popularity of this independent legislative ombudsman has come the increasing danger of the form being adopted but not the substance. Among the reasons for this are the natural desire to adapt the institution to the particular culture and circumstances of each country, the increasing popularity of the institution in the developing countries (many of which are only pseudo-democracies) and their desire to curry favor with, and obtain aid from, a developed democracy. But a more serious reason is that the executive and the administration dislike having their wrongdoings or mistakes revealed in public. Bureaucrats in any organization form a phalanx of loyalty to protect their reputation. So they capture the ombudsman institution by making it part of the executive side of government and diluting its powers. They prefer an inside institution that they can control or, at least, influence. The end result has been a dilution and distortion of the legislative or classical ombudsman concept.

EARLY ALTERATIONS

When the institution was first transplanted from Sweden and Finland, a number of significant alterations were made. These were said to be necessary adaptations to fit the different conditions of the recipient country. But were they really? Or were they instead dilutions or erosions of the original concept? For instance, New Zealand decided to levy a small charge for each complaint. Though this did not alter the essence of the plan, it was a serious limitation for poor citizens, who needed the ombudsman's services the most.

An omission from the first and subsequent adoptions, that also did not sabotage the essence of the original, concerns the power of the Swedish and Finnish ombudsmen to prosecute officials in the courts and their laudable custom of making unannounced inspections of governmental activities and institutions. More importantly, the early adoptions eliminated the Swedish and Finnish ombudsmen's supervision of the courts, an elimination said to be necessary to prevent them from interfering with the historic independence of the courts. Yet the courts are as independent in Sweden and Finland as elsewhere in the democratic world. Besides, in their courts the ombudsmen only handle complaints about procedure, not substance. So a strong case can be made for the supervision of courts elsewhere (see Rowat 1992: 527–538).

Another alteration that almost escaped notice was the insistence in early writings that the institution must be headed by a single person. This was said to give 'the human touch', and evoked images of a white knight riding to the rescue of the downtrodden citizen. However, it has led to the unworkable view that the white knight should be the citizens' advocate. Ombudsmen are expected to be neutral and to side with administrators when a complaint is unjustified, thus gaining their cooperation in accepting the ombudsmen's recommendations. The institution in Sweden has several ombudsmen, each specializing in a different segment of the administration.

This insistence on a single ombudsman compounded a problem that has bedevilled the transfer of the institution. It was said that Sweden and Finland were small countries, and that the institution would not work in a populous country because it would have to turn into a large and unwieldy bureaucracy just like the ones it was supposed to be supervising. It was also maintained that a single ombudsman could not have the expert knowledge needed to supervise the whole administrative side of government. Yet several populous countries have successfully adopted the institution with a commission at its head, each commissioner specializing in one area of administration.

The problem of adjusting the institution to fit the conditions of populous countries has resulted in many alterations of the original concept, some retaining the essence of the original but some constituting a dilution or erosion. Among those retaining the essence were the adoptions at the state or local levels of government in federations, where such adoptions were particularly popular. At an early date, state and local schemes were adopted in Canada, Switzerland and the United States, but not at the federal level. Australia is an outstanding example of a federation that has adopted schemes at both the state and national levels. In the UK and France, one alteration was the requirement that complaints must first go to one's member of parliament, then be referred to the ombudsman, with the results going back to the complainant through the member. Was this cumbersome arrangement a desirable limitation? The answer seems to be 'no', because it cut down drastically on the number of complaints in relation to population. Other populous countries have adopted the scheme without this requirement.

Another adjustment to meet the fear that the institution would be too big and unwieldy was to appoint specialty ombudsmen to handle the complaints against particular agencies where the need seemed to be greatest. There were two precedents for this. At an early date, Germany and Norway had already set up ombudsmen for the armed services. These specialty schemes became popular at the federal level in Canada and the USA but also for institutions where citizens were at the mercy of the management, such as for hospitals, homes for long-term care, the armed services, jails and the police. Where they were set up by legislation on the same pattern as the original general plans, they met the essence of the definition for they were independent of the organization being complained against. But because they satisfied the greatest needs, they had the unfortunate effect of lowering the political pressure for an overall plan. This helps to explain why Canada and the USA have not so far adopted general legislative plans at the federal level. Their existence also made it easy for agency heads, without legislative sanction, to set up grievance officers, call them ombudsmen and pretend that they were the genuine article.

One could conclude about these early alterations and adaptations that, rather than being necessary adaptations, they were diluting, if not eroding, the original Swedish and Finnish institution. However, where they were set up by legislation they did manage to preserve the essence of the original schemes. Hence, by the time that Gerald Caiden edited his book in 1983, the definition of the legislative ombudsman – including the characteristics essential to that definition – had become well established as the desirable model to be followed. This was partly due to the influence of Walter Gellhorn, a Professor of Law at Columbia University, who in 1966 published a thorough international study, *Ombudsmen and Others*, and a smaller book, *When Americans Complain*, recommending the scheme for the USA. He also drafted a model state law which became the template for the five state plans in the US (plus those in Puerto Rico and Guam). He was also influential in getting the powerful American Bar Association to pass a resolution in 1969 defining and urging the adoption of what has come to be known as the 'classical' legislative scheme. This resolution has had a wide influence beyond the borders of the United States.

By 1983, the concept had gained such worldwide popularity that the word 'ombudsman', when used alone, was automatically taken to mean an independent officer of the legislature empowered by law. It was replacing 'homegrown' terms such as parliamentary commissioner or citizens' defender, even in juridical and other languages. For instance, even though in New Zealand's law the title was 'Parliamentary Commissioner of the Administration (Ombudsman)', soon the word ombudsman was always used by the press and public. It has become an international word, like taxi or hotel. But it was beginning to be used by the heads of so many new executive and nongovernmental complaint bureaus that its essential characteristic of independence was often ignored. Hence it is not surprising that New Zealand passed a law in 1991 prohibiting the use of the title ombudsman by others unless the chief ombudsman gives his permission (Robertson 1993). Likewise, the British Ombudsman Association refuses to admit new members unless they meet the essentials of its definition.

LATER DISTORTIONS OF THE CONCEPT

North America is known as the land of *faddism*. In the late 1960s, the word 'ombudsman' burst upon the USA and Canada with such force that it became wildly popular as the new buzzword. In reviewing Gellhorn's two definitive books on the subject in 1966, *Time* magazine noted that by the end of the year, the word had not yet appeared in Webster's dictionary. However, two rival publishers wrote letters to point out proudly that it had already appeared in their dictionaries. Yet few people actually grasped the scheme's essential characteristics. So it is not surprising that a state governor announced that he was going to be the state's ombudsman, or that when the scheme was proposed for the federal level in Canada, the then-Minister of Justice John Turner said that Canada did not need a national ombudsman because he himself acted in that capacity.

The result of the concept becoming so popular was that, by the end of the 1970s, the scheme had been adopted by nine Canadian provinces (all except PEI) and by four American states (Hawaii, Nebraska, Iowa and Alaska). In the US, ombudsman bills were pending in many other states and at the national level. However, then the movement mysteriously ran out of steam. Why? Seemingly, the opportunity to create legislative ombudsmen in the US was a golden one when the US is compared with the parliamentary countries of the Commonwealth. In these countries, the prime minister as chief executive makes all important appointments, sits in the legislature and controls the majority. So, it is surprising that the legislature is able to ensure the independence of an ombudsman. As with the legislative auditor and the electoral commissioner, a special legislative measure was required. But with the separation of powers in the US, it seemed easy for the legislature to set up independent ombudsman offices.

One reason so few were created may have been the passage of the Inspector General Act in 1978 and its later amendments. It provided for independent inspectors-general for an increasing number of federal agencies, and was copied at the state level. However, the focus of these ombudsman-like offices is on auditing – for fraud, waste and mismanagement – and on complaints from internal whistleblowers, rather than from citizens with personal grievances.

A more compelling reason is that in the US the chief executives and heads of agencies have an independent power to appoint. It was all too easy for them to hijack the term by appointing their own officers to handle citizen complaints and calling them ombudsmen. The ones appointed by chief executives came to be known as executive general ombudsmen, and the ones by heads of agencies as executive specialty ombudsmen. Soon, executive, general and specialty ombudsmen began to appear instead of the genuine article at the local, state and federal levels of government. In fact, as Rowat's statistical study has revealed, by 1996 their numbers had grown so large that they greatly outnumbered legislative ombudsmen. By then, at all levels of government in the United States, there were 21 general and 53 specialty legislative ombudsmen for a total of 74, but the numbers of general and specialty executive ombudsmen had grown to 83 and 138, for a total of 221, or three times the number of legislative ombudsmen (Rowat 1997: Table 2, 5–7).

In other words, the ubiquitousness of executive ombudsmen in the US meant that the key characteristic of the ombudsman institution, its independence, was being ignored. The offices of executive specialty ombudsmen could hardly be distinguished from ordinary complaint bureaus, with no questions asked about independence. To paraphrase Bernard Frank, a leading advocate of the classical plan, Americans loved the word ombudsman but not the institution. And so the legislative ombudsman movement in the US quickly declined. But this was not true elsewhere. Rowat's statistics for 1996 show that, in other countries, while there were 170 general and 48 specialty legislative ombudsmen, there were only 13 general executive and 17 specialty executive ombudsmen. Adding the 1996 figures for all legislative and executive ombudsmen gives totals for governmental ombudsmen of 295 in the US, 248 in other countries, and nearly 550 in the whole world (Rowat 1997, Table 2, 5–7).

In the United States, there are now four kinds of executive ombudsmen: (1) those appointed by an agency to deal with internal employee complaints, often called workplace or employee ombudsmen; (2) those appointed by the head of an agency to deal with the public; (3) those appointed by a chief executive (such as a governor or mayor) to handle complaints against a specific agency such as child care; and (4) those appointed by a chief executive for complaints from the public against all agencies. The first three types are often referred to as executive specialty ombudsmen because they supervise a specific agency. Though the degree of independence of executive ombudsmen tends to vary with tradition and politics, it is probably greatest for the last two types because, being in the chief executive's office, they are more independent of the agency being complained against.

This large number of executive ombudsmen naturally poses a problem for the United States Ombudsman Association (USOA), which was founded as an association of legislative ombudsmen. Some executive ombudsmen were anxious to appear more legitimate by joining the Association and patterning themselves, as far as possible, on the genuine article. The Association, wishing to accommodate them and perhaps influence them to become more independent, invented for them the category of Associate Member (non-voting). However, they kept knocking at the door until finally the USOA admitted them as full members and gave them equal representation on its board of directors. Was this a mistake? It certainly helped to legitimize the executive ombudsmen, and the USOA now faces the danger of being captured, or at least heavily influenced, by the interests of the executive ombudsmen.

THE UNIVERSITY OMBUDSMEN

Because of the popularity in North America of the idea that grievances ought to be remedied in a democracy, the second distortion of the original concept came with its expansion, first to the universities, and then to other non-governmental entities such as hospitals and newspapers. At first, the proponents of an ombudsman for university students tried to follow the original concept of independence by having the ombudsman created by law of the board of governors or resolution of the academic senate (as the closest equivalents to a legislature), and by having the students share in the ombudsman's appointment and budget. For example, this was the case at Carleton University in Canada, where the powers and procedures of legislative ombudsmen were taken as the model.

But soon, in both Canada and the US, university ombudsmen were appointed by the president, who usually chose a member of the faculty without any participation by the students. The guarantee of independence was lost, as these ombudsmen could easily be suspected of being in the president's pocket. However, the classical model exerted a strong influence on them and many succeeded in establishing a tradition of independence. By the year 1996, there were at least 83 university ombudsmen, of which only 13 could be said to be legislative – eight in the USA and five in Canada (Rowat 1997: Tables 5, 7). The net result was that the distinction between legislative, governmental and other ombudsmen was obscured. All were indiscriminately called ombudsmen, and so the concept became further distorted. University ombudsmen formed their own organizations in both Canada and the United States. They set the pattern for the use of the word in the quasi-governmental and private sectors.

The university adoptions came mainly in the early 1970s, just about the time the feminist movement was at its height. So another strange result was the distortion of the word itself. By the time the feminist movement hit the universities in North America, the word was already well established in English. Yet the movement claimed that it was not gender-neutral and in the university schemes altered it indiscriminately to ombudsperson (plural, ombudspeople), ombud, ombuds (plural, ombudses), or even ombudsbuddy or ombuddy. Mysteriously, some maintained that the plural should be 'ombudsmans', to void the ending in '-men', or that the singular of the word was acceptable because it was Swedish, and so should be used as the plural.

By then there were several legislative ombudsmen who were women and they refused to agree, arguing that the word was so well established in law and language that it was gender-neutral. To them, changing it to ombudsperson was as unnecessary as changing the word woman to woperson, or changing the British phrase for speed bump from 'sleeping policeman' to 'sleeping policeperson'. Yet the feminist usages have continued in the nongovernmental sector and, in fact, were greatly expanded by the founders of the Corporate Ombudsman Association in its literature. The casual way in which the word has been altered has contributed to its disrespectful, 'dumbing down' usage. It even tortures English grammar by using the singular for the plural, even though the regular plural form is very useful as a linguistic device to avoid the awkward 'her/his' construction in the singular.

THE CORPORATE OMBUDSMEN AND THE OMBUDSMAN ASSOCIATION

The greatest distortion of the classical model was the appointment of so-called ombudsmen by business corporations in the US to settle disputes within the corporation (though sometimes they dealt also with customer complaints). Professor Larry Hill has dubbed them 'wannabe' ombudsmen (Hill 1997). This development mushroomed so fast that, in 1988, Mary Rowe, one of its advocates, estimated that there may have been as many as 8,000 corporate ombudsmen, often called by another name such as liaison officer, internal mediator, work problems counselor, dialog specialist or personnel communications (Ziegenfuss 1988: Foreword). It came about as part of the sudden appearance and popularity of the Dispute Resolution (DR) movement. In effect, the movement hijacked the word ombudsman for its own purposes. It quickly developed its own ombudsman jargon, involving a whole system within the corporation, not grievances by the public as with the classical ombudsmen.

This system is designed largely to prevent expensive corporate litigation in the courts and it involves complete confidentiality on the part of the ombudsman so as to avoid having to release files to the courts, though in the case of employee whistleblowers it has helped to prevent retaliation by their superiors. This was the very antithesis of the power of publicity given to the classical ombudsman, who uses it if necessary to gain redress or reform in important cases and who only keeps the complainants' names confidential if they so wish. But the complainants often want as much publicity as possible in order to force redress or reform. The DR system also involves mediation as a primary device, whereas with the classical scheme the main objective is to secure fairness and justice through investigation or the threat of it. Though legislative ombudsmen often use mediation, it is mainly to settle minor cases of misunderstanding between the complainant and the administration.

A leading theorist in providing the basis for calling 'dispute resolutionists' ombudsmen appears to have been J.T. Ziegenfuss (1988: 17). Ziegenfuss saw the ombudsman as a 'formal troubleshooter' in any type of organization – one who is formally recognized and funded and may have authority based on law, though it is not explained how in a corporation this authority could be based on law. The assumption is that in a corporation one can be made neutral by being formally designated by the management as 'neutral'. This became the basis for a popular phrase in the literature, 'designated neutral'. The plain fact is that in a corporation, an ombudsman cannot be completely neutral because the ombudsman is employed by and therefore ultimately beholden to the top management. Saying, as in management jargon, that the ombudsman is 'staff' rather than 'line' does not resolve this problem. Nor does arguing, as some theorists do, that they are neither line nor staff. The literature is also characterized by its moralistic tone: it is full of injunctions to the ombudsmen regarding what they 'should' or 'ought' to do. These injunctions later became the basis for the code of ethics adopted by the Corporate Ombudsman Association, after it was organized in 1984.

The website of its successor, The Ombudsman Association, stated that it was organized by 'seven people who shared a vision'. The vision appears to have been to turn the growing numbers of corporate dispute-settlers who had appropriated the name 'ombudsman' into a legitimate profession. The founders would do this by having their members adopt a code of ethics and standards of practice, and take study courses. They also make them aim to resemble the well-regarded and popular legislative ombudsmen through stress on neutrality. Due to the need for neutral, objective dispute-settlers, this was, of course, a laudable objective. The organizers of the first corporate ombudsman conference defined ombudsman vaguely 'as one skilled in dealing with reported complaints to help achieve equitable settlements' (Ziegenfuss 1988: 19).

The Corporate Ombudsman Association was so successful that within eight years it decided to extend its scope by changing its name to The Ombudsman Association (TOA). It used the term '*organizational ombudsmen*' to mean all nonlegislative ombudsmen, and made them eligible for at least associate membership. But this was a bad mistake. In the first place, 'organizational ombudsmen' is meaningless because legislative (like executive) ombudsmen are part of an organization and are thus also 'organizational'. Worse still, it puts all other types of ombudsmen – executive, university, and other nongovernmental – in the same bag as corporate. The code of ethics and standards of practice treat them all as though they were corporate ombudsmen and part of the DR movement.

Thus a TOA brochure asks: 'What is an Ombudsman?' and inconsistently replies, not with the well-established definition of a legislative ombudsman, as one might expect, but with its own all-encompassing yet vague definition of an 'organizational' ombudsman:

> An organizational ombudsman is designated as a neutral or impartial dispute resolution practitioner, whose major function is to provide confidential and informal assistance to managers and employees and/or to clients of the employer: patients, students, suppliers or customers. Organizational 'ombudspeople' work in a variety of environments, including corporations, schools and universities, healthcare facilities and in government agencies [...] An ombudsman abides by the Code of Ethics and standards of practice of The Ombudsman Association, or another ombuds association'. (The Ombudsman Association, n.d.)

Note that the statement says 'abides' but must mean 'should abide', since no qualifications are required for membership other than to undertake to abide. There are no penalties for not abiding, even though they are called professionals. Apparently, TOA had a near-monopoly on the word 'ombudsman', because one could not be called an ombudsman unless one adhered to the Code of Ethics and standards of TOA 'or another ombuds association'. Note also that all types of ombudsmen are covered, except perhaps governmental ones who deal with citizens, even including customers of corporations. Yet citizens are, in the same sense, 'customers' of the government.

The Code of Ethics and standards of practice are both aimed at corporate ombudsmen who deal primarily with internal employees and disputes, without recognizing that the circumstances and objectives of other types of ombudsmen are very different. This difference is glaringly true of the executive ombudsmen, because they are governmental. Unlike corporations whose customers can take their trade elsewhere, the state has a monopoly on the use of power, including the power of life or death over its members. Hence, fairness, justice and the prevention of wrongdoing are of paramount importance to both the ombudsman and the citizen. This obviously requires neutrality from ombudsmen who must not only be, but clearly appear to the complainant to be, independent of the organization being complained against. Hence the executive ombudsmen ought to have their independence protected by legislation, rather than being treated as equivalent to corporate ombudsmen. Yet the old Corporate Ombudsman Association seemed to gobble them up, under the new name, without a trace of indigestion. If TOA did not actively welcome them into its ranks, its very existence, with its insistence that ombudsmen could achieve neutrality without legislative protection, tended to legitimize them, even to legislators, who therefore did not see the need to make them legislative. Moreover, calling itself THE Ombudsman Association implied that there was no other. Yet the United States Ombudsman Association, which was founded to represent the legislative ombudsmen, had been in existence for 15 years.

In recent years TOA has vigorously pursued an international membership. On its website it boasted that 20% was international. The website offered information in seven languages and encouraged foreign members to attend its conferences and courses. This development has serious implications for the venerable International Ombudsman Institute (IOI), which has represented the legislative ombudsmen internationally since 1974. It has an enviable reputation for the excellence of its publications, yet it operates on a shoestring. TOA was supported by private corporations which also paid handsomely for employees' course fees. It was flush with money by comparison.

In April 2005 TOA joined forces with the University and College Ombuds Association to become the International Ombudsman Association (IOA). Because this new association will soon dominate the international scene, it poses a real threat to the IOI and the classical concept. In fact, it may not be too long before a new human rights ombudsman from a developing democracy mistakenly arrives at an IOA conference under the impression that IOA is the international association of legislative ombudsmen.

THE AMERICAN BAR ASSOCIATION

Sadly, the influential American Bar Association (ABA) has recently aided and abetted the distortion described above by reversing its stand, taken in 1969, that the ombudsman is governmental and the ideal is legislative. With the adoption in 2001 of its 'Standards for the Establishment and Operation of Ombudsman Offices', it has redefined the meaning and nature of an ombudsman to favor the characteristics advocated by TOA for corporate ombudsmen and to include all kinds of complaint handlers who choose to call themselves ombudsmen. To do this, it had to dilute and generalize its definition so much that it became vague and virtually meaningless. In fact, one is tempted to say that, with the ABA's adoption of the new Standards, its 1969 gold standard had suddenly become dross.

Thus the preamble to the Standards opens with this vague definition:

> Ombudsmen receive complaints and questions from individuals concerning people within an entity or the functioning of an entity. They work for the resolution of particular issues and, where appropriate, make recommendations for the improvement of the general administration of the entities they serve. (American Bar Association, 2001)

A main problem with the rest of the Standards is that they lay out a number of essential requirements of an ombudsman and then, inconsistently, say either that ombudsmen should aspire to meet these requirements or that there are types of ombudsmen who need not meet them. For instance, after stating that ombudsmen must be independent and neutral they add that ombudsmen can be advocates. To the classical ombudsman, '*advocate ombudsman*' is an oxymoron. They say that all ombudsman records are confidential. Yet classical ombudsmen must be able to publicize government wrongdoing. They say that ombudsmen must not address issues pending in judicial or administrative proceedings. Yet the laws for classical ombudsmen do not prohibit them from doing so. Worse still, the Standards define a classical ombudsman as any public-sector ombudsman who receives complaints from the public or internally. This mistakenly includes executive ombudsmen. Curiously, they provide that only ombudsmen with jurisdiction over two or more agencies should be created by law. Yet many specialty ombudsmen for single agencies have been created by law. In fact, they outnumber general ones in the US in the ratio of 2:1 (Rowat 1997: Tables 1, 5).

The classical ombudsmen's power to investigate so as to get at the files and facts is one of their main functions, and one that certainly distinguishes them from dispute-resolution practitioners. Yet the Standards list it as only one of multiple, optional functions. Most worrying of all is that, rather than asserting that independence from the agency being complained against is an essential characteristic of an ombudsman, they recognize that ombudsmen who are part of an agency cannot be truly independent by telling them they should 'aim' to be neutral.

The venerable USOA did what it could to stem the tide of 'wannabe' ombudsmen. It had representatives on the committee that drafted the Standards, but it was a joint committee of the ABA Sections of Dispute Resolution and Administrative Law, and they were overwhelmed by the sheer numbers on the committee and especially in the two ABA sections. So, after three of its past and current presidents had sent letters of opposition to the chairs of the two sections, the whole USOA Board decided to oppose the Standards. Supporting this opposition was the Canadian Ombudsman Association and the ABA's own Section of Labor and Employment, with a membership of over 22,000 lawyers (USOA 2001). Also opposed was Bernard Frank, one of the authors of the original ABA standards, who had been applauded by the ABA just the year before for helping to establish the concept worldwide. Other long-time advocates of the classical plan who voiced their opposition were Larry Hill and Don Rowat, both of whom had published extensively on the subject.

In a last-ditch letter to the President of the ABA (31 July 2001), Don Rowat wrote:

> It is hard enough to get the newly emerging democracies to accept the classical concept without the help of one of the most powerful organizations in the United States to weaken and water it down. Because of the popularity of the classical concept and hence the word itself, quasi- and fake ombudsmen have appropriated the word in order to enhance their own prestige. Other advanced democracies have insisted on limiting the use of the word [...] the definition of the governmental legislative ombudsman should take priority over the others because it is the ideal at which they should aim. Just at a time when the emerging democracies in Latin America and Eastern Europe are giving their new ombudsmen the serious function of protecting human rights, if the ABA proceeds on its present path, widening the definition of ombudsman to admit all comers who like the word is likely to make the US the laughing stock of all advanced democracies, nearly all of which have a national ombudsman.

One could also argue that one profession has no business laying down standards for another. However, all this opposition to the ABA's Standards was to no avail, because the DR practitioners who had appropriated the title of ombudsman were so anxious to legitimize their profession and because the number of lawyers supporting the DR movement was so large.

Unfortunately, in July 2005 the Coalition of Federal Ombuds, consisting of both legislative and executive specialized ombudsmen for federal agencies, decided to adopt the new ABA Standards along with additional Guidance Notes for federal offices. Since most of the Coalition's members are executive ombudsmen who have a vested interest in their own preservation, this is not surprising. So there is little hope that they can be persuaded to adopt instead the United States Ombudsman Association's recently revised standards, which still accord with the classical legislative concept.

This is not to say that the hundreds of executive governmental and university ombudsmen and the thousands of corporate ombudsmen in North America are not doing a tremendous job of resolving minor complaints and disputes within organizations. However, it is to say that, in calling them ombudsmen, we have downgraded the original concept of an independent, fearless official fighting to remedy government wrongdoing against a helpless, hapless citizen. The fact that there are so many other types of ombudsmen with less demanding requirements obscures the importance of having absolutely independent ombudsmen in both the public and private sectors, for the well-being of democracy.

THE HUMAN RIGHTS OMBUDSMEN

Another distortion of the concept appeared with the new democracies in the developing world after the collapse of the USSR. They were naturally anxious to adopt Western democratic devices, especially institutions which protect the citizen against the state. Because of the favorable international reputation of the legislative ombudsman, it became a popular choice. They found it easy to copy the similar legislative provisions from the Western democracies and to add as an objective the protection of human rights. By the time Gregory and Giddings edited *Righting Wrongs* in 2000 to update Caiden's two volumes (Caiden 1983), it was necessary to add several new chapters on the new human rights ombudsmen.

However, because of the importance of protecting human rights in these countries, the ombudsman procedures have had to be made more legalistic, cumbersome and time-consuming. This is what happened to the early state schemes in India, whose aims included monitoring politicians and rooting out political corruption (Rowat 1984: 28). Thus the informality and flexibility of the typical ombudsman's procedures for settling minor cases have been lost. Furthermore, the life-and-death importance of the human rights function overshadows the bread-and-butter administrative function. Some schemes are even aimed solely at protecting human rights. In her comprehensive worldwide study, Linda Reif calls them all 'hybrid ombudsmen' (Reif 2004: 393).

A more serious problem is that the ombudsman only makes recommendations, while the need to protect rights in these countries is so pressing as to require binding decisions such as are made in the West by *human rights commissions*. In some cases, so-called ombudsmen are given this power – but then they no longer fit the definition of an ombudsman. This is why the human rights commissions are not classified as ombudsmen. They are instead a kind of administrative court. Hence the case for separate schemes for human rights and maladministration is strong. My conclusion about the hybrid ombudsmen, then, is that they are so relatively new, so varied in powers and functions and so much in danger of being made toothless by political machination, that only time will tell how successful they will be. Meanwhile, we should always be careful to distinguish them from the classical model.

WHAT SHOULD BE DONE?

Since the alterations, erosions and distortions of the classical concept are already well entrenched in the USA, there is of course no longer any use trying to restrict the use of the word to the legislative scheme. But the various types of complaint handlers now using the word are so different that we should be careful to distinguish them from one another and not confuse them with the preferred legislative model. We should always use descriptive adjectives with the word, thus: general or specialty legislative ombudsman; general executive or agency (or specialty) executive ombudsman; long-term care, hospital, or press ombudsman; university legislative or executive ombudsman; and corporation internal (employee or workplace) or customer ombudsman. As for the word itself, at least the legislative ombudsmen should stand their ground and insist that only the unaltered word ombudsman, including ombudsmen as the plural, should be used in their associations' names and literature.

Furthermore, there needs to be more discussion in the advanced democracies of the merits of the ombudsmen's supervision of the courts as in Sweden and in Finland. Because of the need to foster judicial independence in order to protect human rights, the new democracies have been experimenting with giving the human rights ombudsmen jurisdiction over the courts. Their success needs to be studied by thc advanced democracies. It would be instructive if one of the advanced democracies (or perhaps a state in a federation) became brave enough to confront the conventional wisdom of judicial independence by giving the ombudsman jurisdiction over the behavior of judges. After all, ombudsmen are not a real threat to judicial independence, because their conclusions are not binding.

In addition, steps should be taken to restore the classical concept to its former luster. The key ingredient of the classical model's success is its prescription by law, always with provisions designed to ensure its independence. All other types of ombudsman should emulate this model as closely as possible. For instance, executive ombudsmen, both general and specialty, should lobby their legislature or city council for a law or bylaw to ensure their continuity. University, school, hospital, other institutional and corporate ombudsmen should similarly lobby their board of governors or directors for a bylaw, so as not to be subject to the influence or whim of the president or chief executive officer. Besides internal ombudsmen, corporations should appoint an ombudsman for complaints from their customers, as the nationwide banks in Canada have done.

However, the Canadian banks have recognized that an ombudsman appointed by a single bank can never be regarded as truly independent, and so in 1996 the Canadian Bankers' Association set up an independent ombudsman to hear appeals from the individual banks. There was already a precedent for such a system in other advanced countries, including Britain and Australia (Rowat 1997: 10–13). The Canadian banking scheme was so successful that in 2002 it was emulated by the main associations of firms in the financial and insurance industries (Rowat 2003: 47).

This system of an ombudsman for a whole industry, called an industrial ombudsman, is likely to be extended further in the advanced democracies, either by the industrial associations themselves or by legislation making it mandatory. Such a system is also needed for the professions. Although the legal, judicial, medical and other professions usually have internal systems for hearing complaints, like the police, they are notorious for protecting their own, and need an independent ombudsman chosen by a body representing both the profession and the public.

In view of the downgrading of legislative ombudsmen in the USA, particularly by the TOA and the ABA, what should be done so that the USA will not be so out of joint with the rest of the democratic world? Firstly, because of the recent criticisms of corporate governance in the US, customer and industrial ombudsmen as well as ombudsmen for professional associations deserve to be taken more seriously. More specifically, what can and should the new IOA and the ABA do?

The old TOA is to be lauded for insisting on as much neutrality as possible by ombudsmen within an organization, and for the good work it has been doing with its training of the wannabe ombudsmen. But its successor should no longer pretend that all non-classical ombudsmen are much the same. It should do this by abolishing the word 'organizational' from its literature and vocabulary. It should always use an adjective to describe each type of ombudsman and should stop treating the others as though they were corporate ombudsmen. More important, it should stop admitting governmental executive ombudsmen to its membership, even as Associate Members, and should change its name to the International Nongovernmental or Private-Sector Ombudsman Association, or some similar name, instead of implying that it is the only ombudsman association. It would thus leave the USOA and the IOI their traditional roles of representing governmental ombudsmen in the USA and abroad.

Regarding the ABA, it should at once appoint a new ombudsman committee with a generous allocation of USOA members to revise the Standards into separate ones for governmental and nongovernmental ombudsmen, or, if not separated, to revise them so that: (1) legislative ombudsmen are preferred as the ideal; (2) the Standards say that all governmental specialty ombudsmen should be legislative (except perhaps for internal ones that do not deal with the public); and (3) other inconsistencies favoring corporate internal ombudsmen are removed. Moreover, rather than downgrading the importance of legislative ombudsmen, the ABA should go out of its way to encourage the creation of more – more general ones at the state level and more specialty ones at the federal level. It is surprising that the US has so few general state ombudsmen, whereas all the states in Australia and all provinces in Canada (except tiny P.E.I.) have them. This effort should include protecting the independence of the existing executive ones at the federal level by lobbying Congress for them to become legislative.

Since there are now so many types of ombudsman and since the bare word ombudsman can no longer be taken to mean legislative ombudsman, the Canadian Ombudsman Association has recently changed its name to Canadian Council of Parliamentary Ombudsman (but should change the last word to Ombudsmen). The USOA should consider similarly changing its name to the United States Legislative (or Governmental) Ombudsman Association. And the IOI should likewise change to the International Legislative (or Governmental) Ombudsman Association.

These reforms may seem far-reaching, but they are necessary if the United States and the IOI are once again to become leaders in ombudsmanship.

REFERENCES

American Bar Association (2001). *Standards for the Establishment and Operation of Ombudsman Offices* 6.

Anderson, D.R., & Stockton, D.M. (1990) (Eds). *Ombudsmen in Federal Agencies: The Theory and Practice*. Washington, DC: Administrative Conference of the United States.

Angrick, W.P. (2004). *Report of Vice-President, North American Region* (p. 4). International Ombudsman Institute Conference, Quebec.

Belsen, S. (1997). 'Where is Darwin now that we need him? The Ombudsman in Evolution' (p. 12). Keynote speech at the Ombudsman Association Conference, Montreal. Reprinted in Reif (1999) below.

Caiden, G.E. (1983) (Ed). *International Handbook of the Ombudsman*. 2 vols. Westport, CT: Greenwood Press.

Farrell-Donaldson, M.D. (1993). 'Will the Real Ombudsman Come Forward?' In L.C. Reif, M. Marshall, & C. Ferris (Eds), *The Ombudsman* (pp. 65–75). Edmonton: International Ombudsman Institute. Reprinted in Reif (1999).

Hiden, M. (1973). Ed. & foreword, D.C. Rowat. *The Ombudsman in Finland: The First Fifty Years*. Berkeley, CA: Institute of Governmental Studies, University of California.

Hill, L.B. (1997). 'American Ombudsmen and Others; or, American Ombudsmen and "wannabe" Ombudsmen' (p. 19). Address delivered at the Meeting of the American Bar Association Section of Administrative Law and Regulatory Practice, Washington.

International Ombudsman Institute (2004). *Information Booklet* (p. 14). Edmonton: International Ombudsman Institute.

Kimweri, M.G.J. (1993). 'The Effectiveness of an Executive Ombudsman'. In L.C. Reif, M. Marshall, & C. Ferris (Eds), *The Ombudsman* (pp. 37–64). Edmonton: International Ombudsman Institute.

Meltzer, L. (1998). 'The Federal Workplace Ombuds'. *Journal on Dispute Resolution* 13 (2), pp. 549–609.

Ombudsman Association (n.d.). *Information Pamphlet* (p. 6). Dallas: Ombudsman Association.

Reif, L.C. (1999) (Ed). *The International Ombudsman Anthology*. The Hague: Kluwer Law International.

Reif, L.C. (2004). *The Ombudsman, Good Governance and the International Human Rights System*. Leiden: Martinus Nijhoff.

Reif, L.C., Marshall, M., & Ferris, C. (1993) (Eds). *The Ombudsman: Diversity and Development*. Edmonton: International Ombudsman Institute.

Robertson, J.F. (1993). *Protection of the Name 'Ombudsman'*. Occasional Paper 48 (p. 6). Edmonton: International Ombudsman Institute.

Rowat, D.C. (1984). 'The State Ombudsmen in India'. *Indian Journal of Public Administration* 1, pp. 1–32.

Rowat, D.C. (1985). *The Ombudsman Plan: The Worldwide Spread of an Idea*. Lanham, MD: University Press of America.

Rowat, D.C. (1992). 'Why an ombudsman to supervise the courts?' *Ombudsman Journal* 10, pp. 27–37. Revision of a paper given at the 1991 Ombudsmanship Congress, San Juan, Puerto Rico. Reprinted in Reif (1999).

Rowat, D.C. (1997). *A Worldwide Survey of Ombudsmen*. Occasional Paper 60 (p. 28). Edmonton: International Ombudsman Institute.

Rowat, D.C. (2003). 'The New Private-Sector Ombudsmen'. *Policy Options*, November, pp. 46–48.

Rowe, M.P. (1991). 'The Ombudsman's Role in a Dispute Resolution System'. *Negotiation Journal*, October, pp. 353–361.

Rowe, M.P. (1995). *Options, Functions and Skills: What an Organizational Ombudsperson Might Want to Know*. Pamphlet (p. 16). Dallas: The Ombudsman Association. Reprinted from *Negotiation Journal* 11 (April 1995), pp. 103–114.

USOA (2001). USOA participation on ABA ombudsman committee. http://www.usombudsman.org/ABA.htm.

Ziegenfuss, J.T. (1988). Foreword M. Rowe. *Organizational Troubleshooters: Resolving Problems for Customers and Employees*. San Francisco: Jossey-Bass.

14

The Civilizing Mission of Public Administration

GERALD E. CAIDEN

INTRODUCTION

As might be expected in an increasingly turbulent environment, public administration lately has been experiencing a very bumpy journey. Old hands take all this in their stride, knowing that their craft is sound, things will eventually right themselves and they will make a smooth landing. They have been through all this before, several times in fact, although this time the disturbance seems more severe than ever before. In contrast, the inexperienced are frightened, certainly apprehensive and fear for their safety, imagining the worst: that the craft has not been built to take such punishment, that bits and pieces may be falling off to jeopardize the whole journey and that despite assurances to the contrary, they may be lost and doomed.

For the old hands, this is just another test. From the prospect of globalization, international cooperation and the dire need for universal action to tackle many of the current challenges facing humanity, the future beckons and the means of transportation will need to be remodeled and adjusted accordingly. The inexperienced, what with the crumbling of communist ideology, the loss of faith in socialism and the wholesale cutbacks in public sector budgets and employment, are experiencing a sinking sensation and worry that just at the time when history demands greater intervention in public affairs, so the instruments for achieving that goal have been hamstrung, short-changed, and thwarted by narrow, self-interested and short-sighted forces (Caiden 1991a). Unless current trends are quickly reversed, the world seems to be heading toward disasters that may well overshadow anything that has happened in the past. Unfortunately, nobody can forecast with any accuracy how the craft of public administration will fare in future storms and whether humanity will progress to a brighter future or will suffer worse than it ever has done, from disasters of purely human design and execution.

PUBLIC ADMINISTRATION IN TROUBLE

Public administration, however it is defined, whatever it includes and whatever one would like it to achieve (Caiden 1971a) has not been doing that well in recent decades, even though it probably has been obtaining better results than ever before, simply because the perceived gap between prospect and performance seems to widen. Indeed, in several parts of the world, it has regressed. Why?

Firstly, the tasks now set before public administration seem overwhelming and beyond human capacity to perform satisfactorily at this stage in history. Here is just a brief list of such tasks: preventing war and reinforcing the peace, preventing governments decimating their own citizens, combating international and internal terrorism, reducing worldwide poverty and human suffering, alleviating both natural and man-made disasters, and heading off crises before they get out of hand; however, this list could be extended to cover a whole host of other issues. In any event, either the know-how is missing or the political will to act is too weak, or countries continue their outdated beggar-thy-neighbor policies, so that things drag along without much effective action being taken (Caiden 2004b). Thus, where once the world wholeheartedly fought smallpox and polio, it takes only half-measures to ward off the spread of AIDS and the possible outbreaks of new forms of influenza.

Secondly, the requisite resources to enable governments, public administration or any other social institution to make an effective impact on contemporary challenges fall far short of requirements. Leadership is just not up to many of the tasks emanating from the human predicament. People generally are not willing to sacrifice sufficient time, money and effort. They have turned inward to personal rewards and away from communal service. Already the international community has retreated from the relatively modest goals of the Millennium Agenda, because countries are unable to find the resources or unwilling to make them available to benefit the whole of humanity and not just their own residents. The wealthier nations once pledged to spend a certain portion of their GNPs to helping their poorer brethren, but few have lived up to their promise and while they continue to pledge financial assistance, few actually deliver what they promise.

Thirdly, the political will to stand up and be counted is weak. Instead, the political arena panders to a selfishly-inclined populace, finds the exercise of power too tempting to resist its corrupting effects, tends to give away the store of public investment for temporary relief, manipulates information to gloss over bad tidings, and often disinherits a proven professional competence for a questionable pottage of fads, fancies and allures of the moment that, repeated often and loud enough, promises sure and instant relief (Caiden 1997b). When criticized for falling down on the job, the political arena readily shifts the blame from its own shortcomings to defenseless, community-minded public services struggling to do their best in the circumstances, in some cases cut to the bone but having to cope with more and more demanding clients.

This transfer in blame has been aided by one of those historical shifts in global ideology from communal to more individual concerns after a mid-century shift the other way. That trend was halted and then reversed by a disillusion with collectivism, totalitarianism and autarchy. So it has been easier to convince those who want to be convinced that private enterprise is a more reliable agent of development than public initiatives, that government is more of a problem than a solution, that the public sector without the pressure of market forces is somewhat parasitic and that public servants are too often excessively bureaucratic, incompetent, wasteful, unproductive and inefficient. The overly simplistic remedies proposed include cutting down if not cutting out government, letting market forces rule, sharing out public business, reducing public welfare and restoring self-reliance, and downplaying public service at least for the time being (Caiden 2004a).

In adopting such alluring prescriptions, public administration has been weakened despite accompanying efforts to strengthen both public policy-making and public management by making government more business-like and injecting more intellectualism and rationalism into political passion and partisanship. The traditional core of public administration is being steadily eaten away by narrow technical focuses on its specialized parts that distract from its age-old values and its very essence, which is more than mere improvements in public policy and management. Its mission since the dawn of civilization is just that, enhancing civilization and civilized behavior against the unbridled barbarianism that would otherwise reemerge and has on too many occasions emerged to destroy what has been painfully cultivated at great human cost. What seems to get left out altogether is its embedded philosophy of the golden rule, namely, do not do to others that which you would not have them do to you, i.e., if you cannot do good, at least avoid doing harm and seek the public interest above and beyond partial and selfish interests. This golden rule should of course govern all human behavior, but it is especially incumbent on public administrators because it is so central to human life.

THE CIVILIZING MISSION OF PUBLIC ADMINISTRATION

What has always been the civilizing mission of public administration? Briefly stated, it has consisted of *five elements*, namely, (1) ability to improve personal security and safety, (2) ensure community survival, (3) improve the quality of life for all, (4) provide for the needy, that is, those unable to provide for themselves, and (5) promote the socialization of future generations into pursuing the good life in a good society. Generations that have forgotten these fundamental missions have lived to regret the fact, for they disappeared from history, even the mightiest of empires in their time. Whole societies were wiped out virtually overnight. Huge investments were lost. Years of pacification suddenly without warning gave way to violence, civil war and genocide. Public administration, instead of being a force for good, declined into an instrument of evil, cruelty, immorality, injustice and remorseless slaughter on a grand scale with thousands of willing agents carried along by a bestiality to which they had been blinded (Caiden 1971b).

So, just as public administration has the potential to achieve great good, wondrous works, universal amenities, impressive public services, humanitarian deeds and individual blessings, so it can demonstrate the very opposite, as it has done in virtually every stage of human history. But thanks to the contemporary information revolution, where once public administrators may have been forgiven for acting in ignorance (for not knowing the ramifications of their actions, for being deceived by their political masters, for being shielded from the consequences of their decisions), this no longer holds true. No public administrator today can plead the Eichmann defense or escape the damning accusation of the Nuremberg and like trials that one *should* have known, or at least tried to find out, or anticipated the possible evil outcome (Caiden 1997b). That public administration falls short of its civilizing mission is no excuse to ward off social forces that obviously have uncivilizing effects, reward evil, rationalize wrong, justify the wicked and obstruct its civilizing mission.

No public administrators worth their salt can afford to underestimate their civilizing mission and the values it entrenches. Personal security and safety against wild animals may have been achieved over the centuries, but alas still not against other human beings. An off-course missile can kill anyone on the planet. Ruthless criminals, organized and unorganized, violent and non-violent, haunt the streets of major settlements. No one is safe against adulterated food, harmful products, accidents, incurable diseases and computer abuse. Never before has humankind been faced with the prospect of total elimination through the widespread use of weapons of mass destruction in a global war or mutated genes when some selfish scientific research project goes astray or Mother Nature fails to cope with some environmental disaster. The contemporary global society cannot provide for its needy whose minimal basic needs are still not being met, let alone improve the quality of life for every person – not when the gap between rich and poor grows, the planet's bounty is so badly distributed and so many people are denied their basic human rights altogether or are incapable of enforcing them against their exploiters. As to the socialization of the next generation, the world is deeply divided as to what examples to follow, and provides too few exemplary models. Over the ages, public administration has made a dent formally into cannibalism, infanticide, slavery and capital punishment, but it has still to eliminate the worst of human practices (Caiden 1964).

Even where public administration has made such enormous advances over yesteryear, there is a long way to go and much to be done. It is on this global basis that public administration has to be judged. The hopes and aspirations of humanity once raised by the advent of the United Nations and its entourage of global organizations and their associates have been undermined by the disappointing performance of the international community. Without doubt, many international organizations have never adopted or acted on the basic principles and practices of good public administration, some of which are the same principles of good governance such as transparency, accountability and integrity that they preach to everybody else (Caiden 1988). Theirs is seemingly still a privileged insider's world, occasionally graced with hypocrisy, mendacity, absurdity and even incredulity, a circus that mocks real efforts to come to grips with what ails the planet. Whenever they descend to such depths, they speed the day when they will follow so many of their failed predecessors into oblivion.

RESCUING THE PUBLIC SECTOR

Unfortunately, many of these august international bodies have instigated global policies that kill the goose that lays the golden eggs. Their experts have preached antigovernment rhetoric and advocated the downsizing of the administrative state as a universal mantra. They ignore the reality that continents differ, countries differ, and even local circumstances within the same country differ significantly from one another. While their universal doctrines may have been derived from a similar set of countries and their application may well benefit them and some others, their application elsewhere has only made the plight of others worse. These poorer brethren still need to narrow the gap between themselves and their richer brethren and, to do this, they need to *strengthen not weaken their administrative state*, in the ways that the richer brethren managed to do in the past. These poorer countries still have to guarantee a greater degree of security from both external and internal threats, reduce political, economic, social and cultural instability, establish and enforce the rule of law, embark on extensive public works and investment in the public infrastructure, improve external relations and diplomacy and play a greater part in international relations, reform grossly deficient public finances and taxation systems, provide better emergency and disaster preparedness services, enlarge relief to the dispossessed, impoverished and handicapped, boost local urban services and amenities and encourage research and development. All these are traditional public administration activities in which there is already a high degree of universal professionalism and know-how.

To reduce public administration and expect other social institutions to rush in to fill the gap is to put the cart before the horse. As economists are fond of saying, all other things being equal (which is rare), it was those richer countries already with a justifiable reputation for better public administration that fared better as against their poorer brethren, which could not provide a suitable environment in which other social institutions could prosper, let alone take over basic and essential public sector functions. Thus, the Asian tigers have done well compared with other countries in the region, just as the European countries of the former USSR have done better than their Asian counterparts. But this is far too simplistic a picture of the real world. In any event, what is desperately needed in the poorest countries is a strengthening of their public sectors without which they will continue to fall further and further behind the rest of the world (Caiden 2004b).

The question is not public *or* private sector in competition, but public *and* private sectors together in partnership. The one cannot prosper without the other. The public sector has to raise resources from the private sector by borrowing or taxation, probably both. A prosperous private sector depends on law and order, an adequate public infrastructure and government protection and largesse. There are some functions that only one of them can perform, others that one cannot do without the other and still others in which they can share, compete to enhance public choice and avoid excessive monopolization. All this depends on what is locally available and made available through special efforts and external assistance. It could well be that in some places, the public sector has grown too big and been weakened thereby, but it is probably more the case that public resources have to be redirected to where they are most needed rather than be eliminated altogether or transferred to inexperienced, unaccountable and untrustworthy nongovernmental entities dependent on public subsidies and other favors. In any event, one area of government that greatly needs strengthening globally is what has been termed '*the thinking part*', that part within government that increases its future capacity to govern and its ability to prevent disappointment, loss of credibility and legitimacy and widely missing its targets (Caiden & Caiden 2000). Overly rapid privatization in recent decades, particularly in less developed countries, has already begun to reveal shortcomings that demand renationalization and the reimposition of community controls.

This strengthening of the administrative state at all levels of government is likely to revive and restore the time-honored functions of the civilizing mission of public administration, emphasizing security from external aggression and the issue of sheer survival, security from deviants of all descriptions from violent criminals to interfering eccentrics, improvement in the quality and comfort of life for all individuals and the socialization of the next generation from acceptable, behavior-edifying values. Each of these functions has undergone its own metamorphosis in the past 20 or so years, calling not for less governance or public intervention but more. Governments may take on additional activities but there are these that remain timeless, and just as important as ever they have been since the founding of the administrative state in Sumer some 6,000 years ago.

The issue of sheer survival still dogs countries, peoples and cultures. It is not only minorities, who are jeopardized by the tyranny of the majority, but whole states that can still be swallowed up by their neighbors without too much international concern or intervention. Likewise, minorities who want a country of their own, to avoid extermination, can also be abandoned without warning. They are forced to develop a state within a state to provide their own external security. How can any of these build up sufficient self-protection against overwhelming odds? How can they afford to counteract modern war machines? What deterrents can they muster against overwhelming force? Like it or not, they have to devote enormous resources to self-defense and to cultivating allies that will come to their defense in times of trouble. None of this comes cheap, for sophisticated weapons are expensive to obtain and deploy, military training and preparation absorb precious labor resources and dependency exacts a heavy political price. The nature of modern warfare is continually changing and combat plans and methods have to be updated accordingly. Total warfare leaves none alone and involves everyone in some way as do surprise attacks, non-nuclear terrorism, germ warfare, and poison gasses.

Internal security has gone beyond the simple policing of yesteryear to safeguard the community against all manner of threats, from natural disasters (and emergency preparedness) to technological accidents, from white-collar computer criminals to organized international gangs, from hazardous products to hazardous drivers. Urbanization compounds the challenge by herding people close together, offering more opportunities for evil intent and providing ample hideouts. The paradox is that the more security is provided, the less people feel secure – and especially so in the anonymous city where all are strangers to one another, where turnover of neighbors can be fast and where nobody can take proper care of themselves, not even the very wealthy who can afford private protection. Here is another area of governance where coverage is vast and costly to provide, as it is so labor intensive if it is to be well done.

Every generation tries to ensure that the next will not have such a hard time as it had. All parents want a better future for their children than they had. It is not just a matter of a higher standard of living, that is, more material comforts. Today, it is improving the quality of life which again has gone from being content with a simple, rural way of life to adapting to the fast pace of the global tourist who tries to keep abreast of everything in invention, taste and style. This one wants development and that one wants conservation. This one enjoys noise and that one craves for peace and quiet. All want to fly and yet be able to be caught in a rising safety net. All want the latest in medical advances to extend their lives but are not prepared to give up smoking, alcohol and bad eating habits. Everyone wants to live better: those who supply employment, those who are employed and those who cannot obtain employment or be employed. Business may meet economic demand but governance has to meet community needs and, harder still, community aspirations. And to fulfill community expectations, governance has to invest heavily in research and development. All of this takes considerable public financing which in turn requires more economic, efficient and effective money-raising and allocation.

Every generation worries about its future and how the next generation is going to turn out. Every generation curses its legacy and worries about the legacy that it will pass on. How will the next generation behave? How will it fare? Will it have adequate coping abilities? Socialization becomes harder and harder. Parental guidance has many more competitors. The schools are not providing sufficient skills. Commercialism and the mass media demote proper appreciation of the arts and the cultural inheritance of humanity. Despite all the professionalism, children or a significant portion of them still come out unprepared, even 'rotten', meaning they still go too far astray from the acceptable. What should be done about this? 'They' aren't doing enough and probably never could, so pressures on governance just continue to mount.

In the global society, the wealthier countries, the bigger powers, the more advanced peoples have more options than the poor, weak and underdeveloped peoples. As the gap between them grows, not diminishes, it now seems that the gap between the privileged and the underprivileged within them follows suit. Their circumstances are so different. Whereas for the fortunate, the administrative state can be reduced and alternatives strengthened, the unfortunate may have to strengthen the administrative state until other social institutions reach the capability of assuming a wider role in contemporary society. In other words, they may still have to walk before they can run, let alone catch up, if ever they will (Caiden 1994b).

Some countries and peoples have done exceedingly well over the past two decades, coming from right behind until now they figure high on human development indices, while others – no matter what attention is given them and no matter how much external aid they have received – still languish. The focus on governance rather than government gives us more clues as to why development has accelerated in some regions of the world and why it has actually receded in other regions. At least, we are now asking the right questions even if we still cannot provide right answers. In any event, the administrative state still plays a central role everywhere. It can be diminished in some fortunate countries but it definitely needs strengthening elsewhere, and in all countries some areas of the administrative state can be diminished but other areas still need to be expanded. Much depends on their own peculiar circumstances and how much government intervention their people demand and are prepared to tolerate. So the main question is, what is public administration, the administrative state, government and governance being repositioned, reinvented, reengineered and reformed for? What kind of a future does each society at the different levels of government seek to shape for itself? How do they want their tomorrow to differ from today? What changes in direction do they want to make, for what purpose, for whom? From what do they wish to retreat? Where do they want to go? Why? How soon?

CONTINUING TO PUSH FOR DEMOCRATIZATION

But what is the point of strengthening the public sector if it falls into the wrong hands (Caiden & Caiden 2000)? Crimes against humanity do not just happen by accident. They have to be planned and executed. Thousands if not millions of people participate or know from their relatives, friends and neighbors who do participate what is going on, even if they are silenced in a vast conspiracy to deceive the victims. At least, the chances are greater in a democracy that moral indignation will sooner or later trigger a reaction of disgust and protest that will call for cease and desist and immediate remedial action. But if autocratic bureaucratism continues to operate as usual, not much can be expected to change in practice. So it is not so much the forms of democracy that have to be in place but the whole bloodstream of all public administration (including intelligence, military, police, correctional and custodial branches) that has to flow with a democratic spirit, with a sense of right and wrong, justice and mercy, fairness and fair play, and with due respect for human rights and dignity, public accountability and openness. Neutral professionals, impartial, objective technicians, experts in getting things done can serve any master (Caiden 1996); but democratic public administration requires principled agents loyal to democratic humanitarian values, protected whistleblowers and dedicated ombudsman offices (Caiden 1982b).

Much lip-service is paid to these highfalutin' notions but little is done to institutionalize them. The fear of being unjustly victimized, unless one plays by the rules by which the official game is actually being played, still haunts too much of public administration even in the best exemplars of democracy, particularly in highly sensitive areas where secrecy prevails and where group-think dominates. Officials keep their noses clean even while dirtying their hands and steer clear of making waves that might upset their peers and superiors. Thus, public harm is done and hidden, brought to light only too late. And the cover-ups can be elaborate, rewarding villains and excommunicating angels. This is not the way democratic administration is supposed to operate, but without the will to make it operate otherwise, bad things happen in a formal democracy that could and should have been avoided (Caiden et al. 2001).

Another exhibition of official failing is 'research for hire', where what purports to be independent and impartial is actually financed by public bodies to reach acceptable conclusions or confirm what is already being done or contemplated. There is no real scholarship, no imaginative thinking, and no questioning of given assumptions; nothing that the hirer cannot live with. It is a staged product. Should the hirer make a mistake, the researchers can be stopped in their tracks, their support cut off, their findings suppressed, their reputations sullied by others only too willing to do the hirer's bidding. This is a very sophisticated form of deceit common to all officialdom, democratic or otherwise. Unproven fads and fancies take flight this way with doctored evidence and slanted assumptions, paving the path for self-deception and later outrage when an unsuspecting public eventually discovers the truth (Caiden 1994a).

Why does this occur in the first place? All public administration is under pressure to come up with something different, something more glamorous than the routine, something that speeds questionable political agendas, the quick fix. Despite building independent power, public administration remains beholden to its political masters of whatever stripe who come and go in a shorter tenure than the professional public servants. The political masters want to make a lasting reputation for themselves while they can, which may be quite fleeting, while others have probably more selfish ends in mind, exploiting public office for all that they can get out of it, taking credit only for the good and casting the blame for the bad on incompetent assistants (Caiden 1982a). Public administrators have little choice in the unenviable position they are placed in, sometimes having to shelter unfit officials placed over them about whom they can do little. Whereas professionalism sorts out the unfit, democratic elections supposed to do that job do not always perform so well, better maybe than autocratic processes but far from perfectly. It is a well-kept secret how often a good administration gets saddled with a poor political executive and has to await replacements. Worse still, even in a democracy a well-run public administration can be ruined by incompetent political executives who misuse their offices; only after the damage has been done and later exposed does the innocent and ignorant public find out, too late to prevent avoidable disasters.

RESTORING THE CREDIBILITY OF PUBLIC ADMINISTRATION

Public administration is by no means the only social institution that has been losing credibility. Public opinion is probably much tougher than it used to be, for good reason. Some institutions are in much greater trouble than public administration, and have even greater difficulty restoring public trust. Nonetheless, public administration has done relatively little research to find out why it has been losing credibility. Clearly, the public has been disappointed, as have public leaders in and out of government and also many insiders who can see where performance could have been improved some time ago. Expectations are probably too high and governance promises too much. The better public administration performs, the more unrealistically the bar is raised: the more public administrators sprint, the more they are expected to sprint even faster on the treadmill of human hopes and aspirations (1980). Not enough is done to remind people just what can and cannot be done, how enormous some of the challenges before humanity now are, how much is at stake and how many limitations have to be confronted.

Having said all that, the last time the civilizing mission of public administration was given a chance was some 60 or so years ago following a cruel Great Depression and an even crueler World War II, the likes of which have not been seen since. The price was very high. Hopefully, humanity will not have to pay a similar or worse price for the next chance for public administration to prove its valuable contributions to advancing civilization. To restore the credibility of public administration requires lowering human expectations or raising performance. There is little wrong in aspiring human expectations as long as they come within reasonable bounds and are realistic in the sense of being attainable within a lifetime. From this standpoint, the Millennium Agenda still holds; if not by 2015 then within the lifetime of children just entering their span on this planet. They still may not enjoy as many years as some of the residents of the most fortunate countries who can look forward to reaching age 90 or more in relative comfort, fairly well looked after and capable of taking advantage of their liberty to express themselves.

In those fortunate countries, public administration has done well despite all the carping criticism by those who will never be satisfied and those who demand even better performance. The danger has been and continues to be complacency in its professionalism and its failure to adequately combat the ideological assaults on its very being, or rather its being in certain activities, particularly business ventures and welfare (Caiden 1997a). When, some 30 years ago, the first warnings were apparent that public administrators were paying insufficient attention to public complaints, they failed to take stock and question where they might be going wrong. They were perhaps too sure of themselves and ignored pleas that they institutionalize administrative reform as an ongoing enterprise (Caiden 1991a). They stuck too long with proven expertise that in fact was falling behind the times. They were too bureaucratic, uncreative and slow-moving (Caiden 1991b). And when the political reaction transpired, they had few answers and fell victim first to cutback management, a precursor to much stronger challenges to their style, inefficiency and *raison d'être*. Since then, the switch to private entrepreneurship and the New Conservatism from without, plus the challenges of the public policy field (much of which sees itself as outside public administration) and the New Public Management movement from within, have done much to dispose of any complacency and to begin the long process of a complete overhaul and repositioning if not transformation of the public sector. In these fortunate countries, public administration is getting its new act together (Caiden 1994a).

It is in the less fortunate countries where international efforts are most needed to raise the standards of public sector performance. Until that is achieved, not much progress is going to be made elsewhere in these countries whose peoples are going to rebel in any way they can to protest at their being left further and further behind on the global scale. The widening gap can no longer be hidden from them. The information revolution has seen to that. Those who are able will leave for better climes elsewhere, legally or illegally. Those left behind will show their resentment and vent their frustrations on those whom they will hold blameworthy, particularly foreign exploiters, corrupt leaders, rotten governance and deficient public services. The rot will spread beyond national borders until eventually even the fortunate countries will begin to suffer, too, if their public consciences do not prick them long before.

Within the fortunate countries, people are beginning to understand the limitations of beggar-my-neighbor policies and not-in-my-backyard stances. But when will they enlarge their vision to understand that what is truly new in human history is the global society? Are we not all our brothers' keepers? Do not brothers now encompass all humankind, every resident of the planet, not just my country's residents, my immediate neighbors and my next of kin? Are we all not public servants? Do not the same motives, ethics or obligations enjoin everybody to serve one another decently, honestly, willingly, obligingly, without putting oneself first every time and always? Does not the 'public' in public administration have in this global age a meaning beyond the public sector? Does not the civilizing mission of public administration need renewal and revitalization? Is there any indication that this may indeed come about? Is humanity about to revive the golden rule, however expressed?

A BRIGHTER SIGN

Nothing succeeds like natural disaster to impress on people the need for effective public action, the absence of which leaves them to their own devices. Some of their efforts, alas, only make the situation worse, as when they panic and work at cross-purposes. Other efforts do ameliorate the situation, as when they instinctively cooperate and act selflessly. Until the mid-nineteenth century or so, all seemed to be in the hands of the gods or fate, beyond human intervention. Memories of particularly traumatic disasters, such as fires, floods, earthquakes and comets lingered in folklore for many centuries afterward, and occasionally one would be immortalized in literature, as was the 1755 Lisbon earthquake. Before the advent of the administrative state and the establishment of dedicated NGOs, not much was done or could be done to avert or prepare for such natural disasters or rescue their victims.

Meantime, worse human-caused disasters have befallen humankind, far overshadowing natural disasters. Wars and accidents along with engineered Stalin/Mao-type starvations have taken a much heavier toll in human life. Looking back less than half a century, countries were abandoned to their own devices and too often relief came too late for those who died needlessly. Such was the tragedy of the 1976 Tangshen earthquake in China, and of earthquakes in Peru (1970), Iran (1990), and more recently in Japan, India and Turkey as well as of those carried away by floods in Asia, Africa and Europe. But there has been a significant difference. In time, the global ramifications of such horrifying events have prompted more and more international actors to intervene, notably the UN family of specialized agencies, regional associations of states, friendly countries, prosperous countries, religious affiliates, international NGOs, affected business organizations and a host of charities marshalling individual donations. The burden is now shared.

Perhaps the best illustration is the 26 December 2004 undersea earthquake and accompanying tsunami in the Indian Ocean. Offers of aid and assistance poured in and emergency teams and supplies were rushed to badly affected areas. Promised donations far exceeded expectations. It was a most impressive demonstration of international concern, that highlighted oft-overlooked lessons.

Firstly, countries or rather governments and public administrators who had taken disaster preparedness seriously and had taken precautionary measures fared better than those who had ignored the emerging academic subdiscipline of emergency preparedness and its widely accessible literature, or at least had given insufficient attention to what knowledge has accumulated over the past half century. Their unpreparedness was obvious and inexcusable, even taking into account their professed lack of means. They had forgotten that much of traditional administration is in the nature of insurance against risk. One invests in the hope of never having to claim, or when the inevitable does occur, the claim compensates but at least the services are there when needed.

Secondly, irrespective of disaster preparedness, countries with adequate operating facilities close by disaster zones came off best. They had in place coastal and civil defense systems, open airports and usable access routes, hospitals and medical supplies, police, military, fire stations, public works facilities, food and water reserves, and the like. They had not stinted on public amenities; they had invested heavily in public infrastructure and maintained high levels of public safety, employing many public professionals 'just in case', as insurance. They could mobilize instantly, coordinate local joint activities and organize volunteers. In short, they had put greater emphasis on traditional public service values than on economy and efficiency, admittedly at a higher standing cost. They had services and supplies on hand that they had hoped never to have to deploy.

Thirdly, the military proved its worth as a backup civil service. The military had equipment that local authorities could not afford, staff that could be ordered to do whatever had to be done and undertake work that others were reluctant to do, spare supplies on hand that could be diverted and an authority that almost no other body possessed. The non-military uses of the military were crucial and its professionalism and versatility proved decisive in national emergencies. This civil capacity of the military is too often overlooked and undervalued. If countries are going to put so many resources into the military, they might as well get as much non-military return as they are able.

Fourthly, the information revolution showed just how dated many unrevised official bureaucratic procedures had become. Concerned individuals did not wait for official channels to open or for public officials to act. They improvised, cut out red tape and proved resourceful. Given incentives and motivation, plain simple folks were turned into reliable, responsible, trustworthy and valuable public and community servants. No doubt there were incidences of looting, theft, greed, discrimination, corruption and selfishness, but the surprise was not that there was so much as so little. People did come together and help one another and behave responsibly. They could be trusted to do the right thing by instinct. They acted in good faith. They did not need to be managed and told what to do so much as to be encouraged, assisted and fitted into the bigger picture. Their initiative could be relied upon and their cooperation made the task of public administration that much easier.

Finally, why don't people behave so well in normal times? Disaster brings out the worst in some, but it also brings out the best in many. Is it because people see an immediate purpose in living/being, an obvious cause, a confined focus of intellect and energy, an inner sense of satisfaction in just doing the right civic thing? Do they understand that under the skin, all are much the same, that when disaster strikes, all are in the same predicament and all must help without distinction, discrimination, hatred or favoritism?

WHAT LIES AHEAD?

Nobody can know with any certainty. The future will be different from the present and from what is expected. There will be innovations and creativity that will surprise and transform the world as we know it, in untold ways. Unforeseen events, happenings, tragedies will intervene to turn things around. New ideas, values, heroes, saints and villains will arise that will change directions. People will adjust and move on, just as they did with the 2004 Indian Ocean earthquake. Most institutions are built to take the new into account and although things will change, much will not change that quickly or sharply from the present. Resources such as time, energy or labor cannot be conjured up from nowhere or summoned on demand. Maybe in life-threatening emergencies they can, but not for long, before things revert to where they were before. Patterns are not easily disrupted and people tend at first to resist anything novel, for they are creatures of habit. So, amidst change, there is likely to be much continuity although there may be sharp breaks too. In short, it is not unreasonable to expect the future to be much like the present or a projection of the present.

Then, account has to be taken of cycles of attention, activity, interest, warfare, business and disease, some short, some lengthy, some regular, some irregular, not exactly predictable but fairly persistent and expected. These cycles may be contradictory, erratic, parallel or linked. All this makes the future hazy at best. But looking at periods of 20, 30 and 50 years, one can predict a new world order with some states disappearing and others taking their place, with some international organizations disappearing and others created, with some regimes being overthrown or becoming further entrenched, with some economies collapsing or taking off. In some parts of the world, the administrative state will be strengthened while elsewhere it will be weakened with the ebb and flow of politics. As people grow accustomed to the global society, government intervention is probably more likely to grow than to diminish as more global action is called for to regulate the uncontrollable, the erratic, the unacceptable, the extreme, the unjust and the obstinate.

But as people feel their fate being determined by more and more distant entities, they will try to protect and expand what they can hold on to, their individuality, their private concerns, their privacy and their basic human rights. They will resist further government intervention and oppose what will become more evident to them, namely, the bureaupathologies that accompany the growth of distant entities (Caiden 1991c). As governments experience more limitations on what they hoped to accomplish, they will realize that they had promised too much, that it is unlikely they can deliver, that they do not know how to deliver what they promised, that the price for delivery is too high and that the expectations they built outstrip the possibility of performance. They are going to learn the hard way that they will have to be more realistic as complaints mount and everybody grows more frustrated, disillusioned and demoralized. Yet, paradoxically, they probably will achieve more than has ever been accomplished before, even though everybody will express their disappointments and dissatisfactions.

Some things are predictable. Advances in technology will continue to transform the way public business is conducted. Rapid urbanization will tax municipal services. The welfare state may be cut down as expenses rise. Public employment may become more accessible and more diversified. Corruption will remain a challenge. Public organizations will be required to adopt more inventive ways of raising funds. The public sector will be repositioned to share more operations and activities with other social institutions. Governments will decentralize and at the same time lose more independence to international bodies. Fads and fancies of the moment will continue to have an undue influence over public administration, whose credibility along with that of other large-scale institutions is unlikely to be enhanced by public disenchantment with privatization of public assets.

But then such predictions say more about their author than about what actually is likely to occur. Strangely enough, the study of public administration itself as a distinct discipline may disappear as it fails to gain higher academic standing and other more favored professions absorb it into their fold. Should governance replace government as the center of focus, public administration may fade further and further into the shade (Caiden 1973). Should governments fail to support independent research into public administration, then its academic appeal will diminish and its scholarly pretensions will decline into insignificance (Caiden 1979, 1984). Should any of this happen, then the future will have turned its back on the past. Who then will remember its traditional civilizing mission? Actually, the degrading outcome for civilization will not proceed far before reason is restored and public leaders worthy of the title and common people mired in approaching barbarism at last reverse the downgrading and eclipse of public administration.

To be personal, those of us who continue to uphold the banner of public administration were drawn to it because of our abhorrence of war, violence, terrorism, repression and the deprivation and horrors that accompany revolution. We are reformers. We know what we don't like. We have specific targets in mind. As we looked around we considered the institutions and instruments of civilization, and foremost we chose democracy, liberalism, radical politics and public service and we strove to further tolerance, decency, freedom, human rights, the rule of law, justice, equity, respect, not just for ourselves but for all humanity. What brought us to public service and keeps us here is the civilizing mission of public administration. In our youth, many of us witnessed and experienced first-hand the opposite, the misuse and abuse of public administration to further evil, and we determined to change all that and strive to see that only the public good was furthered. We never expected a joyride. But what we did not anticipate was how much resentment we would provoke, how much we would be vilified and branded as misguided 'do-gooders' and now 'liberals', both terms of denigration. But we still hang in and we will not let go of our dreams and our cherished humanitarian values. We are proud of what we have managed to accomplish in the circumstances. Not as much as we would like to have achieved and would still like to achieve, but the going seems to get tougher and tougher and our critics would like to substitute different values and different objectives to those we want to preserve.

Now many years on from our youth, the problems are more global than national. We are still upset at some of the very things we objected to then, which are now writ large on the world stage. We still abhor war, violence, repression, deprivation, injustice and poverty. And we still oppose reactionary die-hards and revolutionary extremists. We have had to learn much the hard way in our past struggles, and to adapt to changing times. We still have not given up on our fundamental values to make the world a better place for all humanity. We still keep faith with the civilizing mission of public service and public administration.

But alas, the folks who dislike our agenda have also smartened up, and even outwitted us, by belittling our chosen institutions and instruments. They have scorned our enterprise. They have shifted or tried to shift the mission of public administration and they are being quite successful at denigrating much of which we stand for. They believe that what they offer is superior and that we belong to the past. They offer tempting inducements to jump on their bandwagon, even though their way may not be compatible with public administration's civilizing mission and threatens to steer the ship of state back to authoritarianism. Hence, we need to stand firm, protect our cherished values, and resist going with the flow, the latest fads and fancies of the moment, however smartly dressed up. We must stick to what has been proven to work and improve the lot of all humanity, all peoples and all God's children.

REFERENCES

Caiden G.E. (1964). 'In Defense of Public Administration'. *Public Administration Sydney* 24 (3), pp. 224–229. Also in R.N. Spann & G.R. Curnow (1975) (Eds), *Public Policy and Administration.* Sydney: Wiley.

Caiden, G.E. (1971a). *The Dynamics of Public Administration: Guidelines to Current Transformations in Theory and Practice*. New York: Holt, Rinehart & Winston (2nd ed). Revised as *Public Administration*, LA: Palisades Publishers, 1982.

Caiden, G.E. (1971b). 'The Administrative Context'. In P. Lengyel (Ed), *Approaches to the Science of Socioeconomic Development.* Paris: UNESCO, pp. 349–361.

Caiden, G.E. (1973). 'Reflections on the Policy Sciences Movement'. *Public Administration in Israel and Abroad* 12, pp. 132–144, and *Medinah v'Memshal* 2 (1), pp. 122–129.

Caiden, G.E. (1979). 'A Letter from a Self-Styled Iconoclast to his Fellow Public Administration Theorists'. *Dialogue* 2 (2), pp. 4–6.

Caiden, G.E. (1980). 'The Challenge to the Administrative State'. *Journal of Public Administration* 15 (4), pp. 158–168.

Caiden, G.E. (1982a) (Co-Ed). *Strategies for Administrative Reform.* Lexington, MA: Lexington Books.

Caiden, G.E. (1982b) (Ed). *An International Handbook of Ombudsman*. Westport, CT: Greenwood Press. Vol. 1 *Evolution and Present Function*. Vol. 2 *Country Surveys*.

Caiden, G.E. (1984). 'On the Margin'. *Dialogue* 7 (2), pp. 1–6.

Caiden, G.E. (1988). 'The Problem of Ensuring the Public Accountability of Public Officials'. In J. Jabbra & O.P. Dwivedi (Eds), *Public Service Accountability: A Comparative Perspective* (pp. 17–38). New Haven, CT: Kumarian Press.

Caiden, G.E. (1991a). *Administrative Reform Comes of Age*. Berlin: de Gruyter.

Caiden, G.E. (1991b). 'What Really is Public Maladministration?' *Public Administration Review* 51 (6), pp. 486–493.

Caiden, G.E. (1991c). 'Getting at the Essence of the Administrative State'. See A. Farazmand (1994) (Ed), *Handbook on Bureaucracy and Bureaucratic Politics* (pp. 65–78). New York: Marcel Dekker.

Caiden, G.E. (1994a). 'Globalizing the Theory and Practice of Public Administration'. In J.C. Garcia Zamor & R. Khatur (Eds), *Public Administration in the Global Village* (pp. 45–60). Westport, CT: Praeger.

Caiden, G.E. (1994b). 'Revitalización de la Administración Pública'. *Reforma y Democracia* (Caracas: CLAD), 1, pp. 27–48; reproduced (1997) as 'Revitalizing Public Administration'. In A. Kfir (Ed), *Problems in Public Administration*. Haifa University Press.

Caiden, G.E. (1996). 'The Concept of Neutrality'. In H. Asmeron & E. Reis (Eds.), *Democratization and Bureaucratic Neutrality* (pp. 20–44). London: Macmillan.

Caiden, G.E. (1997a). 'The Implications of GA Resolution 50/225'. Originally presented at the UN Meeting of Experts, New York in May. Revised (1999): 'What Lies Ahead for the Administrative State?' In O.P. Dwivedi & K. Henderson (Eds), *Bureaucracy and Its Alternatives in World Perspective* (pp. 295–320). London: Macmillan.

Caiden, G.E. (1997b). 'The Essence of Public Service Professionalism'. Originally presented at the UN Seminar on Public Service Ethics, Salonika and revised and published several times since – most recently in (1999) J. Heuvel & L.W.J.C. Huberts (Eds), *Integrity at the Public–Private Interface* (pp. 21–44). Maastricht: Shaker.

Caiden, G.E., & Caiden, N. (2000). *Toward More Democratic Governance: The Modernization of the Administrative State in Australasia, North America and the United Kingdom*. New York: UN Department of Public Economics and Public Administration.

Caiden, G.E., Dwivedi, O.P., & Jabbra, J. (2001). *Where Corruption Lives*. Bloomfield, CT: Kumarian Press.

Caiden, G.E. (2004a). 'The Erosion of Public Service in the United States'. In P. Reddy, J. Singh, & R. Tiwari (Eds), *Democracy, Governance and*

Globalization: Essays in Honor of Paul Appleby (pp. 37–70). New Delhi: Indian Institute of Public Administration.

Caiden, G.E. (2004b). *The Administrative State in a Globalizing World: Trends and Challenges*. ECOSOC. New York: UN.

15

Spirituality in Public Administration: A Challenge for the Well-Being of Nations A Postscript

O.P. DWIVEDI

SEPARATION OF VALUES AND ETHICS FROM PUBLIC ADMINISTRATION: THE CONTEXT

Traditionally, public administration as a discipline as well as a profession has avoided the discussion about the role of ethics, values, morality, spirituality and religion. The term 'ethics', which comes from the Greek word *ethos*, means accepted customs and traditions of a society; later in Roman times, the term was translated into Latin as *mores* which became 'morality'. Sometimes, the terms 'ethics' and 'morality' are used as virtual synonyms. Nowadays, these two terms refer to good or evil, right and wrong, as well as the appropriate conduct of people in a society. Of course, there are many social scientists who would like to avoid using ethics and morality in the study of human affairs, because of their distaste for anything moralistic or because of their thinking that anyone talking about it must be acting out of self-interest while hiding behind a façade of morality. They also allege that 'the values referred to so frequently in ethical discourse are intangible, beyond measurement, often ambiguous and all too open to various interpretations' (Trompf 1987: 103). And because of this alleged subjective or emotive language, ethical dimensions of public administration and governance have been rarely addressed.

On the other hand, is it not true that ethics and values have always been with us? Or, can anyone deny that the principles used in creating public administration theories and models have been free of the values of their creators? Furthermore, is it not true that there is no human action (Karma) ever undertaken which is not susceptible to blame and praise, or good and bad, and hence influenced by moral reasoning? All these questions and connotations suggest that administration as an activity has never been free from ethical underpinnings. Thus, it is amazing that scholars and researchers examining public policy issues have carried out their research as if values and morality did not matter. Many of them asserted the ideal of value-free research; and if they were teaching, they dismissed the place of ethics or values in their public policy courses. But that vestige of a one-dimensional rationalism is now slowly giving way to a fuller recognition and understanding of the impact and consequences of human values (both personal and organizational) on society in general.

Every serious political philosopher since Aristotle has recognized the important relationship between politics and ethics. The problem came to the fore when the dichotomy between politics and administration was established by the early twentieth century, as it broke the bond between ethics and administration. Consequently, the moral validity and ethical relevance of political action and public policy remained to be reaffirmed. As this situation continued, opportunities emerged for decision-makers to undertake actions in the name of objective reasoning and empirical research, and to dominate the formulation, implementation and evaluation of public policy issues without due regard to ethical implications and moral reasoning.

In this essay, the author touches on a number of broad themes, including the historical context of the chasm between ethics and public administration, the concept of well-being and how it is tied to happiness and spirituality, how the well-being of people affects the well-being of nation-states (which in turn influences the quality of governance, for which statecraft appears to be the essential vehicle), the need for good governance as a prerequisite for achieving the well-being of all, and the role of spirituality in sustaining that prerequisite. The essay concludes with a number of observations.

Separation of Values from Public Administration

By the beginning of the twentieth century, two major events occurred which shaped the future of public administration as a discipline. First there was the emphasis that Woodrow Wilson and Frank W. Goodnow placed on the separation of administration from politics as the single most essential reform in achieving efficiency and removing the objectionable and immoral practices of spoils and patronage besetting the democratic system of governing in the USA. In Woodrow Wilson's words, 'administration lies outside the proper sphere of politics. Administrative questions are not political questions' (Wilson 1887). While Wilson expounded his theory on separation of administration from politics in 1887, Frank Goodnow reiterated similar views in his 1900 book *Politics and Administration.* Other scholars in the USA and in the UK and Germany joined a steady stream of advocates for the dichotomy. This distinction was further strengthened when the first two textbooks on public administration by L.D. White *(Introduction to the Study of Public Administration*, 1926) and W.F. Willoughby (*Principles of Public Administration*, 1927) were published. Through these and by subsequent writings of scholars such as Luther Gullick and Herbert Simon, the discipline of public administration came to be viewed where 'the politics-administration dichotomy was assumed both as a self-evident truth and as a desirable goal; administration was perceived as a self-contained world of its own, with its own separate values, rules and methods' (Sayre 1966). Politics, then, came to be viewed as the domain of values, whereas administration was considered the universe of fact, enshrined in a value-free environment. Thus a stage was set, in the education and training programs and courses of public administration, for the exclusion of ethical issues and value questions (Dwivedi 1988).

The second event which further strengthened the neglect or deliberate elimination of ethics from public administration programs was the rise of scienticism in the discipline. While the roots of scientific analysis in social science disciplines can be traced back to the Age of Enlightenment, slowly the two core elements of scientific method started influencing the philosophical and human sciences. These core elements are rational objectivity and quantification. The main purpose of these scientific elements was and still is to remove biases and fallacies of human thought by searching for 'hard data' which can be measured and then presented in an objective and rational manner. In this context, students and practitioners of public administration are considered to be applied scientists who remain dispassionately aloof from that subjective (and therefore irrational) realm of values and ethical issues. The impact of scienticism was most visible in the two central concerns of public administration: budgeting and public personnel administration. Developments such as 'line item budgeting', 'performance budgeting', 'Planning Programming Budgeting System' (PPBS), 'Zero Based Budgeting' (ZBB), 'Policy and Expenditure Management System' (PEMS), and finally the 'New Public Management' (NPM) have successively and sometimes concurrently dominated the field with the view to increasing efficiency while relying on quantification.

The more complex the governing process became, the stronger the insistence on the use of scientific methodology in providing the analytical framework of the budgetary process. Similarly, in the field of public personnel administration, the emphasis was on objective methods of selection against the backdrop of a highly rational position-classification system. This was achieved in the name of the merit system. It drew its strength from the premise that all factors comprising merit could be quantified. Of course, while the objective was to eliminate patronage, favouritism and incompetence, the result was that the system became too obsessed with quantification, thereby bringing such dysfunctions into the public personnel system as social inequity, biases and minimization of the human element. These examples attest to the fact that scienticism in public administration has dominated the field, and thus it became an end in itself. Robert Dahl elucidated the point further: 'No science of public administration is possible unless: (1) the place of normative values is made clear; (2) the nature of man in the area of public administration is better understood and his conduct is more predictable' (Dahl 1966: 33).

Dahl's lamentation has yet to be responded to, although by the 1980s some scholars (such as James Bowman, Gerald E. Caiden, O.P. Dwivedi, David Gould, M.T. Lilla, John Rohr, Dennis Thompson, Dwight Waldo and others) started questioning the domination of public administration by the methodology and paradigm of scienticism. However, the so-called 'damage' had already been done, in the sense that for several decades teaching, training and research in public administration has tended to treat the question of values peripherally or dismiss it altogether. Efforts during the 1980s were sporadic but it was not until the 1990s that the dignity of men and women, justice, morality and other values emerged as important concerns confronting the discipline of public administration.

With the setting of the above-mentioned stage, delineating a historical review of the separation between ethics and public administration and the need for bringing ethical and spiritual dimensions into governance, the essay examines the need and relevance of good governance as a vehicle for attaining the well-being of all, and examines the cardinal values essential for good governance (as well as certain impediments responsible for poor governance, including a discussion on widespread corruption). The essay next deals with the concept of 'the well-being of all', a concept competing with the other paradigm, 'sustainable development for all' which has overshadowed our world since the publication of the Brundtland Report *Our Common Future* in 1987 (WCED 1987). After analyzing the merits of both concepts (well-being and sustainable development) and a framework for achieving the well-being of all, the essay offers some interpretative explorations and a few propositions concerning the essential role of public administrators in assisting their societies in achieving the well-being of all.

THE WELL-BEING OF NATIONS

In all cultures, philosophers and learned people have debated the nature of the good life and have concluded that happiness and well-being, individually and collectively, is a major indicator of the good life. How people feel and think about their own lives as members of their family and of society is a good indicator of the quality of life as perceived by them. External factors such as income, educational background, family life, place of residence and events do have influence on that feeling but these and other demographic factors have only a modest impact on the well-being of people (Diener et al. 2003). Instead, factors such as personality traits, peace, fulfilment, spirituality and life satisfaction play an important part in their well-being. This is not to say that wealth does not play an important role, because not only do people living in wealthy nations score higher in the measurement of their satisfaction index, but also when poor people receive even a modest increase in their income, their satisfaction level grows. Nevertheless, for poor and middle-income groups, that modest increase is merely a temporary phenomenon because such a nominal increase might simply fulfil their basic human needs and not their desires. Furthermore, there are variations across cultures. For example, Diener et al. reported that Asian-American students were happier when they were closer to achieving academic goals 'whereas Caucasian students were happy when engaging in an activity that was important to them at that moment' (412). In addition, some societies produce higher levels of well-being than do others – a factor of that nation's cultural history, economic prosperity, and good governance.

What is Well-Being?

Is human well-being the same as human welfare? OECD has defined human well-being as more than the sum of individual levels of well-being, which includes equality of opportunities, civil liberties, distribution of resources and opportunities for further learning (OECD 2001: 11). Human well-being in the OECD study encompasses factors such as economic well-being (including the reciprocal value of social 'regrettables' like pollution, crime and divorce), social cohesion (or social capital), better health, and the quality of the environment. Although, the OECD study did not consider in its measurements spiritual or personal fulfilment, virtually all human activity – whether by individuals or collectives – entails patterns of behavior, motivation, and some form of emotional involvement. Such activity affects the mental and spiritual 'health' and well-being (or ill-being) of people. Spirituality, as a special factor, plays an important role in building the inner character of a person, as well as developing norms of behaviour, and sense of purpose in life, strengthening inherited culture and values and supporting interaction within society. Specifically, cultural legacies, identities, practices, and religion play an important role in fulfilment. It should also be noted that economic well-being cannot be based on strictly economic calculation nor can it be determined simply on an aggregate cost–benefit analysis or other consequential or 'outcome' criteria (OECD 2001: 14).

What is well-being? It is a factor of life satisfaction, the sense of happiness, and a reduced level of anxiety and pessimism. For example, Bulmahn reports that in the mid-1990s, as expectations of the merger of East Germany (GDR) with West Germany increased, suicidal mortality in the GDR declined, because 'Eastern Germans are more satisfied today than in 1990 and the share of those who say they are leading a happy life has increased' (Bulmahn 2000: 391). The example of East Germany suggests that modernization and democratization may improve the quality of life, including life satisfaction, and increase the sense of well-being of people. But when it comes to measuring happiness, there exist cultural, racial and individual differences. For example, despite their inferior living conditions older African-Americans in the US reported a higher level of happiness than older whites (Campbell 1976). Furthermore, a study about happiness, materialism and religious experiences in the US and Singapore by William Swinyard and others (2001) found that 'less materially-oriented people are happier than others – both in Singapore and in the United States' (28). It suggests that materialism is not the main source of happiness; instead, happy people look for happiness elsewhere although they might have material possessions. That direction is towards their inner spirituality, religious thoughts, being keenly aware of a divine presence and trying to live by certain cardinal beliefs.

Those cardinal beliefs or values which may constitute the inner elements of well-being include five factors: (1) The most basic is meeting the physical/biological needs. (2) Another is availability of freedom of action, and choices. (3) A third involves opportunities to develop intellectual and/or artistic abilities. (4) A commonality of norms and values being shared with others, especially trust (including whether people trust others or whether people are considered trustworthy, and whether they have trust in government and private institutions). (5) Last but not the least is the satisfaction of 'higher' spiritual needs. It is here where concepts such as Dharma and Karma in Hindu philosophy (discussed later in the essay), as well as the Christian notions of providence and grace become relevant.

Many Western scholars consider well-being a subjective matter because of a well-known association between religion and happiness, although it is not known which particular aspect of religiosity connects with life satisfaction and well-being. And, as faith and religion are subjective matters, the concept of well-being is also seen as a subjective matter. Moreover, there are significant differences among people belonging to different faiths and religions, and hence it is rather difficult to develop a universal model of such a co-relation which can be easily measured and analyzed in a scientific manner. Nevertheless, it has been argued very strongly that 'religious people report being happier and more satisfied with life than irreligious people' (Myers & Diener 1995: 16). Levin & Chatters (1998) have also concluded that religion appears to constitute a therapeutic effect on mental health outcomes, which ultimately relates to satisfaction with life style. Life satisfaction can also be measured. However, between religiosity and spirituality, the major difference is that whereas religiosity may refer to one's relationship with the religion as it is practiced (or the relationship with organized religion), spirituality (to paraphrase Adam Cohen 2002) relates to satisfaction with life as spiritual people feel that their lives have purpose, have understanding about events happening around them, find comfort in their religious beliefs, are willing to help others as they were helped in the past and believe in good Karma. Of course, not all religious beliefs and practices may have the same impact on the spirituality of people or a positive impact on their health. However, one major dimension of spirituality is that it brings goodness into this world. These two dimensions – Karma and spirituality – are discussed later in the essay.

GOOD GOVERNANCE AS THE FOUNDATION FOR ACHIEVING THE WELL-BEING OF ALL

To achieve human well-being, it is crucial to realize that, unless all members of society are able to meet their basic needs and also have a large range of choices and opportunities to fulfil their potential, a nation's overall well-being is not possible. To achieve this objective, statecraft appears to be the essential vehicle through which members of society with the help of public officials could meet such needs and achieve their potentials. The most important of these factors is the existence of good governance, which is a prerequisite for any society to achieve its fullest potential for the good life. Therefore, to achieve the well-being of people, a country ought to usher in an era of good governance by creating conditions for the well-being of its people.

Governance

The concept of governance is as old as human civilization. In essence it means the process of decision-making and the procedure by which such decisions are implemented or not. The term is used in different contexts and varies in perspective among those who govern and others who are being governed. An integral part of this process is the effort to create conditions for 'good governance' which require the prevalence of such fundamental values as accountability, transparency, equity and ethics, which are essential ingredients for the sustenance of a liberal democratic polity. 'Good Governance' or 'Good Administration' is a necessity for any government to achieve the best quality of life for its public. However, what constitutes 'good governance' and how it could be achieved are matters of debate in the public administration literature. At the same time, it is crucial to be aware of the insidious impact of poor governance, corruption and bad management as impediments to good governance.

Governance as a process is of recent origin, and goes beyond the classical functions of government. Different schools of thought derive different meanings from the term 'governance', depending upon the role of process versus activity and control versus rules (Hyden & Court 2002). The term 'governance' involves mechanisms, processes and institutions, through which people articulate their interests, exercise their rights, meet their obligations and mediate their differences. The characteristics of good governance include core values of rule of law, equity, participation, transparency, responsiveness, consensus, economy, efficiency and effectiveness, and above all impeccable accountability. As the people are the source of all power in a democracy, accountability to people is the hallmark of democratic governance (Mohanty, Jones & Rao 2004). It also includes all such governmental measures as guiding, steering, controlling or managing society. In essence – whereas the term 'government' refers to a set of instruments through which people living in a state, believing in and sharing a common core of values, govern themselves by means of laws, rules and regulations enforced by the state apparatus (Dwivedi 2001) – the term 'governance' includes a range of activities involving all cultural communities and various stakeholders in the country, all government institutions (legislative, executive, administrative, judicial and parastatal bodies), political parties, interest groups, non-governmental organizations (including civil society), the private sector and the public at large (Frederickson 1997: 86). The concept is also viewed as the exercise of political power to manage a nation's affairs (World Bank 1992), as well as 'the manner in which power is exercised in the management of a country's economic and social development' (World Bank 1994: vii).

A Framework of Good Governance

The term 'good' is a value-laden term that involves a comparison between two things or systems by using some standard of measure. A government or a system of governance is considered good if it exhibits certain fundamental characteristics. Perhaps the UN Development Program (UNDP) offers the most comprehensive definition and an idealistic model of good governance. Good governance is, among other things, participatory, transparent and accountable. It is also effective and equitable, as well as promoting the rule of law. Good governance ensures that political, social and economic priorities are based on a broad consensus in society and that the voices of the poorest and the most vulnerable are heard in decision-making over the allocation of development resources (UNDP 1998: 3).

From the above characterization, an ideal model of good governance, with ten basic characteristics can be constructed: (1) *public participation* in decision-making; (2) the impartial enforcement of the *rule of law*; (3) *transparency* for access to governing processes (including institutions and information sources); (4) *responsiveness* of institutions to the needs of all stakeholders; (5) *consensus building* among different and differing interests in the society; (6) *equity and fair treatment* assured to all individuals so that they may improve their well-being; (7) effective and efficient *responsibility and accountability* of institutions and officials; (8) *strategic vision of the public good* on the part of the leaders towards long-term perspectives on sustainable human development; (9) substantive *participatory democracy* (not merely formal electoral pluralism) based upon three basic values: fundamental freedom, equality for all, and universal suffrage; and (10) *ethical governance* where governing elites dedicate their lives to service for the public and where amoralism does not reign supreme (Dwivedi and Mishra, 2007).

Good governance and sustainable human development, especially for developing nations, also require conscientious attempts at eliminating poverty, sustaining livelihoods, fulfilling basic needs and offering an administrative system that is 'clean,' and accessible. It is important that these characteristics are not only enshrined in a constitutional document but, most importantly, also practiced in a persistent and consistent manner.

THE ROLE OF SPIRITUALITY IN OPERATIONALIZING GOOD GOVERNANCE

Spirituality can play a crucial role in keeping the system of governance honest and transparent by providing incentive for public officials to serve the public with dignity and respect. How can it be possible? A *spiritually-oriented* public official ought to know that it is his/her Dharma which inspires him/her to serve others. In so doing (that is his Karma), he/she will be fulfilling two duties: one to the self, whereby one seeks inner strength and satisfaction through spiritual action, and the other to the community-at-large whereby one works for the common good. As such, Dharma and Karma combined regulate human conduct and cast individuals into the right character mould by inculcating in them spiritual, social and moral virtues thereby strengthening the ethos that holds the social and moral fabric of a society together, by maintaining order in society, building individual and group character and giving rise to harmony and understanding. Thus, by understanding the precepts and relevance of Dharma and Karma for the management of statecraft, a common strategy for public service spirituality and good governance can be developed. Such a strategy depends much upon how those public officials together (1) perceive a common future for their society; (2) act both individually and collectively towards protecting the common good; and (3) realize that as individuals they have a moral obligation to support their society's goals since their acts will have repercussions on the future of their society (Dwivedi 2002: 48). Finally, a morality-driven model strengthens those broad principles that ought to inform our governmental conduct because they mark the direction towards which those who govern must channel their acts if they are to serve humanity.

These principles include the call for individual spirituality, sacrifice, compassion, justice, striving for the highest good and, specifically for public servants, considering their jobs as a vocation. And while the emphasis on secular government, liberalism and democracy assigns the place of morality to individual conduct and behavior, it has nevertheless acknowledged a continuing tension between the requisites of good governance through its public policy and programs and through the spiritual and moral standards by which they can be measured. Spirituality, deriving from such foundations, thus provides an important base to the governing process. Confidence and trust in liberal democracy can be safeguarded only when the governing process exhibits a higher moral tone, deriving from the breadth of ethical and spiritual sensitivity. Finally, for good governance it is necessary that public officials (elected and appointed) know that there are correct ways of doing things, and that those standards should be adhered to. For these officials, accountability and responsibility should become a moral question, given their awareness that, having been entrusted with the stewardship of the state, they owe special obligations, they have special expectations and they reside in a fiduciary world, and they are moved by a higher cause. It is here that their spirituality and a sense of doing their duty acquire a holistic tone; a tone which may enable them to dedicate their lives to creating conditions for the well-being of their society. Material benefits, possessions and official privileges have been and are going to be transitory illusions; in the final analysis (as demonstrated by Swinyard's study of the USA and Singapore), the well-being and happiness of people will come from how they perceive their inner world, i.e., their spirituality, and their whole approach to life (Swinyard, et al, 2001). Good governance as an operational arm of well-being is possible only when our public officials behave as such.

THE PLACE OF SPIRITUALITY IN GOVERNANCE

By using spirituality in managing government affairs, public officials may overcome such traits of human frailty and base characteristics as greed, exploitation, abuse of power, and possibly mistreatment of people. When we refer to spirituality, we generally mean by it a kind of energy source which (a) is beyond ourselves and transcendent; (b) impels us to search for the purpose of life here and after, as well as why we are here on earth; (c) has an over-arching influence on our sense of right and wrong; (d) empowers us to care for others; and (e) inspires us to act for the common good. Willa Bruce and John Novinson, in an article dealing with spirituality in public service, suggested that an effort ought to be made to operationalize the concept (Bruce & Novinson 1999). In 1987, this author suggested a similar approach regarding the place of morality and spirituality in managing statecraft by stating that 'the moral dimension of governance represents a concern for an improvement in the quality of public service and the conduct of statecraft' (Dwivedi 1987: 707). Although spirituality is supposed to be an integral part of our personal religious views and beliefs, its secular dimension (which is yet to be particularly acknowledged by secular institutions) is crucial in securing public trust. Can it be converted into a moral force to be used for good governance; if so, what path should it follow? One such spiritual path is based on the two precepts of Dharma and Karma which are briefly discussed below:

The Role of Karma in Governing Public Affairs

Karma involves the notion that there is a consequential ethic in any activity performed by an individual; it also means that *each act, wilfully performed, leaves a consequence in its wake*. The law of Karma tells us that every action performed creates its own chain of reactions and events, some of which are immediately visible, while others may take a long time to surface. In the sphere of Karma, a right action, that is, a good or righteous action, generates beneficial results, while an unethical action results in harmful effects. For example, in the public domain, the Karmic law is particularly relevant, as decisions made by public officials are interrelated with and interconnected to what eventually happens within society in general and sometimes even beyond a country's borders. Thus, when an action in the public domain has taken place, those who committed the deed may not face the consequences individually; nevertheless, someone else is going to be burdened with or benefit from their actions. It is in this context that the concept of righteousness or Dharma becomes meaningful.

Our Dharma for Effectively Managing Public Affairs

Dharma entails the principle of righteousness (doing what is correct), involving a system of ethics and moral duty. Applied to governance, while a person who performs a public duty may be capable of both good and evil tendencies, so long as he/she remembers that it is his/her duty to sustain the general welfare of all people, he/she will act in a righteous manner. However, those who do deviate from that righteous path will surely endanger the state, resulting in bad governance. For a public official to act in a *Dharmic* (righteous) manner, it is important for him/her to act in the service of others and to avoid exploiting fellow human beings. Being in public office requires that its incumbents be willing not only to acknowledge the moral responsibility for their actions but also to accept accountability for what they do. The key is in the education of public servants as well as the public in ethical approaches from a critical, reflective and spiritual perspective.

REFLECTIONS

As concluding observations, the author wishes to offer some interpretative explorations and a few general propositions.

Needed: Public Officials with Conscience

The conscience of a person depends largely on character as well as spirituality. Spirituality can lead to mastery over our baser impulses such as greed, exploitation, abuse of power and maltreatment of people. It requires self-discipline, humility, and above all, the absence of arrogance in holding public office. Furthermore, it enables people to centre their values on the notion that there is a cosmic ordinance and divine law which must be maintained. *Spirituality* serves both as a model and operative strategy for the transformation of human character by strengthening the genuine, substantive will to serve the common people. This, the moral leadership, is what the public wants from government officials. The objective of good governance is to create an environment in which public servants as well as politicians in government are able to respond to the challenge of good governance. That challenge for public officials involves a notion of duty, as well as acting morally, responsibly and accountably. If these dimensions can be strengthened in the management of public affairs, it may be possible for a public official to rise above self-interest by placing the collective good above private interest and greed. The strengthening of such a notion creates a shared feeling or spirit of public duty among those who govern.

The Insidious Impact of Fencing Out Morality, Values and Spirituality from Public Administration

There is a general misconception in the field of public policy and administration that the development of public policy and its application are purely an objective and secular endeavour where morality, spirituality and values have no specific role to play; because such factors are mostly emotive, subjective, value-laden and personal in nature. And, as the argument goes, public administration as a domain has no room for such subjective matters. But values and morality are not limited to the personal realm. A democratic society is founded on the principle of the dignity and worth of all people, and moral principles emanate from basic religious values that hold human life both sacred and social. Furthermore, every constitution is generally the embodiment of moral values that guarantee fundamental freedoms, justice, rule of law and the like.

These are the moral foundations on which public policy and its management must be based. Moreover, we live in a world of interdependence in which morality and secularism share and balance one another in the protection and development of human values. And thus, past efforts to fence out morality and spirituality from public affairs and governance, in the name of secularism, public service neutrality and objectivity have contributed to the emergence of an amoral system of public affairs management. Such a situation has shaped and guided humanity for too long, with the result that in many nations immorality, expediency and corruption have become a way of life, and it ought to be changed into an era of good governance and spirituality in public administration.

Demonstrate Social Conscience and Caring Behavior

Demonstration of social conscience and caring behavior by public officials is intertwined with the general concept of good governance and protecting the common good. It is an obligation that human beings owe not only to each other within a society, but also to others living elsewhere. The concept of service possesses two dimensions: the religious and the secular. Historically, world religions have played a vital role in upholding the virtue of serving others.

There is ample evidence for this concept in the major religions of the world (such as Christianity, Judaism, Islam, Hinduism and Buddhism), where people have been exhorted to serve others. This doctrine of service unto others is considered to be the noblest duty and the ultimate concern of all human beings. World religions do agree that to help and serve others is the highest moral purpose of human beings. Furthermore, examples abound in various religious faiths throughout the history of humanity that great souls have devoted their lives to serving others. One can look up to Buddha, Christ and Gandhi as examples of such individuals who devoted their lives to the principles of individual self-discipline, sacrifice, compassion, justice and striving for the highest moral purpose by serving others.

Educating Public Servants to Serve: The Spiritual Approach to Public Administration

Conflicts of responsibility which persons experience within public organizations should not be resolved in an idiosyncratic fashion. In order for an organization to keep the bureaucratic machine in the service of the public, rather than of itself or of special interests, values and principles essential to a democratic political community must provide constant points of reference from beyond the boundaries. If public administrators are to behave in a manner responsive to the wishes of a democratic citizenry, it is essential that policies be established which guide their general course of conduct toward the serving of the public interest. These policies should enforce and reinforce prescribed public service values (Cooper 1982: xiv). But the implication of the difficulty in defining ethical issues for training sessions or classroom instruction is that it is essential to spend considerable time working on it in a variety of ways before asking participants to develop the full range of steps leading to a final resolution of the issues as discussed.

A course on public-service ethics and spirituality should be approached from three angles: classical, legal and environmental. The classical approach emphasizes the philosophical and cultural traditions of a nation. The legal approach focuses on rules, regulations and constraints on individuals to regulate their administrative power and authority. The environmental approach aims at sensitizing public servants to the need to act as guardians of the state, so that its resources are appropriately used and carefully protected; they might act somewhat as Plato's Philosopher Kings (Dwivedi 1988: 124–125). A sense of vocation and spirituality in the service to the public must be instilled unequivocally among public officials and state employees with a proper carrot-and-stick policy. That sense of belief is founded on the premise that governance is a public trust, and working for the government is a public duty that demands the highest level of integrity and behavior as well as such virtues as honesty, impartiality, sincerity and justice.

Spirituality, seen as a process, energizing force and inner strength, can be the greatest source of applying ethics, morality and a sense of belonging to a cadre of dedicated public servants who feel that serving the public is their main mission. On the other hand, a spiritually impoverished statecraft becomes a machine bereft of moral and ethical dimensions. The future of public administration will be bleak without the mantle of spirituality as a guiding force for governance and government workplaces. Only with it, the well-being of all can be sustained.

REFERENCES

Bruce, W. & Novinson, J. (1999). 'Spirituality in Public Service: A Dialogue'. *Public Administration Review* 59 (2), pp. 163–169.

Bulmahn, Thomas (2000). 'Modernity and Happiness: The Case of Germany'. *Journal of Happiness Studies* (1), pp. 375–400.

Caiden, G.E. (2001). 'Corruption and Governance'. In G.E. Caiden, O.P. Dwivedi, & J. Jabbra, *Where Corruption Lives* (p. 19). Bloomfield, CT: Kumarian Press.

Campbell, A. (1976). 'Subjective Measures of Well-being'. *American Psychologist* (February), pp. 117–124.

Cohen, Adam B. (2002). 'The Importance of Spirituality in Well-being for Jews and Christians'. *Journal of Happiness Studies* 3, pp. 287–310.

Cooper, T. (1982). *The Responsible Administrator: An Approach to Ethics for the Administrative Role*. Port Washington, NY: Kennikat Press.

Dahl, R.A. (1966). 'The Science of Public Administration'. In C.E. Hawley & R.G. Weintraub (Eds), *Administrative Questions and Political Answers*. New York.

Diener, Ed, Shigehiro Oshi, and Richard E. Lucas (2003). 'Personality, Culture and Subjective Well-being: Emotional and Cognitive Evaluations of Life'. *Annual Review of Psychology* 54, pp. 403–425.

Dwivedi, O.P. (1987). 'Moral Dimensions of Statecraft: A Plea for an Administrative Theology'. *Canadian Journal of Political Science* 20 (4), pp. 699–709.

Dwivedi, O.P. (1988). 'Teaching Ethics in Public Administration Courses'.

International Review of Administrative Studies 54, pp. 115–130.

Dwivedi, O.P. (2001). 'The Challenges of Cultural Diversity for Good Governance'. Presentation made at the ad-hoc Expert Group Meeting of the UN, New York, 3–4 May.

Dwivedi, O.P. (2002). 'On Common Good and Good Governance: An Alternative Approach'. In D. Olowu & S. Sako (Eds), *Better Governance and Public Policy.* Bloomfield, CT: Kumarian Press, pp. 35–51.

Dwivedi, O.P. and Mishra, D.S. (2007). 'Good Governance: A Model for India'. In Ali Farazmand & Jack Pinkowski (Eds), *Handbook of Globalization, Governance and Public Administration.* New York: Taylor & Francis, pp. 701–741.

Fleishman, J., Leibman, L., & Moore, M. (1981). *Public Duties: The Moral Obligation of Public Officials*. Cambridge, MA: Harvard University Press.

Frederickson, H.G. (1997). *The Spirit of Public Administration* (p. 86). San Francisco: Jossey-Bass Publishers.

Fukuyama, F. (2004). *State Building: Governance and World Order in the 21st Century* (p. 30). New York: Cornell University Press.

Hyden, G., & Court, J. (2002). 'Comparing Governance Across Countries and Over Time: Conceptual Challenges'. In D. Olowu, & S. Sako (Eds), *Better Governance and Public Policy* (pp. 13–33). Bloomfield, CT: Kumarian Press.

Leland, P.J., & Denhardt, K.G. (2005). 'Incorporating Spirituality into the MPA Curriculum: Framing the Discussion'. *Journal of Public Affairs Education* 11 (2), pp. 121–131.

Levin, J.S. and L.M. Chatters (1998). 'Research on religion and Mental Health: An Overview of Empirical Findings and Theoretical Issues'. In H.G. Koenig (Ed), *Handbook of Religion and Mental Health.* San Diego, CA: Academic Press, pp. 33–50.

Lilla, M.T. (1981). 'Ethos, Ethics and Public Service'. *Public Interest* 63 (Spring), pp. 3–17.

Mohanty, P.K., Jones, K., & Rao, S.J. (2004). *Good Governance Initiatives in Andhra Pradesh 2003.* Hyderabad: Centre for Good Governance.

Myers, D.G. and E. Diener (1995). 'Who is happy?' *Psychological Science* 6 (1), pp. 10–19.

Nef, J. (1998). 'Administrative Culture in Latin America: Historical and Structural Outline'. *Africanus*: *Journal of Development Administration* 28 (2), pp. 19–32.

OECD (1982). *Aid and Environment Protection: Ten Years after Stockholm.* Paris: OECD Development Committee.

OECD (2001). *The Well-being of Nations: The Role of Human and Social Capital.* Paris: OECD, Centre for Educational Research and Innovation.

Rohr, J. (1978). *Ethics for Bureaucrats: An Essay on Law and Values*. New York: Dekker.

Sayre, W. (1966). 'Premises of Public Administration: Past and Emerging'. In C.E. Hawley & Ruth G. Weintraub (Eds), *Administrative Questions and Political Answers*. New York: D. Van Nostrand, pp. 103–106.

Swinyard, William R., Ah-Keng Kau, and Hui-Yin Phua (2001). 'Happiness, Materialism, and Religious Experience in the US and Singapore'. *Journal of Happiness Studies* 2, pp. 13–32.

Thompson, D. (1985). 'The Possibility of Administrative Ethics'. *Public Administration Review* 45 (4), pp. 555–561.

Trompf, G.W. (1987). 'The Ethics of Development: An Overview'. In S. Stratigos & P.J. Hughes, *The Ethics of Development: The Pacific in the 21st Century* (pp. 102–129). Port Moresby: University of Papua New Guinea Press.

UNDP (1997). *Corruption and Good Governance.* Discussion Paper 3. UNDP, New York: UNDP.

UNDP (1998). *Good Governance and Sustainable Development.* New York: UNDP. Online at http://www.undp.org/docs/un98-1.pdf.

Wilson, Woodrow (1887). 'The Study of Administration'. *Political Science Quarterly* 2. Reprinted in J.M. Shafritz & A.C. Hyde (Eds), *Classics of Public Administration* (pp. 11–24). Pacific Grove, CA: Brooks/Cole.

World Bank (1992). *Governance and Development: The World Development Report.* Washington, DC: World Bank.

World Bank (1994). *The World Development Report.* Washington, DC: World Bank.

World Commission on Environment and Development (WCED) (1987). *Our Common Future.* New York: Oxford University Press.

Notes on Contributors

Demetrios Argyriades is a graduate of the London School of Economics and Political Science, and the Sorbonne. He started his career in Britain and Greece and in 1967 joined the ranks of the international public service, working first for the OECD and then the UN Secretariat. During the past twelve years, he has served as a consultant to many international agencies in human resources development, public service reform, ethics and good governance. He taught at New York University from 1975, and is still currently teaching at John Jay College, CUNY, as well as other universities in the USA and abroad.

Steven E. Aufrecht is Professor of Public Administration at the University of Alaska, Anchorage. His research interests are in accountability and ethics, as well as cross-cultural administration. He has been a Fulbright Scholar in Hong Kong, and recently a visiting professor at Portland State University and the People's University of China, in Beijing.

Catherine Burke is Associate Professor at the School of Policy, Planning and Development of the University of Southern California. Burke's research focuses on organization and systems design, management theory and leadership, using the Stratified Systems Theory and Systems Leadership Theory. She has been a consultant to large public utilities, city and county governments, and several non-profit social service organizations in Britain and the USA. She served on the Board of Directors of Commonwealth Industries Inc. (now Aleris International) from 1995 through 2004.

S. Colleen Byron is a doctoral student and faculty associate at Arizona State University. Before returning to graduate school, she worked for ten years in the fixed income management field, where she specialized in accounting and trading systems.

Gerald E. Caiden, in whose honor this Festschrift is published, is a graduate of the London School of Economics and Political Science. He has served on the faculties of London University, Carleton University, Australian National University, Hebrew University, University of California in Berkeley and Haifa University, and has published very extensively in public policy, governance, administration, ethics and public service reform. Over the years, he has frequently acted as consultant, researcher and editor for several international organizations and is currently Professor of Public Administration at the University of Southern California.

Jeffrey I. Chapman is the Foundation Professor of Applied Public Finance at Arizona State University. He was the Director of the Sacramento Center at the University of Southern California, Director of the School of Public Affairs at Arizona State University, and has served as Interim Dean of the College of Public Programs, also at Arizona State. He has authored or edited four books and has published in such journals as *Public Administration Review*, *The Journal of Urban Economics, Public Budgeting and Finance*, *National Tax Journal*, *The University of Southern California Law Review* and *Public Finance Quarterly*.

Denise Conroy is Senior Lecturer in Public Policy at the Queensland University of Technology, Australia, where she has taught since 1977. She was a former Commonwealth Public Servant in the Australian Bureau of Statistics (1964–77), specializing in public finance and labor markets. She has served on the boards of state, national and international professional bodies, including the Institute of Public Administration Australia and the International Association of Schools and Institutes of Administration, as well as on many government advisory boards and committees.

O.P. Dwivedi, Order of Canada, PhD, LL D (Hon), is a Fellow of the Royal Society (Canada). He teaches public administration and environmental policy/law at the University of Guelph, Canada. He is a past President of the Canadian Political Science Association (Ottawa), past President of the Canadian Asian Studies Association (Montreal), and a former Vice President of the International Association of Schools and Institutes of Administration. He has authored, co-authored or edited 32 books and over 115 articles and chapters in books and scholarly journals.

Leo W.J.C. Huberts is Professor of Public Administration and Integrity in Governance at the Department of Public Administration and Organization Science, at the Faculty of Social Sciences of the VU University Amsterdam, the Netherlands. He is director of a research group on Integrity in Governance at his department and co-founder and co-chair of the Study Group on the Integrity and Ethics of Governance of the European Group of Public Administration (EGPA). Recently, he published a book with Van Montfort and Doig on rule-breaking government, *Is Government Setting a Good Example?* (2006). Together with Maesschalck and Jurkiewicz, he is co-editor of a volume on *Ethics and Integrity of Governance* (2007).

Joseph G. Jabbra received his *Licence en droit* from the Université St Joseph and his PhD in political science from the Catholic University of

America, Washington, DC. He is President of the Lebanese American University in Beirut and Byblos. Previous to that he served as Academic Vice President of Loyola Marymount University, Los Angeles, and as Vice President, Academic and Research, St Mary's University, Halifax, Nova Scotia. He is author or co-author of eleven books. He has also published thirty-two scholarly articles and book chapters, more than twenty-six book reviews in both English and French, and has delivered numerous conference papers and keynote addresses. He belongs to fifteen professional societies and holds the position of Rapporteur-General of the 27th International Congress of Administrative Sciences (IIAS), which will be held at Abu Dhabi, UAE, in July 2007.

R.B. Jain is a former Dean of the Faculty of Social Sciences and Professor, Head of the Department of Political Science, University of Delhi, as well as Professor and Head of the Department of Public Administration at Punjabi University, India. He is currently National Fellow of the Indian Council of Social Science Research at the Indian Institute of Public Administration, New Delhi. He has been a visiting professor at various universities in Canada, the USA and Germany, and has lectured as guest professor in a number of universities and research institutions worldwide. A former editor of the *Indian Journal of Political Science* and member of the editorial board of the *Indian Journal of Public Administration*, he has written extensively on comparative public administration, public policy and electoral reform, good governance, e-governance and bureaucratic corruption. He has recently been honored by the Indian Institute of Public Administration, for his contribution to the discipline.

Yong-Duck Jung studied at the University of Southern California. He was a research scholar at the London School of Economics and Political Science and the Free University of Berlin, and has served on the Faculty of the Seoul National University. He has acted as President of the Korean Association for Public Administration and of the 'Seoul Declaration' Drafting Committee of the 6th Global Forum on Reinventing Government. He has published more than 100 articles on public administration and public policy and has consulted for academic journals, including *Governance* and the *Korean Public Administration Review*. Currently, he is the President of the Korea Institute of Public Administration (KIPA).

Mohammad Mohabbat Khan is Professor in the Department of Public Administration, University of Dhaka, Bangladesh. He obtained his MPA from Syracuse University and the University of Southern California (USC), and PhD from the School of Public Administration, USC. He taught and did research at several universities in Bangladesh, Jordan, Nigeria, Singapore and the USA. He has published several articles in journals and contributed chapters to edited volumes in the areas of governance, public sector reform, corruption, ethics and gender. He was a member of the Bangladesh Public Service Commission, a constitutional body, for a period of five years.

Min Su Kim is an instructor at the School of Public Affairs, Arizona State University, Tempe. He holds a Master's degree in Economics from Arizona State University and is currently a doctoral candidate at the School of Public Affairs, Arizona State University. He teaches introductory econometrics and public affairs economics, and has research interests in local public finance.

Stephen K. Ma, a Fulbright Senior Specialist in Public Administration, is Professor of Political Science and Director of the Institute for Executive Leadership at California State University, Los Angeles. He has authored/co-authored or edited/co-edited eight books, in English and Chinese. His research articles have appeared in *Pacific Affairs*, *Asian Survey*, *Journal of Contemporary China*, *Chinese Public Administration*, *Asian Journal of Political Science*, *International Journal of Public Administration* and *Policy Studies Review*. He has contributed to the *Handbook of Economic Development* (1998), *Administrative Reform and National Economic Development* (2000), *Where Corruption Lives* (2001), and *Administrative Culture in a Global Context* (2005).

Chester A. Newland teaches at the School of Policy, Planning, and Development, University of Southern California, where he is the Duggan Distinguished Professor of Public Administration. He is a Fellow and past Trustee of the National Academy of Public Administration. He is a past President of the American Society for Public Administration (ASPA) and a past Editor-in-Chief of *Public Administration Review*. He has also traveled extensively for consultancy missions on governance and public service reform in several parts of the world, notably the republics of the former Soviet Union.

Jon S.T. Quah is Professor of Political Science at the National University of Singapore and co-editor of the *Asian Journal of Political Science*. He has published widely on anti-corruption strategies and administrative reform in Asian countries. His most recent book is *Curbing Corruption in Asia: A Comparative Study of Six Countries* (2003).

Donald C. Rowat is Professor Emeritus of Political Science at Carleton University, and a graduate of the University of Toronto and Columbia University. Over the years, he has written and edited comparative studies on public administration, administrative secrecy, local government, federal capitals and the ombudsman, the latter being *The Ombudsman: Citizen's Defender* (1968) and *The Ombudsman Plan* (1985). He is an honorary member of the United States Ombudsman Association, and has received an award from the International Ombudsman Institute for outstanding service to the ombudsman institution.